Building on Ruins

Frank Salmon

Building on Ruins

The Rediscovery of Rome
and English Architecture

ASHGATE

Published by
Ashgate Publishing Limited
Gower House
Croft Road
Aldershot
Hampshire GU11 3HR
England

Ashgate Publishing Company
131 Main Street
Burlington
VT 05401-5600
USA

British Library Cataloguing-in-Publication Data
A catalogue record for this book is available from
the British Library

Library of Congress Card Number: 00-110861

ISBN 0 7546 0358 X

Produced for the publisher by
John Taylor Book Ventures
Faringdon, Oxfordshire

Typeset in Columbus by
Tom Knott, Mears Ashby, Northampton

Printed in Belgium

Contents

Building on Ruins is published in the series
REINTERPRETING CLASSICISM: CULTURE,
REACTION AND APPROPRIATION
edited by Caroline van Eck, Vrije Universiteit, Amsterdam

IN THE SAME SERIES

Producing the Past
Aspects of Antiquarian Culture and Practice 1700–1850
Edited by Martin Myrone and Lucy Peltz
Preface by Stephen Bann

Sir John Soane and the Country Estate
Ptolemy Dean

Allan Ramsay and the Search for Horace's Villa
Edited by Bernard D. Frischer and Iain Gordon Brown

The Built Surface (two volumes)
Edited by Christy Anderson and Karen Koehler

List of illustrations

Dimensions given for drawings refer to the whole sheet.

Colour plates   BETWEEN PAGES 112 AND 137

I William Pars: *A View of Rome Taken from the Pincio*, 1776, 38.4 × 53.4 cm (15⅛ × 21 in) (Yale Center for British Art, Paul Mellon Collection, B1977.14.4704)

II Thomas Jones: *An Excavation of an Antique Building Discovered in a Cava in the Villa Negroni at Rome*, 1777, 40.7 × 55.2 cm (16 × 21¾ in) (© Tate, London 2000)

III Domus Aurea, Rome: Detail of the east wall, niche and apse of Room 119 (Photo: Paul Meyboom)

IV John Soane: Elevation of the building storing the sacred waters of the Nile, Temple of Isis, Pompeii, 1779, 67.5 × 44.5 cm (26½ × 17½ in) (By courtesy of the Trustees of Sir John Soane's Museum, detail of 45/3/2)

V George Hadfield: Bird's-eye restoration of the Sanctuary of Fortune, Praeneste, 1792, 100 × 290 cm (39⅜ × 114⅛ in) (British Architectural Library, RIBA, London, Hadfield [8])

VI Robert Adam: Imaginary Roman ruins, 1755–7, 34 × 33.3 cm (13⅜ × 13⅛ in) (By courtesy of the Trustees of Sir John Soane's Museum, Adam vol.56, no.98)

VII Thomas Hardwick: Part of a wall of the Hadrianic house discovered in the grounds of the Villa Negroni, 1777, 65 × 45.5 cm (25½ × 18 in) (British Architectural Library, RIBA, London, E3/26/2)

VIII Christoffer Wilhelm Eckersberg: *The Forum in Rome*, 1814, 31.5 × 41 cm (12⅜ × 16⅛ in) (© National Gallery, London)

IXa John Goldicutt: *Specimens of Ancient Decorations from Pompeii*, 1825, Pl.15 (By permission of the British Library, 560*.d.9)

IXb Henry Parke: Pompeian mosaics, 1821, 20.3 × 24.8 cm (8 × 9¾ in) (British Architectural Library, RIBA, London, W5/43/35)

Xa Joseph Woods with Richard Sharp: Elevation of the building storing the sacred waters of the Nile, Temple of Isis, Pompeii, 1818, 24.8 × 20.3 cm (9¾ × 8 in) (British Architectural Library, RIBA, London, Y3/63, 4/3)

Xb Henry Parke: View inside the House of Sallust, Pompeii, 1821, 37 × 54.8 cm (14½ × 21⅝ in) (British Architectural Library, RIBA, London, W5/43/2)

XI Charles Robert Cockerell: *An Idea of a Reconstruction of the Capital and Forum of Rome*, 1819, 47 × 97 cm (18½ × 38¼ in) (Courtesy of Sotheby's)

XII James Pennethorne: Restoration of the Forum Romanum, 1826, 75 × 132 cm (29½ × 52 in) (Collection of Lady Annabel Goldsmith)

XIII Charles Robert Cockerell: The Great Theatre, Pompeii, semi-restored, 1832, 44 × 82 cm (17¼ × 32¼ in) (British Architectural Library, RIBA, London, E2/11)

XIV Joseph Michael Gandy: *A Scene in Ancient Rome*, stage design for the opening of Shakespeare's *Titus Andronicus*, mid 1820s, 18.5 × 29 cm (7¼ × 11½ in) (Yale Center for British Art, Paul Mellon Collection, B1975.4.1203)

XV Atrium of the Reform Club, London, designed by Charles Barry, 1838–41 (Photo: Martin Charles)

XVI Decimus Burton: Perspective drawing for the Arch and Screen at Constitution Hill, London, c.1826, 62.5 × 105 cm (24⅝ × 41¼ in) (British Architectural Library, RIBA, London, W14/13)

XVIIa Charles Edge: Plan for the completion of Birmingham Town Hall and its environs, 1846, 64.7 × 94.3 cm (25½ × 37⅛ in) (Birmingham City Archives, Ms. 1703/15/12)

XVIIb 'Mr Ingram': Decorative scheme for the order and coved ceiling coffers inside Birmingham Town Hall, 1855 (Birmingham City Archives, BCL Plan 208)

XVIII The Fitzwilliam Museum, Cambridge, designed by George Basevi from 1835, viewed from the south (Photo: Fitzwilliam Museum)

XIXa George Basevi: Elevation of a doorway for the principal gallery of the Fitzwilliam Museum, Cambridge, c.1843–5, 56 × 77 cm (22 × 30¼ in) (Fitzwilliam Museum)

XIXb Lithograph of the tessellated pavement designed by Henry Pether for the courtyard of the Royal Exchange, London, 1844 (Reproduced by courtesy of the Mercers' Company, London)

XX Lithograph of the perspective of a design for the Royal Exchange, London, by Thomas Leverton Donaldson, 1839 (Guildhall Library, Corporation of London)

Black and white figures

CHAPTER 2

Preface and acknowledgements

The subject of this book has preoccupied my research interests for more than a decade. When I began exploring individual aspects of it in papers and articles, I think it is fair to say that cultural and architectural studies of later eighteenth- and early nineteenth-century British Greek Revivalism far outweighed any similarly specific work on the Roman inheritance of the same period. There was little, moreover, to parallel the degree of attention given to the nineteenth-century French architectural response to Roman antiquity, as exemplified in the series of great exhibitions mounted by the Ecole nationale supérieure des Beaux-Arts in Paris, Rome and Naples from 1981 to 1992. That this is no longer the case is due to a resurgence of scholarly interest in the subject of the British and Roman Antiquity which has occurred during the last five years. The 'Grand Tour' exhibition held at the Tate Gallery and Palazzo delle Esposizione in Rome in 1996–7 provided the opportunity for the public to see a superb collection of artefacts connected with travel to Italy and a catalogue which, when taken together with conferences held in London and Rome, refocused the attention of numerous scholars on the key issues which the Grand Tour raises. Also in 1996 came the smaller but complementary exhibition 'Imagining Rome: British Artists and Rome in the Nineteenth Century', held at Bristol City Art Gallery at the end of a Leverhulme-funded research project at the University of Bristol – a project which also resulted in a volume of essays, *Roman Presences*, edited by Catharine Edwards and published in 1999. Two further studies which appeared in 1997 both deal with cultural questions which relate closely to the architectural issues discussed in this book: Philip Ayres' *Classical Culture and the Idea of Rome in Eighteenth-Century England*, and Norman Vance's *The Victorians and Ancient Rome*. In this context should also be mentioned J. Ingamells' *A Dictionary of British and Irish Travellers in Italy 1701–1800, Compiled from the Brinsley Ford Archive*, published in 1997 by the Paul Mellon Centre for Studies in British Art. The late Sir Brinsley's archive, the product of more than half a century's diligence, had always been open to bona fide scholars, but the extraordinary synthesis of notes and letters achieved by John Ingamells for the published version has set eighteenth-century Anglo-Italian studies onto an altogether new footing. Just as I was pleased to have been asked to contribute entries on many of the architects for the Dictionary, so I hope that the present book will be a useful addition to the broad range of scholarly endeavour mentioned above, especially in what I shall argue is the no less interesting period of the early nineteenth century.

In working on this project over a considerable period of time and in several different countries I have naturally incurred a large number of debts to individuals and to institutions whom I would like to thank here. Before that, however, I should like to place on record two of my greatest fortunes: first to have been born into a family which has proved wholly supportive on every level in all its generations, and second to have married into another. I am hugely grateful in particular to my late grandparents, my parents, Neil and Joyce Salmon, and to my brother Dr Tom Salmon. To my wife, Catharine MacLeod, I owe much more than the dedication of this book can begin to signify. She has selflessly shared the enthusiasms and burdens it brought from first to last, despite having had more important things to do. It was my friend, Hugh Eveleigh, who awakened and fostered my interest in the world of Classical Antiquity twenty years ago, and the generous support of Eve and Rudolf Bamberger and of Professor Stuart Lingo in Florence helped open the door to an academic career for me. I received great encouragement as a young scholar from Dr Cinzia Sicca and Professor Edward Chaney, and learned to appreciate the value and techniques of reading architectural drawings during a magical afternoon with Professor Michael Hirst in 1986 at the Casa Buonarroti, Florence, with free access to all Michelangelo's drawings held there. I would also like to thank, here, my former colleagues in the University of Manchester School of Architecture, John Archer and Dr David Yeomans, for the guidance and practical help they have offered me since I joined the University in 1989.

The following instititutions and individuals in this country have been unfailingly generous in assisting my researches. In London: the British Architectural Library at the Royal Institute of British Architects, and especially the staff of the Institute's Drawings Collection; the staff of Sir John Soane's Museum; the Department of Greek and Roman Antiquities at the British Museum, especially Dr Ian Jenkins; the staff of the Print Room at the Victoria & Albert Museum; the staff of the Corporation of London Record Office; the staff of the Prints and Drawings Collection at the Guildhall Library; and the Mercers' Company, especially its Archivist and Curator, Ursula Carlyle. Elsewhere in England I thank: the staff of the Birmingham City Archives in Birmingham Central Library, and Anthony Peers of Rodney Melville and Partners, author of the Conservation Plan, on the basis of which Birmingham Town Hall will shortly be restored to life; the staff of Birmingham City Museum and Art Gallery; the staff of the Fitzwilliam Museum, Cambridge, especially Professor Jim Marrow and Andrew Morris; the staff of the Local History section of Liverpool Central Library; the staff of the Walker Art Gallery, Liverpool, especially Joseph Sharples; the staff of St George's Hall, Liverpool and Peter de Figueiredo, Historic Buildings Inspector for English Heritage in the North-West Region.

In Italy I must likewise thank: the staff of the British School at Rome, especially the Librarian, Valerie Scott; the Soprintendenze of Rome and Pompeii; the Biblioteca Apostolica Vaticana and the Archivio Segreto, especially Monsignor Charles Burns; the Gabinetto Nazionale delle Stampe, the Archivio di Stato, and the Archivio Vicariato, all in Rome; the Accademia Nazionale di San Luca, Rome, especially Professor Angela Cipriani; the Accademia Parmense di Belle Arti, espcially Professor Guglielma Manfredi, and also Professor Gianfranco Fiaccadori, who introduced me at the Academy; the Accademia di Belle Arti in Bologna, especially Professor Silla Zamboni; the Archivio di Stato and the library of the Accademia delle Belle Arti in Florence.

In the United States of America I would like to express my gratitude to: the Yale Center for British Art, where I was privileged to hold a fellowship in 1993 (at the Center I especially thank Dr Julia Marciari-Alexander); the Getty Center for Research, Los Angeles, especially Beth Ann Guynn in the Special Collections; the John Work Garrett Library, Johns Hopkins University, especially Judith Gardner-Flint; the Cooper-Hewitt Museum, the Pierpont Morgan Library and the Department of Prints and Illustrated Books of the Metropolitan Museum of Art, all in New York.

Among other friends and colleagues I owe an incalculable debt (as do all who work in this field) to Sir Howard Colvin. Sir Howard's *Biographical Dictionary of British Architects 1600–1840* (3rd edn, New Haven and London, 1995) has been my daily companion, but he has also been unfailingly generous on a personal level in freely providing me with much additional information, especially on the Royal Exchange in London. For help with that subject I also thank John Watts of the Royal Exchange and Ann Saunders of the London Topographical Society. Among architectural historians, I have had frequent reason to be thankful for the advice of Professor Joe Mordaunt Crook, Professor Andor Gomme, Professor Alistair Rowan, Dr David Watkin and Professor John Wilton-Ely. At an early stage of my research I was fortunate enough to meet the doyen of early nineteenth-century Roman topographical studies, Professor Ronald Ridley of the University of Melbourne, who has since proved a most generous mentor to me. Professor David Armitage of Columbia University has been a constant source of useful information and provocative ideas during the gestation of this book. Dr Clare Hornsby and Alex Clark offered

me accommodation in Rome, use of an excellent library and good advice at a crucial stage. Other colleagues I must thank for particular advice or assistance are: Professor Danny Abramson (John Soane); David Alexander (prints of antiquities); Dr James Anderson (John Gwynn); Professor Dana Arnold (Decimus Burton); Janine Barrier (the Académie de France à Rome and the Peyre family); Dr Ian Bristow (Pompeii); Dr Janet Delaine (Roman bath buildings); Professor Tim Fulford (Romantic literature and periodicals); Dr Iain Gordon Brown (Robert Adam); Charles Hind (C. R. Cockerell); the Honorable Julia King (George Hadfield); Professor Dr Valentin Kockel (eighteenth- and nineteenth-century models); Professor Brian Lukacher (J. M. Gandy); Professor John Marciari (the Osborn Collection at the Beinecke Library, Yale University); Professor Michael McCarthy (Theodosius Keene); Peter Miller, of Ken Spelman Bookshop, York (John Soane); Drs Eric Moormann and Paul Meyboom (the Domus Aurea); Charles Nugent (Victorian novelists and Roman images in the Whitworth Art Gallery, University of Manchester); Hugh Petter (the British Academy in Via Margutta, Rome); Dr Eleanor Tollfree (architecture in Napoleonic Paris); Dr Geoffrey Tyack (James Pennethorne); Professor David Van Zanten (early nineteenth-century French architects); Professor Andrew Wallace-Hadrill (Pompeii); Dr Mark Wilson Jones (the Roman Corinthian order); and Dr Roger Woodley (Robert Mylne).

I should like to thank my colleagues in the School of Art History and Archaeology at the University of Manchester, especially the staff of the G.ten photographic unit for their excellent work, and those who incorporated some of my duties into their already onerous schedules in order to give me an opportunity to write at an important stage in 1999. I am indebted in particular to Professor Roger Ling for his constant interest in my work on Roman Antiquity, and to Dr Mark Ledbury for help with my photographic order at the Ecole nationale supérieure des Beaux-Arts. Dr Kate Danter has assisted me in a number of practical ways, and the graphic presented in Appendix C was kindly prepared by Mark Wisbey.

This book could not have come to fruition without the commitment shown to it by Ashgate Publishing Limited. The Art History Commissioning Editor, Pamela Edwardes, and Dr Caroline van Eck, editor of the 'Reinterpreting Classicism' series, both went well beyond the call of duty in their efforts to ensure that a tight timetable could be met without loss of substance. Sarah Walsh was assiduous in her copy editing and, in John Taylor and Alan Bartram respectively, I have had an excellent production manager and designer. The inclusion of colour plates here is largely due to a generous grant from the Paul Mellon Centre for Studies in British Art. I am very grateful to the Advisory Council of the Centre for providing this, and, in particular, to the Director of Studies, Dr Brian Allen, for the support he has given me throughout. I owe the first part of my title to the artist Catherine George's acuity during a discussion of my book's subject over breakfast at the British School at Rome.

Paul Valéry once said that 'You don't finish a poem – you abandon it', a sentiment which in my experience might be applied equally to academic books. In this case, readers should know that the artificial timetable of the British universities' Research Assessment Exercise led to the curtailment of my project, specifically in the area of the cultural milieu in which the English revival of Roman architectural forms occurred in the 1830s. Those gratefully mentioned above have all done their best to advise me, however, and I take responsibility for any errors and misconceptions which may remain.

Manchester and Blackheath   June 2000

ABBREVIATIONS

BAL	British Architectural Library (Royal Institute of British Architects), London
BCL	Birmingham Central Library
BM	British Museum, London
CLRO	Corporation of London Records Office
Colvin	H. Colvin, *A Biographical Dictionary of British Architects 1600–1840*, 3rd edn, New Haven and London, 1995
CUL	Cambridge University Library
Envois (1981)	*Pompéi: Travaux et envois des architectes français au XIXe siècle*, Paris and Naples, 1981
Envois (1982)	*Paris – Rome – Athènes: Le voyage en Grèce des architectes français au XIXe et XXe siècles*, Paris, Athens and Houston, 1982–3
Envois (1985)	*Roma antiqua: Envois des architectes français (1788–1924) – Forum, Colisée, Palatin*, Rome and Paris, 1985
Envois (1992)	*Roma antiqua: 'Envois' degli architetti francesi (1786–1901) – Grande edifici pubblici*, Rome, 1992
Fleming	J. Fleming, *Robert Adam and his Circle in Edinburgh and Rome*, London, 1962
Harris and Savage	E. Harris, assisted by N. Savage, *British Architectural Books and Writers, 1556–1785*, Cambridge, 1990
Ingamells	J. Ingamells, *A Dictionary of British and Irish Travellers in Italy 1701–1800, Compiled from the Brinsley Ford Archive*, New Haven and London, 1997
LCL	Liverpool Central Library
Mazois	F. Mazois [and F. C. Gau], *Les Ruines de Pompéi*, 4 vols, Paris, 1824–38
Ms./Mss	Manuscript/s
RIBA DC	Royal Institute of British Architects Drawings Collection, London
SM	Sir John Soane's Museum, London
Taylor and Cresy	G. L. Taylor and E. Cresy, *The Architectural Antiquities of Rome*, 2 vols, London, 1821–2
V&A, PDP	Victoria & Albert Museum, London, Department of Paintings, Drawings and Prints
YCBA	Yale Center for British Art, New Haven

The term 'restoration' (or 'restored') refers in this book to reconstruction of ruined buildings as paper exercises, not to restoration in any physical sense.

In general measurements are given in the form in which they were made, but for the purposes of comparison metric measurements have been taken as the control. The following standards are used:

English foot	30.5 cm
Paris Royal foot	32.5 cm
Vicentine foot	35.7 cm

Figures are rounded up to the nearest millimetre. Measurements in Antoine Desgodetz's *Les Edifices antiques de Rome* (1682) are given in both Paris Royal feet and modules, the module being half the diameter of a monument's column immediately above its base. Each module is divided into 30 parts, and sometimes beyond that into fractions of a part. Since in some cases only the value of the module is expressed in Paris Royal feet, it is then necessary to convert Desgodetz's modular measurements first into Paris Royal feet and from there into metric for comparative purposes.

COLUMNIATION AND THE CORINTHIAN ORDER

Where the number of columns forming peristyles is given, a column standing at the corner junction of the front and the side has been counted twice. In a study such as this, there is a danger that the appearance of the Corinthian order may appear to be simplistically equated with Roman, as opposed to Greek architecture. Where appropriate, the origin of particular examples used has been discussed in the text. Readers should appreciate, however, that for all their advances in understanding the chronology and topography of Rome, the knowledge of architects throughout the period covered in this book inevitably fell far short of the knowledge we have acquired since. Early examples of the Corinthian order, such as that at the Temple of Apollo Epicurius at Bassae of the late fifth century BC, were obviously identified as 'Greek', but from the beginning of the Hellenistic period the issue becomes far less clear. A full explanation of Neo-classical understandings of the origins of the Corinthian order would require a book-length study. The best summary, based on the evidence studied in researching this book, appears to be that architects in general thought of the Corinthian order as the quintessential Roman order, although within that overall position opinion ranged between two poles of thinking: that the refinement of the order was *the* great Roman contribution to Classical architecture, or that it was a sign of the 'Greek Revivalism' they knew emperors such as Augustus and Hadrian to have been interested in.

Roman buildings generally appear under the names by which they are currently identified. However, eighteenth- and nineteenth-century names appear when used by architects and antiquarians writing at the time or, of course, in quotations. In these cases, the modern name is inserted in brackets where it is felt this will aid the reader in identifying the monument. The list below gives the most commonly confused examples in Rome, the inverted commas denoting traditional common appellations. For further detail see entries on individual monuments in N. Thomson de Grummond, *An Encyclopedia of the History of Classical Archaeology*, 2 vols, London, 1996.

In the case of Pompeii, the numbering system for properties (identified by their doorway) within their *insulae* (blocks) and of the *insulae* within regions of the town follows that in *Pompeii: pitture e mosaici*, the definitive encyclopaedia currently in course of publication (Rome, 1990–).

- Temple of Castor and Pollux (or Dioscuri): Temple of 'Jupiter Stator'
- Temple of Vespasian (or Vespasian and Titus): Temple of 'Jupiter Tonans'
- Temple of Saturn: Temple of 'Concord' or of 'Fortune'
- Temple of Portunus: Temple of 'Fortuna Virilis'
- Temple of Hercules Victor: Temple of 'Vesta'
- Basilica of Maxentius (or of Constantine): 'Temple of Peace'
- Forum Transitorium: Forum of 'Nerva'
- The Baths of Trajan and the Domus Aurea (The Golden House of Nero): 'Baths of Titus' or 'Palace of Titus'
- Forum of Augustus: includes the 'Arco de' Pantani'
- Round Temple at Tivoli: Temple of 'Vesta' at Tivoli

Introduction

Although this book is concerned with English architecture during a specific period of time, the years from about 1750 to 1840, it is in no sense a comprehensive survey. Its focus is on British interest in, and use of, ancient Roman architecture, a topic it approaches from the point of view of travel and of archaeological study. The importance of travel lies in the fact that, during the period under discussion, almost every architect of note went to study in Rome, mixing there not only with fellow British students but also with architects of other nationalities, particularly with the French. Once in Rome, all engaged predominantly in the study of antiquities, broadly speaking an archaeological activity. British students were deeply influenced by foreign contemporaries, especially by Giovanni Battista Piranesi and a number of French students in the early part of the period, but by the end of the eighteenth century they had developed distinctive approaches to the ruins of Roman Antiquity which reflected the way that architectural practice had developed in Britain. After relative uniformity of attitude in the second half of the eighteenth century, however, major changes in the approach to Roman ruins took place among the numerous British students who reached Italy in the fifteen years or so after 1815. This was largely in response to the great advances in Roman archaeology and topography which had taken place during the Napoleonic period, in the aftermath of which the British made important but hitherto little recognized contributions of their own. In view of this, it is somewhat ironic that, while Roman studies have for long been seen as an underpinning factor of English architectural design in the second half of the eighteenth century, no similar attempt has been made to contextualize the return to explicit use of Roman models evident in public buildings of the 1830s such as Birmingham Town Hall (Fig.1). That is the gap which, by concentrating on the later part of the period, this book sets out to fill.

In this day and age, when it is possible to visit Roman ruins during a long weekend while having no notion of Roman history, let alone any interest in modern parallels, it is easy to underestimate the reverence for those monuments felt by British visitors in the eighteenth and nineteenth centuries, when the association of ideas formed so important a part of the intellectual outlook of an educated person. Moreover, given our present-day preoccupation with academic discourse, it is hard for architectural historians to place themselves in the position of architecture students of that period, for whom the early stages of pupillage had involved a daily diet of studying and drawing the Classical orders of the major Roman (and Greek) monuments, until they knew them in intimate detail. When they got to Rome, the students saw the ruins first and foremost as pieces of buildings, to be physically pored over, perhaps imaginatively restored and certainly made use of in various ways in new buildings. In this book, therefore, careful consideration has been given in Part I to the surviving evidence of how British architects responded when confronted with the remains of Roman buildings, and in Part II to the evidence of how they responded when confronted with the problem of designing English public buildings in the 1830s and into the 1840s. In general, theoretical writing has been set aside, except in cases such as John Soane's Royal Academy lectures, where it relates directly to the tradition of travel to Italy and to first-hand study of antiquities. This is not to say that discourse was unimportant in England during this period, of course, but rather that archaeology represents a hitherto understated, perhaps even a better way of understanding architectural developments. It would be hard to explain the formal appearance of English Neo-classical architecture in terms of a coherent or logical body of theory, as one can attempt to do with French architecture, for example, whereas most English Neo-classical buildings can be understood in terms of their archaeological sources or inspirations.[1]

A broader acknowledgement of this point might, perhaps, have saved the four important buildings reappraised here in Part II from the peculiar marginalization they suffered in architectural history during the second half of the twentieth century. In survey accounts they have often been viewed with indifference (Birmingham Town Hall, the Fitzwilliam Museum, Cambridge), greeted with hostility (the Royal Exchange) or, in the case of St George's Hall, explained as an example of contemporary Prussian Neo-classicism transplanted to Liverpool. The problem is one of historiography. These buildings do not fit with the definition and chronology of Neo-classicism promoted in John Summerson's great and still standard survey, *Architecture in Britain 1530–1830*, which closes with a chapter on the contending Greek and Gothic Revivals. Nor do they fit comfortably within the survey which picks up where Summerson left off, Henry-Russell Hitchcock's *Early Victorian Architecture in Britain*, in which they are described as occupying a 'curiously isolated historical position'.[2] At best these buildings tend to be regarded as the

1. Birmingham Town Hall, designed by Joseph Aloysius Hansom, Edward Welch and Charles Edge from 1831.

initiating examples of a 'Graeco-Roman' manner, persisted with throughout the Victorian era by architects doggedly working outside the mainstream. This is conceptually a long way from the treatment of them in historical accounts produced before the particular architectural character of the twentieth century impinged on judgements of the nineteenth. In Albert Richardson's insightful *Monumental Classic Architecture in Great Britain and Ireland* of 1914, for example, they were identified as the 'culmination' and 'most cogent expression' of a Neo-classical tradition stretching back to Lord Burlington in the 1730s.[3]

There seem to be two interrelated reasons, other than a failure to appreciate the impact of revitalized Roman archaeology after the Napoleonic period, why these buildings have lost their historical contexts and thereby the 'validity' of their expression. First, the significance attributed to two events which took place in 1836: the selection of Charles Barry's Gothic design for the new Palace of Westminster, and the publication of A. W. N. Pugin's powerfully polemical and pedagogically attractive *Contrasts*, which signalled the 'end of the

history of English Neo-classicism', as Summerson once told an Italian audience.[4] Second, the failure to appreciate the wider historical and cultural ramifications which flow from recognition of the possibility that the Grand Tour, too often isolated as an eighteenth-century phenomenon, was resumed by the British after 1815 and underpinned a renewed phase of enthusiasm for things Roman. Thus it was Hitchcock's assumption that Puginian rhetoric represented common public opinion which led him to judge the very Roman façade of George Basevi's Fitzwilliam Museum as 'quite irrelevant' in the mid 1830s, when, in fact, the strength of feeling for Roman antiquity in Cambridge at that time was such that 90 per cent of University Senate members who voted endorsed Basevi's design (see Pl.xviii).[5] As the chapters in Part II of this book will show, it is the Palace of Westminster competition which was exceptional in that decade, other competitions for major public buildings in England resulting in designs which drew overall forms and details very largely from ancient Roman architecture.

The argument in this book, therefore, assumes a clientèle

and a public receptive to the idea that analogies with the buildings of ancient Rome might serve their modern architectural purposes. There is no need here to rehearse the well-known background to this attitude in eighteenth-century education, historiography and the Grand Tour.[6] It is necessary, however, to reiterate the idea that the continuities in the pattern of British travel to Italy after 1815 outweighed the differences. If, for example, one were to make a narrow definition of the Grand Tour as an aristocratic institution – and note that First Lords of the Treasury (Prime Ministers) such as the 2nd Marquis of Rockingham and the 2nd Earl of Shelburne had visited Rome and become important patrons of Neo-classical art – then it should be noted also that there was no diminution in the percentage of aristocrats visiting Rome in the second and third decades of the nineteenth century, and that among the travellers were future Prime Ministers Viscount Melbourne, Lord John Russell and George Canning, this last memorialized by Francis Chantrey in the guise of a toga-clad Roman orator (Fig.2).[7] In truth, however, travel to Italy was never solely an institution of the aristocracy and gentry, even in the eighteenth century. Middle-class travellers and artists represent two further constituencies, both of which also returned to Italy in the aftermath of the Napoleonic wars, albeit in increasing numbers. Until the advent of the railways, both the means of travel and the itineraries pursued represent important continuities between the eighteenth century and the early nineteenth. Moreover, while the interests of post-Napoleonic wars travellers may have diversified, it was the associative value of the antique which remained pre-eminent, as one later eighteenth-century traveller, writing in 1819, made clear:

the object particularly pointed out to us in Italy is the recollection of former times, and a comparison of those times with the present; to restore to our minds the classical studies of our youth; to visit those places recorded in history as the residences of illustrious characters of antiquity or rendered interesting by historical facts and anecdotes; to admire and reflect upon those remains of polished architecture and sculpture which the hand of time has fortunately spared.[8]

The full and useful exploration of the associative relationship between ancient Rome and nineteenth-century Britain, recently published, need not be repeated in detail here.[9] It is worth noting, however, that two of the most popular pieces of contemporary English literature of the 1830s and 1840s were undoubtedly Edward Bulwer-Lytton's novel *The Last Days of Pompeii* and Thomas Babington Macaulay's poetic *Lays of Ancient Rome*. Roman analogies came readily to historians, philosophers and social commentators such as Macaulay, John Stuart Mill and Thomas Carlyle (in, for example, *Past and Present*), and among the numerous school Roman histories which began to appear were some with illustrations (Fig.3). The world of Rome and the deeds of its heroes, especially of Republican heroes like Lucius Junius Brutus and Marcus

2. Francis Chantrey: Marble figure of George Canning as a Roman orator, Westminster Abbey 1834.

Curtius, were thus brought visually close even to those who did not travel.[10] At the higher scholarly level, new impetus was given to the study of ancient history at Cambridge, in particular, by the introduction of a Classical Tripos in 1822. It was at Trinity College, Cambridge, moreover, that both Julius Hare and Connop Thirlwall were teaching when, in 1828, they published the first two volumes of the *History of Rome*, translated from the second and much revised edition of the Prussian diplomat and historian Barthold Gottfried Niebuhr's *Römische Geschichte* which appeared between 1827 and 1832.

In its critical approach to source material, scrupulously attempting to separate fact from myth for the first time, Niebuhr's great work represented a milestone in the historiography of the Roman Republic. The immense enthusiasm with which it was received in British academic circles culminated in the appearance from 1838 of its English progeny, *The History of Rome* by the Rugby schoolmaster (and shortly afterwards Oxford Professor of Modern History), Thomas Arnold. Comparison of Roman Republican and contemporary history came readily to Arnold, as his preface indicates:

There is no shelter for you here. Return!" The soldiers quickly rallied round their general, under whom they had so often fought victoriously, and whom they considered as invincible. The enemy were repulsed; and the combat being renewed the next day, they were totally defeated. Soon after, Camillus returned to Rome laden with the spoils of conquest; but no successes abroad could allay the dissensions at home.

The youngest daughter of Fabius Ambustus, being married to a plebeian, envied the honours of her elder sister, who was the wife of a patrician. She, therefore, prevailed on her father to excite the people to assert their equal right with the patricians to the consulate. The law for creating a plebeian consul being agitated, the senate strongly opposed it, and forbade Camillus, who was at that time dictator, to lay down his office. But while Camillus was dispatching public affairs, the tribunes ordered that the votes of the people should be taken on their favourite measure; and the dictator vehemently opposing it, they sent a lictor to arrest him, and conduct him to prison. Such a mark of indignity raised a greater commotion than had yet been seen in Rome; and the patricians boldly repulsed the lictors, while the people cried out, "Down with him! down with him!"

B. C. 162.

By the advice of Camillus, who vowed to build a temple to Concord, in case peace was restored, a law was passed, that, in future, one of the consuls should be chosen from the plebeians. At the same time, also, they created from the patricians a prætor, who supplied the place of the consul in his absence. The number of prætors, in after ages, was increased to sixteen. There were likewise two curulic ædiles created, who had the care of the public games, and of the corn and provisions taken in war.

U. C. 396.

Camillus, after resigning the dictatorship, and building a temple to Concord, died of the plague in the eighty-second year of his age, with the reputation of being the second founder of Rome. He never gave a battle which was not followed by a complete victory; besieged a town without taking it; nor led forth an army, which he did not bring back laden with spoils, and covered with glory.

A gulf having opened in the forum, which the augurs affirmed would never close up till the most precious things

The Judgment of Brutus.

Curtius leaping into the Gulph.

3. J. Robinson: 'Ancient History', 1824, illustrations in the Forum showing the judgement of Brutus and Marcus Curtius leaping into the chasm: Republican heroes credited with saving Rome. Images like these reached the desks of English schoolchildren.

Our own experience has thus thrown a brighter light upon the remoter past … it is not claiming too much to say, that the growth of the Roman Commonwealth, the true character of its parties, the causes and tendencies of its revolutions, and the spirit of its peoples and its laws, ought to be understood by none as well as by those who have grown up under the laws, who have been engaged in the parties, who are themselves citizens of our kingly commonwealth of England.[11]

The idea of England as a 'kingly commonwealth' under William IV and the young Victoria points to the way that Roman associative thought of the 1830s incorporated contemporary English political ideology. It would be just as simplistic, however, to draw straightforward conclusions about

this along party lines, as it would to suggest that the nationalistic Gothic Revivalism of the Palace of Westminster was peculiar to one of the political factions of the early 1830s. There was, perhaps, a tendency for Roman analogies to come more readily to those of Liberal persuasion, and certainly the form of England's earliest truly civic building, Birmingham Town Hall, should be seen against the background of the contemporaneous passage of the Great Reform Bill, which extended the franchise to a modest but symbolically very significant degree. However, in the face of the very same political development, the Tory *Quarterly Review* exhorted its readers:

The Romans after a great calamity did not waste their energies in complaints nor bury them in gloomy torpor; and they surrounded with public honours the man who, whatever were his errors, had the redeeming quality of not despairing, even in the last emergency of the fortunes of his country. That heroic spirit saved the state in many emergencies, which a faint-hearted people would have considered as desperate.[12]

Similarly, while the Royal Exchange competition may be seen as highlighting political tensions between the mercantile power of the City of London and the legislative power of Westminster, the competition for St George's Hall (which overlapped with that for the Exchange) proceeded on a distinctly bipartisan basis, in which a fitting expression for the entrepreneurial character of Liverpool came before party allegiances. What can be said in general terms, however, is that these buildings show the appropriation of Roman paradigms by the rising urban middle classes, in some cases working to establish new identities at the time of the Municipal Corporations Act (1835) which increased their self-government to such a significant extent. Aristocrats and gentry who retained an interest in Classicism found a new outlet for their preference in the Italianate or revived Renaissance idiom, introduced by Charles Barry, for instance, at Trentham for the 2nd Duke of Sutherland, and in the more public forum of the Travellers' Club in Pall Mall.[13]

Although much new research has been carried out on the personalities and factions behind the commissioning of the four buildings to be discussed in Part II, a full exploration of the cultural background against which these architectural developments took place lies beyond the scope of this book. It is essential to understand, however, that the eighteenth-century tendency to compare ancient Rome with modern Britain continued in the nineteenth, if one common prejudice against these buildings is to be countered. This is the idea that they are no more than feeble 'copies' of their models, unimaginative responses by generally second-rate architects to the stylistic dilemmas they faced. In this regard, architectural historians appear to lag behind their art historian colleagues, who long ago went beyond the notion that history paintings by Jacques-Louis David or sculptures by Antonio Canova were 'slavish and hence stillborn imitations of Graeco-Roman antiquity'.[14] Historians of British architecture have also lagged behind historians of French and German architecture of the same period, or rather looked in different directions. The opprobrium often heaped on buildings such as Birmingham Town Hall is rarely found in critical responses to, for example, Leo von Klenze's Grecian Walhalla near Regensburg (1830–42) or to Charles Abric's Roman Palais de Justice at Montpellier of 1846 (Fig.4), no doubt because these buildings are understood in terms of Bavarian and French political, cultural and architectural frameworks.[15] A parallel understanding is necessary for the English examples, if the perception of them as either meaningless or anachronistic is to be overcome. That understanding can be found, not in contemporary polemic such as Pugin's (the nationalism of which has perhaps led

historians to treat Britain in terms which are too insular), but in similarities of outlook between British architects and their Continental counterparts. Abric, for example, studied in the Paris atelier of François Debret and at the Ecole des Beaux-Arts, before travelling to study in Rome in 1828. In these respects he differed little from his near English contemporary Basevi, architect of the Fitzwilliam Museum (see Pl.xviii), a pupil in the office of John Soane and at the Royal Academy Schools, before he travelled to study in Rome in 1816.

In 1835, the year in which Basevi won the Fitzwilliam Museum competition, Debret (and in fact fifteen other European architects, including von Klenze) were elected the first Corresponding and Honorary Members of the new Institute

4. *Palais de Justice, Montpellier, designed by Charles Abric, 1846.*

of British Architects, a clear indication of the personal, ideological and professional bonds which existed between English architects and their French, German and Italian counterparts. The foundation of the Institute towards the end of the period under discussion here, together with that of the Royal Academy near the beginning of the same period, also serves as a reminder that this was the time when the figure of the professional architect emerged and became established in Britain. The system of pupillage, thought to have begun in the office of the elder James Paine in 1756, made possible the choice of an architectural career at an early age, while remuneration and the ability to contract for building further determined independence.[16] Through bodies like the Academy and the Institute, architectural ideology effectively moved out of the immediate ambit of the educated aristocracy and gentry, and many British architects broadened their horizons by looking to the international centres of architectural study, in Paris and in the city where the French had their academic outstation, Rome. Travel almost instantly became a vital part of the new professionalism of many British architects. By 1790, James Playfair could speak of his forthcoming journey to Rome as being for the purpose of 'improvement in my profession', a phrase which became commonplace in the first thirty years of the nineteenth century.[17] This link was emphasized by William Chambers in the 1791 edition of his *A Treatise on the Decorative Part of Civil Architecture*, where, drawing from notes prepared two decades before in case he was called upon to lecture at the Royal Academy, he stated that 'it seems almost superfluous to observe, that an architect cannot aspire to superiority in his profession, without having travelled', before going on to describe the objects of such travel: first 'the venerable remains of ancient magnificence' and then Italian Renaissance masters.[18] The ultimate institutionalization of the connection between travel and professional success came with the foundation, also in 1791, of the Architects' Club in London, a condition for membership of which was perceived to be 'a Candidate having *been in Italy*'.[19]

It is the combination of travel and archaeology as essentially central parts of architectural education which, arguably, ought to dictate definition of the difficult term 'Neo-classicism' in relation to British architecture. At its narrowest chronological span, this term has been held to apply to architecture of the period, *c.*1750–1805, while at its widest it has been extended back to *c.*1714 (to incorporate the phase generally known as 'Neo-Palladian') and forward to 1830.[20] The most common definition, however, is that canonized in Summerson's *Architecture in Britain 1530–1830*, in which (along with the closely related Picturesque) Neo-classicism forms Part Five of the book, covering the decades from 1750 to 1830. It is fundamentally important to recognize that there is a distinction to be drawn between the study of Roman Antiquity which largely took place on paper, on the basis of what could be seen in books or in imported collections of drawings, and that which took place in relation to the physical fabric of Antique remains. The 'Neo-classicism' of early eighteenth-century England and Ireland (whether it is the version of the 3rd Earl of Shaftesbury and of the Surveyor of the King's Works in the 1720s, Sir Thomas Hewett, which was called 'Greek', or the version of the 3rd Earl of Burlington, based on Palladio's restorations of the Roman Baths and other paper sources in the 1730s) was architectonically quite different from the responses of architects who had studied the remains with their own eyes.[21] Some British architects had done this before 1750, of course, and some did so after 1840, but it was only between those two boundaries that it was more or less de rigueur to do so, and that two-dimensional paper representations of Antique architecture took second place. As this book will show, it was first-hand study which led to the picturesque and endlessly inventive use of Roman ruins in the later eighteenth century and to the more literal use of Roman models, underpinned by archaeological scholarship, in English public buildings of the 1830s. The Greek Revival, the undeniably dominant Classical idiom in the years from about 1810 to 1830, did not represent the end of Neo-classicism, but rather paved the way for its culmination in a final 'Roman moment' in England, with buildings which boldly answer, in particular, their Parisian and other French siblings.

Part I
Studying Rome

Chapter 1
The later eighteenth-century background

We are apt to praise and form greater ideas of ruins than we should perhaps have had of the buildings when whole. (Joseph Michael Gandy, letter from Rome of 1796)[1]

On the morning of 27 November 1776, a 'wet cold gloomy day', the English architectural student Thomas Hardwick arrived in Rome in the company of the engraver Christopher Norton and the Welsh painter Thomas Jones. Norton, returning to the city which had effectively been his home for the previous sixteen years, conducted the two new arrivals from Piazza del Popolo to Via Condotti and then through the backstreets around Piazza di Spagna to the home of James Byres, Scottish architect turned antiquarian. After lunch with Byres, the party proceeded to the Caffè degli Inglesi on the corner of Piazza di Spagna and Via Due Macelli, to find no fewer than eighteen British artists (along with the resident Irish antiquarian Matthew Nulty) taking postprandial coffee.[2] Thus Hardwick took his place in the large English-speaking community of expatriate and student artists which thrived in Rome in the second half of the eighteenth century.

The centrality of a visit to Italy in the education of ambitious young British architects in this period can be deduced immediately from a glance at statistics such as the number of students found in the coffee house on that afternoon in 1776. From the arrival of Robert Taylor in about 1740 until the departure of Robert Smirke in 1804, it is possible to identify over fifty such architects studying in Italy, a great increase on the handful who had travelled in the preceding half century (see Appendix A). These men established a continuous British architectural presence in the Italian states until 1798, when the French invasion of the peninsula made the journey inadvisable. The Treaty of Amiens of 1802 aided a brief resumption of the tradition, until worsening Anglo-French relations after the Battle of Trafalgar in 1805 left Italy effectively inaccessible to British travellers for a decade. As Hardwick found, there could be considerable overlap between the different individuals involved, with up to five architectural students resident in Rome at any one time. It is striking to note, moreover, that the list of travellers includes most of the men who subsequently dominated British architectural taste and practice in the last four decades of the eighteenth century and first three of the nineteenth: William Chambers, Robert Adam, Robert Mylne, George Dance the Younger, James Wyatt, Thomas Harrison, John Soane, Joseph Michael Gandy, Charles

Heathcote Tatham, William Wilkins and Robert Smirke. There are, of course, significant absentees from this list, such as Henry Holland, Samuel Pepys Cockerell and John Nash in the metropolis, and John Carr and James Gandon in the provinces. Some of these architects seem, however, to have felt the disadvantage of having no first-hand experience of Italy. Holland sponsored his assistants Christopher Ebdon and Tatham to go to Italy, effectively on his behalf, in 1776 and 1794 respectively, while Cockerell's pupils Joseph Kay and Thomas Martyr (not to mention his son Charles Robert) were encouraged to go in the first years of the nineteenth century and, much later (in 1824), Nash sent James Pennethorne. One can well understand why in 1773, for the frontispiece to their *Works in Architecture*, the Adam brothers commissioned Antonio Zucchi to paint the allegorical 'Student conducted to Minerva, who points to Greece, and Italy, the countries whence he must derive the most perfect knowledge & taste in elegant architecture' (Fig.5). Moreover, Zucchi's configuration of the Mediterranean map, in which Italy is placed above Greece, indicates the dominance of travel to Italy and also symbolically suggests that the Romans had not only inherited the architectural mantle of the Greeks but had surpassed their achievements.

Against the overwhelming evidence for the importance of travel to Italy of the numbers and personalities mentioned here, the counter arguments of a small minority of architects in the mid 1760s seem almost insignificant. However, they point to a telling assumption about such travel and are therefore worth considering. A vociferous critic of the Italian experience was one of the four architect founder-members of the Royal Academy, John Gwynn, who, in 1766, had written:

where is the necessity of this parade of going to Rome[;] is there a building, or even a fragment of a building in Greece or Italy, of which we have not accurate draughts and measures? and is it not from these resources that every modern building is compiled without variation, and without the least attempt at novelty or invention? ... But this being the case, what becomes of genius and invention, is the farce of an architect's having been at Rome to supply the want of these, and [the exclusion of] every attempt of introducing novelty and elegance, because it is not of foreign extraction[.]³

Gwynn's nationalism, bordering on xenophobia, finds its visual counterpart in Charles Churchill's caricature 'Arrivd from Italy', in which the victor of the competition to design Blackfriars Bridge over the Thames, the Scot Robert Mylne, is seen serving up to the English public the unpleasant 'tricks' he had learned at Rome (Fig.6). At the heart of Gwynn's objection to Italian travel, however, was the issue of ancient architecture, the surveying and recording of which he felt to be an impediment to modern invention. This point was echoed the following year, when the elder James Paine commented that 'in our time, when all the finest examples of ancient architecture are faithfully given by numbers of ingenious persons, what more can be learned by going abroad, than that those very ruins are in a less perfect state now, than when they were drawn and measured a century or two ago'.[4] The notion promulgated by both writers, that the archaeological record of ancient Roman (and Greek) architecture was in some sense complete by the middle of the eighteenth century, was, in fact, profoundly out of step with the activities of the British architectural students who, even at that moment, were flocking to Rome and for whom the study of Antiquity evidently outweighed all other considerations. They and their successors put great effort into surveying the ruined buildings of Rome and its eastern empire, but this method of study only represented one aspect of their approach to Antiquity. Of no less significance were the topographical and capricious drawings of ruins made, in particular, by Robert Adam in the 1750s and by those who followed him. An understanding of the relationship between these different modes of study and their connection with later eighteenth-century British architectural design is the principal purpose of this background chapter. First, however, it is necessary to consider the distinctive character of British architectural travel which developed in this period, the practical framework of which not only conditioned student activities in relation to the Antique but also established patterns which, it will be argued later, were resumed in the years between 1815 and 1835.

The nature of architectural travel and association

In the second half of the eighteenth century it was very uncommon for architects to travel prior to completion of their pupillage around the age of 21, or after having established themselves in business in their later twenties. The great majority of those listed in the first part of Appendix A were therefore relatively youthful and impressionable. In this respect they corresponded with the typical young Grand Tourist, but it is a great mistake to think that these two groups of traveller can be readily equated. The supervised Grand Tour, undertaken by young aristocrats and gentry in order to complete their educations, involved a range of experiential objectives, of which acquiring architectural expertise formed a small part in some cases. By contrast, students intent on a professional architectural career were travelling to obtain specific aesthetic and technological skills, equivalent to those sought by painters and sculptors.[5] Architectural travel should be distinguished from the Grand Tour in terms of its different

social and financial circumstances, its particular itineraries and its broadly academic basis (whether in terms of connections with Italian academies or with influential architectural personalities encountered in Italy). These differences were so marked that it would really be better to avoid use of the term 'Grand Tour' altogether as a description of the travels of architectural students.

While the fact of being on foreign territory may have diminished the rigour with which British social protocol was enforced at home and facilitated a certain fluidity between individuals from different classes, there is no doubt that the distinction between the Grand Tourist and the emergent professional architect was already apparent at the beginning of the period under discussion here. When the 25-year-old Robert Adam reached Italy in 1755, he wrote: 'if I am known in Rome to be an architect I cannot enter into genteel com-

5. Francesco Bartolozzi's print after Antonio Zucchi: 'A Student conducted to Minerva', c.1773. The goddess points the student of architecture towards Greece and, set over it, Rome.

6. *Charles Churchill: 'Arrivd from Italy', c.1761. The print satirizes Robert Mylne's success in the competition to design Blackfriars' Bridge, London, so soon after his return from Rome. Below the arch Mylne is seen riding back to Edinburgh, laden with Italian academic honours.*

pany'. This was not simply Adam's own snobbish perception of his social position; Richard Hayward, who kept a list of British visitors to Rome from 1753 to 1775, noted that Adam (together with a 'painter' named Capel who arrived at the same time) arrived as 'gentlemen, Rather than studiants'.[6] Adam's letters, the only ones among several surviving collections written by later eighteenth-century British architects in Italy to have been substantially published, represent an important source of information about architectural study activity on the peninsula, but Hayward's comment points to the dangers inherent in taking the experiences they describe to be typical. With capital of £5000 and an expenditure of £800 to £900 per annum while in Italy, Adam was wealthy even by the standards of some of the foremost aristocratic Grand Tourists.[7] Accordingly, he took a manservant to Italy

with him and engaged a valet and a Parisian chef in Rome; he bought his own carriage in the summer of 1755; he employed Charles-Louis Clérisseau as his personal assistant (retaining the French architect after leaving in 1757 until 1760 when James Adam arrived in Rome), and he employed four other draftsmen. The Casa Guarnieri where he lodged (or *Palazzo*, as Adam termed it) had been occupied two years previously by the 2nd Earl of Dartmouth and Frederick, Lord North, a future Prime Minister. Later, James Adam also lived at the Casa Guarnieri, was painted by Pompeo Batoni like many a Grand Tourist, and described himself as socially compromised when caught at a dinner with the architectural student George Dance, the painters Nathaniel Dance and Gavin Hamilton, and the engraver Robert Strange, none of whom kept carriages or assumed the title *Cavaliere* as he did.[8]

7. *Theodosius Keene:*
Drawing of the Forum
Romanum, with the Temple
of Castor and Pollux, 1775.

By contrast, Robert Adam's fellow Scot and contemporary in Rome, Robert Mylne, lived on an annual salary of £30 from his father, having travelled part of the way to Rome on foot, as James Stuart had done before him and Robert Smirke and others were to do afterwards (although in 1803 it took a 'good share of Aristocracy' in Smirke to watch his 50-kg (120-lb) portmanteau being carried on the head by a female porter as they walked from Lerici to Sarzana!).[9] Walking was a common form of travel for architectural students within Italy: for example, the six-week expedition from Rome to Naples undertaken by James Stuart, Nicholas Revett and the younger Matthew Brettingham with Gavin Hamilton in 1748 was accomplished entirely on foot, an unthinkable hardship for Grand Tourists.[10] The majority of the students were supported by modest parental allowances, although some private patrons, such as Lord Leicester (who supported Brettingham's visit to Italy) were generous with their protégés.[11] Sixty pounds per annum was the sum commonly allowed, an amount identical to the living expenses provided by the Royal Academy's three-year Travelling Studentship, established in 1774 with money from the Society of Dilettanti, taken up by John Soane in 1777 and George Hadfield in 1790.[12]

Sixty pounds was not a negligible amount on which to survive for a year, but the students frequently found their resources stretched (lodging for a year in Rome, for example, cost approximately half of their salary). Even the prudent

Soane returned to Britain after only two years on the Continent with debts of £120.[13] As a consequence, many sought employment from Grand Tourists whilst in Italy. Mylne supplemented his income by serving as architectural tutor to three Grand Tourists and by acting as draftsman to the antiquarian Richard Phelps for his proposed book on the antiquities of Sicily.[14] In terms of the income they might gain, however, students of architecture were disadvantageously placed by comparison with sculptors and painters. A sculptor such as Joseph Nollekens could fare well from the trade in repaired or made-up ancient statues, while painters could earn good money through commissions for portraits or selling landscapes. Architects were occasionally employed to produce topographical or measured drawings, an example of which can be found in a sketch of the Arch of the Septimius Severus made in 1775 by Theodosius Keene for the amateur architect Sir Roger Newdigate and presented to the client for comment prior to being drawn up neatly.[15] Keene was a competent draftsman, as a print-like topographical view of the Temple of Castor and Pollux in the Forum shows (Fig.7), but architects could hardly hope to compete commercially in this field with the numerous British painters, especially the outstanding watercolourists who were in Italy at the same time (Pl.1). In terms of commissions for specifically architectural work, the best that young architects could hope for from British patrons they met in Italy was to produce designs for buildings in the hope of future preferment or, more often, for small parts of buildings such as chimneypieces.[16]

These financial details are important, in that they circumscribed the activities of architectural students in Italy. That a large proportion of the average three to four years spent in the country was devoted to residence in Rome was no doubt partly due to the relative economy of staying in one place. Certainly, architects were not adherents of the standard itinerary of the Grand Tour, with the emphasis it placed on moving between Italian cities at different times of the year to take advantage of climatic conditions and to witness particular festivals. In fact some saw the festivals as a distraction from serious study: Stephen Riou complained in 1753 that the 'airy noisy joys' and 'killing pleasures of the expired Carneval' had ruined Rome in the spring for one who had 'tasted of what makes this great city the most enchanting to the lovers of the arts'.[17] Residence in the Eternal City also provided the opportunity for students to familiarize themselves with the villas, sanctuaries, tombs and other Roman remains of the surrounding Campagna. After his first winter in Rome, Charles Heathcote Tatham systematically set aside one day each week in the spring of 1795 for expeditions of up to 24 km (15 miles) distance outside the city and, in 1803–4, Joseph Kay kept a diary specifically documenting his 'excursions' around Rome, including day trips to Tivoli and Ostia and longer visits to the Alban Hill towns to the south.[18] A trip to Spoleto to see the well-preserved Temple of Clitumnus could be undertaken

8. Measuring the Temple
of Juno, Agrigento, from
Richard, Abbé de Saint-Non,
'Voyage pittoresque de
Naples et de Sicile',
published in 1785.

from the Rome base and included the Apennine scenery and falls of Terni and Narni; but antiquities on the east coast or in the north, such as the Arch of Trajan at Ancona and the amphitheatre at Verona, tended to be seen by the students when travelling to or from Rome at the beginning or end of their Italian sojourns.

The case of Naples and southern Italy was somewhat different. Three times the size of Rome and with a volcano which obliged foreign visitors in this period with relatively frequent eruptions, the city of Naples was a social and physiological phenomenon. The presence of the politically and culturally adept Sir William Hamilton as British ambassador from 1764 to 1800 further ensured the importance of the city as a place of residence for Grand Tourists. For architectural students, however, Naples had little to offer in terms of Roman architecture since the pronaos of the Temple of Castor and Pollux, incorporated into the church of S. Paolo Maggiore, had col-

lapsed in the 1688 earthquake.[19] It offered even less in terms of modern buildings, invariably spoken of dismissively by the British. Naples was, nonetheless, the base from which important expeditions had to be made: to Pozzuoli, Baia and Cuma in the Campi Flegrei, and increasingly to the Vesuvian towns of Herculaneum and Pompeii. Moreover, in that it provided the major point of access to Paestum and Sicily, Naples played an important role in introducing British students to Greek architecture, since so few (perhaps just ten per cent) went on to Greece itself.[20] For these reasons almost all of the British architects who visited Italy stayed at Naples, some only for a matter of days but many for a period of a month or so.

The limited resources of most young British architects in Italy had a material effect on the way they studied ancient architecture, especially once they had travelled away from Rome and other large centres. The great expeditions organized by the Society of Dilettanti and other wealthy anti-

quarians to examine ancient sites were very well equipped. James Dawkins's journey to the Levant with John Bouverie and Robert Wood in 1750 took place in 'a ship hired for us in London, and fitted out with every thing we could think might be useful', namely a library of Greek historians and poets, books on antiquities and travel writings, gifts with which to bribe local landowners and a variety of surveying instruments.[21] Visual evidence of such well-resourced projects is offered by the Abbé Richard de Saint-Non's expedition to the Kingdom of Naples and Sicily (Fig.8). The Abbé's team of antiquarians and artists erected scaffoldings and swarmed all over the Temple of Juno at Agrigento with their rods and lines, while he and his companions (including two ladies) sat comfortably beneath an awning, fresh provisions on the table and a troupe of Sicilian horsebacked bagpipers serenading them. Most architectural students had to make do with a good deal less equipment, often no more than a case of drawing instru-

ments and some rulers. The cost of erecting scaffolding lay beyond the means of the students, as comments from Gandy and Smirke confirm.[22] Ladders could easily be hired in Rome though, and a 1779 drawing by the French artist and collector Louis-François Cassas showing two students somewhat precariously measuring the entablature of the Temple of Vespasian doubtless represents an almost daily occurrence in the Forum (Fig.9). Travelling in the countryside the students were faced with less favourable circumstances for surveying work. At Paestum, Smirke found that ladders could only be obtained from a town several miles distant and at prohibitive cost. It is no surprise to find that the drawings which survive from his studies at the site are topographical views.[23] Absence of survey drawings and the emphasis placed on other forms of study of ancient architecture might be seen, then, partly as a reflection of these practical considerations.

A further respect in which architectural students differed

9. Louis-François Cassas: View of the Forum Romanum, 1779, with two students measuring the Temple of Vespasian.

from young Grand Tourists lay in the academic milieu in which they moved. Most of the major Italian cities had fine arts academies; some, like those in Florence and Rome, of historic fame by the middle of the eighteenth century. British architectural students doubtless joined compatriot painters and sculptors at the Accademia del Nudo, the life class run by the Accademia di S. Luca in Rome, a study facility to which, even after the foundation of the Royal Academy, architects had no access in London. The design teaching offered by the Italian academies was too elementary, however, for students who had already completed apprenticeships in Britain.[24] A sense of how the British rated themselves in comparison with Italian students can be gained from the fact that, in the *Concorso Clementino* (one of two periodic open competitions run by the Accademia di S. Luca), they thought only of entering the most senior of the three classes, thereby competing with young Italian architects on the verge of entering practice.[25] Victory in such competitions offered a sign of professional success with no equivalent in Britain, at least until the foundation of the Royal Academy. The winning students became a greater focus of public attention in Rome than all but the most distinguished or notorious Grand Tourists, receiving their medals at a splendid ceremony in the great hall of the Palazzo Senatorio on the Capitoline Hill, its walls hung with crimson damask (Fig.10). When Robert Mylne won first prize in 1758, the 'King of England' (James Francis Edward Stuart, the Old Pre-

tender) was on the dais: 'Think on my heart when I received the news [of my victory],' Mylne had written to his brother, 'thump, thump, thump, I feel it yet.'[26] Such success did not go unnoticed in Britain either, as is evident from the appearance of Mylne heading for Edinburgh on horseback with his 'Medals Deplomas/Deplomas from Rome' in Charles Churchill's caricature (see Fig.6).

As someone with gentlemanly pretensions, Robert Adam would not have dreamed of entering one of the Italian *concorsi*. In common with almost a third of later eighteenth-century British students in Italy, however, he was interested in the status conferred by elected membership of Italian academies.[27] The academies maintained social divisions by distinguishing between *dilettanti*, who were generally elected to honorary status, and *professori* or professional artists. In the case of the Accademia di S. Luca, election as *Accademico di Merito* gave British travelling architects the same status as resident Italian professors, including the right of attendance at the monthly meetings and of involvement in setting subjects for and in judging the *concorsi*. According to the standard history of British architecture of this period, the students' participation in the architectural thought of Italian academies was thus 'at least as important to English architecture as the advantages gained from the measurement of antique buildings'.[28] That this was really so may be doubted, however. British architects were generally elected to academies in passing through cities or, in the case of Rome, when they were on the point of returning home. Even the participation of British expatriate members in the theoretical and policy discussions of the Accademia di S. Luca can be shown to have been relatively insignificant.[29]

The connection between the Accademia di S. Luca and Roman antiquities could hardly be ignored by architects visiting the city. Although it had no formal responsibility for the ruins, the institution's base was the domed church of SS. Martina e Luca which stood right on the northern edge of the Forum, overlooking the submerged Arch of Septimius Severus (Fig.11) and the new premises, to which it removed in the 1790s, were in Via Bonella, which ran between the Forum and the 'Arco de' Pantani' (next to the Forum of Augustus). It can be suggested, however, that the ideological and pedagogical approaches of the Academy lagged behind the intensified study of Antiquity in later eighteenth-century Rome. The leading Italian personality in this regard was undoubtedly Giambattista Piranesi, *Accademico di Merito* from 1761 and a notable presence at meetings until 1766. Subsequently, Piranesi's attendance declined significantly. He was entirely absent during the last six years of his life (except for a visit to a meeting held on 11 October 1778, less than a month before his death), and he never held more than minor office.[30] By contrast, the dominant architectural personality in the Academy at this period appears to have been Clemente Orlandi, *Principe* (President) in 1757 and in 1769–70; he was also acting in that role

11. Giambattista Piranesi: Veduta of the Arch of Septimius Severus. The Church of SS. Martina e Luca beside the Arch was the seat of the Accademia di S. Luca for most of the later eighteenth century.

12. Clemente Orlandi: S. Paolo primo Eremita, Rome, 1767–72.

for twelve months from May 1772 during the absence in Spain of Anton Rafael Mengs. Orlandi was not a prolific architect, but his design ideas emerge clearly enough from his academic *morceau de réception* and from his design for the church of S. Paolo primo Eremita, built between 1767 and 1772 (Fig.12).[31] Both show him to have been a devotee not merely of the Roman Baroque tradition, perpetuated in the middle of the eighteenth century by the *Principe* Ferdinando Fuga, but of the Borrominesque form of Baroque universally condemned by British architects. Orlandi's conservatism evidently came to a head in the *Concorso Balestra* of 1773. He set as the subject the problem of unifying architecturally Piazza del Popolo, and was no doubt influential in the award of the prizes to Domenico Lucchi (a pupil of a Roman architect) and Saverio Marini from Naples, whose designs drew respectively on Pietro da Cortona's S. Maria della Pace and on St Peter's, among other sources.[32] Entirely overlooked was the entry of Thomas Harrison of Chester, who manipulated the ancient Roman elements of the triumphal arch and the Pantheon dome with consummate skill to produce an innovative Neo-classical design (Fig.13). Harrison petitioned Pope Clement XIV to have his designs displayed alongside those of the winners, and the public support he received was such that the Pope, in an unprecedented move, compelled the recalcitrant Academy to elect the English student *Accademico di Merito*.

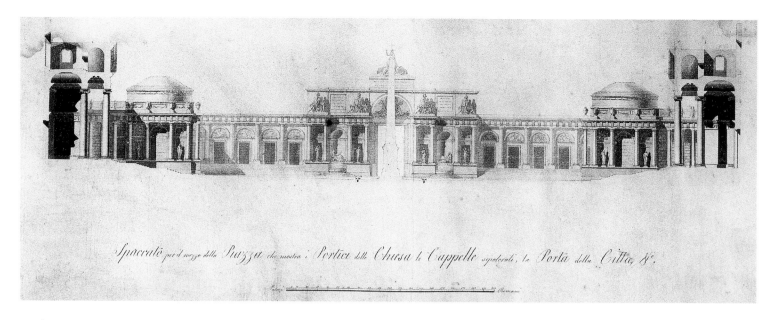

Spaccato per il mezzo della Piazza che mostra i Portici delle Chiesa le Cappelle sepolcrali, la Porta della Città, &c.

13. Thomas Harrison:
*Design for the Piazza del
Popolo, prepared for the
Concorso Balestra at the
Accademia di S. Luca, 1773.*

Harrison's ideas bear witness to the influence not of the Accademia di S. Luca but of the only foreign academy of any size and significance in later eighteenth-century Rome, the Académie de France, housed from 1725 in Palazzo Mancini on the Corso. The French system of architectural education was the envy of British students. From 1720 to 1793 the Académie royale d'Architecture in Paris organized competitions culminating in the *Grand Prix* (or *Prix de Rome*), through which successful students could be sent to Palazzo Mancini for four years as *pensionnaires* (students with a stipend) of the French state. Although directors of the Académie de France were automatically elected to the Accademia di S. Luca, the official relationship between the two institutions was not as close in the second half of the eighteenth century as it had been since the late seventeenth, nor were French architectural students such conspicuous participants in the Italian *concorsi* as their British counterparts. This might be seen not just as a reflection of differing national academic circumstances but also of the different approach to design adopted by the French students. The eclectic treatment of antique forms, which marked the arrival of a new design approach in the 1740s, had its origin in the work on paper of Jean-Laurent Le Geay in Rome, and was reflected by the *pensionnaires* who followed him, especially in their designs for scenic backdrops or temporary structures erected for the biannual Rome Festival of the Chinea.[33] By 1749 Le Geay and his followers had returned to Paris, where they may well have associated with the avant garde Ecole des Arts, set up in the Rue de la Harpe by Jacques-François Blondel. The influence of their ideas was quickly apparent in the Académie royale d'Architecture itself. In the 1746 *Grand Prix* competition, Gabriel Turgis was premiated for the design of an Hôtel of typical early eighteenth-century French character, drawn from the vocabulary of Jules Hardouin Mansart and Robert de Cotte.[34] By contrast, Marie-Joseph Peyre's win-

ning design for a fountain of 1751 presented a far more adventurous and inventive treatment of Classical motifs, including the use of the Doric order. More striking still was Charles de Wailly's 1752 winning design for the forecourt to a great palace (Fig.14). The single-fornix triumphal arch, with free-standing Doric columns and the quadriga placed on a surmounting drum, represent an innovatory recombination of forms drawn from Roman ruins. Moreover, de Wailly's careful pictorial use of light to create a sense of distance and scale points towards the development of an architectural sublimity in design ideas to match that being created around 1750 by Piranesi in the views of Roman monuments published in *Varie vedute* and *Antichità romane*.

Some British students, notably William Chambers (but probably also Robert Mylne), were familiar with these French advances from having studied at Blondel's Ecole des Arts in Paris, and established lifelong friendships with fellow students Peyre, de Wailly and Julien-David Leroy. For many more, it was in Rome that the connections were made. Chambers, like the Adams after him, associated with Clérisseau, Laurent Pecheux (also a friend of George Dance and tutor to Robert Adam) and the sculptor Augustin Pajou.[35] All of these men, of course, studied in the circle of Piranesi, whose personal inspiration and printed works represent a touchstone for the European study of Antiquity in the second half of the eighteenth century. Rome at this time functioned as an international community of students, working together, tracing each other's drawings and exchanging prints. In the absence of a physical base to match the Palazzo Mancini, the Caffè degli Inglesi, with Piranesi's fantastical Egyptian wall decorations, might be considered the seat of an unofficial British artists' 'academy'. The records of the annual Eastertide census in Rome, in which at least half of the architects listed in Appendix A feature, show them almost without exception to have been resident

in the streets of the three parishes of S. Andrea delle Fratte, S. Lorenzo in Lucina and S. Maria del Popolo nearest the Piazza di Spagna (see Pl.1).[36] The Caffè, as Thomas Hardwick found on his arrival in Rome, was the point of interchange for British artists and antiquarians, a place as essential to their lives as the salons were to the Grand Tourists.[37] It was there that the British could always be contacted by their colleagues of other nationalities, where working parties could be assembled and ideas discussed.

Roman ruins: the archaeological approach

The process begun in Rome by what was known even at the time as 'L'Ecole de Lejeay' has been described as nothing less than the 'dissolution of the Vitruvian vocabulary'.[38] While caprice played an important part in this, as will be seen later in this chapter, it was by no means an entirely wilful development. The belief that Graeco-Roman architecture had functioned within an invariable framework of rules, as set out by Vitruvius, may have been discarded, but in its place came the idea that a freer disposition of architectural elements was itself sanctioned by ancient practice. Archaeological enquiry and recording were therefore important components of the later eighteenth-century study of Antiquity, components which were in line with the Enlightenment tendency towards quasi-scientific investigation, precise observation and categorization.

The work central to the mid-eighteenth-century understanding of ancient Roman architecture was Antoine Desgodetz's *Les Edifices antiques de Rome dessinés et mesurés très exactement*, published in Paris in 1682 after its author had been dispatched to Rome eight years earlier by the Académie royale d'Architecture.[39] The book comprised descriptive text interleaved with 137 plates, which showed twenty-three Antique monuments in Rome, together with the Temple of 'Vesta' at Tivoli and the amphitheatre of Verona. It had superseded the sixteenth- and earlier seventeenth-century surveys of these ruins and achieved canonical status, both in terms of the minute measurements and in terms of the character of architectural ornament it presented. By the middle of the eighteenth century, however, Desgodetz's work was subject to criticism on three fronts: its inconsistent modes of representation; the inaccuracy of its measurements; and its almost exclusive concentration on the religious and civic architecture of Rome itself. Although Desgodetz's essential visual approach did not differ from the standard Renaissance technique of rendering the buildings and their details orthographically, of central importance to his archaeological and scholarly claims were the images with which he generally opened his account of each monument. Some of these, such as those of the Temples of Hercules Victor, of Saturn and of Antoninus and Faustina, purported to show just the surviving Antique elements, with Medieval and more modern accretions stripped away and a few wisps of foliage introduced to suggest ruination.[40] It would have been clear to any student visiting Rome, however, that these plates were not objective records of the monuments. In the case of the Temple of Castor and Pollux in the Forum, for example, the overall form of the three columns and entablature shown by Desgodetz reflected what did survive, but he had restored all the carved elements to perfect condition (Fig.15, compare with Fig.7). Desgodetz also depicted two courses of a travertine podium beneath the columns which the early nineteenth-century excavations would show did not exist in this form. In the case of some temples, such as that of Portunus, Desgodetz showed the entire podium restored. In other cases, such as that of the Temple of Mars Ultor, the podium was not shown at all (in fact no restoration was undertaken). This inconsistency no doubt reflected the different extents to which Desgodetz had been able to open

15. Antoine Desgodetz:
*Elevation of the Temple of
Castor and Pollux, Rome,
from 'Les Edifices antiques
de Rome', published in 1682.*

OPPOSITE
16. Thomas Hardwick:
*Entablature of the Temple
of Castor and Pollux, Rome,
1777–9.*

Entablature to three Columns in the Campo Vaccino at Rome.

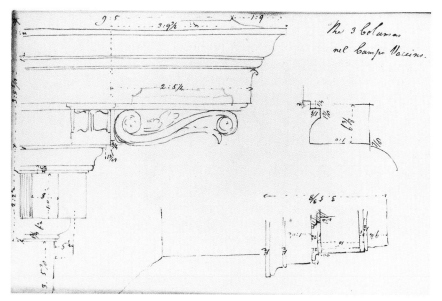

excavations at the bases of the monuments, but it was also perceived as a point of fallibility once visiting architects began examining the extant remains with their own eyes.

The second respect in which Desgodetz's canonical status was called into question after 1750 was the famed accuracy of his measurements and consequent disposition of architectural ornament. In 1760, with the columns of the Temple of Castor and Pollux threatening to collapse, the Roman Conservatori had scaffolding placed around the monument. Piranesi, in a letter addressed to Robert Mylne in London, described this opportunity, 'one of the most rare occasions', to study one of Rome's greatest buildings at close quarters and in reasonable safety. He declared that Desgodetz was not 'so exact as he is considered to be, not even tolerably accurate'. To prove his point, he had taken several Englishmen up to the entablature

and there, 'on the spot with Desgodetz in my hand, have shown them that this author has varied all the ornaments and consequently has altered most of the dimensions'.[41] It is hard to see today where Desgodetz might have erred with the mouldings and his measurement of the capital height, at 66⅓ modular parts (1.610 m), is only 5 mm lower than the survey of the Temple made with the latest equipment and published in 1991. The modern study has shown, however, that with other monuments, such as the Hadrianeum, where he erred by 20 cm with the width of the abacus, Desgodetz invented measurements in order to complete his restorations.[42]

The final regard in which Desgodetz's work was called into question at this time concerned the limited nature of its subject matter. With many more architects travelling to Italy and, in a few cases, further afield in the Mediterranean, the idea that the ruins in the capital city alone could serve as a microcosm of Roman architectural practice throughout the empire could no longer be maintained. Moreover, Desgodetz's text had effectively isolated Roman religious and civic architecture from other types of building, such as tombs and domestic property. Although the stuccoed and painted decoration of such spaces had fascinated European antiquarians and architects since the Renaissance, the excavations of the later eighteenth century at Herculaneum and Pompeii, especially, but also in Rome, fired the enthusiasm of visiting students (Pl.II).

The refinement and extension of the grammar of Roman architecture, then, lay behind the labour which many British architectural students invested in surveying and recording Roman ruins in the second half of the eighteenth century. A full revision of Desgodetz no doubt lay in the minds of some, although in the event the seventeenth-century plates were reused unaltered in a French reprint of 1779 and in George Marshall's English translation (1771–95). Robert Adam was one of the first architects to make a concerted attempt to revise Desgodetz, deploying Clérisseau, the Belgian Laurent-Benoît Dewez, Agostino Brunias and two other Italian draftsmen to this purpose for a year in 1755–6.[43] Surviving sketchbooks and letters from a number of British students testify to detailed surveying campaigns, but the architect who perhaps came nearest to arranging his data in publishable form was Thomas Hardwick in the late 1770s. Hardwick compiled an album, now in Baltimore, in which his measurements were laid out as though for the engraver, the ornaments economically tipped in with ink as a guide (Fig.16).[44] The neat measurement Hardwick gave here for the ten mouldings comprising the architrave of the Temple of Castor and Pollux was 3 ft 6⅜ in, a measurement he preferred to take from a 'model' (presumably a cast) rather than rely on the memoranda he had taken on site, where he recorded the same measurement as 3 ft 5 in before amending it to 3 ft 4¾ in. Reliance on a cast, in which slight increases of scale are possible, was a mistake in this case, since Hardwick's initial measurement was astonishingly a mere 2 mm away from a survey of the monument made in

1989.[45] What this shows, however, is that students felt some uncertainty about the minutiae of measurements made on timber ladders 15 m (50 ft) or so above the ground, where parallax distortion was likely to occur if the eye was not exactly level with the element being measured. The quest for absolute 'accuracy' was, in fact, an obsessional but perhaps ultimately a rather futile aspect of the study of antiquities, since, albeit within much smaller margins than their sixteenth-century predecessors, different architects came up with different results on the same monument. Hardwick's one-time working companion, John Soane, for example, measured the height of the architrave of the Temple of Castor and Pollux as 3 ft 5⅜ in, 12 mm higher than the most recent survey (Fig.17).[46] What can be said, however, is that these architects returned home satisfied that they had verified the grammar of Roman architecture for themselves.

British architects were, of course, by no means the only students who engaged in this form of archaeological study. In the mid 1750s the *pensionnaires* Peyre, de Wailly and Pierre-Louis Moreau-Desproux began work on a 'supplement' to Desgodetz, focusing on the Baths of Diocletian (it was Peyre who, in 1779, was to instigate the reprinting of *Les Edifices antiques de Rome).*[47] Interest in the Roman thermal complexes represents an important part of later eighteenth-century study of the antique, since it indicates the expansion of the vocabulary of Roman forms beyond Republican and Augustan religious architecture to incorporate the huge-scale *opus caementicium* architecture of later imperial Rome. The principal published source on the bath buildings remained Palladio's sixteenth-century reconstructive drawings, published by Lord Burlington as *Fabbriche antiche* in the 1730s. The importance attached to the baths can be judged from the fact that copies of a set of measured drawings of the Baths of Caracalla, made by James Byres with two or three other architects, can be found among the papers of visiting students such as Hardwick and Richard Norris.[48] One British architect, however, set out for Rome with the express intention of revising *Fabbriche antiche* through first-hand surveys: Charles Cameron, author of *The Baths of the Romans* in 1772, may not have fulfilled his ambitious project, but the studies he did carry out in Rome were certainly exceptional among architectural students from Britain.[49] Cameron obtained permission to make excavations at the 'Baths of Titus' on the Esquiline Hill in support of his project. In fact, although he did not know it, he was exploring the remains of Nero's Golden House below the Baths of Trajan. One of his points of entry to the subterranean rooms of the palace was high up through the south wall of Room 119 (Fig.18). This room, evidently unknown to earlier explorers of the Golden House and not properly surveyed again until the 1920s, is today recognized as one of the most important in this most important of Roman buildings (Pl.III).

A less original but similar case to Cameron's is the excavation at the base of the Colosseum, organized in 1777 by Hardwick and reported to the Society of Antiquaries, in which Hardwick corrected Desgodetz's assumption that the amphitheatre stood on a six-step stylobate.[50] Permission to make such excavations had to be sought from the Reverenda Camera Apostolica, at the head of which was the Cardinal Camerlengo (the papal 'Chamberlain'). From 1763 to 1799 this office was held by a single man, Cardinal Carlo Rezzonico, but the day-to-day management of the Roman monuments lay with the Commissarii delle Antichità, of whom there were four in this period: Ridolfino Venuti (1744–63), Johann Joachim Winckelmann (1763–8), Giovanni Battista Visconti (1768–84) and his son Filippo Aurelio Visconti (1784–99).[51] Under Venuti and the Visconti, in particular, a structured system was established to govern the excavation, the export and (particularly after the foundation of the Museo Pio-Clementino in the early 1770s) the preservation of antiquities.[52] While the quest for potentially lucrative objets d'art was encouraged, however, there appears to have been little willingness on the part of these authorities to sanction disruptive physical interventions intended for purely archaeological or architectural purposes.

OPPOSITE
17. John Soane: Measured details of the entablature of the Temple of Castor and Pollux, Rome, 1778–80.

18. Domus Aurea, Rome, Room 119, the upper part of the south wall. This is precisely where Cameron broke through to become the first architect-scholar of modern times to enter this important Roman room.

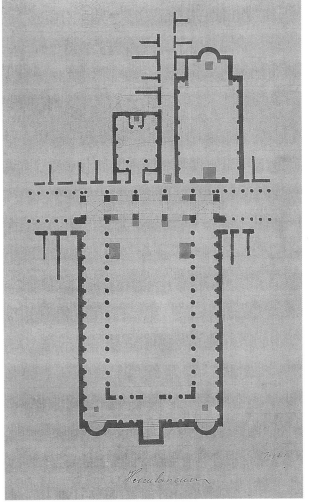

19. A plan of the Basilica at Herculaneum, perhaps based by William Chambers on a French source in the 1750s.

20. James Stuart, Nicholas Revett, Robert Wood and James Dawkins meeting at the Monument of Philopappus in Athens, May 1751. Revett and Stuart (who looks directly at the viewer) are dressed in Turkish costume. Dawkins converses with Revett, while Wood studies the Monument.

Indeed, Ludovico Mirri's 1774 clearance of parts of the Golden House was one of the very few major projects undertaken by an Italian antiquarian primarily for academic reasons in the second half of the century.[53] Such explorations did not form part of the excavation business, in which capital raised by the sale of two-thirds of the sculpture found in one dig was invested in employing the forty or so men needed to carry out the next. Most British architectural students could not, in any case, have afforded this kind of capital outlay.

What Cameron's excavation does indicate, however, is a quest for novelty through investigation of hitherto under-explored types of ancient architecture and places. This was doubtless one of the attractions of the Campanian excavations, although students travelling to Herculaneum and Pompeii were constrained by both administrative and physical problems. Keen to protect their patrimony, the Bourbon authorities in Naples placed notorious restrictions on access to and study at the sites. Soane's studies of the Temple of Isis complex at Pompeii, so he told his Royal Academy audience when lecturing much later, were made 'by stealth by moonlight', although the nineteen pages of memoranda and sketches

on Pompeii which survive in his notebooks suggest that he enjoyed better access to the site than he claimed (Pl.iv).[54] Much of the tour of Herculaneum took place in stifling tunnels 2 m (c.6 ft) high and 1 m (c.3 ft) wide, up to 20 m (c.60 ft) deep in the solidified lava and mud which had flowed over the town in AD 79. At Pompeii, the covering of volcanic ash and *lapilli* was more easily removed, but the excavations tended to be back-filled once objets d'art had been extracted and paintings cut from the walls.[55] As a result of these restrictions, the British visual record of the Campanian towns is a disappointing one in the 1750–1800 period, with the possible exception of Soane's work at Pompeii. Chambers's papers, for example, contain a plan of the subterraneous Herculaneum Basilica and two adjacent buildings, the Galleria Balba and the Augustalium, but this appears to have been traced or closely derived from the French architect Jérôme-Charles Bellicard's plan in Charles-Nicolas Cochin's *Observations sur les antiquités de la ville d'Herculanum*, which appeared both in French and in English translation in 1753 (Fig.19).[56] Instead of the cross vaults carried on a portico across the front of the building, however, Chambers's plan appears to correspond more closely with the recent discovery that the Basilica had quadrifrontal arches at either end.

The quest for novelty, coupled with the desire to obtain a fuller and more accurate record of ancient architecture, underpinned the famous expeditions further east in the Mediterranean which form such a feature of later eighteenth-century archaeological endeavour. One can only speculate on the discussions between Robert Wood, James Dawkins, John Bouverie, James Stuart, Nicholas Revett, Matthew Brettingham and Gavin Hamilton which took place in Rome in late 1749 and early 1750, or those between Wood, Dawkins, Stuart and Revett when they met again in Athens in May 1751 (Fig.20). Their outcome, however, is evident enough in Wood's *The Ruins of Palmyra* (1753) and *The Ruins of Balbec* (1757), and in Stuart's and Revett's first volume of *The Antiquities of Athens*, which appeared in early 1763, thanks in part to the support of the Society of Dilettanti. The effect of Stuart's and Revett's work was to set up a new canon of ancient Greek architecture.[57] Wood's two books on second- and third-century public architecture on the eastern fringes of the Empire, on the other hand, showed that the Romans had been capable of inventive novelties not to be found in the architectural canon derived from ruins in Rome itself. 'Discoveries' included the remarkable third-century round Temple of Venus at Balbec, with its podium and entablature of concave curves, and the arch at Palmyra, which gave evidence of Roman planning ingenuity in the way it concealed the change in axis from the principal street to the Temple of the Sun (Temple of Bel) outside the walls (Fig.21).

Wood and Stuart, probably the two prime movers in these expeditions, shared the view that the 'principal merit of works of this kind is truth'.[58] They organized excavations around the bases of the monuments under study and produced measurements claiming accuracy to within hundredths of an inch. In these respects they self-consciously emulated Desgodetz. The key point of difference, however, lay in their use of actual state topographical views, to provide 'authority for our measures' and 'reasons' for every element of their restorations (Fig.22).[59] The extent to which the 'actual state' views of their draftsman, Giovanni Battista Borra, really were topographically precise may be open to question: in the image of the Palmyra arch, for example, the ruined elements appear to have been conveniently arranged in the foreground so as to confirm the restoration of each element of the structure's mannerisms: the pedimented aedicules without columns or pilasters, and its frieze of horizontally arranged acorns (see Fig.21).[60] Nonetheless, this was a new mode of representation for ancient ruins, one quickly adopted by Robert Adam, who went further in bringing actual state and restored elevations together on single plates in his *Ruins of the Palace of the Emperor Diocletian at Spalatro in Dalmatia* of 1764.[61]

If topographical representation of the ruins moved British archaeological study of Roman architecture on to a new footing, in one important respect little had changed from the seventeenth-century approach of Desgodetz and his sixteenth-century predecessors. This was the way in which the structures were shown when restored to their supposed original condition, where they appear as orthogonal elevations (see Fig.21) and occasionally as geometrical sections. One new graphic technique, deployed by Hardwick and others, was the use of wash to distinguish surviving elements from those hypothesized. In Richard Norris's 1769 elevation of the Temple of Antoninus and Faustina, for example, dark grey wash was used for the pediment and podium imagined by the architect, while pale grey wash served to mark the depth to which the columns of the pronaos were buried (Fig.23). This small advance, however, was surely developed as a record of the extent of the monument's submergence with which an architect might return home, rather than as a new way of visualizing the structure when whole. Ancient Roman buildings continued to be seen generally in later eighteenth-century Britain in restorations void of the contexts of neighbouring architecture or surrounding landscape, and void of the vitalizing power of the perspective.[62]

The few large-scale restoration projects which were undertaken by British students in this period should be seen in much the same light, based as they are on Renaissance and Baroque drawings. Edward Stevens's restoration of Pliny's Villa at Laurentinum, used in illustration of Thomas Sandby's fifth Royal Academy lecture on architecture (delivered 1770–98), was made not in Italy (as Soane later supposed) but as

21. Giovanni Battista Borra: Restoration of the arched gateway at Palmyra, drawn for Robert Wood's 'Ruins of Palmyra', published in 1753.

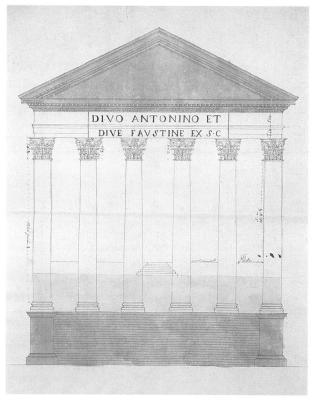

22. *Giovanni Battista Borra: Actual state view of the arched gateway at Palmyra, drawn for Robert Wood's 'Ruins of Palmyra', published in 1753.*

23. *Richard Norris: Elevation of the Temple of Antoninus and Faustina, Rome, 1769. Norris used dark grey wash to denote the Temple's hypothetical pediment, podium and frontal steps, and pale grey wash to show how deeply its columns were buried.*

an academic exercise in London, deriving its character from earlier restorations by Vincenzo Scamozzi and Jean-François Félibien.[63] A more complicated case is that of George Hadfield's extraordinary restoration of the Roman Republican Sanctuary or Temple of Fortuna Primigenia at Praeneste, since Hadfield certainly spent some months in the summer of 1792 either residing at or making visits to the site over which the town of Palestrina and the Palazzo Colonna-Barberini had been built from the fifteenth century (Fig.24 and see Pl.v). Hadfield's set of drawings, which does not include an actual state plan or plans of the surviving Antique elements, only partially survives, making full assessment of his project difficult. It is clear, however, that he was aware of Pietro da Cortona's restoration, published with an extensive text in Josefo Maria Suarez's *Praenestes Antiquae* in 1654, and that he increased the temple's scale and grandeur 'far beyond reality' in a frankly Piranesian manner.[64] Moreover, the choice of a bird's-eye perspective lends the drawings a strangely artificial model-like or theatrical character, heightened in the case of the 'topographical' view by the scale of the only human figures included, who appear as though at the front of a stage

to which the town forms the backdrop. The sheer size of Hadfield's restoration drawing (Pl.v) also suggests that his work had more to do with imaginative fantasy than with archaeological exactitude. At a width of 2.9 m (9½ ft), it only stands comparison, among images produced by British architects in later eighteenth-century Italy, with Robert Adam's 2.75 m (9 ft)-wide fantastical design for a palace, prepared in Rome in 1757.[65] These exceptional images serve as reminders that beyond the specifically archaeological surveying lay a quite different range of responses to Roman ruins among British architectural students during this period.

Roman ruins and architectural invention

In a letter written during his homeward journey from the Mediterranean in 1757, Adam described Robert Wood's 'taste', in a phrase now famous, as 'hard as Iron & as false as Hell'.[66] Adam can hardly have objected to Wood's efforts to extend the vocabulary of Roman architecture, a motivating feature of his own diversion to study Diocletian's Palace at Split a few months earlier. What he meant by 'hard', presumably, was that the archaeological fidelity attempted in *The Ruins of Palmyra* had resulted in decontextualized or coldly academic restorations, images which were 'false' because they lacked the passionate engagement with the grandeur and fertility of invention he believed to have been characteristic of the Roman architectural imagination itself, and which he wished to emulate in his own design work. He had found that work for a revision of Desgodetz, even with the proposed addition of topographical plates, 'retarded more material studies'.[67] By the time of that project's abandonment, Adam, under the influence of Clérisseau and Piranesi, in particular, had developed a creative response to Roman ruins which prioritized the ruin as an object and architectural invention over more strictly archaeological objectives.[68] This approach had far-reaching consequences, both for the development of British Neo-classical

architecture and for the ways in which students subsequently studied in Rome during the second half of the century.

The surviving corpus of Adam drawings relating to Roman ruins embodies an extraordinary exploration of graphic possibilities, ranging from straightforward topography to pure fantasy. In the album now at Penicuik House most of the drawings conform with the title page inscriptions, which indicate that they are 'Italian Views' and 'Views of Antiquity in and about Rome & other parts of Italy'. One drawing, however, formerly attributed to Adam but now to Clérisseau, demonstrates that something other than topographical study was taking place (Fig.25). The drawing is a 'view' of the remains of the eastern apse and platform of the Temple of Venus and Rome, seen from an elevated point in one of the galleries of the Colosseum. An instructive comparison can be made with a drawing executed from an almost identical position thirty years later by Willey Reveley (Fig.26). Reveley used one of the semi-submerged ground-level arches of the Colosseum to frame his view and he foreshortened the perspective, so that the front of the platform of the Temple of Venus and Rome was omitted. In other architectural respects, however, the drawing appears to be a faithful piece of topography. By contrast Clérisseau, in a demonstration of visual selectivity, simply ignored the inconvenient Medieval intrusion on this view of the convent of S. Francesca Romana, with its tall campanile. This selective approach became a notable feature of the approach to drawing among subsequent British students. In his 1778 study of the church of S. Agnese fuori le Mura, for example, Soane removed later Christian elements which interferred with what he took to be a Roman basilica.[69]

The next step after selective viewing in the depiction of ruins in the Adam circle was the transposition of actual ruins into fictitious contexts, in a manner somewhat akin to the *capricci* of the painters Giovanni Paolo Pannini and Hubert Robert.[70] Then there are sketches of 'ruins', in which elements which clearly have their origins in the remains of real struc-

*25. Charles-Louis Clérisseau:
View of the Temple of Venus
and Rome, Rome, 1755–7.*

*26. Willey Reveley: View
of the Temple of Venus and
Rome, Rome, 1784–9.*

tures were recast into new forms (Fig.27). In this image, for example, Adam derived a ruin with a pair of Doric columns and a high attic from the remains of the (Corinthian) Forum Transitorium, combining it with an arch developed from the 'Arco de' Pantani', geographically approximate but not adjacent to the Forum Transitorium. Finally, the largest group of drawings of this pseudo-topographical nature are those represented by Pl.vi from Adam Album 56 in Soane's Museum. In drawings such as this, Adam experimented with the generic vocabulary of Roman architectural forms, coffered vaults for example, in 'ruins' which were entirely invented. The stoical Roman soliders, introduced on a carved relief in the foreground, seem to serve the purpose of 'authenticating' Adam's imagination. It might appear strange that, with the actual ruins of Roman Antiquity before his eyes, Adam should have invested so much energy in imagining and drawing fictitious ruins such as this, but the end objective, of course, was not to achieve a topographical record but a *modus operandi* for the architectural creativity which lay ahead. In this context it is significant that Album 56 concludes with seven drawings of interior or semi-interior spaces, in which Adam imagined entire precisely the sort of building complexes he had imagined ruined (Fig.28 and see Pl.vi). His vision of 'ancient Rome' here was intimately related to that of Piranesi in the *Prima parte di architetture, e prospettive inventate*, and surely also to the sketching trips undertaken with Piranesi to Hadrian's Villa at Tivoli, the Baths of Caracalla, the Appian Way and Albano in the summer of 1755.

A number of conclusions emerge from this summary analysis of ruin drawings within the Adam circle which are of importance in the context of this book, because Adam was a central figure in the establishment of a tradition or 'cult' of the ruin among eighteenth-century British architects, which was to carry over into the early nineteenth century in the teaching and work of architects such as Soane. Moreover, it is important to recognize Adam's approach in order to appreciate the different ways the ruins would be represented by younger nineteenth-century architects, an essential prelude to understanding the different architecture which resulted. The first

LEFT
27. Robert Adam: Imaginary
ruin, based on the Forum of
Nerva and the 'Arco de'
Pantani', Rome, 1755–7.

ABOVE
28. Robert Adam: Imaginary
Roman Building, 1755–7.
This 'building' reflects
Adam's experimentation with
the forms and light effects of
Roman ruins, real or, as seen
in Pl.VI, imagined.

point to note about Roman ruin drawings in the Adam circle, seen most vividly in Clérisseau's 'view' of the Temple of Venus and Rome (see Fig.25), is the way the ruin was isolated from its historical and chronological contexts through the process of selectivity. Adam was little concerned with the historical specificity of the architecture he studied. For example, his reference to 'Domitian's Palace' at Split, instead of Diocletian's, three months before he used the site as the base for establishing his reputation for 'archaeological' research, demonstrates a striking lack of interest in the fact (clearly denoted by the emperors' names) that he was dealing with very late Imperial Roman architecture, not Flavian architecture dating from more than two centuries earlier.[71] Other architects were not quite as cavalier, but it is important to recognize that, as has been well observed elsewhere, for later eighteenth-century architect-travellers such as Adam, history meant more 'a world of places, not of times, a world whose essential structures were topographical, not temporal'.[72] In this context it is significant to note the relative lack of success enjoyed by William Newton in endeavouring to produce the first full and annotated English translation of Vitruvius, a scholarly endeavour begun perhaps with the architect's visit to Italy in 1766–7 but not completed until after his death in 1790.[73] The interests in the ruins of British architects visiting Italy for a few years and seeking a vocabulary of form for their working careers at home were not the same as those of long-term Rome residents, such as Piranesi, and few seem to have entered fully into the intellectual antiquarianism and polemics of his *Le antichità romane* and *Della magnificenza ed architettura de' Romani*.

A second observation on Adam's response to Roman ruins concerns the subject matter of the drawings. It is significant to note the limited degree of interest they show in trabeated architecture, just at the time when Marc-Antoine Laugier, in his *Essai sur l'Architecture* (1753), was exciting Europe with a theory of design around the principle of trabeation which would rapidly be incorporated into the polemics of Greek Revivalism. In Adam's drawings, however, stone columns and their entablatures (pieces of the very temple buildings of the first and early second centuries which form the greater part of the canon established by Desgodetz) play a part, but it is the Roman *opus caementicium* architecture of the second to fourth centuries which predominates: the towering piers, superimposed arches, apses, domes and coffered or stuccoed vaults of baths, basilicas and sepulchral chambers. Seen in this context, Adam's shift from the idea of a revision of Desgodetz to that of studying the baths may be seen as reflecting a reduction of dependence on the orders, soon to be a characteristic of the Adam style of architecture and of interior decoration in particular.

With the exception of drawings on blue-grey prepared paper which required white heightening, a technique he seems to have acquired from Jean-Baptiste Lallemand and which was used throughout a jointly produced album of almost entirely invented ruins in landscape settings,[74] Adam generally depicted the stone or brick-faced concrete masses of his preferred ruins in pen and brown or grey watercolour. Sometimes golden-yellow washes were used for columns and pale blue to capture Italian skies, but the red porphyry sarcophagi and other such accoutrements, which make occasional appearances, come as a surprise (see Pl.VI). Adam's palette, acquired partly from Clérisseau but also from the ferrous gallnut ink and occasional red chalk of Piranesi's drawings, became a standard element in the representation of Roman ruins among later eighteenth-century British students. Ruined buildings

in the city of Rome had been bleached of colour, of course, by centuries of exposure, but new archaeological discoveries, such as those at Pompeii, opened the possibility of new aesthetic ideas for any student prepared to accept, on the evidence of his own eyes, that Winckelmann's view of colour as an impediment to the beauty of form may not have been shared by the Romans. Soane's notes indicate that he was aware the columns of the quadriportico behind the Great Theatre at Pompeii had been painted blue, red and yellow, yet he passed no positive or negative comment on the Roman use of architectural colour in general. When he used washes to capture the character of the Temple of Isis and its surrounding buildings, he used the conventional brown and straw colours (see Pl.IV).[75] In the case of interior decoration, discoveries at Pompeii and in Roman excavations, such as that of a late Hadrianic house in the grounds of the Villa Negroni witnessed by Thomas Hardwick in 1777, left no doubt as to the rich paint colours deployed by the Romans for walls and ceilings (see Pl.II and Pl.VII).[76] Naturally there were some instances in which these colours were emulated in later eighteenth-century British interiors, the outstanding example being Joseph Bonomi's remarkable gallery of 1787 for the Dilettante 4th Earl of Aylesford at Packington Hall, inspired

by publications of the 'Baths of Titus' (Nero's Golden House) over the previous decade. In 1762, however, Adam, had found himself 'at a loss' when looking for indications of Roman colouring among the hundreds of ruin drawings with which he had returned from Italy. Shortly afterwards he abandoned *all' antica* ceiling designs and refined the low-relief stucco on pink or green pastel-tinted ground with which his name would become synonymous and which was adopted by James Wyatt and numerous other figures.[77]

A final point which may be inferred from drawings of Roman ruins by Adam and those who followed him in the second half of the century is the high value they attached to the ruin as a ruin. 'We are apt to praise and form greater ideas of ruins than we should perhaps have had of the buildings when whole,' wrote Gandy from Rome in 1796 in a letter quoted as the epigraph to this chapter. The ruin had become a greater stimulus to the imagination of architects than any attempt at visual restoration. Lack of interest in using archaeology as a means of creating images of Roman buildings in their complete states, beyond the frigid restorations of Desgodetz or Wood, corresponded with lack of interest in creating buildings which were literal versions of Roman examples. Instead, elements of ruined buildings and ornamental

30. Richard Dubourg: 'Du Bourg's Museum', London, c.1818. A group of visitors are shown a very large model of the Colosseum. The display was thematic (with tombs on the left here) as well as pseudo-topographical (with the Arch of Titus on the right, placed as though across the Via Sacra).

details were gathered eclectically to produce new forms for modern-day patrons (Fig.29). Adam's Saloon at Kedleston Hall, situated behind a south front modelled on the Arch of Constantine, is a *locus classicus* for this process: the hemispherical Pantheon dome was given the coffers of the tunnel-vaulted aisles of the Basilica of Maxentius, while the four niches with their lozenge coffers (disposed like the niches around the vestibulum of Diocletian's Palace at Split) are versions of the back-to-back apses of the Hadrianic Temple of Venus and Rome (see Fig.25).[78] Paintings of ruins by the artist William Hamilton, inset above the doors, serve as reminders of the sources by which the new building has been inspired, their capricious character a reminder that the process in train was creative rather than strictly mimetic.[79] With its central oculus, external glazed door to the south and north door to the top-lit Entrance Hall, the forms of the Saloon at Kedleston are enlivened and given variety by the way in which the light falls across them. It is arguable that one of the most important lessons architects like Adam learned from drawing great fragments of Roman *opus caementicium* structures was how to manipulate building mass and to handle spatial composition under changing conditions of light.

The British fascination with ruins manifested itself in a number of different guises in the eighteenth century, of course.[80] In the context of the present study of travel, archaeology and visual representation, a significant form to note is the physical representation of ruins found in the later eighteenth-century Italian tradition of architectural model-making, largely centred on the Neapolitan Giovanni Altieri and on Antonio Chichi. The latter made a series of thirty-six models of famous buildings in Rome, including antique examples such as the Arch of Titus.[81] These almost always reproduced the ruin in its actual state and were made of cork in order to give an impression of marble or travertine surfaces pitted by centuries of decay, or of the rough texture of *opus incertum*. The Society of Antiquaries was an early repository for these objects in London, receiving the Temple of 'Vesta' at Tivoli from the expatriate dealer Thomas Jenkins and then, in the late 1770s, an Altieri model of the Colosseum from Thomas Hardwick.[82] The models were presumably expensive, making Hardwick's acquisition an unusual event. His Roman contemporary, Soane, by contrast, purchased his first models (the round temple at Tivoli by Altieri and the Arch of Constantine) only in 1804, when he was an established professional on the eve of becoming Royal Academy Professor.[83] As a young architect, however, Soane had been able to refresh his

31. Joseph Michael Gandy:
John Soane's house at 13
Lincoln's Inn Fields, London:
a view of the dome area by
lamplight, 1811.

OPPOSITE
32. Charles Heathcote
Tatham: Fragments of
Roman architecture brought
to England by the architect
and published in his
'Etchings' in 1806.

memory of the Roman ruins by visiting Richard Dubourg's cork model museum in London (doing so, in fact, a month before its destruction in 1785 in a fire caused by a misadventurous demonstration of Vesuvius erupting). By 1798, Dubourg had opened a second model display (Fig.30). Here the London public and architectural students alike, deprived by that time of access to Italy by the French invasion, could enjoy a vicarious visit to the ruins, with the Tivoli round temple set high on its cliff edge and the Arch of Titus (the only restored monument in the display) straddling its Sacred Way.

Cork models, which may have been at scale but were not at actual size, were of little help to practising architects, however, except as a spur to memory. Of far greater utility were the casts, or even marble fragments with which some managed to return from Italy and which others went to considerable lengths to acquire at a distance. Fragments and casts offered material records of Roman buildings which few could expect to see again during their lifetimes, and a permanent source to which reference could be made for the minutiae of measurement or for ornamental detail. There is some evidence that casts of the major monuments in Rome were not easily come by: moulds were apparently not retained, putting anyone who wanted a cast to the expense of arranging the procedure anew, and the requisite permit could be hard to obtain. In 1760, George Dance took advantage of the rare scaffolding of the Temple of Castor and Pollux to have a cast made of the order, reporting that he had had to save up money especially and that 'It was never modelled before. I had the greatest difficulty to get permission to have it done.'[84] Nonetheless, Edward Stevens, Willey Reveley and James Playfair are all known to have compiled cast collections in Rome, while in 1776 Christopher Ebdon dispatched from Leghorn to his London employer, Henry Holland, seventy casts of ornamental fragments and larger pieces such as the order of the Temple of Vespasian.[85] Soane's first casts evidently came from the 1795 sale of Playfair's effects. He also bought seventeen lots of casts at the sale of Reveley's belongings in 1801, including the capital and entablature of the Temple of Castor and Pollux.[86] In Gandy's atmospheric watercolour of the Dome area at the rear of 13 Lincoln's Inn Fields (Fig.31), Soane is seen extending his arm across the capital in the direction of the entablature on the west wall, or perhaps towards the Altieri cork model of the round temple at Tivoli. The installation of these casts in this position in 1808–9, immediately to the east of what was then his drawing office, shows how intimately these fragmentary representations of Roman Antiquity were related to the education of Soane's pupils and to his own design activities. The ruined elements of Roman buildings were constantly before their eyes.

Casts were doubtless seen as substitutes for loose real fragments of Roman architecture, but the number of specifically architectural marble pieces which entered Britain in the second half of the century seems to have been relatively small by

comparison with other forms of antique sculpture. The purchase and importation of such fragments was limited by three factors: their availability, their price and their weight. Robert Adam had both the wealth and the social position to have acquired in Rome a room full of 'marbles and plaster casts', including 'capitals, pieces of friezes … all the antique orna-

ments that I am to use in my architecture', but these precious possessions later had to be sold in London, as the Adams struggled to recuperate their losses in the Adelphi crisis.[87] The major collection of architectural fragments to enter Britain in this period was that acquired by Charles Heathcote Tatham for Henry Holland in the 1790s. Political turbulence in Rome, leading to the accelerated break up of private Roman collections and diminishing the effectiveness of the export control system, enabled Tatham to buy marble pieces for about £10 each, dearer than casts but not prohibitively so. He cleverly reduced their weight for shipping by having the backs hollowed out. By 1796, Tatham had 250 fragments, a collection he believed to be smaller only than those built up by Bernard de Montfaucon and Piranesi earlier in the century.[88] On his return to London, he published two folio volumes of prints of architectural ornament, the first of items in Roman and other Italian collections and the latter showing the fragments he had collected for Holland together with some he had purchased himself at the sale of the Earl of Bessborough's effects. Tatham made it clear in his prefaces that his purpose was not to deal with the orders of architecture in a quasi-archaeological fashion, as Stuart and Revett had done, but to diversify knowledge of Roman ornament.[89] Accordingly, the drawings of the fragments were arranged on the plates in an almost random order, deliberately undermining any notion of system and suggesting that it was for designers of talent to forge these architectural letters into new words (Fig.32). It is

significant, though hardly surprising, to note that the list of Tatham's subscribers includes many of the figures who, over the past fifty years, had played leading roles in introducing to Britain a Neo-classical architecture inspired by fragmentary Roman ruins: Bonomi, Samuel Pepys Cockerell, Dance, Gandy, Holland, Hardwick, James Lewis, Robert Mylne, Soane and Wyatt. Significantly, too, the list includes leading Roman figures such as Antonio Canova and the architects Mario Asprucci and Giannantonio Selva. Asprucci designed the temples in the *Giardino inglese* at the Villa Borghese, laid out in the mid 1780s by the Scottish landscape painter Jacob More and the location which, to this day, reflects the extent to which Neo-classical ideas, generated by British architects in Rome and developed at home, had returned to influence practice in their place of origin.[90]

By the close of the eighteenth century, the British architects who had studied in Rome during the previous five decades had established patterns of looking at ruins, of representing them on paper, of collecting fragments or casts of them, and of manipulating all these elements in their design work. Archaeology, largely in the form of the surveying both of extant monuments and of little-known remote sites, played an important part in sanctioning the breaking of previously established rules, in providing the grammar of a new architectural language, and in providing novelty. However, the relative lack of advance in the archaeology of architecture across this period effectively left the ruins free to exert a creative

34. Joseph Michael Gandy:
Extemporary 'prova' of a
Triumphal Arch, for the
Concorso Clementino at the
Accademia di S. Luca, 1795.

Prima Claſſe Primo Premio Giovanni Campana Napoletano

35. Giovanni Campana:
Elevation and section of a
Sepulchral Chapel for the
Concorso Clementino at the
Accademia di S. Luca, 1795.

power over the architect, and there was no thoroughgoing interest in what Roman buildings or cities would have been like in Antiquity.

The strength of the British approach to handling the language of Roman Antiquity by the 1790s, and its distinctiveness from the French approach with which it had shared common roots, can be seen microcosmically in the case of Joseph Michael Gandy. The few surviving drawings made by Gandy in Italy comprise topographical views and six sheets of architectural orders and fragments, drawn large scale with brown and grey washes.[91] In 1795, Gandy was the last British student to compete in the *Concorso Clementino* at the Accademia di S. Luca (Fig.33). The central rotunda in the design for a 'Sepulchral Chapel' he was required to submit drew its Pantheon dome, Roman Doric order, frieze of swags, bucrania and paterae not directly from Roman sources but from the mausoleum at Brocklesby in Lincolnshire, built by James Wyatt between 1786 and 1794 when Gandy was his pupil. In addition to this powerful but eminently buildable design, Gandy's performance in the two-hour extemporary examination at the Academy showed a remarkably sure sense of direction in the handling of Antique elements by comparison with his fellow

competitors (Fig.34). Gandy sketched out the subject set, a triumphal arch, and confidently placed it in a landscape setting, while his rivals struggled to impress with partial plans and paltry orthogonal elevations.[92] The attractive utility of Gandy's responses contrasts with the impossible scale and impractical function of the 'Sepulchral Chapel' schemes of competitors like the Roman architect Giovanni Campana, whose design echoes the visionary images produced by Etienne-Louis Boullée and Claude-Nicolas Ledoux during the Revolutionary period (Fig.35). There is a possibility, in fact, that Campana's design relates to drawings produced ten years previously by Etienne-Eloy La Barre for the *Grand Prix* at the Académie royale d'Architecture in Paris, which appeared in Armand-Parfait Prieur's and Pierre-Louis Van Cleemputte's *Collection des prix que la ci-devant Académie d'Architecture proposoit et couronnoit tous les ans.*[93] Within a year of the *concorso*, however, the young General Bonaparte was given command of an army destined for Italy, and Franco-Italian relations were about to move on to an altogether different footing. This was to have far-reaching consequences, not only for French investigations of ancient Roman architecture but also for the British perception of the ruins and for architecture in England.

Chapter 2
The British and Roman archaeology after Napoleon

Rome will be his head quarters, because it is convenient to fix oneself principally in one place, and Rome, from the multitude of its objects both ancient and modern, and from the society obtained among artists of all nations, who resort thither, is far preferable to any other city.
(Joseph Woods's 'Instruction to a Young Architect', 1828)[1]

When Napoleon's army crossed from France to Piedmont in April 1796, the Italian states entered two decades of political turmoil. The effects of this on the pattern of British travel in the Mediterranean area were inevitably enormous, as can be seen in Joseph Michael Gandy's letters documenting life in the increasingly lawless city of Rome.[2] Gandy believed that George III's sixth son, Prince Augustus, in Rome for much of the 1790s, was organizing for a frigate to evacuate all British residents from Civitavecchia to Corsica as the French marched south to Piacenza. In May 1796, however, the aristocrats and other travellers left without the artists' contingent. At this inopportune moment Gandy learned from London that his patron, John Martindale, had become bankrupt. Having over-extended himself in the speculative purchase of two putative Poussin paintings, Gandy did not have the means to escape from Rome and was still there when the long-expected French finally entered the city early in 1797. He need not have feared for his personal safety, since the five officers billeted in his lodgings treated him with great courtesy, but the occupation of Rome had effectively made him an enemy resident. In May he left with no clear idea as to how he could return home, but he had the good fortune to meet in Florence a diplomatic messenger known to his family, with whom he travelled to London. The impression conveyed by Gandy's letters is of one deserting the lost cause of a city and country in which all of the old certainties had been destroyed.

It is no surprise that, with stories such as Gandy's for evidence, historians have viewed the Napoleonic invasion of Italy as the terminal point for the tradition of the British Grand Tour, conveniently closing with the century itself. There is no denying the fact that, apart from the brief flourish of travel made possible by the 1802 Treaty of Amiens, the period between the Battle of Trafalgar in 1805 and that of Waterloo in 1815 was one in which the British presence in Rome and Italy was minimal. Some long-term residents remained, of course, though men like James Byres had retreated to home territory. There is even evidence that some students, the architects John Newman and Archibald Simpson among them, did make journeys to occupied Italy. On the other hand, the case of the

Scottish Classical scholar Joseph Forsyth served as an example of the dangers which such travel could entail. Having travelled to Rome during the Peace of Amiens, Forsyth was arrested when hostilities resumed and imprisoned until 1814, publishing his *Remarks on Antiquities, Arts and Letters, being an Excursion to Italy in the years 1802 and 1803* in 1813 as a sort of scholarly appeal for liberty to the then Emperor Napoleon. For an historical phenomenon to be described as having ended, however, it is necessary that it should not have restarted in anything like its former guise. Yet, as was suggested in the Introduction to this book, that is more or less precisely what happened in the case of the Grand Tour and of British professional architectural travel to Italy after 1815. The similarities with the later eighteenth-century outweigh the differences, legitimizing treatment of Anglo-Italian relations in the period from about 1750 to 1840 as a single cultural entity. This is not to deny that the war-time hiatus, together with changing social and aesthetic circumstances in Britain, led to different attitudes and emphases among the travellers, but rather to suggest that the fundamental change in circumstances of the post-Napoleonic period still took place within the central preoccupation with Antiquity which had been generated before the wars. Those changed circumstances were, however, very significant, for French government, both in Rome and Naples, had revitalized the archaeology of Roman public and domestic architecture, together with the institutions and publications through which such archaeology was transmitted.

The Napoleonic interlude in Rome and its aftermath

It would be hard to find an example in the history of warfare in which art was more explicitly politicized than the Treaty of Tolentino concluded on 1 February 1797, under the infamous terms of which many of the most celebrated antique sculptures were removed from Rome to Paris. The Papal government's policy on the excavation and retention or export of works of ancient art, carefully constructed during the eighteenth century, was thereby turned on its head and the French action had a material effect on archaeological activity, in that Pius VII and his Secretary of State from 1800 to 1806, Cardinal Ercole Consalvi, stimulated the search for new statuary in order to replenish the depleted galleries of Rome. Furthermore, in 1803 Pope Pius banished the historic cattle market from which the Forum had taken its familiar name of 'Campo

36. George Basevi: A view of the Temple of Portunus, Rome, 1816–19, taken from the south to show the podium as excavated by the French government. Although Basevi concentrates on the Roman elements of a building converted to use as a church, the Christian bell turret on the top left end of the building is shown in faint outline.

Vaccino', and instigated the first systematic clearance of Roman monuments there with the removal of some 4 m (13 ft) of earth from the Arch of Septimius Severus in 1802–3, revealing the base of the monument and the level of the Via Sacra.[3] On an administrative level, the sculptor and recently elected Professor of the Accademia di S. Luca, Antonio Canova, was appointed to the new post of Inspector General of Fine Arts and Superintendent of the Vatican and Capitoline Museums in 1802, taking over some of the responsibilities of Carlo Fea, who had been appointed Commissario delle Antichità in 1801.

France was to have a more direct impact on the archaeology of ancient Rome, however, between June 1809 (when Rome was annexed as one of its *départements*) and 1814 when the French government was expelled. In these five years, many of the ruined buildings of ancient Rome were excavated, in part as a matter of cultural curiosity and in part as a stimulus to the contemporary Roman economy through the provision of labour for its citizens. Napoleon and his government in Rome thus achieved two key objectives: the satisfaction of the long-standing French wish to investigate the Roman past in a more thoroughgoing scientific manner than had been possible under Papal government, and the securing of a degree of popularity for a usurping foreign power.[4]

The structure of French authorities in Rome, although complicated, can be briefly described. After the occupation of the city and its state by the army under the military Lieutenant-Governor General Miollis in 1808, Camille de Tournon arrived in 1809 to serve as Prefect or civil head of the annexed *département*. The ruling council, the Consulta Straordinaria, included Joseph-Marie de Gérando as the member with particular responsibility for arts and antiquities. The Conservatori,

or municipal councillors who had superintended the antiquities in the Italian regime, were suppressed, their responsibilities being transferred to Commissario Fea. The new French council set up successive 'Commissions' to manage the excavation and recording of Roman buildings in 1809 and 1810 respectively before, in 1811, an Imperial Decree established the 'Commission des Embellisements'. The operation of this Commission was affected, however, by a requirement placed upon the Accademia di S. Luca to take responsibility for keeping monuments in a good state of repair and by the arrival from Paris in 1811 of Martial Daru, as the official charged with selecting ancient works of art for requisition by the 'Crown' of Imperial France. In that same year, de Tournon persuaded the Emperor to agree to an annual budget of a million French francs for what might be termed environmental expenditure in the Roman *département*, of which approximately a third was to be put to use for broadly archaeological purposes. Half of the money was provided by the French state and half was to be raised through local taxation. At any one time about a thousand Rome residents were recruited through their parishes to participate in squads excavating and removing spoil. This employment (and the food which accompanied it as part-payment) helped to offset the effects of the suppression of religious establishments which had provided a safety net against widespread poverty in the recent past.

The key architectural figures in Rome during the period of French annexation of 1809–14 were Giuseppe Valadier, Giuseppe Camporese and Raffaele Stern. The first two served as architect-directors of the 1810 and 1811 Commissions, meeting weekly under the aegis of the prefecture and controlling public monuments with a budget of 500,000 French francs, or just over 10 per cent of the *département's* income. Stern's official position was as architect to Daru's department of the 'Biens de la Couronne'. With the support of the Prefect de Tournon and the Commissario Fea, these three architects were responsible for organizing and carrying out the most dramatic archaeological works hitherto undertaken on antiquities surviving in Rome. The street level was lowered in the Forum Boarium, clearing the podium of the Temple of Portunus (Fig.36), while houses built into the adjacent Temple of Hercules Victor were removed. New clearance work was undertaken at the Nero's Golden House on the Esquiline Hill, and on the Palatine. A start was made on the excavation of the Imperial Fora, the central section of the Basilica Ulpia being revealed in the Forum of Trajan. In the Forum Romanum itself, trees were removed and the houses dotted around the site were purchased and demolished, as was the Convent of S. Francesca Romana. The Arch of Titus and the Temple of Saturn were detached from buildings into which they had been incorporated. The three columns of the Temple of Castor and Pollux were cleared to their bases and consolidated. The inscription identifying the Column of Phocas was discovered when its pedestal was excavated. At the Basilica of Maxentius,

37. Bartolomeo Pinelli: The
French excavation and
restoration of the Temple of
Vespasian, Rome, 1810–11.

60,000 cu metres (78,500 cu yards) of earth were carried away
and the pavement and remains of the south portico exposed.
In perhaps the most audacious operation of all, 23,000 cu
metres (30,000 cu yards) of earth and rubbish accumulated
against the east wall of the Tabularium were cleared and the
three columns of the Temple of Vespasian restored. By the end
of the eighteenth century (during which, contrary to common
belief, rubbish had accumulated in the Forum at an accelerated
rate), only the upper few feet of the column shafts, the capitals and the entablature of the building protruded from the
ground. An elaborate scaffolding was constructed around the
ruin, the entire entablature hoisted up, the earth dug away,
the newly revealed podium repaired, the columns straightened
and the entablature replaced (Fig.37).

Associated with this extraordinary phase of excavational
activity was the revival of the idea that Antoine Desgodetz's
Les Edifices antiques de Rome might be revised. As has been seen
in Chapter 1, the eighteenth-century ambitions of Robert
Adam and of Marie-Joseph Peyre in this regard had not been
sustained. Fea and Valadier had a revision of Desgodetz in
mind as early as 1804, when they undertook some excavational work at the Pantheon. Further specific reference was
made to revising Desgodetz again in 1810 but it was decided

instead to produce a wholly new work serving a somewhat
different purpose, the *Raccolta delle più insigni fabbriche di Roma
antica*. This work, chiefly the responsibility of Valadier, was to
appear in triannual fascicules, each one dealing with a single
monument. The first fascicule appeared in 1810 and featured
the Temple of Antoninus and Faustina, no doubt because the
French Académie had organized the excavation of the pronaos
on its own initiative in 1809 before the formal annexation of
Rome by France. Fascicules on the round temple at Tivoli and
the Temple of Hercules Victor in Rome followed in 1813. In
the *Raccolta*, each monument was described in an essay by
Valadier, before the latest antiquarian evidence for its ancient
form, identification and situation was summarized by Filippo
Visconti (Fea's predecessor as Commissario, not reappointed
by Pius VII after his brother, Ennio Quirinio, had sided with
the French and moved to Paris as Keeper in the Louvre).
Meanwhile, Valadier's plates presented architectural data in
the form of the traditional measured plans, elevations and sections. French feet was the unit of measurement used, although
a scale of Roman palms was also provided (see Abbreviations
and terminology). What was new, however, was the degree of
attention given to newly excavated parts of monuments. In
the case of the Temple of Vespasian, for example, Valadier in-

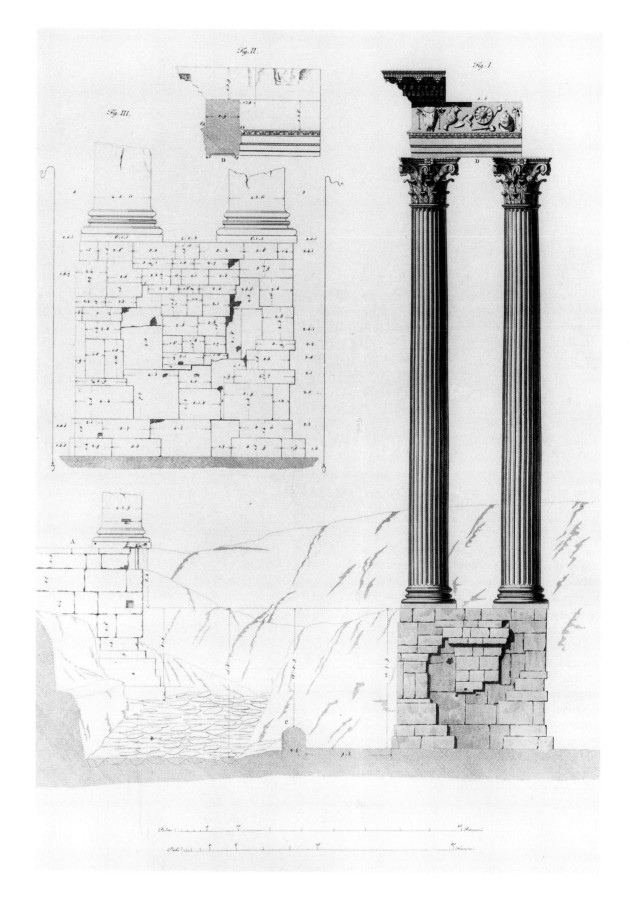

38. Giuseppe Valadier:
Elevation of the restored
Temple of Vespasian, Rome,
from the north, with details
of the podium, from
'Raccolta delle più insigni
fabbriche di Roma antica',
published in 1818.

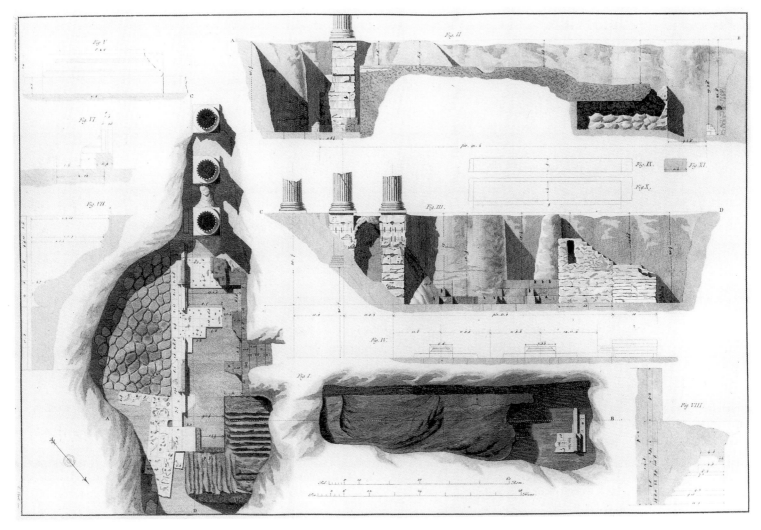

cluded minute measurements for every block of travertine making up the podium which had been buried for hundreds of years and which he and Camporese had reconstructed stone by stone (Fig.38). Moreover, the plate shows the position of the temple in relation to the newly revealed Via Sacra and in juxtaposition with the corner Temple of Saturn. The quasi-scientific objectivity and contextuality of the plates was matched by an almost puritanical absence of restoration. This type of image, a distinct development on eighteenth-century renditions of Roman ruins, might be recognized as the antecedent of the modern archaeological survey. By the time the French departed in 1814, the Forum had begun to take on the appearance of a dusty modern archaeological site rather than a semi-rural arcadia, in which the ox-carts now carried around timber for scaffolding and great stones for repairs to the monuments (Pl.VIII).

The restoration of Pius VII, together with the renewed appointment of Cardinal Consalvi as Secretary of State, brought back to power two men personally and politically committed to reclaiming the ancient Roman inheritance

Napoleon had seized. After the expulsion of the French, care of the Antique monuments initially reverted to Fea, who continued as Commissario delle Antichità until 1836, and to Canova, as Inspector General of Antiquities and Museums. The architect Camporese assisted them, as Superintendent for the Conservation of Museums and Antiquities. In 1816, however, a new General Consultative Committee for the Fine Arts was established, comprising Canova as President, Alessandro d'Este (President of the Vatican Museums), Filippo Visconti as Secretary, the Commissario Fea and the Danish sculptor Bertel Thorvaldsen. By the time of the deaths of Canova and Camporese in 1822 the system had been modified. The President was Monsignor Domenico Attanasio, the business manager of the Cardinal Camerlengo. Visconti remained as secretary, and Fea had become one of two consiglieri, the other being the architect Giuseppe Valadier. The complexity of these committee structures should not mask the fact that in Visconti, Fea and Valadier were three men influencing developments in post-Napoleonic Rome who had served on the various French commissions. This helped ensure continuity, both in the pro-

39. Giuseppe Valadier: Plan and sections of the excavation of the Temple of Castor and Pollux, Rome, from 'Raccolta delle più insigni fabbriche di Roma antica', published in 1818.

grammes of excavation undertaken and in the way the resultant discoveries were disseminated. Thus publication of the *Raccolta* resumed in 1818 with Valadier's fascicule on the Temple of Castor and Pollux, where a second phase of excavation in 1816–18 had revealed the northern end of the podium with two flights of steps, one rising from the ground set at 90 degrees to that leading to the cella entrance (Fig.39). In the same year, Valadier issued his fascicule on the Temple of Vespasian and one on the Column of Phocas. Two final fascicules, on the Theatre of Marcellus (1822) and the Temple of Mars Ultor (1826), resulted from surveys undertaken by Francesco Saponieri. Valadier was, of course, not the only Roman architect to be involved in this archaeological work, and among the publications which appeared independently in the city at this time the outstanding example was Antonio de' Romanis's fine 1822 monograph on the Golden House, *Le antiche camere esquiline dette comunemente delle Terme di Tito*. In addition to the work covered in these publications, the restored papal government was responsible for the remarkable physical restoration of the Arch of Titus between 1818 and 1824. A substantial scaffolding designed by Raffaele Stern consolidated the remaining Roman parts of the structure while its Medieval encumbrances were removed (Fig.40). The 'missing' Roman elements were then supplied according to designs so expertly prepared by Valadier that most visitors today fail to realize that they are looking at a largely fabricated work.

A year after the completion of restoration work on the Arch of Titus, Pius VII was succeeded by the 'ultra puritanical' Leo XII who, according to the British architect Sydney Smirke in 1824, insisted on the draping of nude statues and inhibited academic life classes. Another young architect, James Pennethorne, described the new pope as 'anything but an encourager of the arts', especially in so far as Protestant English were concerned.[5] The great Napoleonic phase of archaeology in Rome was over, although the way in which Roman monuments were studied and the rate of that work had been irrevocably altered.

Roman archaeological societies and British antiquarianism

The Napoleonic period and its aftermath witnessed not only a great change in the physical treatment of the monuments in Rome but also the reorganization of the societies which disseminated new discoveries and interpretations. The Pontificia Accademia Romana di Storia di Archeologia had been founded by Benedict XIV in 1740 and had functioned until 1805. In 1810, however, with Rome under French government and Pius VII imprisoned at Savona, the Academy was re-established under French protection. The meeting place was Ferdinando Fuga's Palazzo Corsini alla Lungara, the temporary home of Joseph-Marie de Gérando.[6] Management of the Academy

quickly passed to Italians, however, for when de Gérando was recalled to Paris in 1811, Canova became President and Giuseppe Guattani Perpetual Secretary (in emulation of their respective positions at the Accademia di S. Luca). The Academy moved its base to the Capitol, where meetings were held every fifteen days and each member was required to prepare a dissertation once a year. It was an international organization, in the sense that its statutes envisaged including 40 'corresponding' members from outside Lazio and Umbria among its 110 members (the total number was reduced to 100 after new statutes were introduced in 1818). It could also elect honorary members. British involvement was small but not insignificant. Two expatriate antiquarians who had braved residence in Rome during the French occupation, Edward Dodwell and James Millingen, were rewarded by election to honorary membership. Francis Henry Egerton (later Earl of Bridgewater), classically educated at Eton and Oxford and a Grand Tourist in 1782–3, became a corresponding member in 1813. The other British corresponding members up to 1840 were: Sir William Gell, John Foster and John Scandrett Harford (all elected in 1817); the architect Charles Robert Cockerell and diplomat William Hamilton (elected in 1818); Richard Burgess (elected in 1833); John Talbot, Earl of Shrewsbury, and the patron of A. W. N. Pugin (elected in 1835); and Patrick Walker (elected in 1836).[7]

Far more significant than the Accademia Romana, however, was the Instituto di Corrispondenza Archeologica, founded in 1829 at the Palazzo Caffarelli, also on the Capitol, and the ancestor of the modern-day Deutsches Archäologisches Institut in Rome. Not only was this a substantially larger academic body, it was also more decidedly international in its outlook. In the 1820s a group of Germans gathered in Rome and led by the scholar Eduard Gerhard had founded the 'Iperborei romani' (the 'Romans from North of the Alps') as an informal society, but by the end of the decade the rapidly advancing nature of Roman archaeological and topographical understanding made clear the need for a more professionally-run international society.[8] The early history of the Instituto di Corrispondenza has recently been examined in some detail, and it is now clear that its foundation came about largely as a result of the relative lethargy of the Accademia Romana and in the face of considerable hostility from the President of that body, Nicola Maria Nicolai, together with certain members of the Papal government.[9] The Accademia Romana had managed to publish only three volumes of proceedings by 1829 and, with the exception of Pietro Bianchi's and Lorenzo Re's paper on the Colosseum, these papers did not discuss the archaeological discoveries made during and in the aftermath of the French occupation. In 1829, therefore, the Hanoverian Chargé d'Affaires in Rome, August Kestner, and the Prussian ambassador, Karl Bunsen (who had succeeded his mentor Barthold Georg Niebuhr in this post in 1816) approached the Cardinal Camerlengo, Pier Francesco Galleffi, about the possibility of

40. George Ledwell Taylor and Edward Cresy: View of the Arch of Titus, Rome, from the west, from 'The Architectural Antiquities of Rome', published in 1821. Taylor and Cresy show themselves on Rafaelle Stern's scaffolding with sketchpad and measuring rod in hand, studying the coffers.

*41. Luigi Rossini: View
across the west end of the
Forum Romanum, from 'Le
antichità romane divise in
cento tavole', published
1819–23. Comparison with
a similar view by Piranesi
(Fig.11) shows the extent to
which the character of the
Forum had changed in the
early nineteenth century.
In this view, the Arch of
Septimius Severus had been
cleared by Pius VII in
1802–3 and the Temple of
Vespasian by the French in
1811. The English Duchess
of Devonshire had sponsored
the removal of a huge
amount of earth from
around the Column of
Phocas in 1817.*

establishing a new society which would publish reports of excavations throughout Europe. The Cardinal agreed to the idea and, in fact, important members of the Accademia Romana (including Fea, Visconti and the precocious antiquarian Antonio Nibby) were supportive of it. Nicolai, however, perceiving the broadly similar objectives of the proposed Institute to his own Academy, denounced its promoters as foreign schismatics and persuaded the Director of the Holy Apostolic Palace to prohibit the printing of its manifesto. The Institute only avoided stillbirth when Bunsen threatened that withdrawal of the consent initially proffered by Galleffi would be taken as a national insult to Prussia.

As founded in 1829, the Instituto di Corrispondenza Archeologica comprised four classes of member (associate, honorary, ordinary and corresponding) and four sections: Italian, German, French and English. Each section had its own secretary, the British representative being James Millingen. Indeed Millingen was, with Gell, an honorary member of the Institute's initial directorate. Meetings were held in Rome every three weeks, which members of other sections present in the city at the time could attend: Lord Lovaine (later 2nd Earl Beverley), Lord Northampton and a Dr George Nott (or Knott), a Canon of Winchester, were among those who participated in the Institute's early days. More importantly, however, the Institute immediately commenced publication of two separate and substantial journals: a *Bullettino* and *Annali*. In addition a volume of *Memorie*, opening with Gell's account of the ruins of the Etruscan town of Veii, appeared in 1832.[10] The *Annali* were published annually but the *Bullettino* was issued as often as monthly. The importance of these publications can hardly be underestimated, since they meant that news of the latest excavations in Rome (and indeed throughout the Mediterranean world) was quickly and comprehensively transmitted to members throughout Europe, along with reviews of the latest publications on all areas of ancient archaeology. The British had major involvement in the new organization. A year after its foundation there were 27 members in the British section, a number which had doubled to 55 by July 1831, more than the 34 German and 48 French members (see Appendix B).[11] By 1836 there were 71 British members. The Institute used the address of a publisher in London (until 1835 Rodwell, Gell's publisher, in New Bond Street, then Bohn in Henrietta Street, Covent Garden). Correspondence on archaeological matters, reviews and drawings could be submitted through the London link. By these means, the study of Roman archaeology was effectively moved onto the footing it has enjoyed ever since: still under the control of the Roman authorities but now with the acceptance of foreign involvement both in Rome itself and at a distance. As has been seen, the British were the keenest participants in and beneficiaries of this development, alongside the Germans.

Among the British members of the Institute were many of those who were to make great contributions to the study of ancient Rome in the first half of the nineteenth century. They include dilettanti such as Henry Gally Knight and Thomas Hope, and aristocrats such as the Earl of Aberdeen and the Duke of Buckingham, this last the sponsor of an excavation on the Via Appia in early 1829 which revealed a fine mosaic pavement.[12] Buckingham was one of a number of English aristocrats who financed excavations in and around Rome in the post-Napoleonic era. The most celebrated case was that of the keen antiquarian Elizabeth, Duchess of Devonshire, to whose enthusiasm the massive clearance of earth from around the column of Phocas in 1817 was due (Fig.41). A different constituency of British member in the Institute was that of important scholars of Roman history and literature such as Thomas Arnold, Julius Hare and Christopher Wordsworth Junior, the latter two attached to Cambridge, where both the University and Trinity College quickly became subscribers to the Institute. Then there were the architects who were members: Charles Robert Cockerell and Thomas Leverton Donaldson.

A British member of the Institute of particular importance was Richard Burgess of St John's College, Cambridge, Chaplain to the English congregation in Rome from 1831 to 1836. In 1831 Burgess published his *The Topography and Antiquities of Rome, Including the Recent Discoveries Made About the Forum and the Via Sacra*. Dedicated to Buckingham for having encouraged and promoted the study of antiquities in Rome, Burgess's work was a response to what he referred to as the 'new impulse' of the 'system of excavations adopted by the French, and continued by the popes after their restoration'. He imagined that his dissertations, if not found to justify their pretensions, would be 'consigned to oblivion', but his attempt to produce 'something between the dry researches of an antiquary and the jejune information of an itinerary' certainly earn him his place in history.[13] Other British antiquarians had published work on ancient Rome in the second and third decades of the century, though none were especially enterprising. The most comparable work to that of Burgess is Edward Burton's *A Description of the Antiquities and other Curiosities of Rome* of 1821 which suffered, in Burgess's eyes, by overhasty preparation and, in more recent opinion, by inadequate scholarship.[14] Although a substantial work of over six hundred pages, Burton's book is more an itinerary based on outdated sources than a well-structured piece of antiquarianism.

Burgess was a frequent companion and thus intellectual beneficiary of Antonio Nibby, the leading young Roman antiquarian from the 1820s. In his assessment of the Forum Romanum, for example, (about which he commented perceptively that 'it can scarcely be said that any one of the monuments remaining … is positively known to be what it is called'), despite introducing all the evidence surviving from antiquity and the various modern arguments, Burgess almost invariably sided with Nibby, even where this led him into error.[15] His book, however, represents an excellent synthesis

in the English language of recent topographical research on antiquities in Rome by an international field of architects and antiquarians. It was Burgess who introduced English readers to Nibby's identification of the 'Temple of Peace' as the Basilica of Constantine, adding that the discovery of a medal in 1828 had shown the building to have been begun by Maxentius. Moreover, in places, Burgess touched on originality. On the problematic issue of the identity of the famous painted rooms of the 'Baths of Titus' on the Esquiline Hill, for example, he recognized that their position beneath the superstructure of the Baths (of Trajan) must have rendered them uninhabitable, and suggested that they were part of 'the house of Maecenas embodied in that of Nero'. Burgess thereby came close to identifying the remains of the Golden House. He was also close to correctly identifying the Temple of 'Jupiter Tonans' as that of Vespasian, three years before Luigi Canina did so in print.[16] Finally, in a useful appendix, Burgess arranged the surviving monuments of ancient Rome in chronological order. This endeavour resulted in some erroneous (though at that time traditional) information, such as the attribution of

the Pantheon to Agrippa and the dating of the Temple of Castor and Pollux to the second century AD, but it nonetheless represented an early attempt to define the characteristics of pre-Republican, Republican and different types of Imperial Roman architecture. This was an important shift in the concept of history, away from the topographical approach common in the later eighteenth century, towards the chronological approach established by the middle of the nineteenth. It is no wonder that, as has already been recorded, membership of the Pontificia Accademia Romana di Storia di Archeologia was added to Burgess's membership of the Institute in 1833.

British architects in Italy after 1815

The great influx of British Grand Tourists to Italy immediately after the conclusion of the Napoleonic Wars was matched by that of British architectural students. In fact, the sense that the architects could hardly wait to return to Italy emerges from the case of C. R. Cockerell, who had been in Greece and the Levant since 1810 and had made expeditions to Sicily in 1812 and 1813. Cockerell's movements closely shadowed the passage of hostilities. He had reached Naples by April 1815 and arrived at Rome on 28 July, just one month after the Battle of Waterloo. The following year it is possible to identify no fewer than nine other British architectural students joining Cockerell in Italy, among them George Basevi, John Goldicutt, Joseph Gwilt, Peter Robinson, Richard Sharp and Joseph Woods (see Appendix A). The number present increased to 13 during 1817, to 17 during 1818 and to the greatest number of 20 during 1819, the individuals involved by this time including Charles Barry, Edward Cresy, Thomas Leverton Donaldson, Philip Hardwick, Ambrose Poynter, John Sanders, George Ledwell Taylor and Lewis Vulliamy. In fact, the figures available suggest that more British architectural students visited Rome in the two decades following Waterloo than had done in the whole of the eighteenth century.

A few of the travellers after 1815, such as Robinson, Woods, Sanders and Lewis Wyatt, were established architects in middle age, perhaps taking advantage of the changed political circumstances to make journeys denied to them earlier in their careers. None of those who had travelled in the later eighteenth century returned to Italy, although it has recently been observed that Soane probably contemplated doing so in 1819.[17] The majority, therefore, were once again young students with an average age of about twenty-five, travelling after completion of pupillage which, as in the later eighteenth century, lasted five years or so from its late teenage inception.[18] These young men financed their travel through a variety of means, all of which paralleled eighteenth-century circumstances. The Royal Academy's Travelling Studentship was taken up by Vulliamy in 1818, five years after winning the Academy's Gold Medal; by Samuel Loat ten years later; and by John Johnson, who won the Gold Medal in 1835. Architectural students such as Thomas Allason, John Peter Gandy and Francis Bedford were employed to act as draftsmen for archaeological expeditions, although it is fair to say that in the early nineteenth century such expeditions were generally made to Greece, rather than to Roman sites. Some of those older British architects who reached Italy after the Napoleonic period took younger students with them to act as draftsmen. Woods engaged Richard Sharp in Paris for this purpose, Sanders took William Purser with him from London, while Charles Mathews was taken to Naples in 1823 in the entourage of Lord Blessington. In the majority of cases travel had to be funded from family resources, and in general the students were better off than their eighteenth-century predecessors. Basevi's expenditure of £710 in just over two years, for example, would have placed him comfortably as a Grand Tourist. On the other hand, the £100 given to George Wightwick by his father barely covered a year in Italy in 1825, and financial constraint prevented him from journeying south of Rome.[19] In such cases, travel could be as hard as it had been for men like Robert Mylne in the 1750s. Indeed, George Ledwell Taylor estimated

that he and Edward Cresy had travelled 4000 miles on foot and only 2120 by conveyance during their two years in the Mediterranean. Although much of their walking was undertaken in Greece and in Sicily, journeys on foot made in Italy included those from Genoa to Pisa and from Loreto to Milan via Ancona, Rimini, Bologna, Venice and Verona.[20] Lodging in Rome, invariably back in the streets around the Piazza di Spagna (see notes to Appendix A and Pl.1), cost between 10 and 20 *scudi* (about £2 to £4) per month, a significant but supportable increase on pre-Napoleonic prices.

In many practical respects, therefore, the late eighteenth-century tradition of British architectural travel to Rome resumed. However, the severing of the umbilical cord which connected many British architects directly to Rome prior to 1800 had led to important changes in the direction of architecture in Britain during the first two decades of the nineteenth century. The way had been opened for the Greek Revival to make its mark in public architecture, largely as a result of interruption of the tradition of travel, coupled to the appearance of the second volume of *The Antiquities of Athens* (illustrating the great monuments of the Acropolis) in 1790, of the second volume of *Ionian Antiquities* in 1798, and in 1807 of *The Antiquities of Magna Graecia*, William Wilkins's survey of the great Doric temples of Sicily. It was perhaps inevitable, therefore, that architects, who were pupils in a London where the new Covent Garden Threatre received a Greek Doric portico and the Erechtheion Ionic order and caryatid porch adorned the new church of St Pancras on Euston Road, would be more inclined than their eighteenth-century predecessors to risk travel beyond Italy and into Greece itself; perhaps as many as half of the total number did so. Access to Athens, the Peloponnese and the archipelago, in addition to Paestum and Sicily, must have heightened the feeling for Greek architecture of many early nineteenth-century students and, in some cases, qualified their reaction to ancient Roman architecture.

It is important to realize, however, that the journey to Greece was a desirable addition to what remained the essential experience of residence in Rome: 'I willingly give up the whole plan and go only to Sicily,' wrote Basevi to his father from Rome in 1818, when it appeared that extension of his previously agreed Italian itinerary to Greece would prove too costly.[21] Very few students were, in any case, able to reach Greece without also travelling through Italy (Francis Bedford, William Inwood's pupil William Railton, and Edward Jones appear to have been exceptional in this regard). There are, moreover, three more key reasons why it may be argued that Rome resumed its position of centrality in British architectural education after 1815: the nature of the individuals involved and of the education they had received; the sustainability of artistic communities in Rome, with all the benefits they brought; and the fact that, in England at least, it could have been predicted that the fashion for the mimetic Greek Revivalism of Smirke, Wilkins and their generation, with its repetitious tendencies, would not retain its hegemonic status for long.

A graphic compilation of individuals who made up the body of British students reaching Rome in the period from 1815 to the mid 1830s reveals a remarkable pattern of inter-relationship, in that so many of them were linked through family connection or pupillage to eighteenth-century architects who had either visited Italy themselves or who had sent others on their behalf (Appendix C). In the latter category, as has been seen in Chapter 1, was Henry Holland, whose former pupil Peter Robinson was among those architects who arrived in Italy in 1816 (and Robinson's own pupil, Robert Wetten, was in Rome in 1830). The principal pupils of Robert Taylor (Samuel Pepys Cockerell and John Nash), may not have visited Italy themselves, but their own pupils did so in the early nineteenth century: Joseph Kay, Thomas Martyr, C. R. Cockerell, Ambrose Poynter and James Pennethorne. William Chambers's students Edward Stevens, Thomas Hardwick and Willey Reveley had all travelled to Italy in the 1770s–80s, followed in turn by Samuel Angell, Philip Hardwick and his pupil Thomas Henry Wyatt after 1815. Similarly, James Wyatt's pupils Samuel Bunce, George Hadfield and Joseph Michael Gandy visited Rome in the late eighteenth century, as did John Peter Gandy, John Foster Junior and Lewis Wyatt in the early nineteenth. The strongest of these cross-generational links between British architectural students who visited Italy, however, was that associated with the name of John Soane, or perhaps, one might say, of Soane's own master, George Dance Junior, whose Italian experiences Soane had himself set out to emulate. Of Soane's twenty-nine pupils, ten are known to have travelled to the Mediterranean (in addition, three of Soane's employees had also been in Italy). Robert Smirke was briefly a pupil of Soane's, and it is significant to note that five of Smirke's own pupils duly found their way to Rome (and, in some cases of course, to Greece). Thus it can be seen that architects such as Taylor, Chambers, Holland, Wyatt and Soane who, in the later eighteenth century, had done so much to establish the basis of an architectural profession in England, had created a sort of school of travel among their pupils and those pupils' pupils, which flourished first in the 1780s and 1790s, then most fully in the years from 1815 to 1830.

Early nineteenth-century architectural students must have felt that the success of their masters was due in part to their first-hand experience of Italy and their consequent ability to meet the requirements of clients similarly steeped in Antiquity. This was a perception strongly reinforced by early nineteenth-century architectural pedagogy. James Elmes's *Lectures on Architecture*, for example, delivered to the Surrey and Russell Institutions in London, the Philosophical Institution in Birmingham, and published in 1821, illustrate the point that the relative excellencies of Greek and Roman architecture remained the touchstone of all architectural education, although

Elmes, who had not travelled abroad himself, depended on John Chetwode Eustace's *A Classical Tour through Italy* (1813) for his account of Rome. The most influential exposition of the value of travel to the Mediterranean had been given in the lectures delivered at the Royal Academy from 1809 by Soane. The extent to which Soane's lectures depended on theoretical ideas originating in the second half of the eighteenth century has recently been revealed in a comprehensive study.[22] Soane believed that the value of abstract ideas of architectural form and meaning promoted by French writers such as the Abbé Laugier and Pierre-François Hugues ('Baron d'Hancarville') had to be married with first-hand study of the remains of Classical Antiquity, in which those ideas had found their highest expression. He therefore explicitly recommended travel to the Mediterranean in both of the sets of six lectures he prepared. In Lecture 3, Soane told his audience that the student's 'only acquaintance with the remains of the structures of the ancients must be obtained by a great sacrifice of time and expense', while in Lecture 12, having itemized texts which should be read and the skills for appreciating painting and sculpture which should be acquired prior to travel, Soane said that the architectural student had 'then only to complete his studies by visiting foreign countries. Thus prepared, the young architect may reasonably be expected … to receive every possible advantage to be derived from the study of the extensive remains with which Rome and the Campagna, as well as many other parts of Italy, abound.'[23]

Soane's lectures were not published during his lifetime and it is a matter of speculation as to who might actually have heard them, since no attendance lists were kept. However, Royal Academy studentship lasted for a maximum of ten years, and Soane read Lecture 3 five times between 1810 and 1820 (once at the Royal Institution). He read Lecture 12 in 1815. On the basis of this evidence it is fair to assume that many of those students who travelled in the decade from 1815 to 1825 had heard their professor's explicit advice that they should do so, his constant reference to ancient Roman exemplars and his criticism of British Greek Revival architecture. Moreover, Soane was by no means alone in insisting on travel to Italy as an essential ingredient of British architectural training. As late as 1846, when he published his *Hints to Young Architects*, Soane's former assistant Wightwick still insisted on reserving four months for Rome in a year's Continental tour, which was 'as ever, important in expanding the taste for the beautiful and picturesque, and in stimulating that professional enthusiasm which can only be excited by beholding the actual realities whose distant features we have previously learned to appreciate'.[24]

Rome was indeed, as Joseph Woods put it in his 1828 'Instruction to a Young Architect' (see the epigraph at head of this chapter), the 'head quarters' for British architectural students travelling in Europe, offering not just quintessential buildings but also 'the society obtained among artists of all nations, who resort thither'. As has been mentioned, expatriate British artists had immediately resumed their habit of residing in the quarter of Rome around the Spanish Steps and were to be found there in even greater numbers than in the second half of the eighteenth century. The viability of the community linked, no doubt, to the even stronger presence in Rome of the French Academy (now established in the Villa Medici just beyond the top of the Spanish Steps), led to the foundation of the little-documented 'British Academy of Arts'. An organization of this name was still in existence in Via Margutta below the Pincian Hill in 1929, when the first volume of a journal called *Annales Institutorum*, dedicated to the various institutions of the city, was published. The Academy disappeared from the records between 1935 and 1936 and its archives do not appear to have survived.[25] It was evidently founded in 1823, however, thereby pre-dating the Instituto di Corrispondenza Archeologica and standing as the first academy of a major European country to be established in Rome after that of France. Its origins can be traced to a group of British artists in the city in 1821 who, according to Woods, organized life classes to occupy the winter evenings, paying for them by a monthly subscription levied among themselves. Although it is the names of painters and sculptors which have been recorded in connection with this group, there were at least twelve British architects in Rome during 1821 and they are likely to have been participants, including the man who later effectively founded the Institute of British Architects, Thomas Leverton Donaldson. On the basis of the students' initiative, funds began to flow in from individuals supportive of their Roman studies: William Hamilton, the Dukes of Bedford and Devonshire, and Sir Thomas Lawrence. There was even a donation of £200 from George IV in 1822.[26] The academy was managed by a committee of seven artists elected from among those resident in Rome at any one time.[27]

According to Woods, the British had decided to set up their own life class so that they 'might pursue their studies unimpeded by the inconveniences attending crowded schools, and without being indebted to the liberality of foreign institutions'. Woods added, however, that the Academy had only a few books and a cast of the Apollo Belvedere, and the intention of Pius VII to offer George IV a base for a British Academy in Rome (first mooted in 1817) had not materialized.[28] Whatever the facts about the elusive 'British Academy of Arts' in 1820s Rome, it is clear that the city had become once again the centre of British artistic education abroad and the place to be aimed at if at all feasible by aspiring students. A comment by the first biographer of the painter Richard Wilson, written in 1824, emphasizes this point:

That Rome is the place, beyond comparison, above all others, for an artist to form himself in, there cannot remain even a doubt. A journey thither, provided nothing else were obtained, would be amply compensated by the acquisition alone of that almost indescribable spirit of enthusiasm almost invariably inspired by the genius of the place; and without which it is in vain to expect anything either great or sublime.[29]

That this was also true for architectural students is suggested by a letter Basevi wrote to his sister in 1817: 'Rome, the eternal city, is the only place for an artist to live in. The climate, the associations, the every thing, lends itself to form the painter, the Artist.'[30]

British architects and archaeology in Rome after 1815

Soane's Royal Academy lectures also provided students with some indication as to the method of study he thought they should pursue while they were in Rome. When illustrating the Classical orders, Soane followed his predecessor, Thomas Sandby, in generally using the plates in the 1650 edition of Fréart de Chambray's *Parallèle de l'architecture antique et de la moderne*. In his second and third lectures, however, Soane made reference to the beautiful measured drawings of the Temple of 'Vesta' at Tivoli, produced by Dance in 1761–2, which he had copied in 1780 (Fig.42). The professor adduced the measurements provided here to show 'many proofs of the inaccuracy of Desgodetz, which it is the more necessary for me to notice to prevent the young artist from placing too great a confidence in his representations', a point to which he returned in Lecture 4 in saying that Desgodetz was not 'the great desideratum required for correctness'. Correctness was important because, as Soane showed, Desgodetz had disproved the belief, reiterated by his contemporary François Blondel in his *Cours d'Architecture*, that the Romans subscribed to a system of fixed architectural proportions determined by harmonic theory. In early nineteenth-century London architectural circles, it was apparent that two key seventeenth-century French texts, one of them still the major 'archaeological' survey of ancient Roman edifices with their variable proportions, were far from satisfactory sources. The student should, as Soane went on to say in Lecture 12, 'from actual mensurations taken by himself, make finished sketches of such structures as are most valuable'.[31]

It was more or less inevitable, therefore, that British students reaching Rome after 1815 should have resumed the surveying of extant Roman remains which had preoccupied a number of their eighteenth-century predecessors. As before, the value of this approach to study did not pass entirely unquestioned among the student body. Soane's own pupil Basevi, who was in Rome at the same time that George Ledwell Taylor and Edward Cresy were carrying out the most comprehensive of all the British measuring campaigns, commented 'may it improve them! I must own I doubt its utility.' Basevi was probably questioning the scale of his compatriots' activities rather than their nature, however, for he had written earlier that he had not yet made any measurements as he was waiting for 'somebody to erect a scaffolding, when I shall pro-

42. George Dance: Measured elevation of the ruined round Temple at Tivoli, 1763. This drawing, sadly rather damaged, acquired its fame partly through Soane's reverence for it.

A GEOMETRICAL ELEVATION OF THE REMAINS OF A TEMPLE AT TIVOLI.

A SCALE OF ENGLISH FEET

pose to take a share in the expense'.[32] Another Soane protégé, Wightwick, writing after Taylor and Cresy had published their magnificent *The Architectural Antiquities of Rome* in 1821–2, advised the student 'not to risk his neck in measuring, for the thousandth time, a Roman ruin', although by his own confession Wightwick 'could not resist the gratification' of measuring and drawing the Temple of 'Vesta' at Tivoli: 'so the ladders were brought, and I kissed the ox-cheeks on its frieze for very joy, embraced the necks of its elegant columns, and nearly broke my own in so doing' (see Fig.42).[33] Wightwick questioned the value of surveying again in his *Hints to Young Architects*: 'It is his sketch and note book, rather than his measuring rod, which should occupy his foremost attention. He requires less to fill his paper with dimensions than his mind with IDEAS.'[34] However, the mechanical and the imaginative cannot be so easily separated and, as will be seen in Chapter 4, it was scholarly archaeological study which underpinned the early nineteenth-century British architects' visionary evocations of Roman Antiquity.

Young British architects in post-Napoleonic Rome were more advantageously placed than their eighteenth-century predecessors with regard both to the issues of expense and of safety involved in making their surveys. The number of British architects present in Rome at any one time made the matter of

finding a colleague with whom the costs of surveying could be shared far less problematic. Preserved in the Rome State Archives are five sets of documents, in which six British architects made eleven separate requests to erect temporary scaffoldings on six different monuments in the nine months between May 1821 and February 1822 alone.[35] It seems reasonable to assume that many more such surveys must have been documented at times. The scaffoldings presumably varied in form depending on the nature of the monument. Thus, for example, Taylor and Cresy had the advantage of the load-bearing scaffolding designed by Stern to support the Arch of Titus during removal of its Medieval superstructure (see Fig.40), whereas John Goldicutt's 1816 surveys of the Temple of Vespasian were made from a sort of painter's cradle, cantilevered out from the entablature of the monuments and accessed by two ladders with a platform at the mid-point (Fig.43). This arrangement, perilous though it may appear to modern eyes, represented a great advance on the exposed ladders used in the previous century (see Fig.9), offering relative security and, through the manoeuvrability of the cradle, avoidance of parallax.

Another advantage enjoyed by British architectural students in the years of Pius VII's restoration, confirmed by the documents which survive, was the unprecedented co-operativeness

43. *John Goldicutt: A sketch showing the scaffolding with the benefit of which the architect was able to make measured drawings of the entablature of the Temple of Vespasian, Rome, in 1816.*

that same evening, in order to legitimize the operation. The British students applied for their licences to the President of the Committee, Monsignor Attansio, or occasionally directly to the Cardinal Camerlengo, Bartolomeo Pacca, but it was invariably Visconti and Valadier who dealt most immediately with the requests, and did so open-handedly. Valadier superintended the construction of the scaffoldings, because he knew how to erect them in a way which caused least damage to the monuments and because he was familiar with the workmen. His support for British endeavours was indispensable and when, in 1825, Sydney Smirke commented that Valadier 'looks like a hog, and *is*, I believe, so near one in character that I have let every opportunity pass of knowing him', the young Englishman's loss was doubtless greater than Valadier's.[37]

It was in this atmosphere of co-operative administration and relatively secure access to the ruins that Taylor and Cresy undertook their monumental survey of ancient Rome in 1818–19. Writing fifty years later in his *The Autobiography of an Octogenarian Architect*, Taylor used almost casual terms when describing the motives which lay behind the exhaustive study of Roman antiquities he had made with his companion:

At Rome we were so enchanted with the ancient buildings, and convinced that they required to be better described, that we resolved at once to measure accurately and draw the different temples, with the view of publishing them when we returned to England … we pursued our object diligently … obtaining permission to erect scaffoldings to each building.[38]

Their contemporaries in Rome perceived their work to be of almost overwhelming intensity, Basevi commenting that 'Mr Cresy and Mr Taylor … are storming the Campo Vaccino, they scarcely leave a stone unmeasured'.[39] This was probably a more accurate characterization of a pair of architects evidently indefatigable in their pursuit of Antiquity. Indeed, the obituary of Cresy which appeared in *The Builder* in 1858 would describe how 'death found him still busy at his post, seated in his library, his Vitruvius open before him, he fell from his chair, pen in hand, ceasing to work only when he ceased to live'.[40]

Basevi's report of Taylor and Cresy 'storming the Campo Vaccino' was made in March 1818, within a month of their arrival in Rome. In May they departed for a summer tour of Greece and Sicily, returning in October and staying in or around Rome until March 1819. It was during this second phase of residence that Taylor and Cresy acquired an exceptionally generous licence signed by Canova, Alessandro d'Este (as Secretary General of the General Consultative Committee for the Fine Arts) and Camporese (as its Architect-Director). The licence permitted them to 'freely draw and measure' under the watchful eye of the 'Public Architects' and their Inspector, Michele Ilarii, fifteen of the most famous surviving monuments of Rome: the three Arches of Titus, Septimius Severus and Constantine; the Temples of Vespasian, Saturn, Antoninus and Faustina, Castor and Pollux, Portunus,

of the authorities. Although the students evidently inundated the General Consultative Committee for the Fine Arts with requests for permission to erect scaffoldings, and monuments such as the Temple of Mars Ultor must therefore have been subject to continuous wear and tear, all of these licences were granted. Indeed, in acceding to Catherwood's and Davies's request to scaffold three temples, the Secretary Visconti commented that he was minded 'always to provide this advantage to students of architecture, the most practical of the fine arts'.[36] Moreover, in October 1821 when it emerged that John Lewis Wolfe had arranged for the construction of scaffolding on the Column of Trajan in the mistaken belief that he had completed the formalities required, Visconti, far from recommending punishment, arranged for the licence to be delivered directly to the young architect's lodgings in Via Gregoriana

TEMPLE OF JVPITER STATOR, ROME.

Details of Order &c.

44. George Ledwell Taylor and Edward Cresy: The order of the Temple of Castor and Pollux, Rome, from 'The Architectural Antiquities of Rome', published in 1822.

45. George Ledwell Taylor
and Edward Cresy: View of
the Temple of Castor and
Pollux, Rome, showing the
podium excavation, from
'The Architectural
Antiquities of Rome' 1822.

Hercules Victor and 'Nerva' (probably that of Mars Ultor); the Columns of Trajan, Marcus Aurelius and Phocas; the Basilica of Maxentius; and the Colosseum. Taylor's sole surviving sketchbook from this period, actually recording the architects' visit to Tivoli to study the two temples there, sheds some light on their working methods. It contains a tiny topographical watercolour view of Tivoli, later worked up for the engraving which appears as Pl.64 in *The Architectural Antiquities of Rome*. There then follow three sides of working surveys of the tetrastyle temple, a building eventually not included in the book because it was 'too much dilapidated to be useful to the architectural student'.[41]

It is clear, then, that Taylor and Cresy took as their departure point the tradition initiated by Robert Wood and James Stuart, in that they commenced their study of a monument with an actual state perspective view. Another respect in which they complied with tradition, in this case a tradition stretching back to the Renaissance, is seen in their inclusion of engraved plates laying out the order of each monument orthographically and in perfect condition (Fig.44). There are two important points to note about this type of plate in *The Architectural Antiquities of Rome*, however. The first is that the measurements were made in units of English feet, inches and lines (twelfths of an inch), thus making available to British architects in print for the first time a compendium of the orders of the major Roman monuments in the units of measurement they used in their architectural design work. The second point is the high level of accuracy achieved by Taylor and Cresy. At 5 ft 3 in and 5 lines, for example, which converts to 1.610 m, their measurement of the height of the capital of the Temple of Castor and Pollux is just 5 mm lower than the survey of the temple published in 1991.[42] That this degree of accuracy is characteristic of the early nineteenth-century phase of surveying more generally is clear from the 1818 issue of the *Raccolta*, in which Valadier recorded the height of the same capital at 4 ft 11 in and 9 lines (Paris Royal), or 1.618 m, a mere 3 mm higher than the modern survey. Given the state of the 1800-year-old masonry, these discrepancies are really negligible. It might be recalled from the discussion in Chapter 1 that Desgodetz, while achieving as impressive a level of accuracy as Taylor and Cresy with the measurement of this particular capital, is now known to have invented measurements elsewhere. Moreover, to take a sixteenth-century woodcut such as Palladio's in *I quattro libri dell'architettura*, we find that at 4 ft 7½ in (Vicentine), or 1.651 m, the Renaissance architect's measurement was 3.6 cm (1½ in) higher than the modern survey. *The Architectural Antiquities of Rome* thus joined the *Raccolta* in establishing a new canonical source for the specific measurements and general proportions of Roman architecture.

Taylor's and Cresy's *The Architectural Antiquities of Rome* is a very significant publication for further reasons. The viewpoints the architects selected for their topographical renditions were often carefully chosen, so as to show the

monuments in their post-Napoleonic state of excavation and as a prelude to a much more explicitly archaeological approach to the ruins than anything undertaken in the eighteenth century. This innovation can be seen especially clearly in the case of the Temple of Castor and Pollux, where the renewed phase of excavation had just concluded, and where the architects in fact provided two views: one from the south-east, but also one from the north-east (Fig.45). The latter, a relatively unusual angle, was chosen in order to reveal the excavation pit in which the temple's columns could be seen standing on travertine piers. This view heralds a plate in which Taylor and Cresy presented a plan with elevations and detailed sections of the frontal arrangement of temple and podium (Fig.46). It is striking to note the similarities between this image and the one published by Valadier in 1818, the same year that Taylor and Cresy were making their surveys (see Fig.39). The English architects seem to have appreciated both the novelty of this type of representation – like an anatomical diagram in the way it peeled back layers of earth – and its ability to convey architectural information. The archaeological evidence had 'disclosed the extent of the front of the temple, which was found to have been octastyle'.[43] It had also shown, as has been seen above, that the columns were supported on travertine piers

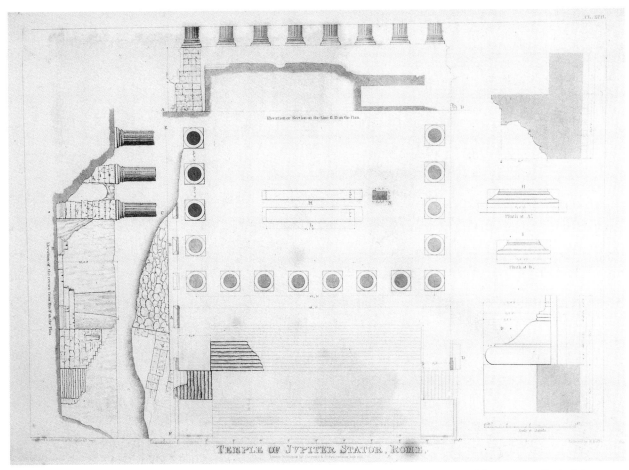

Elevation or Section on the Line G. D. on the Plan.

TEMPLE OF JVPITER STATOR, ROME.

46. George Ledwell Taylor
and Edward Cresy: Plan and
section of the excavation of
the Temple of Castor and
Pollux, Rome, from 'The
Architectural Antiquities of
Rome' 1822.

47. George Ledwell Taylor
and Edward Cresy: The
north elevation of the
Temple of Castor and
Pollux, Rome, restored,
from 'The Architectural
Antiquities of Rome' 1822.
Taylor's and Cresy's belief
that the Temple must have
been approached directly
from the Forum led them
to misinterpret the archaeological evidence of the
lateral steps.

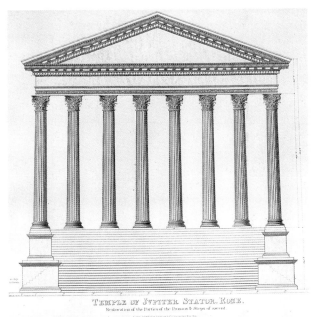

TEMPLE OF JVPITER STATOR, ROME.
Restoration of the Portico of the Pronaos & Steps of ascent.

embedded in the massive tufa and *opus caementicium* podium. The new area of uncertainty, and the point at which Taylor's and Cresy's interpretation differed significantly from Vala-

dier's, concerned the issue of how the cella had been approached from ground level. The excavation had shown that a flight of steps led down from the pronaos to a platform at mid-point in the podium, and that this platform had been accessible from lateral steps leading down to ground level at right angles to the frontal flight. Taylor and Cresy, however, went beyond Valadier in hypothesizing an additional flight of steps between the ground and the platform in the front of the temple (Fig.47). The English architects were evidently unable to countenance the idea that such a grand podium in a Roman temple (the height was some 7 m/23 ft) would not have been given a splendid approach directly from the Via Sacra. Overlooking the evidence provided by Cicero that the building had frequently served as a meeting place for the Roman Senate, they did not realize that its Forum front had had to serve as a rostrum from which announcements could be made. Yet, as early twentieth-century excavations would show, that is precisely how the Temple of Castor and Pollux was disposed, with a high wall at the north end of the podium parallel with the Via Sacra.

The depiction and analysis of excavation pits was only one of the innovatory ways in which *The Architectural Antiquities of Rome* represented Roman ruins. While Taylor and Cresy might have seen that type of image in Valadier's *Raccolta*, there

48. *George Ledwell Taylor and Edward Cresy: Lithographic detail at quarter size of the capital of the Temple of Castor and Pollux, Rome, from 'The Architectural Antiquities of Rome' 1822. Lithography, a relatively new printing technique at this time, was used by the architects to disseminate a new form of image of Roman architecture.*

Measured and Delineated by G.L.Taylor & E. Cresy

T. Kaulkner, Lithog.

TEMPLE OF JUPITER STATOR ROME

THE CAPITAL

One quarter the actual size

PRINTED BY A. FRIEDEL, 13 SOUTHAMPTON ST. STRAND

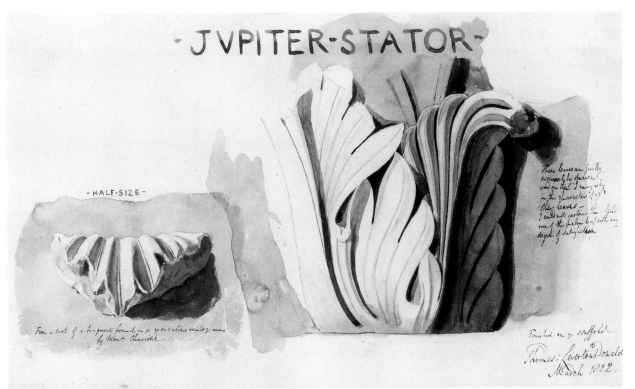

- JVPITER-STATOR -

- HALF-SIZE -

49. Thomas Leverton
Donaldson: Sketch of
acanthus leaves of a capital
of the Temple of Castor and
Pollux, Rome, 'finished on ye
scaffold' March 1822.

appears to be no precedent for their decision to include huge details of the orders and the decorative details of monuments at a quarter of their actual size (Fig.48). These plates provide an instance where a new mode of perception coincided with a new printing technology: that of lithography, patented in England by Alois Senefelder in 1801 but only becoming common in the second decade of the century. The relative ease with which British architects in Rome could scaffold monuments gave them a more intimate acquaintance with the deep, sculptural relief of Roman carving than their eighteenth-century predecesors (who can hardly have been comfortable clinging to their flexing 15-m/50-ft ladders with one hand). A large-scale sketch by Donaldson, for example, 'finished on ye scaffold' in March 1822, shows a detail of the leaves on a capital of the Temple of Castor and Pollux, boldly drawn in ink and given graded shading by the use of overlapping bands of brown wash (Fig.49). Returning to London, architects such as Taylor and Cresy found that they could reproduce the effect of their eye-ball encounters with details such as these through monochrome lithography, which had introduced an hitherto unparalleled grey scale to printmaking. This new printing medium also offered the advantage that architects could transfer the image on to the lithographic stone themselves without depending on the intermediation of an engraver and thereby retaining greater 'fidelity' and 'peculiar character', as John Jenkins and William Hosking found in 1827 when publishing their *A Selection of Architectural and other Ornament*.[44] Jenkins and Hosking went on to give a further reason for their choice of lithography which has nothing to do with aesthetics but which is, nonetheless, clearly significant. It was a good deal cheaper than copper-plate engraving or etching, enabling young architectural students recently returned from Rome to disseminate a vocabulary of form (and promote themselves in so doing, of course) without depending on the liberality of individual patrons or lists of subscribers.

Although Taylor and Cresy held back from stating that they intended their *The Architectural Antiquities of Rome* to stand as a replacement for Desgodetz's *Les Edifices antiques de Rome*, the book must surely have been intended as such, for many years later Taylor expressed his irritation that Desgodetz was still being used as the canonical source.[45] A new edition of Desgodetz, produced by Fea in 1822, presented parallel French and Italian texts, but the revisions to the measurements which Fea knew to be necessary were postponed yet again to a supplementary volume, eventually published by Luigi Canina in 1843. Taylor's and Cresy's work, which contained 130 plates and chapters on fifteen of the ancient buildings in Rome, together with the round temple at Tivoli and the Arch of Trajan at Ancona, thus represented the most comprehensive single survey of this type to have been published on the Roman monuments since the seventeenth century. It displayed extremely accurate measurements on plates which were traditional both in their orthographic presentation of data and in their engraving, and presented images of the ruins in new forms and media. The use of English units of measurement placed *The Architectural Antiquities of Rome* outside the mainstream of early nineteenth-century Roman archaeology, with its inevitable emphasis on French sources, but this is no reason why the book should so often be overlooked today as an important source. Moreover, the provision of an English source book for the major Roman monuments was to become an underpinning factor in the production of Roman architectural forms which occurred in English public architecture during the 1830s.

Taylor's and Cresy's work in Rome, although it took place at the same time that Nibby, Fea and others were piecing together the results of their excavational activities with literary texts in quest of a new level of understanding of Roman topography and chronology, was probably a little too early to have benefited from the work of these Italians, which had yet to reach digestible published form. Although the English students were clearly aware of new developments, they did not or could not synthesize these into a new essay on the history of the Roman monuments. Moreover, they were aiming for a market in England which knew the monuments by names made familiar by older texts and traditions. Thus they continued to call the Temple of Castor and Pollux the Temple of 'Jupiter Stator', even while informing their readers of its probable new identity. Other students were keen to communicate news of such changes to the older architects in London. Basevi wrote to Soane in January 1818, for example, about the discovery of the 'ancient plan of the temple hitherto called Jupiter Stator, but now by all the antiquaries that of Castor and Pollux'.[46] For Soane, who regarded the order of the temple as perhaps the finest of all Corinthian specimens, this might have been a major discovery. Yet he made little of it when talking of the temple to the students of the Royal Academy, simply crossing out a reference to the monument's 'dilapidated state' in the 1817 copy of his second lecture when amending it for delivery in 1819.[47] Soane's marginalia, however, show that he then got himself into a corner by trying to make the three columns compatible with a Temple of Venus mentioned by Vitruvius (presumably the Temple of Venus Genetrix in the as yet unexcavated Forum of Julius Caesar). It was doubtless his professorial sense of responsibility that led Soane into these antiquarian waters, but he was ultimately a typical late eighteenth-century architect, more interested in the ruins per se than in establishing chronological and topographical accuracy. Basevi's concerns as a student in Rome were altogether more precise:

It appears to me that ... of the five or six temples remaining in the Forum, three are decidedly in bad taste and of bad times, after Severus or Constantine[.] The only ones deserving much study are the Temples of Jupiter Stator (now called that of Castor and Pollux), Antoninus and Faustina, and Jupiter Tonnans [Vespasian] ... To be sure the Temple of Peace [Basilica of Maxentius] is a very fine building, as is the Colosseum, but they afford little study for an architect.[48]

The excavations and antiquarian work in the Forum, in particular, then, were leading students away from the *opus caementicium* architecture of the second to fourth centuries which had so inspired Adam and his followers, and back to the trabeated marble architecture of the late Republic and first century AD. This development had considerable significance for the templar architecture someone like Basevi would employ when designing public buildings in England later.

For British students reaching Rome after publication of *The Architectural Antiquities of Rome* in 1822, the very existence of the book made a difference to their approach to study. This can be seen clearly from the case of John Nash's pupil James Pennethorne who certainly knew the book and who, in 1825, as a result no longer saw any point in raising scaffolding 'merely to be allowed to take the general dimensions'.[49] Moreover, while it was assumed that a student should gain an intimate acquaintance with the details of architectural sculpture, Pennethorne found that, in the absence of scaffolding, fallen fragments in museums could fulfil this purpose (the selection of ornament published by Jenkins and Hosking was also made from objects seen in Italian museums rather than in situ). Pennethorne kept a diary and wrote almost weekly to Nash, thereby providing a record of the study method deployed by a young British architect in Rome in the mid 1820s. The emphasis was still generally placed on the monuments of ancient Rome, in spite of the prejudiced Sydney Smirke's 1825 quip that 'to rummage up heaps of Roman brick dust is out of my beat'.[50] Pennethorne began in December 1824 with the Forum of Trajan, clearance and excavation of which had begun in 1811, followed by the Forum of Augustus, the newly reconstructed Arch of Titus, the Arch of Constantine and the Temple of Antoninus and Faustina. Then came the Castel Sant'Angelo (because Pennethorne admired it as a 'subject', though not, he said, for 'architectural' reasons), followed by the Pantheon, a study he earmarked for sending to the Royal Academy exhibition. Although he had assured Nash that he would give proper attention to modern architecture in Rome, after five months Pennethorne admitted that he had not seen any modern villas or palaces, nor even travelled outside the city. He went to some lengths to explain his working approach to Nash, beginning with what he called the 'picturesque' sketch, an actual state drawing of *c*.23 × 38 cm (*c*.9 × 15 in), perhaps made with the use of a camera lucida and generally coloured on the spot. Then he made very large orthogonal outline drawings of specific parts of the architecture, slightly shaded, with 'only the general proportions in measurement to impress them on our mind'. Finally, he proceeded to a restoration drawing, in order to 'follow the ancients through the whole of their designs' and have an 'idea of their grand conceptions'.[51] Pennethorne's success in gaining, through this method of study, a visual idea of the grandeur of ancient Rome will be discussed, alongside the innovative visions of other British architects, in Chapter 4.

Cast collections and models

Before concluding the present chapter the subject of casts and models, touched on in later eighteenth-century contexts, should be returned to. This is partly because it became much more common in the post-Napoleonic period for architects to commission and import to Britain casts of Roman buildings. It is also partly due to the fact that the display of casts and their relationship to design work appears to have changed after 1815. Moreover, an innovation in architectural model-making and display holds further significance for the way ancient Roman architecture was perceived in London during these years.

An inventory of the Royal Academy's possessions made in 1810 lists only nineteen architectural casts, and quite where these were kept at Somerset House remains a mystery as they do not appear in eighteenth-century images of the Academy's 'Cast Room' and 'Antique School'.[52] In his third lecture, read that same year, Soane bemoaned the fact that the architecture student in London 'has no models of ancient buildings to consult, nor plaster casts of their ornaments and component parts to refer to'. Although Soane reiterated this complaint in his sixth lecture (given in 1812 and on three further occasions), in 1814 the Academy introduced drawing from casts of architectural ornament as part of the examination for the admission of students to its Schools.[53] Perhaps this was an instigation of Soane's, for at the end of his sixth lecture he had gone on to say that he was in the process of arranging his own collection of casts and fragments at Lincoln's Inn Fields in the form of a museum which the students could visit on the days either side of his lectures, seeing this as part of his professorial responsibilities. In any event the moment was apposite, for after 1815 the influx of British architects to Rome introduced a corresponding influx of casts to London. Art historians have given due consideration to the effect on artists and the public of the arrival and display of great works of sculpture, such as the Elgin Marbles, in London. For architectural students and other persons unable to travel themselves, the great number of casts of Roman buildings which arrived between 1815 and 1840 must have had a similar impact, especially when the relatively small number of examples made from Greek buildings is considered.

The major collections of casts appear to have been Decimus Burton's 209 casts and Lewis Wyatt's 90, but John Sanders, Basevi, Joseph Gwilt and Samuel Angell are all known to have returned from Italy with some. The increased scale of collecting suggests both that the cost of acquiring casts relative to the income of the travellers had decreased, and that the Roman authorities had become more co-operative in allowing them to be made. To judge from a comment of Basevi, there was still no system for retaining moulds ('they take the mould of the thing ordered and destroy it immediately after') and, according to Pennethorne enquiring on behalf of Nash, prices

50. George Ledwell Taylor and Edward Cresy: Detail of a view of the Temple of Mars Ultor, Rome, showing preparations for cast-making, from 'The Architectural Antiquities of Rome', published in 1822.

varied from £15 for a piece of the frieze relief of the Temple of Antoninus and Faustina to £60 for a set of the entablature, capital and column top of the Temple of Castor and Pollux.[54] In the case of this most famous of Roman temples, Gwilt was able to import to London a set of the moulds themselves, which can surely be presumed to have issued progeny. This exceptional case aside, a number of British architects such as Wyatt followed Gwilt's advice, issued to John Lewis Wolfe, to employ one of Canova's workmen, Benedetto Malpieri, to make the casts for them.[55] The costs of doing this were not huge but, with the exception of Angell and Basevi (who joined forces for an order with the older Joseph Woods), it is noteworthy that the architects who made the commissions came from the pool of established figures who either visited Italy or felt the lack thereof. Unless a monument was under repair or already being surveyed, architects would have had to pay for erection of scaffolding in addition to the costs of labour and materials. Taylor and Cresy provided an illustration of the relatively straightforward platform required for making moulds of the 'foliage and ornament' of the Temple of Mars Ultor (Fig.50). It is possible that the workmen were engaged on an order for Sanders, a companion of Taylor's and Cresy's for much of their time in the Mediterranean, who certainly commissioned casts from this temple as well as from the Temples of Vespasian and Hercules Victor.[56]

In 1823 Sanders sold some of his casts to Sir Thomas Lawrence, who then offered them to the Royal Academy for £250 in his will (an offer the Academy declined).[57] Many of the imported casts, possibly including the residue of Sanders' collection in 1826 and certainly the whole of Wyatt's in 1834, made their way with some inevitability into the possession of Soane. In 1824 Soane had taken the opportunity when rebuilding the rear of 14 Lincoln's Inn Fields to redisplay the casts he already possessed in the 'Corridor' – actually a small top-lit room which he considered threw the sculptural elements of capitals and entablatures into best relief (Fig.51). Some of the greatest pieces of architecture (Soane's casts of the order of the Temple of Castor and Pollux on the end wall, the capital of the Tivoli round temple high on the right, the Erechtheion capital opposite) were thus removed from the immediate ambit of the drawing office to a small room in the 'museum'. While this was consistent with the general development of Lincoln's Inn Fields in this period, however, it can hardly be seen as an indication that Soane wished his pupils to take less notice of the objects. Indeed, in that confined space they perhaps confront the viewer with greater immediacy than they did when displayed with a multitude of other objects in the Dome area (see Fig.31).

Although Soane's Museum stands today as the *locus classicus* for the display of these full-size plaster representations of the ruined grammar of Antiquity, it is important to remember that his house was not untypical in this regard of the houses of other British architects in the 1820s. Gwilt certainly had a 'museum' of casts, and the case of Burton suggests that other architects known to have casts, such as Basevi, Wyatt and Angell, might well have mounted them on their walls in similar fashion.[58] Burton, whose early professional success seems to have precluded a visit to Italy and Greece (though he reached Spain in 1826), initially integrated his casts with domestic life in his Spring Gardens house (Fig.52). The majority of casts in his very large collection were of ornamental details in the Vatican Museums, but important elements, such as the capital seen on the left in the interior view, were evidently among them.[59] When, later in his career, Burton moved home to Bayswater, the casts remained with his office in Spring Gardens, a clear indication that the importance of having these objects always before the eyes in the design context outweighed any notion that they were merely decorative.

It is not known whether Burton's erstwhile employer, Nash, went ahead with the order for casts from Rome priced for him on the spot by Pennethorne in 1825. Certainly they do not appear alongside the Petworth Amazon, Capitoline Antinous, Diane à la Biche and Apollo Belvedere in an image of their intended destination, the gallery of Nash's house at 14–16 Regent Street which so impressed Karl Friedrich Schinkel dur-

53. The Gallery in John Nash's Regent Street house, drawn by Francis Arundale, from J. Britton and A. C. Pugin: 'Public Buildings in London', published 1825–7.

ing his visit to London in 1826 (Fig.53). Above the bookcases of this room, however, Nash had placed glass cases containing his collection of a new type of model: small, finely made plaster representations of ancient buildings restored to their perfect condition. The manufacturers of these iconic objects were Jean-Pierre Fouquet or his son François and, although seventy-six models had appeared in the famous gallery opened in Paris by Louis-François Cassas in 1806, their novelty and status in Britain is reflected in the £1000 price Nash told the diarist Joseph Farington he had paid for his.[60] Nash's collection included the Greek temple seen in the left foreground of Fig.53, the two probably Roman temples behind that and the triple-fornix triumphal arch in the background. It was not unique, in that in 1834 a magnificent set of twenty Fouquet models was purchased by Soane from Cresy and disposed around his museum.[61] The importance of these objects lies both in their subject and their form. They show, in three dimensions, the new tendency of the early nineteenth century to visualize ancient buildings entire, rather than in their ruined states, and their prismatic and eminently portable nature (tiny white objects shining under glass boxes and domes), gave them a quasi-religious aura.

The appearance of the Fouquet models in London, essential though that is to understanding the changing nineteenth-century British response to Antiquity, which will be discussed

further in Chapter 4, does not mean that the late eighteenth-century fascination with the ruin model had entirely disappeared; rather, that it had been supplemented by a new type of representation. The four cork models of Paestum made by Domenico Padiglione and now in Soane's Museum, for example, were acquired in 1826 from the estate of Sanders. Soane established his 'Model Room' with a central triple-deck platform to accommodate both these and a very large cork model of the theatre area of Pompeii, also made by Padiglione and probably purchased by Sanders in Naples.[62] The theatre area had been the focal point of Soane's own Pompeian studies in the late 1770s when the Temple of Isis was being excavated, a factor which doubtless heightened his association with the model. Moreover, it must have been obvious to Soane in the late 1820s that, having baulked at the possibility of a return visit to Italy in 1819, he would never again see the Roman city which had undergone much more substantial clearance since his own visits in 1779. The urban scale of the model doubtless offered some compensation, but it was to much younger architects, such as Soane's own pupil, Henry Parke, that the opportunity of renewed study at the disinterred city was to fall. They took that opportunity, with important consequences both for the archaeological history of the site and for the development of English architecture.

Chapter 3
Pompeii in the Napoleonic and Restoration periods

Pompeii presents to our view and familiar regard, the private dwellings, and much of the domestic life as is immediately connected with them, of a great people; together with their public buildings; not in a detached and isolated state, but as they form an essential part of a populous city.
(James Cockburn, Preface to T. L. Donaldson, *Pompeii*, 1827)[1]

The town of Pompeii had been rediscovered in 1748 and finally identified by name in 1763. The fact that the site was covered with volcanic *lapilli* rather than solid lava meant that the buildings beneath were better preserved and could be more readily excavated than those at the other great Campanian town, Herculaneum. But clearance of the site could hardly be regarded as a systematic process in the eighteenth century. The area around the two theatres and the tombs and housing near the Herculaneum Gate had been left uncovered but, from an architectural point of view, the general policy of backfilling one excavation with the spoil from the next meant that interesting properties like those of Julia Felix, the House of Emperor Joseph II and, outside the walls, the so-called Villa of Cicero were lost almost as soon as they were found.[2]

British architects visiting Italy in the early nineteenth century, however, found an altogether more encouraging situation. The clearance of the Pompeian Forum which was in progress throughout the period from 1813 to the mid 1820s meant that they could study the temples and other public buildings as part of an urban construct, unimpeded by the post-Antique accretions of the public areas of Rome itself. Moreover, knowledge of Roman domestic architecture had remained a 'desideratum' until, in Thomas Leverton Donaldson's words, 'the buried city of Pompeii satisfactorily cleared up every difficulty'.[3] The increased pace of excavational work, the removal of spoil from the site, the careful recording of buildings discovered and the fact that the British enjoyed better access to the site after 1815 than under the infamous eighteenth-century restrictions, were all results of what had occurred during the period 1798 to 1815, for much of which the French exercised direct political control over the Neapolitan State.

The French work at Pompeii

French excavational activity in early nineteenth-century Campania centred almost exclusively on Pompeii. Other sites, such as Herculaneum (where there had been no significant work for decades and where work did not resume until 1827), Stabiae and Puteoli (Pozzuoli) continued to feature in itineraries of the region, but little new excavation was undertaken.[4] Links between France and the Bourbon court of Naples had been close even before Napoleon's invasion of Italy, because Ferdinand IV's Queen, Caroline, was the sister of Marie-Antoinette. But the period from 1796 to 1806 was one characterized by constant shifts in power between the Bourbons and the Bonapartists in Naples, shifts which were mirrored by archaeological activity. When the French (under General Championnet) established the second Parthenopean Republic in Naples in 1798, instructions were given to continue with excavations at Pompeii; two houses adjacent to the Forum facing the south side of the basilica were uncovered, acquiring the popular name of the 'Houses of Championnet' by which they are still known.[5] In June 1799, however, the French withdrew from Naples to consolidate their gains in northern Italy, allowing Ferdinand to return from his refuge in Sicily in 1802. Robert Smirke, who visited Pompeii in May 1804, noted the lack of progress with the excavations, claiming that Ferdinand never visited the site and that the labourers had not been paid.[6] The second flight of the King and Queen to Sicily in 1805 preceded the installation of Napoleon's brother, Joseph Bonaparte, as King of Naples. Two weeks after his arrival Joseph went to Pompeii and decided to resume the excavations with renewed vigour, deploying as many as eighty people for the purpose. In 1807 Joseph appointed the antiquarian Michele Arditi as Director General of the Museo di Napoli and Superintendent of all the Campanian excavations. One of Arditi's first acts was to draw up a scheme to systematize the clearance of Pompeii.[7] Work was concentrated on the area around the Basilica and in the Strada Consolare, leading from the Herculaneum Gate towards the Forum, where the House of Sallust was uncovered between 1805 and 1809.[8] The departure of Joseph Bonaparte to assume the throne of Spain in 1808 did not slow this pace of work at Pompeii. On the contrary, his replacement in Naples was Marshal Joachim Murat, husband of Napoleon's sister Caroline. Murat and Caroline both showed great enthusiasm for furthering the excavations, personally visiting Pompeii every week. They remained in power in Naples until Murat was defeated by the British at the Battle of Tolentino in May 1815. During the seven years of their administration much of the land under which the ancient city lay was acquired for the state. It was also during these years that the number of people employed in clearances reached its maximum of over 600 during the Revolutionary period, the spoil being systematically carried away from the site for the first time, the bulk of it by women and children using baskets balanced on their heads.

The restoration of Ferdinand IV in 1815 (given the new title of Ferdinand I of the Kingdom of the Two Sicilies in 1816) slowed down the pace of excavation once more. The King lacked interest in the fine arts, but this was also politically a turbulent time, during which he was forced to concede a new constitution and to submit to the unwelcome presence of Austrian troops between 1820 and 1826. Without the financial resources supplied by the French, the number of men working at Pompeii dwindled. Just as at Rome, however, where the return of Pius VII had slowed the pace of the French excavations, the momentum which had built up and the continuity of the personnel involved was sufficient to ensure that the work was carried forward. In Naples, Arditi remained the government official ultimately responsible for excavating and recording the site at Pompeii, as well as for granting access to visiting foreign students, until his death in 1838. There was further continuity in the post of the on-site Architect-Director of the Excavations. Apart from a brief period when Nicola d'Apuzzo held the post, from 1809 it rested with the Bonucci family (Antonio, then his nephew Carlo) until 1833.

The period of French occupation and of Bourbon restoration also served to loosen the control exercised over the publication of Pompeian discoveries by the Accademia Ercolanese. In 1811 the Royal Library Prefect, Abbate Domenico Romanelli, set the pattern of early nineteenth-century Pompeian topography by publishing his *Viaggio a Pompei*, a substantial itinerary further expanded in its 1817 second edition. By 1813 two Frenchmen, the Comte de Clarac (tutor to Caroline Murat's children and keeper of Greek and Roman antiquities at the Musée Royal in Naples until the Restoration) and the numismatist Aubin-Louis Millin, had published works about the recent discoveries made in the Via dei Sepolcri. In 1824 Carlo Bonucci himself was the author of another substantial descriptive itinerary, *Pompei descritta*, which went into further editions in 1826 and 1827 (not to mention two French editions in 1828 and 1837).[9] Similar in scope and format was Andrea de Jorio's French *Plan de Pompéi* of 1828, while an illustrated German account of the site was available in *Wanderungen durch Pompeji* of 1825, by the Austrian soldier Ludwig Goro. By far the most important figure in the early nineteenth-century phase of Pompeian excavations, however, was Charles François Mazois, a former pupil of the Imperial architect Charles Percier. Appointed to an official position of Draftsman and granted a pension by Caroline Bonaparte, Mazois lived alongside the site at Pompeii recording the discoveries made. Forced to retreat to Rome after the restoration of Ferdinand, Mazois spent a year writing the anonymous *Le Palais de Scaurus*, a book describing the layout and functioning of an idealized large Pompeian house. In 1816, however, he was allowed back to Naples, where he continued his work of recording the site until his return to Paris in 1819. The first two volumes of his great folio *Les Ruines de Pompéi* were published in 1824, although the individual fascicules had been appearing since 1812: seven were available by 1817 and thirteeen by 1820.[10] *Les Ruines de Pompéi* represents the principal record of the early nineteenth-century excavations, as well as the most comprehensive visual representation to that time of buildings found on the site since its rediscovery in 1748.

Mazois's arrival at Pompeii coincided with excavations carried out by a regiment of French soldiers around the walls to discover the town's full extent. During the years of his residence, extensive work was carried out along the Via dei Sepolcri, whilst at the south-east corner of the site there was renewed clearance of the amphitheatre. The principal achievements, however, just as in Rome, were the clearances of the Forum and of parts of the network of streets linking the theatres to the Forum and the Forum to the Herculaneum Gate (Fig.54).[11] In the Forum, the Temples of Apollo (then called the Temple of 'Venus' or 'Bacchus') and of Jupiter were discovered and uncovered between 1816 and 1817, followed by the Eumachia Building and Macellum (the Market, then called the 'Pantheon') in 1820–23 and the Forum Baths in the mid 1820s. Celebrated private houses excavated included the House of Apollo on the Vicolo di Mercurio from 1810 and the House of Pansa (actually of Alleius Nigidius Maius) in 1813–14, followed by the House of the Tragic Poet in 1825 and the House of the Faun in 1830.[12] In 1826, however, Mazois died prematurely and production of the third and fourth volumes of *Les Ruines de Pompéi* was undertaken by Franz Christian Gau. Like his friend, Jacques-Ignace Hittorff, Gau came from Cologne. As architectural students, the pair had moved to Paris in 1809 in order to study at the Ecole, where Gau became a pupil of Louis-Hippolyte Lebas and of François Debret. Although his foreign nationality made him ineligible for the *Prix de Rome*, Gau nonetheless travelled in the Mediterranean between 1815 and 1821, working in Rome for Barthold Gottfried Niebuhr at the beginning of this period. The third and fourth volumes of *Les Ruines de Pompéi*, which Gau produced respectively in 1829 and 1838, while still based on the work of Mazois, were substantially supplemented by Gau himself and by more recent research and surveys: the drawings of the Forum Baths, for example, were provided by Henri Labrouste.[13]

The British and Pompeii after 1815

This is the background to the excavation and recording of the site at Pompeii against which the history of British involvement needs to be set. In Sir William Hamilton and his circle, Britain had had an extremely conspicuous political and cultural presence in Naples up to the Napoleonic period and this was quickly re-established after the Battle of Tolentino. The key personality was surely the former Cambridge academic and antiquarian, Sir William Gell. During the early years of the nineteenth century Gell had travelled extensively in Turkey and the Greek archipelago, from 1811 to 1813 with the architects Francis Bedford and John Peter Gandy on an expedition sponsored by the Society of Dilettanti. In 1814 he was back in London, where he was knighted in May, but later that year he accompanied Caroline of Brunswick on her journey into exile,[14] reaching Naples in June 1815 and effectively taking up residence in Italy until his death in 1836. Although Gell maintained a home in Rome (the 'Boschetto Gellio', part of a friend's house on the Palatine), it was in Naples that he established himself in a house below the Certosa di S. Martino. Here, he became a renowned topographer and guide for British visitors, serving from 1830 as Neapolitan 'Minister Resident Plenipotentiary' for the Society of Dilettanti. Gell is commonly described as the author of the extremely popular *Pompeiana*, an illustrated account of Pompeii in the early nineteenth century published between 1817 and 1819. However, while Gell made most of the drawings using his camera lucida, the 'literary part' other than the first essay was the work of his 'coadjutor', the architect John Peter Gandy, who returned to England in 1813 after the Dilettanti expedition but was certainly back in Naples by 1819.[15] Their work reached further editions in 1821 and 1824 and a French translation (1827–8) before, in 1830–31 Gell, this time acting on his own, issued two supplementary volumes describing discoveries made at Pompeii since 1819. A second edition followed in 1837, but Gell had died the previous year, leaving unfinished a third series of *Pompeiana*, the manuscripts of which survive at Sir John Soane's Museum.

Beside Gell, the leading British personality associated with Naples was perhaps the Countess of Blessington, whose letters and diaries made her the social historian of the city in the 1820s. Gell and Lady Blessington ensured that the British established what one writer has termed a 'cultural hegemony' in the void left at Naples by the departed French government.[16] When one adds to this the powerful diplomatic presence of men like Sir William A'Court and William Richard Hamilton, it is evident that Campania once again became a key port of call in the British Grand Tour and in the professional travels of British artists. In view of the clearances undertaken by the French at Pompeii there was even more reason than in the later eighteenth century for tourists and architects alike to visit the site. Numerous written accounts, hundreds of sheets of drawings and a number of substantial publications survive as evidence of the visits to Pompeii made by these two constituencies of traveller in the period from about 1815 to 1830. Although the importance of the British architects' studies has been hinted at, notably by French scholars discussing the work of Mazois and of the *pensionnaires* of the Académie de France à Rome in the same period, most drawings have

never been fully catalogued and no detailed analysis has yet been made of them.[17]

Although the evidence of the drawings shows that students visiting Pompeii in the Restoration period enjoyed better access than their eighteenth-century predecessors, problems of this nature still presented themselves. In 1813, Superintendent Arditi had introduced a rule that dilettanti could only visit the town with official escorts (a measure designed to prevent disfigurement of the fabric and theft) whilst artists, although allowed to wander without surveillance, were forbidden to draw.[18] The latter condition must have proved impossible to enforce as the area excavated rapidly expanded, and it was soon replaced by a system of permits which, though tiresome, nonetheless represented a great advance on the situation which had prevailed before. Back in 1803, Robert Smirke had gone to the extreme of seeking the support of the Prince of Wales in his attempt to gain unhindered access to Pompeii. Smirke wrote to his father from Rome:

On the subject of Pompeii nothing I suppose has transpired; I hear so interesting an account of it as to increase much my desire of being able to make some sketches of it when there but I suppose I must be contented with doing every thing of that kind by stealth. Should however my application have been made to the Prince or be made while I am absent from Italy, if the letters are directed to me post restante, Rome, I shall be sure to procure them on my return.[19]

Smirke's use of the term 'stealth', the very word chosen by Soane twenty years earlier to describe the circumstances in which he claimed to have sketched the Temple of Isis, shows how little the situation had changed in the intervening period. It seems that the Prince was never approached or never acted on Smirke's behalf for, after visiting the site in the spring of 1804, the architect commented that Pompeian wall decorations 'might have afforded useful hints, and I have not ceased to lament the neglect of the proposed application to the Prince of Wales upon this subject'.[20]

Arditi's new system, described by Joseph Woods in 1817, offered two types of visit to the site:

We are not suffered (unless a permission to draw have been previously obtained) to go about without a guide, and these take you in regular succession to the soldiers' quarters, the theatres, the amphitheatre, the forum, with its surrounding temples and public buildings, to several private houses, to the street of the tombs, and the villa of Marcus Arrius Diomed.[21]

The guided itinerary, which took five hours to complete, was no doubt sufficient to satisfy the curiosity of most amateur visitors to Pompeii, but it was far from adequate for architectural students, who therefore sought to obtain the licences from Arditi mentioned by Woods. On successive days in 1821, for example, Ambrose Poynter, already incommoded by a large boil developing on his temple, found himself with the additional problem of 'running after the orders for Portici and

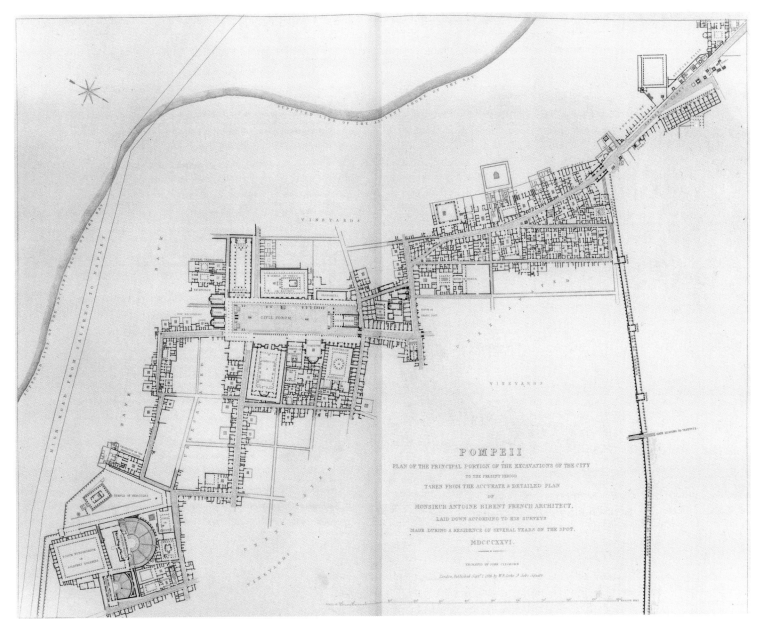

Pompeii' and 'at the Cav. Arditi's for my orders'.[22] Applicants evidently required the support of the British diplomats resident at Naples, and the unofficial backing of Gell could be of assistance. In October 1818 George Ledwell Taylor and Edward Cresy 'called on Sir Henry Lushington and Sir Wm A. Court to obtain permission to draw at Pompeii, and on Sir Wm Gell, who instructed us how to apply, and received us very politely; called also on [Pietro] Bianchi, the architect' (and later Superintendent).[23] This system was still in place in 1825 when Sydney Smirke, 'wishing to make a few sketches at Pompeii … went to Mr Antrobus, Mr Hamilton's deputy, to whom he had given me a letter; he wrote for me to the Marquis here whose duty it is to grant the licences to draw'.[24] But Smirke received no reply after eight days, despite making

four visits to Arditi's office. Finally a visiting Member of Parliament, Mr Western, obtained the licence on Smirke's behalf but, as it was to be shared with some Germans with whom he disdained to work, the architect felt compelled to reapply. Even Gell experienced some difficulty in the late 1820s, when he found one official (whom he declined to name) systematically denying access to excavations made in the three previous years.

The process of obtaining permission to draw at Pompeii thus proved laborious and frustrating for British students but, as with Valadier and the Roman authorities after 1815, Arditi seems to have been generous in granting bona fide students good access. Perhaps a reflection of the difficulties experienced in gaining licences can be found in the fact that a con-

55. Ambrose Poynter: Elevation of a wall in house 'B' at Pompeii (probably in Region VI Insula 2), 1821.

siderable amount of collaborative work was undertaken. In some instances the British were in any case travelling together: Woods, as an established figure in his forties, with the 25-year-old Richard Sharp as his amanuensis, and Taylor and Cresy as peers. Others, however, found benefits in pooling resources with compatriots they met in the large post-Napoleonic English colony in Rome or when visiting Campania. In October 1816 James Hakewill, whose purpose in travelling was primarily to produce a series of topographical drawings for his *Picturesque Tour of Italy*, collaborated with John Goldicutt in the quite different activity of making a measured survey of the Pompeian Forum excavations (see Fig.58).[25] Poynter and Henry Parke, the two young architects among the small group of mourners at the funeral of John Keats in Rome in February 1821, were both at Pompeii in September of that year and working alongside one another, to judge from the similarities of their topographical views and some tracings apparently made by Poynter after Parke's drawings. Co-operation

in the exchange of drawings and information among the British extended well beyond the site: Woods's collection of Pompeian materials contains, in addition to many drawings by Sharp, drawings from Donaldson with watermarks suggesting that they were copied in England after both architects had returned (but before Woods's second departure for Italy). Meanwhile, Donaldson's own album of Greek and Roman sketches contains a plan of the House of the Dancers and other Pompeian details by Parke.[26] British publications on Pompeii at this time also involved an important element of shared endeavour: the first volume of Gandy's and Gell's *Pompeiana* included a plan of the House of Pansa by Charles Robert Cockerell and one of the Forum by Sharp; Donaldson's 1827 two-volume work *Pompeii* made use of drawings by Thomas Allason, Hakewill and Goldicutt, Sharp, Parke, William Wesley Jenkins and, most substantially, of drawings by the military engineer James Cockburn; Goldicutt's own *Specimens of Ancient Decorations from Pompeii* of 1825 included two images supplied by Poynter. In one, Poynter's pencil sketch and detailed colour notes on a Fourth Style wall elevation provided the basis for Goldicutt's hand-coloured plate, although some of the detail was lost in the printed version (Fig.55 and Pl.ixa). John Jenkins, whose visit to Pompeii took place sometime between 1823 and 1825, collaborated with William Hosking in publishing *A Selection of Architectural and other Ornament: Greek, Roman and Italian* in 1827, the title page of which has a Pompeian street as a setting and which contains lithographic details of a painted wall and a floor in the House of Sallust. Finally, the Library of Entertaining Knowledge's *Pompeii: Its Past and Present State*, first published in 1831 as a substantial text with 300 images (its pocket-sized nature notwithstanding), announced in its title its liberal use of Gell and Donaldson, as well as of the obvious French and Italian scholarly sources.[27]

It is not surprising, perhaps, to find that British architects, faced with still somewhat intractable authorities and limited time at Pompeii, should have taken such an open-handed attitude to each other, both when in Italy and when compiling publications in England later. Perhaps more noteworthy, given the recent history of hostilities between their two countries, is the extent to which the British collaborated with their French counterparts. Cockerell was in Naples probably for about three months in 1815, during which time his growing expertise in Classical archaeology made him a valuable contact for those responsible for interpreting the Pompeian excavations.[28] With Mazois, who called him 'mon ami M. Cockerell, architecte d'un grand mérite … qui a fait un long et fructueux voyage en Orient' ('my friend Mr Cockerell, architect of great merit … who has completed a long and rewarding journey in the East'), he discussed the fortifications and theatres of Pompeii, comparing them with Greek examples he had seen. Later Cockerell corresponded with Gau, 'qu'il honorait du nom d'ami' ('whom he honoured with the name of friend'), providing further information on ancient theatre design for the fourth volume of *Les Ruines de Pompéi*.[29] An obituary of Mazois by Donaldson in the second volume of his *Pompeii* makes it clear that the two were acquaintances who had shared information and engaged in debate about the site. Donaldson's own work, especially his hypotheses about the Basilica became, in turn, a source of reference for Gau in the third volume of *Les Ruines*, alongside Gandy's and Gell's *Pompeiana* (to which Gau made even more frequent reference). Gau referred to Donaldson as a 'savant architecte anglais' (a 'knowledgeable English architect') and Donaldson later repaid the compliment by nominating Gau for election among the first wave of Corresponding and Honorary Members of the Institute of British Architects.[30]

An intriguing question, emerging from this background, is that of the extent to which British architectural students sought access to or were obliged to copy the French surveys of Pompeian buildings, as opposed to conducting their own surveys. Among Goldicutt's drawings are a number of traced

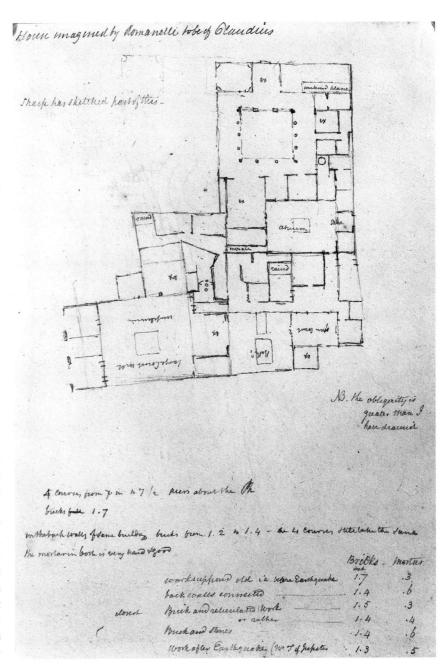

surveys of the buildings in the vicinity of the Forum which were being excavated at the time of his visit, bearing French inscriptions in a hand other than his own.[31] Whilst these may suggest the easy option of second-hand work, however, there is ample evidence that the British studied independently. Many of the drawings in Woods's collection were clearly made in situ in a small sketchbook (subsequently broken up), from which he transferred the information to larger sheets later. A good example is his tiny plan of the 'House imagined by Romanelli to be of Claudius' (the House of the Vestals) (Fig. 56).[32] This property was not a new discovery, having been excavated in the 1770s, but Woods's plan was hand-held (after

56. Joseph Woods: Plan of Pompeian house VI.1.7, the House of the Vestals, 1818.

completing it he added that 'the obliquity is greater than I have drawn it') and annotated with observations on the building's function and construction. Furthermore, Mazois included only a portion of the plan of this property in the second volume of his work, which was devoted to private houses. An even more striking example is a plan of the so-called Academy of Music, excavated only in 1809–10 (Fig.57).[33] Woods traced this plan in or after 1822 but the original was made by Sharp in 1818. Since Mazois did not include this building at all, the British plan may well be the earliest made. It is important to note, moreover, that Sharp's plan included measurements. This is typical of the many British plans of more familiar houses (although strangely Sharp employed millimetres, whereas most used English feet and inches) and it represents a further development on Mazois's published work which provided a general scale (of six different European units of measurement) but featured no figures on individual plates. Measurements made on the ground when the present book was in preparation confirm that Sharp was extremely accurate, although he inadvertently reversed the details of the two northernmost shops on Strada Consolare.[34] His plan also documents lost features of the house, such as the locations of paintings and mosaics, the single pier which stood just east of the tablinum and the platform in Room 16 just to the north of this.

Both in terms of minutiae and originality, it is clear that the surveys of Pompeii made by British architects in the immediate aftermath of the Napoleonic period represent a considerable contribution to the archaeological history of the city. When they are fully catalogued, it is likely that they will also augment present-day knowledge of Pompeian decorative design. Among a finely presented set of drawings by Parke of pavement mosaics, one shows the floor of a shop in Insula 1 of Region VI.[35] The central motif survives in situ, but Parke's drawing demonstrates that its centre has been altered in a subsequent relaying (perhaps in the 1982 restoration of this property) and, furthermore, he included the threshold mosaic which does not survive in situ. Numerous British drawings document both the form and the colour of wall paintings which have deteriorated by long exposure or as a result of the standard technique used for showing them to visitors, described by one architect in 1806, which would horrify modern-day conservators: 'the persons who attend to show these ruins, carry with them a pail of water and a small jug, with which they throw some of it against the walls, and then the colours come out as fresh and as distinct as if they had been but lately done'.[36]

What can be said generally about the corpus of Pompeian work produced by the British in the twenty years following 1815 is that, while it reflected the new interest in Roman public buildings stimulated by archaeological activity in Rome itself, it also exploited the unique opportunities offered by the abrupt termination of Pompeii's existence and the particular

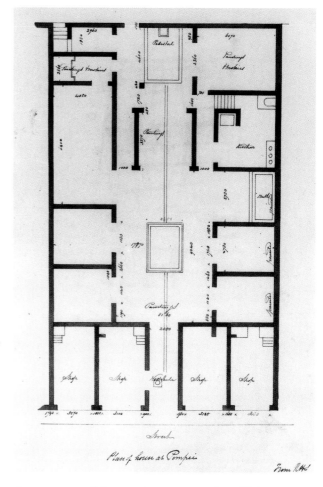

Plan of house at Pompeii

circumstances of its ongoing recovery. In addition to new information on the design and construction of monumental public architecture, the emerging city gave the students insights into Roman urban planning, as well as into domestic architectural and decorative design. In terms of public architecture it is perhaps not surprising that the British concentrated more on the Forum than on the area of the two theatres, 'Soldiers' Quarters' (Quadriportico), Temples of Isis and 'Esculapius' (Jupiter Meilichios) and Triangular Forum which had all been recorded in the eighteenth century. It is true that Woods, whose neat arrangement of his drawings into sets corresponding with the standard itinerary he had described (perhaps in anticipation of a publication on Pompeii), attempted comprehensive coverage of this area of the city, gathering together six sets (forty-three drawings). Meanwhile Donaldson included in his *Pompeii* a survey he had made of the theatre area with William Wesley Jenkins, which purported to show some new clearances. It was, however, the buildings around the Forum, emerging from the ground before the students' very eyes, which drew their attention most.

Goldicutt's Forum plan of 1816 shows, through the use of a pale green wash to indicate areas still buried, that of the public buildings only the Basilica and the three chambers at the

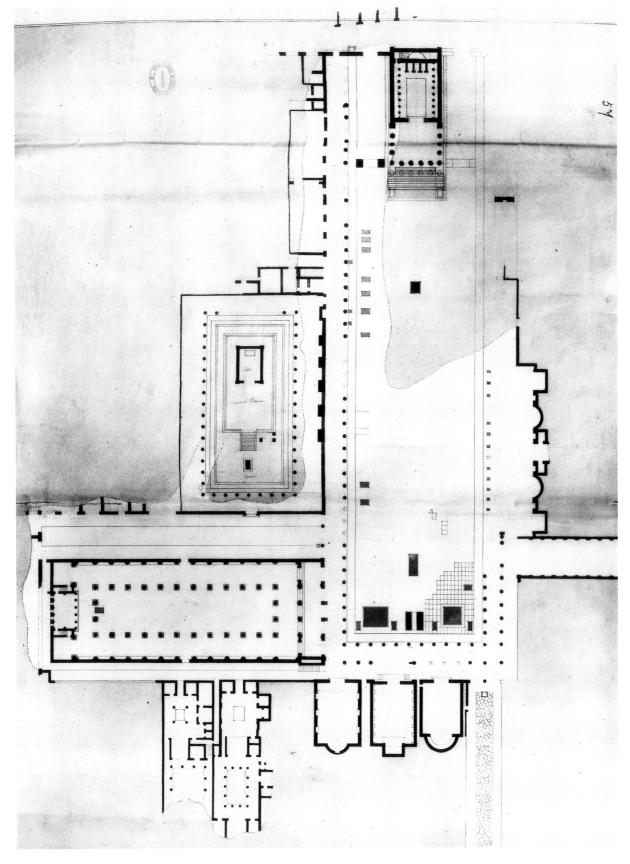

POMPEII IN THE NAPOLEONIC AND RESTORATION PERIODS

south end of the Forum had been fully cleared, along with the eastern flank of the Temple of Apollo and the western flank of that of Jupiter (Fig.58).[37] The same technique of using wash to indicate unexcavated ground appears on an anonymous plan of the Forum in Soane's Museum, dated November 1818, by which time the Temple of Vespasian and Sanctuary of the Lares had been cleared on the east side and a start made on the Eumachia Building (Fig.59). By providing the precise date of November, the anonymous architect of this plan enables us to establish that Richard Sharp's plan of 1818, published in Gandy's and Gell's *Pompeiana*, was made earlier in the year, since Sharp was not yet able to include the Arch east of the Temple of Jupiter. The speed of discovery is further illustrated graphically by a plan preserved at the Ecole nationale supérieure des Beaux-Arts, drawn by the British amateur, Henry Wilkins, and included in his *Suite de vues pittoresques des ruines de Pompeii* of 1819. The copy of this plan at the Ecole was annotated in pencil in 1822 by Jean-Baptiste-Cicéron Lesueur (a friend of Donaldson's), to show the emerging Eumachia Building and Macellum.[38] Lesueur worked alongside his exact contemporary in Italy, Félix-Emmanuel Callet, the only *pensionnaire* of the Académie de France à Rome in the first half of the nineteenth century who made Pompeii, or more specifically the Pompeian Forum, the subject of his obligatory fourth-year archaeological study. It is Callet's plan which shows that all of the buildings surrounding the Forum had been cleared by 1823.[39] Studies such as Callet's, however, did not reach published form, so the 'Plan of the Civil Forum of Pompeii' in Donaldson's book stands as an early example of the completed excavation in printed form.[40]

British students engaged in the debates about identity, date and function which the newly discovered Forum buildings engendered. Gandy and Donaldson, for example, participated in the arguments which sprung up amongst an international range of scholars about the form that the Basilica had taken in Antiquity. The importance of the Pompeian example lay partly in the fact that, as it had to pre-date the destruction of the town in AD 79, it represented a secular public building type from before the supposed decline of Roman architectural taste (in fact it is a Hellenistic building of late second-century BC Republican date). Whilst excavations in the Fora at Rome had revealed a section of Trajan's Basilica Ulpia by 1814, they had yet to uncover the remains of the Basilica Julia (originally a first-century BC building) or the Basilica Aemilia (dedicated in 34 BC, though on the site of two earlier basilicas). Both Englishmen argued that the side aisles of the Pompeii Basilica had had galleries over them, and Donaldson that the central nave would have been open to the sky. Gau, presenting Mazois' reconstruction, took issue with both these hypotheses, rightly as it now seems.[41] However, he erroneously proposed as a result that the building was actually not a basilica at all but the Comitium.

Gau's thoughts about the Forum in Pompeii concerned the individual buildings not just in isolation but also as part of an urban entity. In an interesting passage he distinguished between the civil forum and commercial fora. Unable to accept that public ceremonials and commercial markets could have co-existed in the Roman world, he quite arbitrarily decided that the Pompeian Macellum had been a Pantheon or Hospitium, and then entered into a comparison of Roman and nineteenth-century governmental structures. The architectural unity of Roman civil fora was, in his view, the result of the fact that the number of individuals involved in politics and government administration could be accommodated within a single area of the city. In the modern world, by contrast, whilst the relatively small number of politicians required only a single parliament building, the numerous functionaries occupied departments spread throughout the city.[42] That British minds were working in a similar way is apparent from Donaldson's text, published, it will be recalled, two years earlier than Gau brought out the third volume of Mazois. The English architect, too, distinguished civil or judicial fora from commercial fora, though acknowledging that the two types might be conjoined in smaller cities. The Pompeian Forum was 'surrounded by all the edifices appertaining to public business', and was 'further enriched by votive monuments to the memory of … distinguished individuals'. 'On entering the Forum,' he continued, 'a magnificent assemblage of architectural embellishment opens upon the view – an assemblage which our usages render it impossible ever to realise in the application of architecture to the customs of modern times.'[43] This comment notwithstanding, the principles of Roman forum planning which Donaldson learned at Pompeii (notably the use of an elongated form in place of the Greek agora's square, and the necessity for streets to enter the space boldly but not to traverse it) were, it will be argued in Chapter 8, to be of value to the architect ten years later, when he competed for the commission to rebuild the Royal Exchange in the heart of the City of London.

In addition to comparing Roman and modern civic design, Gau gave consideration to the role played by polychromy in ancient and modern public architecture.[44] He credited Cockerell, Hittorff and Gottfried Semper with giving the public a precise notion of the way colour had been applied to monuments in the ancient world, but first-hand visits to Pompeii inevitably compelled all travelling architects to confront this issue for themselves. What emerges from the British responses is that they were better prepared to respond to colour in mosaic floors than they were when it appeared on architectural elements. Perhaps this was because of a greater familiarity with the former. Woods observed that the fanciful *opus sectile* designs he saw at Pompeii had 'long been in use in modern times, for one sort of ornament or another' but, if this was indeed the case, it did not prevent him from making a detailed comparative study of various forms of *opus signinum* with inset tesserae. Woods also recorded the form and colours

59. Plan of the Forum, Pompeii, November 1818, by an unknown British architect.

PLAN·OF·THE·FORVM·AT·POMPEII

IN·ITS·PRESENT·STATE·NOVEMBER·MDCCCXVIII

60. *Ambrose Poynter:*
Tracing of stucco wall
details in a house at Pompeii,
probably VI.1.7, the House
of the Vestals, Room 43,
1821. No decoration survives
there today. By putting
tracings such as these
together with whole wall
elevations (such as Fig.55),
Poynter was able to bring
home a clear record of the
overall character and small-
scale detail of Pompeian
decorative schemes.

of the *opus sectile* floors of the Temples of Jupiter and Apollo.[45] The pavement of the Temple of Apollo, which did not appear in *Les Ruines de Pompéi* until 1838, was particularly admired by British visitors to the site, Donaldson describing it as 'a very elegant mosaic, the centre compartment consisting of green, white and black marbles, and the border of a Greek meander of black, white, and red mosaic': it is this pavement which features most prominently in Parke's beautiful composite drawing of seven Pompeian examples, a type of image commonly produced by the British (Pl.ixb).[46]

The British response to paint on columns and other architectural elements was rather less enthusiastic than to these coloured mosaics. It needs to be recalled that acceptance that the ancients had painted their architecture at all was still only beginning to gain currency in the immediate aftermath of the Napoleonic period. In Chapter 1 it was seen that colour hardly featured in late eighteenth-century studies of such buildings as the Temple of Isis, carried out by, for example, Soane (see Pl.iv). After 1815 it was a factor which could no longer be overlooked, and there could scarcely be a stronger contrast in this respect between Soane's rendition of the little building where the Nile waters were stored and that of Sharp with its yellow, red and green grounds, preserved among Woods's papers (Pl.xa). As an older architect trained in the 1790s, Woods himself found architectural polychromy especially unpalatable. In his estimation, the Pompeians had produced a 'gross deformity' by placing stucco on the 'slender Greek Doric' stone columns 'of a sober gray colour' around the 'Soldiers' Quarters', and painting their bases red, with yellow and red alternating shafts (blue for the central pair on two sides). Woods revered what he considered to be the pure 'Greek' taste introduced to Roman architecture under Augustus, and this dictated his views on style and dates in Roman architecture. Of the Corinthian columns in the Pompeian Basilica, for example, he wrote:

I incline to attribute all to one time – which will be at the point when the old practices were going out of use and the thick stucco just beginning to come in – There is a degree of Caprice within the Capitals which points out the same – but as they are decidedly Pompeian and Tivolese I cannot imagine them later than early in the reign of Augustus or perhaps a little before.[47]

Colour played, of course, an even more significant role in the painted decoration of Roman domestic architecture, where its appearance raised slightly different questions for students. In the later eighteenth century the number of domestic buildings which were preserved in Rome itself was relatively small. Commenting on this in the Preface to the second volume of *Les Ruines* as a way of highlighting the singular importance of Pompeii, Mazois listed an ancient street near S. Maria Maggiore, the house discovered at the Villa Negroni and houses on the Tusculan and Appian Ways as the few examples in the capital.[48] The later eighteenth-century discoveries at Pompeii, such as the so-called Villas of Cicero and Diomedes outside the Herculaneum Gate and town houses such as those of 'Emperor Joseph' and of the Vestals, had already increased the number of Roman domestic buildings available for study. In the ten years following 1815 it was not just the clearance of *Insulae* 2, 3 and 6 of Region VI from which British students benefited, but also the greater freedom they had to measure and draw, here and within the long-exposed villas and houses as well. Thus it is no surprise to find among Woods's collection of drawings a set of the Villa of Diomedes, mostly by Sharp. The twenty-two drawings include a plan, construction details and coloured records of walls and ceilings within the Villa, which also provided a rich source for Goldicutt and Alexander Roos.[49] Woods and Sharp however, also made copious use of the Napoleonic discoveries, such as the famous Houses of Pansa and Sallust and, as has been seen earlier, the less well-known Academy of Music, in the documenting of which the British were pioneers. Parke's drawing of the House of Sallust is particularly instructive (Pl.xb). The First Style blocks of wall colour are placed in a perspective setting but one which, far from recording the remains as part of a picturesque topographical view (as a painter or amateur visitor might have done), treats the ruined house as a kind of stage set with a receding succession of planes. This specifically architectural approach seems to show a student extrapolating a lesson on the effects of colour for potential later use in the design process.

The greatest interest in Pompeian houses was taken by Parke's 1821 workmate, Ambrose Poynter, to judge from extant evidence. The descendant who later transcribed Poynter's travel diaries said of the architect's time in the Mediterranean: 'in view of his later development [as a Gothic Revivalist] it seems curious that his visit to Pompeii was clearly what might be called the focal point of his journey'.[50] Poynter's Pompeian portfolio shows that he made a systematic study of Roman domestic architecture there. It includes several sides of notes,

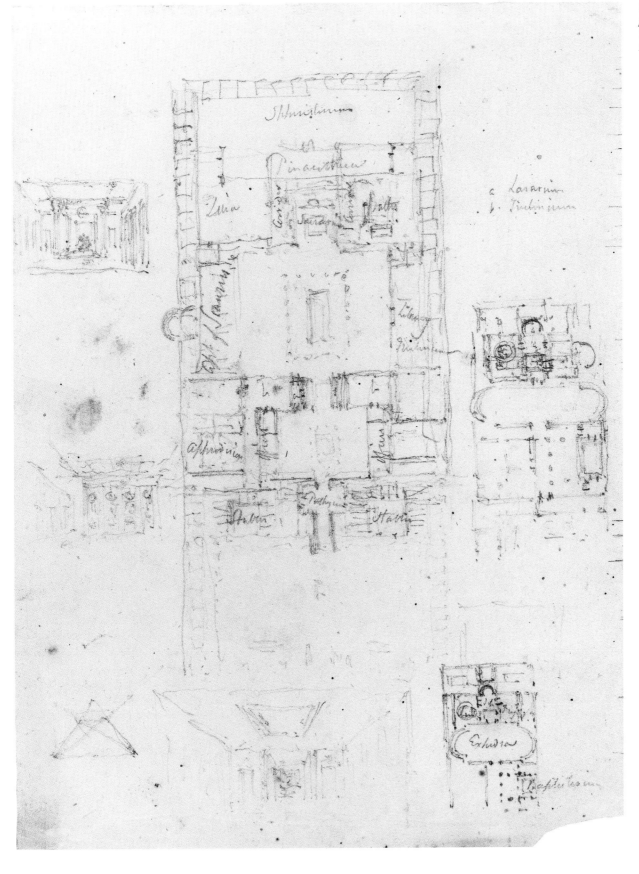

61. Ambrose Poynter: Sketch plan for the hypothetical 'Palais de Scaurus' of François Mazois, 1821.

largely devoted to describing 'the principal object of interest at Pompeii', its houses, in terms of their plan arrangements, practical functions and decorative qualities. A number of the drawings conform with an arrangement of six particular houses which Poynter identified by lettering them 'A' to 'F'. The first of these was the House of Pansa, of which he drew a plan showing areas still buried and a sheet showing pavement designs. From House 'B' Poynter took the elevation of a wall which subsequently appeared in Goldicutt's *Specimens* (see Fig.55 and Pl.ixa). Poynter's House 'C' was that of Championnet I, adjacent to the Forum (of which he and Parke both produced plans). No drawings appear to survive for House 'D', while one drawing with colour notes offers a very rough elevation of the wall of the tablinum of House E. House 'F' was that of the Vestals.[51] Two of the sheets relating to this last house are actually tracings of Fourth Style horizontal and vertical bands of *rinceau*, mythical beasts and lyres, almost certainly made directly from the wall of Room 43, referred to by Poynter as 'one of the most highly finished in Pompei', with a beautiful blue ground, details picked out in golden yellow and a dado of real grey marble (Fig.60). These sheets were numbered, so that they could be put together with the larger-scale elevation of the whole wall (see the example of Fig.55). In this way, Poynter maintained a complete record of the wall's overall and detailed design.

The careful ordering and lettering of his drawings suggests the possibility that Poynter intended to produce a publication on this subject. Certainly his notes attempted to synthesize the archaeological evidence that he had gathered and it is clear that he had familiarized himself with the literature, including Mazois's *Le Palais de Scaurus*, published in 1819 and made more topical by the appearance of a second edition in 1822. In fact, one of Poynter's sheets of sketches represents a remarkable attempt to visualize Mazois's House of Scaurus (Fig.61). The apartment of Scaurus, with that of his wife Lollia on one side and the 'aphrodisium' for more discreet encounters on the other, appears to the left (or west) of the plan. The library, triclinium and bath complex face it from the east, with the pinacoteca and spheristerium (an indoor court for ball games) across the north end of the house. All this follows the verbal description provided by the French architect, though Poynter could not work out how to fit in the exedra, with its twin hemicycles, and alternatives for the plan for this part of the house were experimented with on the right-hand side of the sheet. Poynter's notes go into some detail on the arrangement of rooms in actual Pompeian houses. However, his general view on Roman domestic design as exemplified by Pompeii was not favourable. He commented that, in *Le Palais de Scaurus*, Mazois 'naturally introduces many apartments not to be found in the mediocre city of Pompei', and he interpreted the general use of the Tuscan order (rather than the Corinthian) in atria as a further sign of Campanian impoverishment. Poynter was also critical of Roman ventilation and lighting, saying

that the houses could only have been suitable for summer living. Finally, his views on interior decoration were somewhat equivocal. In that it was seen as a poor substitute for marble revetment, First Style painting was disapproved of, and other Styles were in 'bad taste', primarily because their colours were 'as gaudy as possible'. On the other hand, Poynter thought the presence and execution of central figures in the Fourth Style very appealing and his comment that the decorative detail of the paintings was 'usually valuable' presumably lies behind the fact that he went to the extent of tracing some such detail directly from the walls.

Poynter's assessment of Pompeian wall decoration was typical of that of many other British architects who studied at Pompeii in the decade following 1815. Woods, for example, considered the preference for 'bad plaster' over 'good stonework' to be 'depraved', but conceded that some of the decoration was 'graceful', and that 'if we were to compare them with the decorations of the walls of any city in modern Europe, the advantage would be greatly, very greatly in favour of Pompei'.[52] Although there is no evidence that the British discriminated between the different Styles of painting represented by the walls of Pompeii, it is clear that whatever they perceived to be in 'bad taste' they associated with the post-Augustan age, using Vitruvius' famously sour chapter on the developing 'decadence of fresco painting' in Book 7 of his treatise to support this view (the treatise was commonly believed to have been written later than the third decade BC now ascribed to it). Since Vitruvius's criticisms were aimed at the depiction of objects, including the elements of architecture, in fantastic forms which had no basis in reality, it was presumably precisely those aspects of Third and Fourth Style painted decoration which the British had in mind when they spoke of bad taste.

It is striking to note that belief in the artistic supremacy of the Augustan period dictated the distinction between good and bad Roman taste in painted decoration, as in architecture more generally. In this regard, at least, the studies of Pompeii (and of Rome itself) made by early nineteenth-century British architects can be seen as continuous with those of their later eighteenth-century counterparts. In most respects, however, their achievements were of an altogether different order. The depth of detail in their work, on Roman domestic architecture and interior design as well as on Roman public architecture in its urban contexts, placed them alongside Callet and other *pensionnaires* of the Académie de France à Rome such as Abel Blouet, Félix Duban and Henri Labrouste as pioneers in the examination and documentation of the rapidly emerging site at Pompeii in the first three decades of the century. Moreover, in the breadth of its scholarship and the extent of its illustration, the corpus of publication produced by British architects and antiquarians during this period is surely of an importance second only to that of Mazois's and Gau's monumental *Les Ruines de Pompéi*.

Chapter 4
The vision of Rome after 1815

While the eye contemplates the wreck of grandeur, let the imagination effect its restoration. (George Wightwick, on visiting the Forum in 1825)[1]

The Napoleonic excavations and clearances at Rome and Pompeii, their continuation by the restored Italian governments and improved access to the monuments themselves were all contributory factors to a significant change in the perception of Roman architecture among British architectural students arriving in Italy after 1815 from that of their eighteenth-century predecessors. Those making renewed surveys now focused not just on the measurement of columns, capitals and entablatures, but also on how temples, in particular, had risen on podia from street level and had been accessed. In their *The Architectural Antiquities of Rome*, George Ledwell Taylor and Edward Cresy illustrated the excavations in plan and perspective, using images which were typologically new in early nineteenth-century Britain. By depicting the anatomy of the ruins in such detail, they reminded readers more forcefully that these ruins were members of what once had been a whole body. Meanwhile, their typologically innovative lithographic plates of carved details of Roman buildings represented another aspect of Roman architecture which now preoccupied the British: the sculptural richness of the architecture, rather than the minutiae of its measurements.

Taylor and Cresy did not respond, however, to one highly important development which was occurring in the British response to Roman Antiquity, even as they went to print: the use of the perspective in restoring buildings or, indeed, in visualizing parts of entire cities. While their perspectives of the ruins in 1818–19 offered an audience wider than a purely architectural one images of the changed face of post-Napoleonic Rome (like those of contemporary topographically-inclined painters such as Samuel Prout and Charles Eastlake), the restorations of Taylor and Cresy retained the steely orthographical detachment of Robert Wood (see Fig.47).[2] If *The Architectural Antiquities of Rome* provided British architects with the data they needed to be able to build in emulation of Roman monuments, it was perspective visions of the Forum Romanum and of street and domestic scenes at Pompeii which offered more immediate inspiration both to architects and to potential clients unaccustomed to reading architectural surveys. The visions which form the subject of this chapter occupy a dual position: on the one hand they testify to British involvement in the great advances in Roman topographical

understanding achieved during the two decades after 1815 among Italian, French and German antiquarians; on the other hand, they lead towards a more imaginative engagement with Antiquity, which the public at large loved to revel in, especially through their reading of Edward Bulwer-Lytton's *Last Days of Pompeii*, the most popular novel of this period after Walter Scott's *Waverley*. The British visions did not function in isolation from the touchstone of architectural study in Italy, which remained the Académie de France and the activities of its *pensionnaires*. As will be seen, however, in certain respects the greater degree of liberty from academic rules enjoyed by British students worked to their advantage.

Restoration in the French *envois* from Rome

By the time that British students began arriving back in Rome in 1816, their French colleagues at the Villa Medici had a clear curriculum for their studies of Antiquity set out by the newly formed Académie des Beaux-Arts and the Institut de France. The idea of regularizing architect-*pensionnaires'* activities in Rome appears to have originated with Marie-Joseph Peyre and his younger brother Antoine-François in 1778, when the then Académie royale d'Architecture decided that its students in Rome should make survey and restoration drawings of antiquities for display in Rome and for subsequent dispatch for assessment and exhibition in Paris (hence the term 'envois', used to describe these projects).[3] Studies of the Theatre of Marcellus by Antoine-Laurent-Thomas Vaudoyer and, after a rule change in 1786–7, of Trajan's Column by Charles Percier survive from the late eighteenth-century, but it was in 1799 that the system which would effectively continue until 1960 was set in place. The progress of each student during the first three years of his time in Rome was to be assessed through *envois* comprising details of ruined buildings at one quarter of their actual size. Only in the fourth year were *pensionnaires* permitted, indeed required to make a full restoration study. In order to do this, they were provided with a small budget to assist with the physical exploration of the remains of the chosen site. Then, on the basis of actual state surveys, they progressed to drawn restorations as they imagined the building or complex to have been in its ancient state, made on paper of a stipulated large size. From 1815 the Academy intended that these fourth-year *envois* should be systematically engraved, but in the event publication resulted

62. Giovanni Pardini: The Temple of Venus and Rome, Rome, actual state and semi-restored sections, from Richard Burgess, 'The Topography and Antiquities of Rome', published in 1831.

63. Louis-Sylvestre Gasse: Restoration elevation of the Forum of Augustus, Rome, 1803–5. The rules of the Académie forbade perspectives and obliged architectural students to use orthographical elevations such as this. As a result, the Forum appears isolated from any urban or topographical context.

only from private initiatives. Thus Guillaume-Abel Blouet's *Restauration des Thermes d'Anthonin Caracalla à Rome* of 1828, although dedicated to the Beaux-Arts section of the Institut, was not an official production. It is important to bear in mind that, while interested foreigners would undoubtedly have been aware of the nature of French architectural training in Rome in relation to antique buildings, and would have been able to see the drawings on display at the Villa Medici, they could not refer to more than a handful of these works in published form.[4] Nonetheless, the French approach undoubtedly influenced the British. Richard Burgess's ground-breaking 1831 *The Topography and Antiquities of Rome*, for example, included a survey of the Temple of Venus and Rome undertaken by the author's architect-collaborator, Giovanni Pardini, leading to a wholly new type of image in the context of British guidebooks to Rome (Fig.62). This temple was 'the fashionable antiquity of the city' (as a result of renewed excavations in 1828), but it can hardly be coincidental that it was also the subject of Léon Vaudoyer's *envoi* of the previous year, with its comparable restoration section.[5]

The earliest *envois* of the nineteenth century, such as Jean-Antoine Coussin's 1802 study of the Temple of Hercules Victor in the Forum Boarium and Louis-Sylvestre Gasse's of the Forum of Augustus, in 1803, followed a standard format, with simple sheets containing a topographical view of the ruins, an actual state plan, and restored plans, elevations and sections (Fig.63).[6] There are two crucial points to note here. First, although restored elevations such as that by Gasse could achieve a degree of scenographic depth, they still isolated the Roman buildings from any urban or other context. Second, there were no perspective views, since these were prohibited by the Académie until late in the nineteenth century. Where these *envois* did differ from previous representations, however, was in the way they emphasized new excavations around the monuments. Coussin, for example, included an indication of the little dig he had undertaken at the base of the peristyle of the Temple of Hercules Victor. In 1809 a rapid stride was taken in this direction with Jean-François-Julien Ménager's study of the Temple of Antoninus and Faustina. Initially given permission to survey the temple by the government of Pius VII in 1807, Ménager proceeded to excavate the entire pronaos in 1809 at the Académie's behest, after the French had occupied Rome (although before the Consulta Straordinaria had been fully established). Ménager made his neatly redrawn survey notes, including a very beautiful and detailed sheet of plans and sections of the excavation pit, as an integral part of his submission (Fig.64).[7] Thereafter, Achille Leclère's 1813 study of the Pantheon, Pierre-Martin Gauthier's of the Basilica of Maxentius (1814) and Jean-Louis Provost's of the Temple of Vespasian (1815), all reflect the fact that French excavation or other clearance work had been in progress on these monuments during the period when they were *pensionnaires*.[8]

One of the most topical of the immediately post-Napoleonic studies was that made of the Temple of Castor and Pollux by Jean-Tilman-François Suys in 1816. As has been seen in Chapter 2, initial explorations were made around the podium of the temple in 1813, but the most revealing excavations did not take place until 1816–17 when they were witnessed by Taylor, Cresy and many other British students. The work of Suys falls between these two periods and shows an otherwise unrepresented stage in the dawning comprehension of the Temple's form. His reconstruction proposed an octostyle building with fifteen columns to each flank, thus following the restoration of Andrea Palladio who, in turn, had taken this prescription from Vitruvius (Fig.65). Suys also proposed a podium approached by straight flights of steps at either end and, as a result, a cella with front and back entrances.[9] Even as Suys returned to Paris, however, another *pensionnaire*, Auguste Caristie, was engaged in reconstructing the form of the Temple. Financed by the Count de Blacas, Caristie made excavations of the podium in March 1816 and spring 1817 (although it is unclear precisely how this related to the official excavation being carried out at the same time by the Commissario delle Antichità, Carlo Fea).[10] Caristie's study of this individual monument subsequently became part of a larger study of the entire Forum as excavated between 1809 and 1819, published in Paris in 1821 as *Plan et coupe d'une partie du Forum Romain* and dedicated to his former master, Percier. Caristie's reconstruction of the Temple (Fig.66) placed thirteen columns in its flanks, incorporated the discovery of fourteen lateral steps to a mid-point platform in front of the Temple and removed Palladio's notion of a rear (southern) approach to it, which Suys had emulated.

As the case of the Temple of Castor and Pollux shows, ongoing excavation work had come to bear close relationship to the way in which the *pensionnaires* and other French architects and antiquarians visually reconstructed Roman buildings during the first two decades of the nineteenth century. While the accuracy of the restorations steadily rose, however, they continued to depict the buildings in a way which isolated them from any urban context, either within the Forum, if that was their location, or in the city at large. This was a problem caused in large part by the Académie's prohibition of perspectives of the restorations. The lack of vitality was exacerbated, moreover, by the Académie's additional refusal to allow the architects to include historical figures in their elevations or sections.[11]

Roman Forum restorations after the Napoleonic excavations

The early nineteenth-century British vision of Rome developed against the background not just of the French *envois* but also of the studies of the leading Italian topographers of the period, in particular in relation to their work on the Forum Romanum. The first major publication on the history and dis-

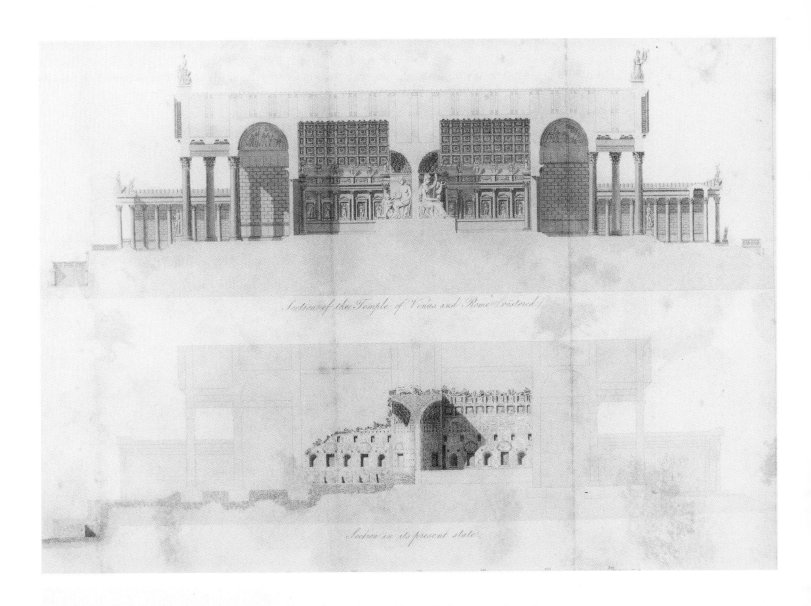

Section of the Temple of Venus and Rome restored.

Section in its present state.

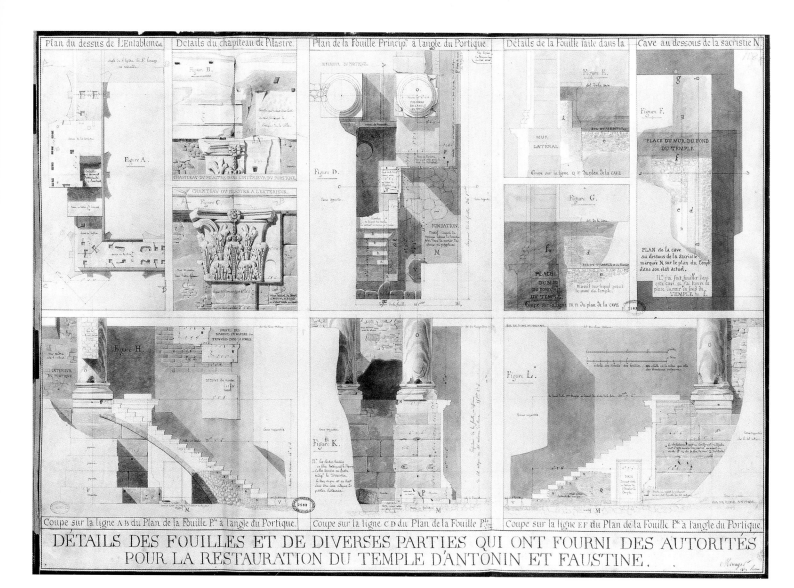

DÉTAILS DES FOUILLES ET DE DIVERSES PARTIES QUI ONT FOURNI DES AUTORITÉS POUR LA RESTAURATION DU TEMPLE D'ANTONIN ET FAUSTINE.

64. Jean-François-Julien Ménager: Details of the excavation of the pronaos of the Temple of Antoninus and Faustina, Rome, 1809. Ménager included the excavation he had been permitted to make as an integral and beautiful part of his set of drawings.

position of the Forum to be published after the excavations of the Napoleonic period was Antonio Nibby's *Del Foro Romano*, which appeared in 1819. At the same time as writing this book, however, Nibby was in the process of producing the fourth edition of Francesco Nardini's seventeenth-century *Roma Antica*, a fact which certainly affected his interpretation of the site. Most significantly, Nibby remained committed to Nardini's belief that the Forum had been situated effectively on a north-south axis, directly between the Capitoline and Palatine Hills, bounded to the north by Basilica Aemilia (turned through 90 degrees from its actual position) and, in Nibby's case, to the south by some 800 Roman feet by the Basilica Julia (Fig.67).[12] At the foot of the Capitoline Hill Nibby retained the traditional identification of the Temple of Vespasian as that of 'Jupiter Tonans', and he noted the position of the Temple of Concord, the podium of which had been discovered in the summer of 1817. This meant that he had to find a new identification for the Temple of Saturn (pre-

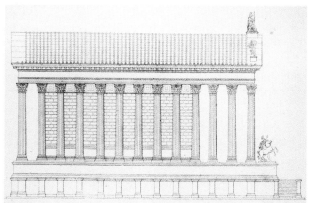

viously thought to have been that of Concord), which he settled on calling the Temple of 'Fortune'. Further to the south, hypothetical Temples of Vespasian and Saturn were separated by the Clivus Capitolinus and Arch of Tiberius. The east side

DU TEMPLE DE JUPITER STATOR.
AU QUART DE L'EXECUTION.

65. Jean-Tilman-François
Suys: Restoration plan,
elevation, and other details
of the Temple of Castor and
Pollux, Rome, 1816.

OPPOSITE, BOTTOM
66. Auguste Caristie:
Restored east elevation of
the Temple of Castor and
Pollux, from 'Plan et coupe
d'une partie du Forum
Romain', published in 1821.

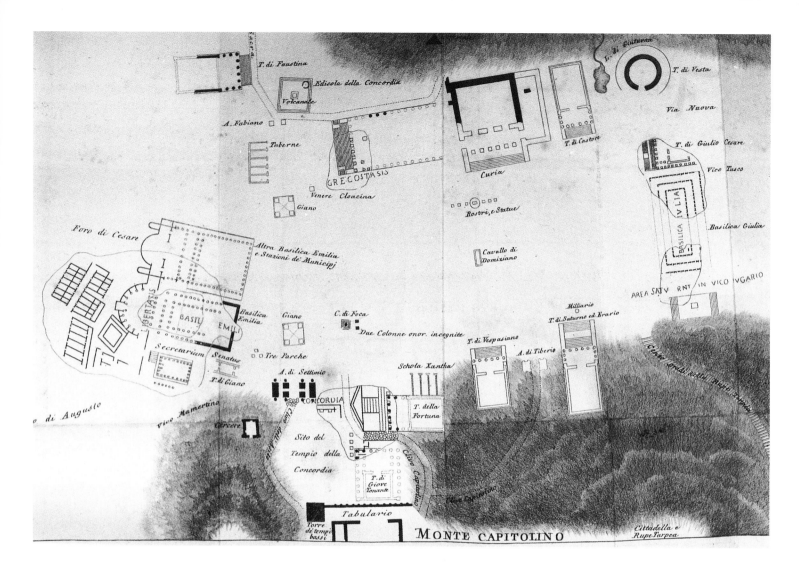

Labels in the plan image (as visible): T. di Faustina, Edicola della Concordia, Volcanale, A. Fabiano, Tuberne, GRECOSTASIS, Venere Cloacina, Giano, Foro di Cesare, Altra Basilica Emilia e Stazioni de' Municipj, LIBERTATIS, BASIL. EMIL., Basilica Emilia, Giano, Secretarium Senatus, T. di Giano, A. di Settimio, CONCORDIA, Vico Mamertino, Carcere, Sito del Tempio della Concordia, T. di Giove Tonante, o di Augusto, Tabulario, Torre de' tempi bassi, MONTE CAPITOLINO, C. di Foca, Due Colonne onor. incognite, Tre Parche, Schola Xantha, T. della Fortuna, Clivo Capitolino, Clivo Espiatorio, Rostri, e Statue, Cavallo di Domiziano, Curia, T. di Castore, Milliario, T. di Vespasiano, A. di Tiberio, T. di Saturno ed Erario, AREA SATV RNT IN VICO IVGARIO, G. di Giuturna, T. di Vesta, Via Nuova, T. di Giulio Cesare, Vico Tusco, BASILICA IVLIA, Basilica Giulia, Cittadella e Rupe Tarpea

67. *Antonio Nibby: Plan of the Forum Romanum, from 'Del Foro Romano', published in 1819. North here is to the left (actually the bottom left).*

OPPOSITE

68. *Carlo Fea: Plan of the Forum Romanum, published in 1827. North here is to the top (actually the top left).*

69. *Auguste Caristie: Plan of the Forum Romanum, from 'Plan et coupe d'une partie du Forum Romain', 1821. North here is to the bottom (actually the bottom right).*

of Nibby's forum was almost entirely bounded by what he called the 'Graecostasis' (actually the Temple of Castor and Pollux), the Curia (the 'Temple of Augustus') and a hypothetical Temple of Castor.

Since this east side of Nibby's Forum is of particular relevance for the work of one British architect, it is worth describing the grounds on which he determined its layout. In editing Nardini he had been tempted to accept the new archaeological evidence which suggested identification of the surviving three most famous columns as part of the Temple of Castor and Pollux.[13] But in *Del Foro Romano* he discounted this proposed identification on the grounds that the Temple was known to have fronted the Forum. He knew that the building with the three columns had faced north and therefore it would have been its side, rather than its front, which would have faced a Forum oriented on a north-south axis. On the basis of comparison with the marble plan of Rome and coupled to the discovery of *fasti* in the recent excavation, Nibby thus concluded that the surviving columns (which he showed in black)

were part of the east peristyle of the 'Graecostasis'. In fact the Graecostasis (the area where foreign ambassadors waited prior to their appearance before the senate in the Curia) was an open area at the base of the Capitoline Hill which lost its function with the dismantling of the Republican Comitium under Julius Caesar and was subsequently incorporated into the area around the Temple of Concord.

Nibby's great rival as archaeologist and antiquarian was the Commissario Fea who, in 1827, published a Forum plan dedicated to the Cardinal Camerlengo Pietro Francesco Galleffi (Fig.68). Better drawn than Nibby's and differing in many details (with, in fact, as many errors), Fea's plan continued to orientate the Forum on a north-south axis, placing the Basilica Julia a great distance from the Arch of Severus. However, Fea had made the post-Napoleonic identification of the Temple of Castor and separated the building (no.23 on his plan) from the Curia and Comitium, placing these two buildings on opposite sides of the 'Graecostasis' (nos 26, 29, 28). Although Fea incorrectly supposed that the steps of the pronaos had led

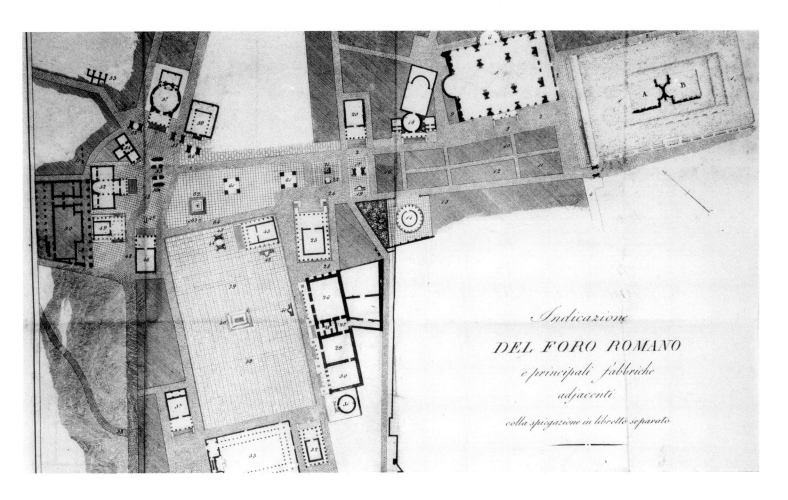

Indicazione
DEL FORO ROMANO
e principali fabbriche
adjacenti

colla spiegazione in libretto separato

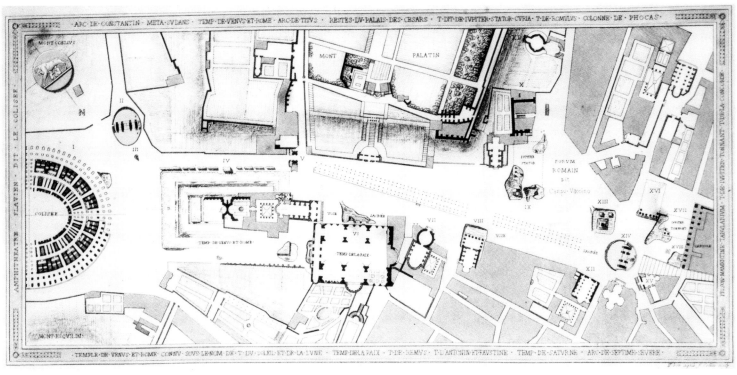

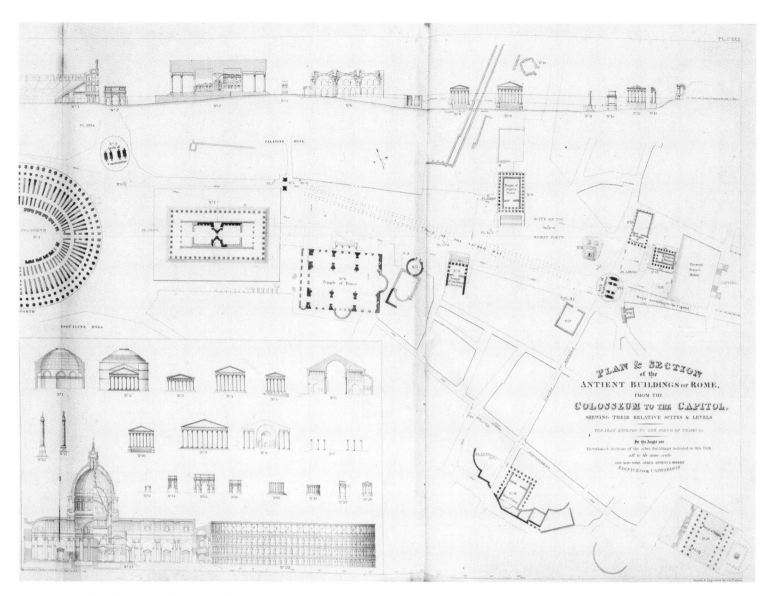

70. *George Ledwell Taylor and Edward Cresy: Plan of the Fora area of Rome (with elevations and inset), from 'The Architectural Antiquities of Rome', 1821–2. North here is to the bottom (actually the bottom right).*

directly down to the Forum in two flights, he appears to have been the first person to hypothesize the correct number of eleven columns in the lateral peristyles of the Temple.

It is striking to note that the two Italian antiquarians seem to have taken little note of the work carried out contemporaneously by foreign architects on the site. Caristie's work, although not published until 1821, can hardly have been unknown to Nibby and certainly not to Fea. In his plan (Fig.69) the Frenchman placed the legend '*Forum Romain*' on what is now known to be the site of the Basilica Julia and the direction in which he believed the Forum to have extended thus remains unclear. However, the elongated rectangle of the plate on the west-east axis, the extension of the Sacred Way directly from the Arch of Severus to that of Titus and the inclusion of the entire space from the Capitoline Hill to the Colosseum suggests that Caristie had a sense of the real disposition of the Forum and its eastward extension. Taylor and Cresy had

similarly conceived the Forum space as extending from the Capitol to the Colosseum in their plan, the first serious English attempt to lay out the topography of the heart of the ancient city (Fig.70). Indeed, they had gone further in adding the area of the Imperial Fora, thereby conceptualizing the entire administrative centre of ancient Rome as a single urban entity. Taylor's and Cresy's work appears, however, to have been unkown in Rome during the 1820s. Only one Italian antiquarian, Stefano Piale, seems to have accepted the re-orientation of the city's most important civic space at this time. In a paper read to the Accademia Romana di Storia di Archeologia in 1818, Piale argued that Nardini's orientation of the Forum should be turned through 90 degrees, even though the overall extent of the space would thereby be halved. For Piale, the Forum had extended from the Arch of Severus eastwards to the Temple of Antoninus and Faustina, much as we now know it did. Given this orientation, Nibby's objection to

71. Luigi Canina: Detail of plan of the Forum Romanum, from 'Descrizione storico del Foro Romano', 1834. North here is to the right (actually the top right).

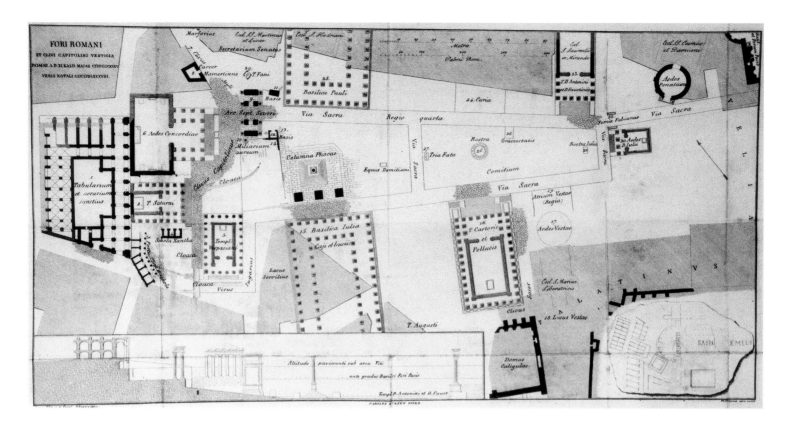

72. Karl Bunsen: Plan of the Forum Romanum, from 'Annali dell'Instituto di Corrispondenza Archeologica', 1835. North here is to the top (actually the top left).

the identification of the Temple of Castor and Pollux disappeared and, moreover, Piale concluded that the Comitium had been an open area rather than a covered building.[14] Six years later, Piale read a further lecture to the Accademia Romana in which he agreed with a suggestion made by the founder of the Iperborei Romani, Eduard Gerhard, that the Basilica Julia had been placed far too far from the Column of Phocas by Nibby.[15] Not only had Piale reorientated the Forum, then, but he had also begun the process of defining its southern boundary at the very point where Fea, Nibby and all previous topographers had believed its axis to have extended south between the Capitoline and Palatine Hills. Piale's papers were not published until 1832–3 and his views may thus have been unknown to those outside the Accademia Romana. Fea, however, continued to ignore them, and it was not until Luigi Canina published his *Descrizione Storico del Foro Romano* in 1834 and Karl Bunsen his *Forum Romain* in the 1835 *Annali dell'-Instituto Corrispondenza Archeologica* that Piale's definition of the space was officially recognized (Figs 71 and 72). Bunsen, however, rejected the orientation of the Basilica Julia proposed by Nibby and Fea, turning it through 90 degrees from its actual position, and Canina identifyed the Temple of Castor and Pollux as the Curia (see III on Fig.71). Despite this aberration, Canina's work is important, in that it sought to distinguish clearly the different phases of architectural history which overlay each other on the same site. He was also first to identify the Temple of Vespasian correctly.[16] This was the state

of antiquarian knowledge on the Forum emanating from the Camerlengato and the Accademia Romana at the time that two young British architects, Charles Robert Cockerell and James Pennethorne, were making their visionary restorations of the principal urban space of the ancient city.

The British vision of the Forum Romanum

Cockerell was in Rome throughout the second half of 1815 and returned there from northern Italy for a second stay from late 1816 to Spring 1817. It was probably during the latter period that he made the initial studies for his restoration of the Forum, subsequently reproduced in a number of engraved versions. It also seems likely that the work was commissioned by Elizabeth, Duchess of Devonshire, who, in early 1818 wrote to the architect in London about the 'beautifull drawing of the Forum Romanum w[hich] you was so good as to do for me' and saying how greatly the drawing and accompanying 'valuable explanation of it' had been admired in Rome.[17] Preserved in the British Museum are six drawings which represent stages of Cockerell's work. Four are topographical views, all showing the Forum from east to west, one from the unusual high vantage point of the tower of the church of S. Francesca Romana. The state of excavation of the monuments shown, the sketchy nature of the drawings and the fact that at least one of the sheets has been torn from a sketchbook, all suggests that these drawings were made in situ by

73. Charles Robert Cockerell: Topographical sketch of the Forum Romanum east to west, probably made in the winter of 1816–17.

the architect when in Rome (Fig.73).[18] Moreover, it was this angle of view that subsequently became the basis on which Cockerell developed his great vision of the epicentre of the Roman world. The two remaining sketches in the British Museum show the restored view. One appears to represent the very first stages of Cockerell's thoughts (Fig.74).[19] It was executed on two pieces of paper stuck together, the left part showing the Tiberian Palace on the Palatine Hill only in the barest outline. The Temple of Castor and Pollux, beside it, similarly appears in outline and as a prostyle rather than a peripteral building. The second restoration sketch in the British Museum, with its circular Temple of Vesta in the foreground, is close to the image passed to the engraver Giacomo Rocruè in Rome (Fig.75).[20] This print was probably made in 1818, because when the Duchess of Devonshire wrote to Cockerell in February of that year, the possibility of employing a different engraver, Vincenzo Feoli or his assistant Giorgio Baltezar, was under discussion. The final episode in the genesis of Cockerell's vision came back in London where, in 1819, he prepared a magnificent watercolour version of the work, nearly a metre (*c*.3 ft) wide, for exhibition at the Royal Academy (Pl.XI).[21] For this work the architect allowed his imagination a freer reign, introducing elements such as the circular peristylar court in the foreground, not present in earlier versions and for which there was no archaeological evidence (it may come, in fact, from the foreground of Cockerell's earlier restoration of ancient Athens). This great vision represents the endpoint of a conception of ancient Rome which had begun with the abandoned Forum and ruinous buildings shown topographically in Fig.73. Its impact at the Academy seems to have been instantaneous, since the Gold Medal subject set that same year and won by Sydney Smirke was a restoration of Pliny's Villa at Laurentinum. The Gold Medal competition was intended by the Academy in London to test the design skills of the students and their potential for careers as public architects, not their feeling for Antiquity, and this was the only restoration of ancient architecture among the many public buildings and monument subjects set during the period covered by this book.[22]

The painting displayed by Cockerell at the Royal Academy was described as 'An Idea of a Reconstruction of the Capital and Forum of Rome, from an elevated point between the Pallatine Hill and the Temple of Antoine & Faustina from the existing remains, the authorities of ancient writers, and the descriptions of Piranesi, Nardini, Venuti and others'.[23] Cockerell's sources, then, were largely eighteenth-century ones (certainly his work predated Nibby's fourth edition of Nardini, and Piale's third edition of Ridolfino Venuti's 1763 *Topografica della antichità di Roma*) and he was working a little too early to have benefited from Caristie's considered work on the Forum or, of course, from that of Taylor and Cresy. Cockerell thus made the traditional assumption that the axis of the Forum had been north-south. Presumably he chose the east to west viewpoint because the ruins were more suggestive

L'antico Foro Romano di C. R. Cockerell   Giacomo Rocchi incise

from that angle, with the Capitol towering in the background, or perhaps because it reduced the amount of hypothetical restoration necessary at the southern end of the putative Forum which was entirely built over in the early nineteenth century. As Burgess, who accepted Nibby's orientation of the Forum, was to write later, in the search for a boundary towards S. Giorgio in Velabro, 'the particles of evidence are like atoms diffused through a vast expanse'.[24] Rocruè's print (see Fig.75) was produced with a key to the buildings shown, enabling a clear picture of Cockerell's topography of the Forum to emerge. He accepted Fea's new identification of the Temple of Castor and Pollux, calling it 'formerly' the Temple of 'Jupiter Stator'. By placing ten columns in its flank he settled on a number not given by any other authority, but he seems to have been the first person to reconstruct correctly from the archaeological evidence the way the steps of the podium descended to the Forum. The surviving Ionic pronaos of the Temple of Saturn was transformed into a Corinthian building by Cockerell, who also anticipated Nibby in reidentifying it as a Temple of 'Fortune'. But whereas Nibby retained the traditional identification of the Temple of 'Jupiter Tonans', Cockerell, who left Rome a few months before the discovery of the podium of the adjacent actual Temple of 'Concord', decided to give it that dedication. Everyone knew that there had been a Temple of Saturn in the Forum, but nobody knew where it was. Cockerell opted for the tradition which placed this building just to the north of the Arch of Septimius Severus, near the site of the Curia, making it continuous with the Basilica Aemilia. At the centre of the Forum, roughly in the position of the Column of Phocas (which Cockerell did not include), he proposed a blocky structure as the 'Tribune or Rostra'. In the placement of the Temple of Jupiter Feretrius on the southern summit of the Capitoline Hill and that of Jupiter Capitolinus on the northern peak, Cockerell followed tradition (although Burgess later argued at length and correctly that these two buildings should be reversed).

Cockerell's Forum restoration was made for personal reasons as well as in order to court the patronage of the Duchess of Devonshire. It was not his first study of this type. He had already made and had had engraved a similar restoration of ancient Athens, two impressions of a print of which his father received in London in the spring of 1816.[25] Moreover, it is known that the months he spent in Rome and Florence at this time were ones when Cockerell experienced serious doubt about his fitness for an architectural career, telling his father that he felt qualified only to be 'professor of the beautiful in architecture', a sentiment with which the construction of so sublime a vision fits well.[26] What is clear, though, is that the image he had created of ancient Rome permeated Europe during the ensuing two decades. At least three re-engravings quickly followed: the Royal Academy exhibit was engraved in London in its magnificent full size by John Coney in 1824. Meanwhile, a new version after Rocruè was

OPPOSITE
74. Charles Robert Cockerell: Restoration sketch of the Forum Romanum east to west, 1816–17.

75. Giacomo Rocruè: Engraving of Charles Robert Cockerell's restoration of the Forum Romanum, c.1818.

LEFT
76. Thomas Babington Macaulay: 'Lays of Ancient Rome with Illustrations Original and from the Antique by George Scharf Jun.', 1847 edn. Cockerell's Forum Restoration is used to illustrate the city of Rome in the lay 'The Prophecy of Capys'.

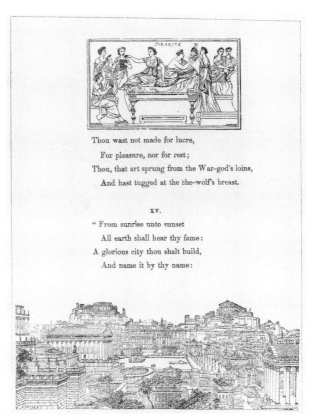

engraved in Rome, probably also in the 1820s, by Pietro Parboni and Giuseppe Acquaroni, published by Tommaso Cuccioni and dedicated to the German engravers Franz and Johannes Riepenhausen. Somewhat smaller in size, this copy also had a legend which followed Rocruè's, except that the Temple of Saturn had now become that of 'Fortune' or 'Concord'. A third engraving (again after Rocruè but further reduced in size and of more rectangular shape) was produced by Alexandre-Charles Dormier, probably in Paris in 1842, published by D. A. Audot, this time with a key to only twelve rather than sixteen buildings. Copies of these prints can still readily be found with dealers in London and Rome, suggesting how much more common they must have been in the first half of the nineteenth century. Moreover, versions of Cockerell's restoration appeared in various other contexts in the first half of the nineteenth century.[27] Probably its most seminal distribution came in the 1847 edition of Thomas Babington Macaulay's *Lays of Ancient Rome*, for which the illustrations were prepared by George Scharf (Fig.76). There it was given a period-specific identity, as 'Rome in the Augustan Age, a Restoration by C. R. Cockerell R.A.', but served as the visual companion to Macaulay's hugely popular attempt to invent what he assumed must have been the lost Latin poetry of the Republic.[28]

Arriving in Rome ten years after Cockerell, another British architectural student, James Pennethorne, found that his predecessor's Forum restoration was still a great source of debate

77. James Pennethorne:
Restoration of the Forum
Romanum, north to south
1825. At the left extremity is
the Arch of Fabianus, no.25
on Fig.78. Pennethorne
gained honorary election to
the Accademia di S. Luca on
the strength of this image,
a scholarly yet visionary
response to post-Napoleonic
advances in archaeological
understanding

78. James Pennethorne:
Sketch plan of the Forum
Romanum with an
explanation of its
topography, in a letter to
John Nash, 1825. North here
is to the left (actually the
bottom left).

in the city. It was partly to emulate Cockerell, but also to 'render himself a name' and 'to get into the academy' (the Accademia di S. Luca) that, in the early months of 1825, Pennethorne worked intensively on his own restoration drawing of the Forum (Fig.77).[29] It has been seen in Chapter 2 that Pennethorne developed his method for studying the remains of Antique buildings in general by making perspective sketches, outline elevations and restoration drawings. The young architect's diary, letters to his master John Nash and a memorandum facilitate an equally full understanding of the processes by which he came to produce this important image of the civic centre of Rome in its ancient state. Within a week of his arrival in Rome on 10 December 1824, Pennethorne was already studying and sketching 'an idea of the restoration' of the newly excavated Forum of Trajan.[30] The unusual degree of attention paid by Pennethorne to the process of making restorations might be seen as a reflection of the activities of the French *pensionnaires* in preparing their *envois*, but Nash had instructed him not to fraternize with other artists and he did not, in fact, visit the French Academy and see the 1825 exhibition of drawings until after he had completed his own restoration of the Forum Romanum. Evidently, however, he did know Caristie's published Forum plan, which he later described as 'very good though I fear rather incorrect'.[31] Moreover, he asked Nash to send from London a tracing of Taylor's and Cresy's plan and section of the Forum (see Fig.70) in its 1818 excavated state. He had brought a sketch of this engraving with him, but now needed 'the scale and all parts <u>very particular</u> [sic]'.[32] This suggests, of course, that while Pennethorne appreciated the importance of *The Architectural Antiquities of Rome*, the book was not readily available in Rome itself.

A letter of 22 February 1825 provides important information on the progress of Pennethorne's work. Not wishing to rely on Caristie and lacking sufficient detail from Taylor and Cresy, he was proceeding to acquaint himself with the latest antiquarian thought on the disposition of the Forum. He had acquired Nibby's recently published *Del Foro Romano* and also obtained a copy of Cockerell's restoration, 'which is more a restoration of the Capitol than the Forum & I take mine on the other side purposely not to interfere with him'.[33] In the same letter he announced to Nash that his Forum would be bounded to right and left respectively by the Temple of 'Jupiter Tonans' and the 'Graecostasis' (the Temple of Castor). Pennethorne's diary reveals that his on-site studies, reading of Nardini, Nibby and Fea, and sketching for the Forum restoration took place between 4 and 15 March, the final drawing being completed on 23 March.[34] On 17 April he dispatched to London the Forum plan and perspective, together with a detailed memorandum on the whole scheme.[35] Since the final plan is now lost, a roughly sketched version which he included in this letter (Fig.78) has become a central document for the interpretation of the whole restoration.

Pennethorne justified his decision to conceive of the Forum as lying effectively on a north to south axis by pointing out that this would locate it more precisely along the valley between the Capitoline and Palatine Hills. Like some of the Italian antiquarians, he was also concerned that the east to west view would have made the ancient world's grandest urban space little more than a wide street. Pennethorne thus determined on the erroneous traditional axis and on a viewpoint which 'supposes me standing on the Basilica Emilia' (nos 21–2 on his sketch plan).[36] He next began the process of trying to square what he could learn from Roman writers, ancient coins and medals, the Severan Marble Plan (then in the Capitoline Museum), the contemporary antiquarians he had read and his own observations about the site and form of individual buildings.

His starting point was the senate house or Curia (no.2 on his plan), generally thought at that time to be identified with the 'Temple of Augustus' at the foot of the Palatine Hill.[37] The central importance of this building in Roman political life led him to posit a road in front of it, bisecting the Forum east to west (approximately where the modern Via del Foro Romano runs) and leading to the Clivus Capitolinus through the Arch of Tiberius (no.11). By chance this hypothesis resulted in placement of that arch only thirty or so metres (*c*.98 ft) to the south-west of the position which it was found by excavations of 1900 to have occupied. From the identification of the 'Temple of Augustus' as the Curia, however, it followed for Pennethorne that the adjacent ruins of the Temple of Castor were in fact those of the 'Graecostasis' (no.1). In Pennethorne's hands the 'Graecostasis' became the dominant building of his entire restoration, situated in the front left foreground, the famous three columns interpreted as second-century architecture of the time of Antoninus Pius 'in whose time architecture flourished extremely … but this is only conjecture & on no authority'.[38]

In Pennethorne's restoration, the south boundary of the Forum was closed by just two buildings: the entirely misplaced Temple of Julius Caesar and the long flank of the Basilica Julia (nos 7 and 8 on his plan). While the Basilica does indeed close the south side of the Forum, its excavation (which began only in 1849) showed it to have been situated perhaps 150 m (164 yd) further north than Pennethorne had hypothesized on the basis of his assumption about the Forum's axis. On the west side of the Forum, however, the architect had more physical evidence with which to work. In the front right part of his restoration Pennethorne depicted the conjunction of the three temples which remain distinctive features in front of the Tabularium today. At the extreme right he reconstructed the Temple of Concord (no.16 on his plan). The substructures of this Tiberian building, with its highly unusual plan of a pronaos set against the transverse axis of its cella, had been discovered and tentatively identified in an excavation by Fea in the summer of 1817.[39] Neither Caristie nor Nibby nor Taylor and Cresy were able to supply any details of its form

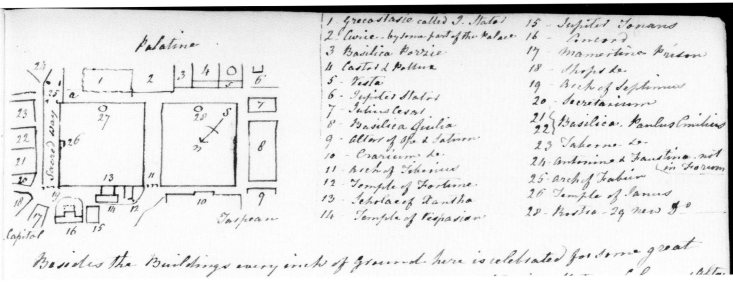

on their plans dated up to 1819 and, as noted earlier, the Temple does not appear at all in Cockerell's restorations, but six years later Pennethorne had sufficient information, perhaps from an early Imperial medal, to draw a convincing reconstruction.[40] The identification of the real Temple of Concord, however, presented him with the same problem Cockerell had faced of what to call the Ionic portico of the Temple of Saturn, known as the Temple of 'Concord' until that point

in time. Pennethorne noted that some antiquarians had begun referring to it as the Temple of 'Fortune' (Nibby, in fact, since Fea opted for the 'Temple of Juno'). But the British student chose to identify it instead as the Temple of Vespasian (no.14 on his plan). The celebrated three columns and frieze with sacrificial implements, traditionally called the Temple of 'Jupiter Tonans', thus remained unchanged (no.15). Since this structure is the real Temple of Vespasian, however, had Pen-

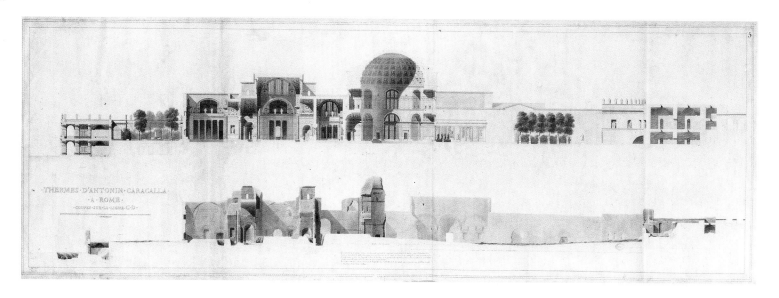

79. Guillaume-Abel Blouet:
Longitudinal sections of the
Baths of Caracalla, Rome,
1825–6, showing the central
block in its actual ruined
state and as restored.

nethorne chosen the only other option available to him he would unwittingly have become the first person to have identified it correctly, predating Canina in this by nine years. Standing in front of the Temple of Concord and spanning the Via Sacra was the Arch of Septimius Severus (no.19 on Pennethorne's plan). As a substantially surviving monument the evidence for the position of this structure was irrefutable, and Pennethorne followed Cockerell in envisaging the Republican Fornix Fabianus (no.25) in a parallel position to that of Severus in front of the Temple of Castor (front left on Fig.77, right on Fig.75), a position near to where very recent scholarship suggests it may indeed have stood.[41]

There is no doubt that on one level Pennethorne intended this work to stand as an exercise in classical archaeology. He had read some of the latest antiquarian accounts of the Forum, and it was Nibby's identifications and suggested positions of monuments which actually lay behind his rather naïvely regularized plan. But he also engaged with some of the same primary or secondary sources the antiquarians had used in their work, and made some first-hand observations of both the long extant and newly excavated fabric. By these means he had been able to make what he told Nash was 'as correct & perfect a restoration as is now possible'.[42] Perhaps this was indeed a fair claim: ten years later the French *pensionnaire* Jean-Amond Leveil reached broadly similar conclusions through analysis of the same sources. Leveil had studied the site for two years whereas Pennethorne had taken just seventeen days, and the French student, moreover, wholly overlooked the (by then) more recent reorientations of the Forum by Bunsen and Canina.[43] But Pennethorne's relative haste is not without its significance. He did not consider all of the evidence available to him, either in documentary or in physical form. Nash's injunction against becoming involved with foreigners notwithstanding, his failure to consult with Fea, Valadier or Canina (Rome's leading architect-experts on the ruins) seems indicative of a lack of scholarly rigour. He evidently overlooked Part Four of Valadier's *Raccolta delle più insigni fabbriche di Roma antica*, which had presented the latest research on the Temple of Castor, including its definitive identification. It also seems unlikely that, having asked Nash to send Taylor's and Cresy's carefully surveyed plan of the Forum, Pennethorne waited until it arrived before commencing and completing his own study. He ignored the Column of Phocas, newly prominent in 1825 following its excavation seven years previously. All of this suggests that Pennethorne was entertaining other ideas than purely archaeological ones. An alternative attitude does, in fact, emerge in the same letter to Nash in which he reported that his restoration was as accurate as possible, when he went on to say: 'until I laid it down on paper I could not picture to myself so numerous and so magnificent an assemblage of buildings as were in this place'. More is learned about Pennethorne's views on the purpose of restoration drawings from a letter of 23 January 1825:

it is not from the remaining parts but from the study of the … whole building when perfect that I ought to derive the greatest advantage – for though the drawing [of] the remains is absolutely requisite yet it is I think secondary & mechanical compared to the exertion of the mind in the former. For the labour of the hand must be subject to the understanding.[44]

Here, then, is the very antithesis of Joseph Michael Gandy's eighteenth-century view that greater ideas could be formed from ruins than from the imagined restoration of a ruined building. In the mid 1820s Pennethorne believed that imaginative restoration was the direct way to reach a full appreciation of the sublimity of Roman architecture. Given this context, it is perhaps not surprising that when preparing a much larger and coloured version of his Forum restoration for presentation to the Accademia di S. Luca in 1826 in support of his candidacy for honorary election, Pennethorne suppressed the

strictly 'archaeological' elements of the drawing and amplified its emotive power (Pl.XII). He increased the size of the space by removing the Basilica Julia from the background altogether. The inclusion of a new foreground, with groups of Roman figures near a circular temple, served to increase the sense of scale in the painterly manner being deployed at that same time by artists such as John Martin and J. M. W. Turner. As Pennethorne's biographer has aptly put it, the true subject now 'is the idea of ancient Rome, not ancient Rome as it actually was'.[45]

On 26 April 1825, shortly after finishing his initial Forum restoration, Pennethorne went to see the exhibition of the French *pensionnaires* at the Villa Medici which, he reported to Nash, 'has made me discontented with all I have done'.[46] The work on display in 1825 probably included one of the most celebrated of all post-Napoleonic *envois*, Blouet's study of the Baths of Caracalla (Fig.79). Possibly on display at the same time was the second- and third-year work of Félix-Jacques Duban and Pierre-François-Henri Labrouste respectively. However, the British student amplified his comment only by mentioning the French manner of sepia colouring, which he seems to have wished he had deployed for his own drawing. With the benefit of hindsight, it can be argued

that neither Pennethorne (nor Cockerell) had anything to be ashamed about in comparing their work with that of their French counterparts. Wonderful drawings though they are in many respects, the early nineteenth-century *envois* nonetheless remain relatively dry archaeological exercises, insisted upon by the institution of the Académie and produced by students who, on the evidence of their coeval activities, were at least as interested in the possible uses of the Renaissance re-interpretation of Classicism as they were in Antiquity. The prohibition on preparation of restored perspectives and inclusion of historical figures were clearly factors which inhibited the development of a fuller vision of the past in France, although architects such as Jacques-Ignace Hittorff, Duban and Labrouste did their best to overcome this in their graphic work outside the confines of the Académie.[47] The English vision of Rome was altogether more emotive, and the power of the images created by Cockerell and Pennethorne is clear when they are compared with the slightly naïve illustrations provided in 1834 by even as eminent an Italian architect and antiquarian as Canina (Fig.80).

Cockerell and Pennethorne were certainly not the only British architectural students in Italy to have attempted such restorations. Ambrose Poynter was preparing a restoration of

80. Luigi Canina: Perspective of the Forum Romanum restored, from 'Descrizione storico del Foro Romano', 1834.

the Forum of Trajan in the mid 1820s, which he had to abandon under pressure of work, while Francis Arundale showed a Restoration of the Forum and Palatine, and a Restoration of the Mausoleum of Hadrian at the Royal Academy in 1830 and 1831 respectively. Even provincial architects, such as S. J. Walker of Nottingham, entered into the archaeological spirit of the moment, as can be seen from his restoration of the Forum, prepared in 1832 and published in 1837 with a dedication to the Duke of Newcastle (Fig.81). In Walker's case, however, the archaeological content of the restoration was limited, to judge from the bizarrely asymmetrical podium of the Temple of Castor and Pollux, the incorrect plan of the Temple of Concord and a number of introduced porticoes for which there was no authority.

Imaginative array: the case of Donaldson

These English architects' visions have their counterparts in the less archaeological and more imaginative visions of the ancient world created as a kind of parallel to objective reality. Perhaps the greatest and most famous example of such works is Karl Friedrich Schinkel's vast *Blick in Griechenlands Blüte* ('A view of Greece in its prime'), a 'restoration' scene of Greeks temple-building at Halicarnassus, painted in the same year that Pennethorne was working on his Roman Forum restoration.[48] It has been shown that, around this time, Schinkel was greatly impressed by his encounter in Paris with the work of the former *pensionnaire* Jean-Nicolas Huyot, when he saw Huyot's collection of archaeological drawings. What marked Huyot out from contemporary *pensionnaires* was precisely his pioneering attempt to 'discover and restore the whole monumental layout of cities in terms of their public institutions' rather than concentrating on the proportioning and decoration of individual buildings.[49] Huyot's most celebrated early work was his restoration of the Temple of Fortune at Praeneste, made in 1811. In the mid 1820s it was Huyot who inspired younger

architects like Labrouste to conceive of the architecture of the ancient world as occupied by ancient people with material concerns, and his influence certainly also extended over impressionable young English students. During his first period of residence at Rome in 1819, Thomas Leverton Donaldson had become intimate with the then resident *pensionnaires*. The friendship which sprung up between him and the Grand Prix winner of that year, Jean-Baptiste-Cicéron Lesueur, gave him access to the Villa Medici where he saw, and was allowed to copy, a version of Huyot's restoration of Praeneste which, he said, 'made a deep impression on my imagination'.[50] Indeed, since a copy of Huyot's work could be found at the Villa Medici at this time, it might also be wondered whether Cockerell earlier and Pennethorne later might also have seen it. By 1821, when Donaldson returned to Italy from Greece and Asia Minor, Lesueur was presumably beginning work on his own *envoi* of the Forum of Trajan, and had just been joined in Rome by Blouet, whose friendship with Donaldson pre-

sumably also dates from their time together in Rome.[51] It was in these contexts that the English architect prepared the 'Temple of Victory' drawings which were to gain him honorary admission to the Accademia di S. Luca in 1822 and a gold medal at the 1861 Paris Exposition Universelle, and about which in 1876, under very different architectural circumstances in Britain, he was to publish a French memoir (Fig. 82).[52]

In their scale, Donaldson's drawings reflect the circumstances under which his French companions laboured, but freed from the restrictions of the rules of the Académie des Beaux-Arts he was able to develop an imaginative array of buildings of quasi-forum character. The plan of the complex (on three levels with temple and theatre at the top, palaestra and academy opening from a columnar area below that and nautical amphitheatre and stadium below that) derived from Huyot's restoration of Republican Praeneste. But for architectural forms Donaldson wished to marry the 'purity' of

Greek (Doric) architecture to the 'magnificence' of Roman. Accordingly he created a vision of buildings of Hadrianic date but situated at Messene, an outreach of the Roman Empire in the south-west Peloponnese, a site he had admired when travelling with John Lewis Wolfe and William Jenkins. His sepia drawings include the perspective illustrated here, looking across the area with the triumphal column between academy and palaestra buildings as a ceremonial procession takes place. Donaldson's drawings mark the point where British architects began to translate visions based on careful study of archaeological evidence into designs of an urban or civic nature, an important point underpinning the studies which form the Part II of this book.

The 'Temple of Victory' was displayed at the Royal Academy in 1824, the same year that Coney's full-scale engraving of Cockerell's Roman Forum restoration was published. Pennethorne is not known to have displayed his restoration on his return to London in 1826, but it seems very likely that such a striking image, on the basis of which he had gained honorary membership of the Accademia di S. Luca, would have been shown to interested parties. Arundale, as has been noted, showed his restoration of the Forum at the Academy in 1830. To London audiences with access to the Academy, these visions of ancient Rome must have been extremely striking, as they remain today.

British restorations of Pompeii

The grip of ancient Pompeii on the popular imagination, paralleling that of Rome, had already begun in the late eighteenth century. It is visible, for example, in Jacob More's 1780 painting *Vesuvius in Eruption*, now in the Scottish National Gallery and subtitled 'The Last Days of Pompeii'. More's interest, however, lay largely in the sublimity and colour of the erupting volcano rather than in the town, seen on fire in the middle distance, or the fate of its inhabitants, a few of whom creep away in the foregound.[53] For the Abbé de Saint-Non's monumental *Voyage pittoresque de Naples et de Sicile* of 1781–6, the *pensionnaire* Louis-Jean Desprez executed a series of four Pompeian restorations which depict events taking place before the town's destruction.[54] In two, scenes of sacrifice are seen being enacted at the Temple of Isis in AD 79. In another, the quadriportico and Great Theatre are shown in restored perspective, while a fourth plate of more domestic character has a family at home in the courtyard of the Villa of Diomedes. These images are of a type quite unlike anything else among the hundreds of engravings in de Saint-Non's work, however, and it seems that no other Antique site had the power to bring out this imaginative reaction in the French artists. Indeed, it is striking to note that Hubert Robert's 'restoration' of the Temple of Serapis (Macellum) at Puteoli (Pozzuoli) in de Saint-Non 'restored' the edifice to a slightly less dilapidated state of ruin. The changing circumstances of the early nineteenth century, however, made the imaginative restoration of Pompeii much more common. It is also important to note that, from the outset, Mazois's great work on the site had included restoration drawings, although those in volume two of *Les Ruines de Pompéi*, which deals with private houses, show greater interest in construction details than in the daily lives of Pompeians.

British architects visiting Pompeii after 1815 seem soon to have begun to add restorations to the archaeological drawings they made there. As in Rome, Cockerell was a significant figure in this respect. Among the miscellaneous drawings in the British Museum that may be associated with his studies at Pompeii in late Spring 1815 are two restorations of the Doric

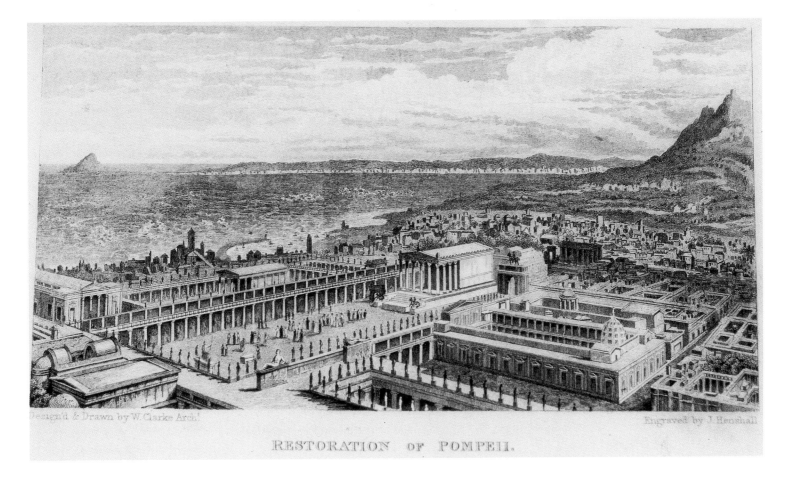

Design'd & Drawn by W. Clarke Arch.t   Engraved by J. Henshall

RESTORATION OF POMPEII.

Temple in the Triangular Forum, with views out to sea beyond (Fig.83). Cockerell's valuable contribution to Mazois's essay on the theatres at Pompeii had made him an internationally-acknowledged expert on the subject, and in 1832 he worked up a restoration of the Great Theatre at Pompeii for display at the Royal Academy (Pl.XIII).[55] In this magnificent drawing the theatre's scenae frons and seating are seen perfect, but through a rubble-strewn break in its rear wall. The fact that Cockerell showed this drawing to the London public fifteen years after returning from Italy is probably a reflection of the growing enthusiasm for visions of ancient Roman civilization permeating society at that time. More specifically, it may have been a response to the appearance at precisely that moment of two new popularist publications on Pompeii: William Clarke's two volumes for the Society for the Diffusion of Useful Knowledge and the two supplementary volumes of *Pompeiana* by Sir William Gell.

Clarke's 300 illustrations showed the ruins in their actual state, but the frontispiece was his 'Restoration of Pompeii', a bird's-eye view westwards over the Forum towards the sea (Fig.84). This image was juxtaposed with Cockerell's by now famous restoration of the Roman Forum (newly engraved by T. Bradley), which served as the frontispiece to the second volume. Comparisons of the two fora were not uncommon by the end of the 1820s, Joseph Woods noting for example that 'the Forum [of Pompeii] was certainly magnificent. What then may we imagine those of Rome to have been, where the size of the parts, and of the whole, the materials and the architecture, were so much superior.'[56] Gell's new volumes of *Pompeiana* also contain images of the city restored. In the original 1817–19 volume, Gell had included five images of restorations: the Herculaneum Gate; the atrium of the House of Pansa; two views of the Forum; and the atrium of the House of Sallust.[57] The images are, however, either eerily depopulated or, when figures are present, enervated. In the 1832 volumes the seven restorations are of much more enlivened character, such as that of a sacrifice taking place at the Temple of Fortuna Augusta in front of the busy street (Fig.85). The restoration is credited to Gell and it relates to a drawing in the British Museum, showing the Temple and its urban context from almost exactly the same angle and with many of the same features (Fig.86).[58] This drawing is particularly fascinating and important, because it shows how the artist perceived the site whilst actually there. He used his pen to outline the existing ruined urban fabric, but took the pencil to superimpose the spectral presence of a restoration. As with Cockerell's restoration of the Pompeii Theatre (though that was made several years after its author's return to England), antiquarians

84. William Clarke: Bird's-eye view of the Forum of Pompeii, restored, from 'Pompeii: Its Past and Present State; Its Public and Private Buildings', first published in 1831.

85. William Gell: The Temple of Fortuna Augusta, Pompeii, restored perspective, from 'Pompeiana', first published in 1832.

and architects could literally see the grandeur of ancient Roman architecture whilst looking at and through its ruins, an apposite fulfilment of the exhortation of George Wightwick quoted as an epigraph at the head of this chapter.

Perhaps more striking than these restored images of public spaces in Pompeii were the images of the Romans in their private houses, which began to appear. The relatively good state of the ruins at Pompeii made imagining such houses pristine and occupied by their luckless inhabitants an easy task for the reading and travelling public, and by the 1830s this had become an interest which Gell happily supported. Thus, among the restored views provided in the 1832 volumes of *Pompeiana* are two plates which juxtapose actual state and restored images of the House of the Tragic Poet (Figs 87 and 88).[59] In the restoration a lady sits in the vestibulum talking to a standing male figure whilst a servant enters the atrium bringing refreshment: the scene could almost be taking place in a London Regency Drawing Room. Gell provided the visual counterpart to a sense of the immediacy of the past felt by many British visitors to the site in the early nineteenth century, typified by Lady Blessington: 'On finding myself

occasionally alone in some apartment of the dwellings in Pompeii, the paintings still fresh and glowing on the walls … I felt as if intruding, an unbidden guest, in some mansion, whose owners had but lately left it'.[60]

Rome and Pompeii in London

In the second half of the nineteenth century, scenes of ancient Rome and Pompeii were to prove highly popular subjects in Victorian academic painting.[61] Even in the 1820s and 1830s, however, the British vision of ancient Rome, built up partly from archaeological evidence and partly from the imagination, was by no means exclusive to architects and antiquarians, to those who saw the Royal Academy's exhibitions or even to Grand Tourists. The surge in popularity of plays with Roman subjects ensured that, whether or not one had travelled to Italy, scenographic representations of ancient Rome were quite common. These formed the backdrops to established masterpieces, such as Shakespeare's *Coriolanus* and *Julius Caesar*, but, as a recent study has shown, many new plays on Roman subjects were also in repertory in the immediate after-

math of the Napoleonic period, especially at Drury Lane, and 'everybody would have recognised the distinctively Roman sets'.[62] Some idea of what these sets must have been like can perhaps be gained through the series of stage designs produced by Joseph Michael Gandy during the 1820s. Having given up hope of a successful architectural career, Gandy was seeking alternative outlets for his extraordinary skills of draftmanship. Two such potential outlets were the illustration of literary texts and the design of stage sets (Pl.xiv).[63] The watercolour reproduced here has a printed label reading: 'Titus Andronicus Act I Scene ii – The Tomb of the Andronicii before the Capitol of Rome, Titus Andronicus, his sons, prisoners etc'.[64] Gandy clearly wished to show the London theatre-going public a sublime image of the Forum from a viewpoint similar to that adopted by Pennethorne. Individual monuments are recognizable although, no doubt for compositional reasons, they have been moved a good deal from their actual positions and in relation to each other. Approached up a flight of steps, the Forum is seen as bounded to the left by the Arch of Septimius Severus. In the middle distance stand the Temples of Saturn and Vespasian (the latter with its distinctive frieze) and, away to the left, the peripteral Temple of Castor and Pollux, given thirteen columns in its flanks (as proposed by Caristie). In the background, between the Capitol (right) and Palatine (left), the Aventine Hill rises.

In addition to the theatre, London crowds were entertained in the early nineteenth century by the panorama, or 360-degree painting, the invention of which is credited to Robert Barker in about 1785.[65] Barker's building in Cranbourne Street, near Leicester Square, erected in 1793, provided a central location in the capital where he could display such paintings to a paying public keen to gain a vicarious experience of or to 'revisit' a place without the necessity of travel. In 1817 Barker opened a view of Rome from the tower of the Capitol and, seven years later, after Barker's son left his interest in the Leicester Square building to John and Robert Burford, a panorama of Pompeii was displayed with a leaflet of descriptive text given particular authority by the involvement of Thomas Leverton Donaldson. As late as 1844, the architect Frederick Catherwood's panorama of Balbec was being shown by Burford at Leicester Square. It should be noted, moreover, that the panoramas were by no means exclusively

86. William Gell(?): The Temple of Fortuna Augusta, Pompeii, evidently the drawing on which Fig.85 was based.

87. William Gell:
Topographical view inside
the House of the Tragic Poet
Pompeii, from 'Pompeiana',
first published in 1832.

88. William Gell:
Restoration of the House of
the Tragic Poet, Pompeii,
from 'Pompeiana', 1832.

London phenomena. Once it had closed in 1818, for example, Barker's and Burford's 'Rome' was transferred to Edinburgh. Meanwhile, a Liverpool panorama (the second in the city in fact) opened in 1825 with a view of Naples, familiar to many as the base for their expeditions to the Campanian excavations. It was but a short step for the British vision of ancient Rome, created in these different media and reaching an increasingly wide audience, to be translated into built form.

1 *William Pars: 'A View of Rome Taken from the Pincio', 1776.*

11 *Thomas Jones: 'An Excavation of an Antique Building Discovered in a Cava
in the Villa Negroni at Rome', 1777.*

III *Domus Aurea, Rome: Detail of the east wall, niche and apse of Room 119,*
perhaps entered for the first time since Antiquity by Charles Cameron in 1768–9.

PART·OF·THE·TEMPLE·OF·ISIS·AT·POMPEIA·

IV *John Soane: Part of the Temple of Isis, Pompeii, 1779. Soane's use of brown watercolour reflects the almost monochromatic perception of ancient Roman architecture among later eighteenth-century British architectural student travellers.*

v *George Hadfield: Restoration of the Sanctuary of Fortune, Praeneste, 1792.*
This unusual and huge drawing, nearly 3 m (9½ ft) wide, is perhaps the most
remarkable fabrication of a Roman site undertaken by a British architect in the
eighteenth century.

VI *Robert Adam: Imaginary Roman ruins, 1755–7.*

VII *Thomas Hardwick: Part of a wall of the Hadrianic House discovered in the grounds of the Villa Negroni, 1777 (see Pl.II).*

VIII *Christoffer Eckersberg:* View of the Forum, Rome, 1814. *In this painting, the eighteenth-century 'Campo Vaccino' has begun to take on its modern appearance as a dusty archaeological site as a result of the Napoleonic clearances.*

OPPOSITE
IXa *John Goldicutt: An illustration of a wall from* Specimens of Ancient Decorations from Pompeii, *1825.*

IXb *Henry Parke: A collection of Pompeian mosaics, 1821.*

43

Pompeii
Side building of Temple of Isis
(principally from A.H.)

Marked 7 in plan

xa *Joseph Woods and Richard Sharp: Part of the Temple of Isis, Pompeii, 1818. Woods's and Sharp's response to Roman architectural polychromy leads to an entirely different record of this structure from that of Soane forty years earlier (see Pl.IV).*

xb *Henry Parke: View inside the House of Sallust, Pompeii, 1821. Parke has treated the ruined building as though it were a painted stage set, rather than topographically.*

xI *Charles Robert Cockerell: 'An idea of a Reconstruction of the Capital and Forum of Rome', shown at the Royal Academy in 1819.*

XII *James Pennethorne: Restoration of the Forum Romanum, 1826 version.*

XIII *Charles Robert Cockerell: The Great Theatre, Pompeii, shown at the Royal Academy in 1832. The restored theatre and scenae frons are viewed through the deliberately 'ruined' rear wall.*

XIV *Joseph Michael Gandy: 'A scene in Ancient Rome', a stage set design for
the opening scenes of Shakespeare's 'Titus Andronicus', painted in the mid 1820s.*

OPPOSITE
XV *The atrium of the Reform Club, London, designed by Charles Barry,
1838–41, with its mosaic floor.*

XVI *Decimus Burton: Perspective drawing for the Triumphal Arch and Ionic
Screen at Constitution Hill, London, c.1826.*

OPPOSITE

XVIIa *Charles Edge: Plan for the completion of Birmingham Town Hall and its
environs, 1846. Blue is used to denote Hansom's and Welch's work (except for the
northern projection for the organ, which Edge had added in 1836–7). Red
denotes Edge's proposed additions of 1846.*

XVIIb *'Mr. Ingram': Decorative scheme for the order and coved ceiling coffers
inside Birmingham Town Hall, 1855. The distortion of the cornice at the right
of this drawing is due to its poor condition.*

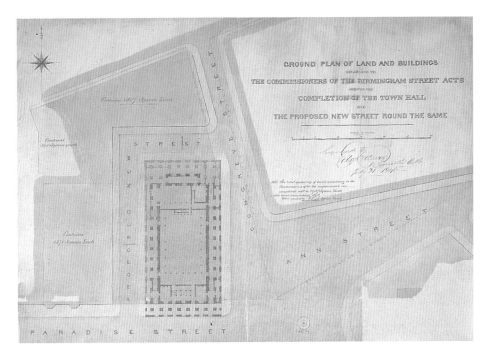

XVIII *The Fitzwilliam Museum, Cambridge, designed by George Basevi
from 1835.*

OPPOSITE
XIXa *George Basevi: Elevation of a doorway for the principal gallery of the
Fitzwilliam Museum, Cambridge, c.1843–5.*

XIXb *Lithograph of the tessellated pavement designed by Henry Pether for the
courtyard of the Royal Exchange, London, 1844.*

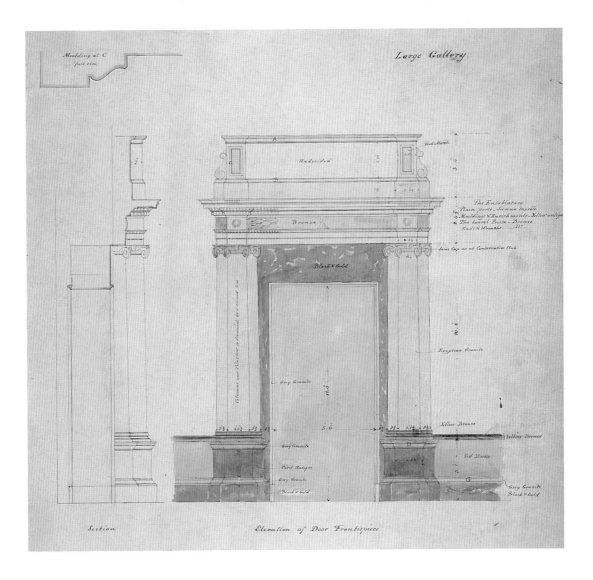

Moulding at C
full size

The Entablature
Plain parts Sienna marble
Mouldings & Enrichments Yellow antique
The laurel Frieze Bronze
Ends & Wreaths Do.

Same Caps as at Conservative Club

Red Marble

Undecided

Bronze

Black & Gold

Egyptian Granite

Grey Granite

Yellow Bronze

Grey Granite

Verd Antique

Grey Granite

Black & Gold

Red Marble

Grey Granite

Black & Gold

Section

Elevation of Door Frontispiece

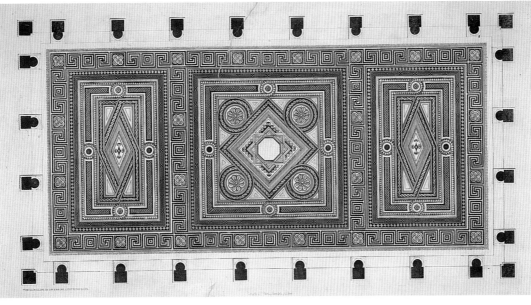

xx *Lithograph of the perspective of a design for the Royal Exchange, London, by Thomas Leverton Donaldson, 1839. The architect showed two drawings of this design at the Royal Academy in 1840.*

OPPOSITE
xxi *James Pennethorne: Perspective of a design for the Royal Exchange, London, shown at the Royal Academy in 1840.*

XXII *St George's Hall, Liverpool, designed by Harvey Lonsdale Elmes*
from 1840.

OPPOSITE

XXIIIa *Harvey Lonsdale Elmes: Interior elevation for the Concert Hall in St*
George's Hall, Liverpool. This drawing probably post-dates Elmes's introduction
of red Aberdeen granite for the columns in 1844.

XXIIIb *Charles Robert Cockerell: Interior elevation for the Concert Hall in St*
George's Hall, Liverpool, 1851. Cockerell introduced more colour to the interior
than Elmes had intended, as well as Renaissance architectural features such as
balusters.

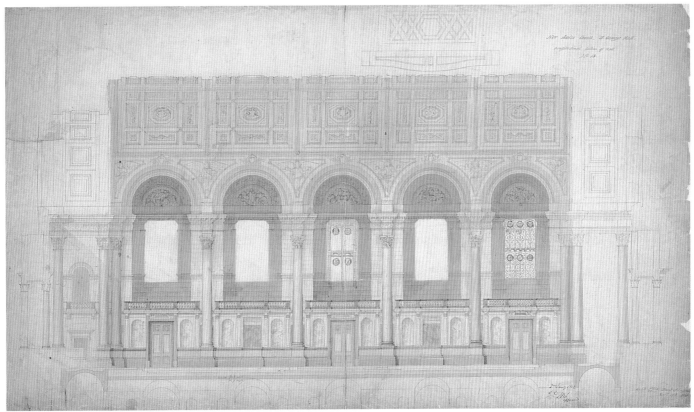

New Assize Courts. St George's Hall.
Longitudinal Section of Hall.
No 13

xxiv *John Goodchild: A fantasy of St George's Hall, Liverpool, under construction, 1854.*

Part II
Building Roman

Chapter 5
Architecture in England in the 1830s

In proportion as pseudo-Greek is in the ascendant, so is Roman art slighted, and falling into disrepute; but it is well to remember this truth, that we, who approximate nearer the wealth of old Rome than any other modern nation, not only do not rival her greatness and taste in our edifices, but are actually falling behind other states, whose resources are as limited as ours are boundless. (The Quarterly Review, 1835)[1]

The decade from 1830 to 1840 was one of the most complex, indeterminate even (in the eyes of some historians) and yet one of the most stimulating in British history. The short reign of William IV and the accession of the young Queen Victoria meant that this was a time with little of the certainty (or torpor) associated with the courts of long-standing monarchs. In political terms, the voices of a wider sector of society came to be heard, either through the ballot box after the modest extension of the franchise under the Great Reform Bill of 1832, or through organized and sometimes violent public dissent. Yet, the enormous economic and social problems facing the country notwithstanding, reform took place in an atmosphere fundamentally supportive of the institution of the monarchy, and the foundations of Victorian Imperial prowess were set in place. Thomas Arnold's description of the country as a 'kingly commonwealth' in the 1838 preface to his *History of Rome* was thus not a comparison made without thought, and surely represented an opinion shared by a significant sector of the educated middle classes.

In architectural terms this decade was certainly one of change as well. John Nash and Sir John Soane died in 1835 and 1837 respectively, and architects of the generation who had travelled to the Mediterranean during the Peace of Amiens, such as Robert Smirke and William Wilkins, were at the height of their careers. It was the time, however, when those who had been educated during the Napoleonic Wars and had perhaps travelled afterwards were looking for opportunities to develop the ideas of their own generation. Moreover, these men differed from their predecessors, in that it was they who moved their profession onto an altogether new footing by founding the Institute of British Architects. This institutional development, and the stylistic debates of the time, both bear a closer relationship to their continental parallels than has perhaps hitherto been recognized.

Architectural problems of the 1830s: Gothic and Greek

The year 1836 has frequently been taken as a turning point in the history of English architecture. In February of that year, four commissioners reported on the ninety-seven entries they had received for the design of the new Palace of Westminster and their preference for the ideas of Charles Barry was confirmed by Barry's appointment as architect in the summer. Barry's success in adopting the 'Gothic or Elizabethan' style stipulated in the terms of the competition was due in part to his employment of Augustus Welby Northmore Pugin, whose *Contrasts: or, A Parallel between the Noble Edifices of the Fourteenth and Fifteenth Centuries and Similar Buildings of the Present Day; Shewing the Present Decay of Taste*, though in preparation since about 1831, was published in the same year. There is no doubt, therefore, that the year 1836 marks a turning point in the history of the Gothic Revival. Pugin's powerfully polemical text and plates moved the long-standing debate on the use and value of medievalizing architectural forms and ideas on to a new level. At the same moment, the conditions of the Palace of Westminster competition, which had been announced in 1835, appeared to indicate to those who debated them in printed form the end of the consensus that Classical architecture was the correct form for English public buildings. One modern writer has commented that 'it is probably impossible to overestimate the importance of the Houses of Parliament as an architectural monument in England's history … the fact that this was such an important structure determined that its rebuilding would have a profound effect on all official architecture to follow'.[2] Whether this was really so, however, is a matter which might be called into question. The Palace of Westminster itself is open to various interpretations, and the public buildings erected both in the provinces and the capital, which form the focus of Part II of this book, suggest that it had little immediate impact.

After the destruction of much of the old Palace of Westminster in October 1834, the Prime Minister, Viscount Melbourne, turned for assistance to Robert Smirke, the youngest of the three architects who had been 'Attached' to the Office of Works prior to its rearrangement in 1832. Smirke provided temporary accommodation for the two Houses and prepared drawings for rebuilding in his 'Tudor' style, which found favour with both William IV and with Sir Robert Peel, Prime

Minister for the first three months of 1835.[3] A Select Committee appointed to consider the matter further, however, having at first favoured Smirke's plans concluded in June not only that an open competition should be held but also that 'the style of the buildings be either Gothic or Elizabethan'. There were two simple grounds on which the Members of Parliament made this recommendation: that these styles were indigenous to England and that they were appropriate in the context of the neighbouring Westminster Hall and Abbey.[4] While the focus on urban context shown here represents in itself an interesting development in English architectural theory, it is the nationalist argument which is of greater significance, in that it raises the question of what might constitute 'Englishness' in 1835.

The nuances of meaning surrounding the design of the new Palace of Westminster have been the subject of many thoughts among historians. At one extreme lies the idea that the building was a people's palace, marking the emergence in England of a middle-class, anti-establishment aesthetic, a change from an aristocratic to a democratic art. At the other lies the argument that the building was even more clearly a royal palace than its predecessor, the architecture and decorative programme of which symbolized the continuing ascendancy of monarchy, aristocracy and church.[5] Yet another view is that Whigs and Tories agreed on the choice of 'Gothic or Elizabethan' styles, the Whigs looking for a symbol of measured reform and continuity, the Tories for one reaffirming traditional values.[6] However, both the Whig and Tory Prime Ministers, Melbourne and Peel, had supported Smirke's plans, while both of their parties more broadly evinced strong interests in Classical architecture at this time. One of the commissioners, George Vivian, discussing ten publications on the affair anonymously in the Tory *Quarterly Review* in February 1837, criticized the stylistic restriction placed on the competition by the Select Committee and argued that Roman or Renaissance forms, as naturalized by Inigo Jones, Christopher Wren and Lord Burlington, would serve better than 'the fantastic incongruities of the Tudor' or even than 'the superior purity of a Grecian style which prevailed when arches and domes were not invented'.[7] The Whigs, for their part, when given a free hand two years later, employed the same architect, Barry, to work in the very different idiom of the Italian *cinquecento* for the Reform Club. In fact, about the only thing that can be stated with certainty about the symbolism of the Palace of Westminster is that the radical faction, to judge from statements made in the *The Westminster Review*, wanted a Neo-classical building on a new site with a semi-circular chamber, following the example of the Parisian Chambre des Députés. This, it was argued, would be an appropriate physical embodiment of the government of a free people.

The circumstances surrounding the competition for the design of the new Palace of Westminster were ones which were particular to that project. One should be wary of extracting from this case principles general to the country as a whole, or even to London as a city. Outside Westminster a much more central debate, both in the five years before and the five years after the fire there, concerned the nature of Classicism in English architecture, more specifically still the nature of the Greek Revival. The history of the British Greek Revival has been chronicled in considerable detail, from its origins in seventeenth-century travel accounts through to the production of the key archaeological books in the later eighteenth and early nineteenth centuries which made possible a revival of Greek ideas in built form.[8] It is the term 'British' which needs to be taken with care, however, for in the two countries of the British Isles in which Greek Revivalism was most readily received, England and Scotland, its chronology was not quite the same. The baseless Greek Doric, the proportions of the orders of the temples at Paestum, the Ionic orders of the Erechtheion, the temple on the Illisus or at Priene, all appeared in England earlier than in Scotland, and although by 1820 the idiom was in full flow both in London and in Edinburgh, by 1830 it was beginning to peter out in the English capital. During the 1820s virtually all major public building projects had been Greek in form. Smirke began the British Museum in 1823 and erected the General Post Office in St Martin's-le-Grand from 1824 to 1829 (Fig.89). Smirke, the Inwoods, Francis Bedford and others grafted Greek porticoes and details onto the rectangular bodies of the Classical churches erected for the Commissioners of 1818, both in London and in the provinces. With the Fishmongers' Hall by Smirke's pupil Henry Roberts, of 1831–4, and Philip Hardwick's propylaeum at Euston Station, however, the capital witnessed the last of its literally 'Greek' monuments.[9] This was hardly so in Scotland, where Thomas Hamilton and William Playfair continued to work in Edinburgh and Alexander 'Greek' Thomson had not even started in Glasgow.

The rise and decline of the Greek Revival in London and England between the 1790s and 1830s can also be traced through the arguments evinced for and against it by architects and antiquarians. In 1795, Charles Heathcote Tatham had written from Rome in response to a letter from Henry Holland:

It is with great pleasure I read your remarks on the subject of Greek architecture gaining ground in England ... surely no arguement can be offered that Roman Architecture either for adaptness, beauty and proportion exceeds the Grecian from which all Historians inform us the former copied and took its origin.... The Parthenon and Temple of Minerva ... will I believe in the opinion of most of our professors rank higher, as true examples of art and magnificence in architecture, than all the Triumphal arches or even temples that the Romans ever erected.[10]

Shortly afterwards, with the publication in 1804 of Thomas Hope's *Observations on the Plans and Elevations designed by James Wyatt, Architect, for Downing College, Cambridge*, the case was made for the rejection of the later eighteenth-century Neo-classical style and the freeing of younger architects like

Wilkins and Smirke to introduce Greek orders and forms to major buildings. Foremost among those objecting to this approach, however, was John Soane. In his Royal Academy lectures, Soane stressed that Greek architecture was to be studied for the qualities which might be abstracted from it rather than imitated, an idea he had inherited from Julien-David Leroy. Soane's views on Greek Revivalism were well enough known in public circles from his attack on Smirke's work at Covent Garden Theatre which brought about the temporary suspension of the lectures in 1810–11. In the privacy of his study, however, the professor noted to himself in 1820: 'It is not by applying the model of a Grecian Choragic Monument … not by decorating our public buildings with the appearance of pagan temples … that a true taste for architecture will be produced. No, it is to the artists of the rising generation we must look.'[11] Soane was far from alone in these thoughts. In 1822 J. B. Papworth published an excerpt from a letter written by 'Athenian' Stuart to Sir Joshua Reynolds, in which Stuart had expressed his 'fear … that many will be content to copy what they find detailed in [The Antiquities of Athens], without regard to the why and wherefore that governed either the ancients or myself', to which Papworth added that 'the apprehension is verified by the practice of the day'.[12] By the early 1830s it was, as Soane had predicted, younger architects such as the 25-year-old Francis Arundale, who were involved in this argument: 'it is with regret that we see Greek forms introduced in situations wholly at variance with the purpose for which they were originally intended.'[13]

The major issue facing those who, by the early 1830s, were questioning the dominant Classical idiom of the previous decade, was that of the new direction which might be taken. Arundale's comments were made in the context of an argument that England should return to the models provided by Palladio which had been so successfully adapted, in his opinion, by Jones, Wren and Sir William Chambers. His suggestion was prescient, not of a Palladian revival strictly speaking, but of the renewed interest in Italian *cinquecento* practice shown by Barry in his Travellers' Club in Pall Mall, begun in 1830, and even by Soane in his design of 1830 for the State Paper Office in Duke Street. There was certainly a constituency of thought during the 1830s which held that this represented a legitimate direction for the country to proceed with its public architecture, as has been seen above in the attack on the design of the new Palace of Westminster made in *The Quarterly Review*. But those making this case were ahead of their time, and their preferred idiom was not to burgeon until the 1840s. In its 1835 review of Hope's *An Historical Essay on Architecture*, the *Quarterly* was clear that the Greek Revival could no longer serve as the basis of public architecture which would adequately represent England in an international context. The Inwoods' St Pancras Church showed that 'no ideas of composition at all adequate to our exigencies can be derived from [ancient Greek buildings]', and the possible alternative of 'the

happy inventions of modern [that is Renaissance] Italy' were again held up for consideration. A third option, however, was to be found in ancient Roman architecture, to which the journal urged architects to give renewed attention: 'The architect of the present day may continue to observe as much Grecian severity of character as he chooses; but he ought to know that he has at his command resources, drawn from old Roman magnificence … far greater than Greece can furnish.'[14]

Architectural problems of the 1830s: The individuality of Cockerell

If the recommendations of *The Quarterly Review* were to be taken as an invitation to eclecticism in the use of Classical architecture, they could well serve as a description of the work of Charles Robert Cockerell, except that Cockerell did not draw the line at Italy when compiling his tremendous fund of post-Medieval formal sources. Cockerell's position as a designer is inevitably of concern in the context of the present study, and will be considered in further detail when building projects of the 1830s with which he was involved come under discussion in the following chapters. The question which should be addressed now, however, is how the architect came to derive his inimitable approach to Classical design. By inclination and experience Cockerell had acquired perhaps the greatest understanding of ancient architecture among post-Napoleonic British students of architecture. As has been seen, he was also the creator of some of the most captivating and influential visual recreations of Athens, Rome and Pompeii (see Pls XI and XIII). Given these factors, it might have been expected that he would be a leading figure in a situation in which the literal use of archaeological precedent was encouraged by patrons. Indeed, Cockerell's collaboration with Playfair on the design of the Scottish National Monument in Edinburgh from 1824–9 suggests he was not disdainful of the literal use of even so distinctive an ancient monument as the Parthenon. It is a project begun in 1829 and continuing through the following decade, however, that best shows the development of other priorities in the architect's oeuvre, the design process for Cambridge University Library.

The part of the University Library in Cambridge which Cockerell finally came to build from 1837 was the residue of a series of three competitions held in 1829, 1830 and 1835–6. In the limited first competition of 1829, the University specified no style for the quadrangular building complex required, which was to include four schools, four museums, three lecture rooms and various offices in addition to the library. In a letter to the Vice-Chancellor, however, Cockerell 'presumed that the Grecian style is most appropriate to a classical institution'.[15] Suitability within the academic context had been one of the grounds advanced by Hope in 1804 in support of Wilkins's Greek scheme for Downing College in Cambridge, but in the intervening period the Gothic cause had been gath-

89. *The General Post Office by Robert Smirke, St Martin's-le-Grand, London, built 1824–9 (demolished 1912).*

ering strength. Wilkins himself had produced Gothic work for Trinity, Corpus Christi and King's Colleges, while Thomas Rickman's and Henry Hutchinson's New Court at St John's College was still under construction in 1829. The first competition for the University Library was, accordingly, in essence a Greek-Gothic battle, with Wilkins submitting a Greek scheme but Rickman and Hutchinson, and Decimus Burton submitting designs in both Greek and Gothic idioms. Cockerell proposed a Greek Ionic order as the controlling external feature of his quadrangle. The east front, facing on to the Senate House lawn, was given an unpedimented decastyle portico (the pediment was reserved for the first floor library behind the portico), while the south and west façades had attached colonnades (Fig.90).[16] However, the introduction of small Pantheon domes on the four corners and the use of an attic which Cockerell described as deriving from the Forum of Nerva (the Forum Transitorium) in Rome, hinted at a range of Classical sources extending beyond the Greek alone. In a much less worked-up alternative scheme, Cockerell proposed building the Law and Divinity Schools in a block which would mirror James Gibbs's Senate House, but which would have an open portico in the manner of that of Octavia at Rome, creating access to the front of King's College.[17] It is unknown whether Cockerell knew that Gibbs himself had suggested that the Senate House might be paired in this way, that Stephen Wright had also proposed it, or that Soane had almost carried out such a scheme in 1791. Although this alternative proposal was enthusiastically received by at least one member of the Library Syndicate, Cockerell's principal submission was the one selected.

Cambridge University, having realized that the scale of the envisaged project was likely to incur unsustainable costs, decided to hold a second competition in 1830, asking architects to concentrate on the western half of the site, since the old library building at right angles to the Senate House, refronted by Wright in 1754–61, could be retained for the foreseeable future. The architects were also asked to work 'in the Grecian style'. Cockerell, however, prepared a Roman scheme much in the manner of Gibbs, with a giant order of Corinthian pilasters governing east and south elevations and a hexastyle

Corinthian portico replacing Wright's façade (Fig.91).[18] The Corinthian order used by Cockerell here was of mature Roman character, although juxtaposed with the use of Doric friezes between the two storeys of the east, south and west ele-vations, which continue as baseless Doric colonnades linking the main body to the Senate House and south entrance. A fur-ther noteworthy point about this, perhaps the most Roman of all Cockerell's designs, is that the surviving perspective

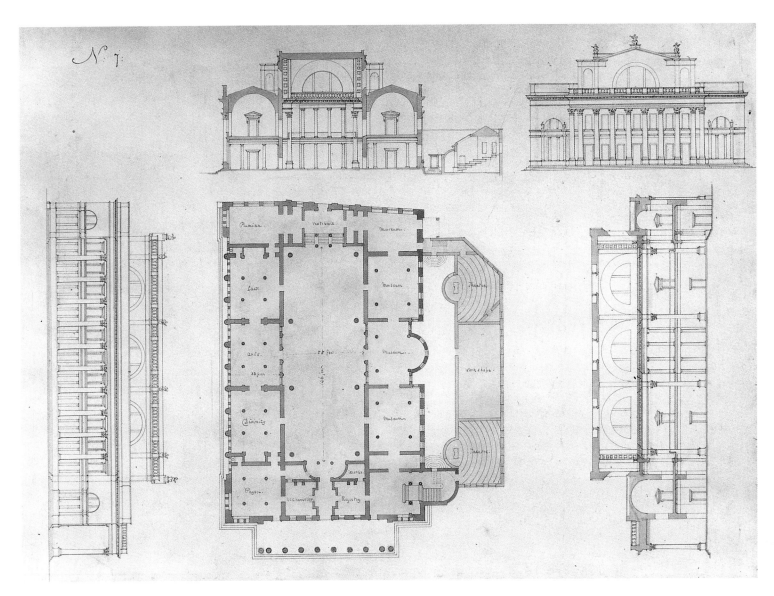

N.º 7

sketches associated with it differ from those produced in connection with other schemes in that they give far greater emphasis to urban context. King's College Chapel and, in one view, Great St Mary's Church, are all brought into play around a central, Forum-like space. This, coupled to the rather static and historicizing character of the views, perhaps suggests that his restoration of the Forum Romanum discussed in Chapter 4 was not far from Cockerell's mind. Rickman and Hutchinson complained that Cockerell had plagiarized the portico they had designed in the first competition and the matter degenerated into published exchanges of invective.

By the time that the University decided to hold a third competition for the Library in 1835–6, Cockerell's ideas had greatly increased in complexity. A diversion from his central design ideas was caused by the Syndicate's speculation that a covered hall rather than an open court might be placed at the centre of the ensemble. Cockerell briefly developed two

schemes in response, both retaining the unpedimented portico across the east elevation from the first competition but in other respects quite new. In one of the schemes, Cockerell retained the Forum Transitorium attic in addition to the Ionic colonnade (reduced in length), but introduced huge Italianate belvederes at each corner and a Mansard roof or dome, which may owe something to the Basilica at Vicenza.[19] In the alternative scheme, aptly-named the 'thermal' design by the architect's biographer, the forms of Roman baths and late basilicas were adopted quite literally. The decastyle east portico (now in the Corinthian order) was used to front a building with a great covered court (Fig.92). The use of such Roman motifs in elevation has an English precedent in Lord Burlington's designs of the 1730s for the York Assembly Rooms, Chichester Council House and proposed Houses of Parliament.[20] The sudden change in Cockerell's draftsmanship, however, seen in diminished scale and minimal use of shading, suggests that this was

OPPOSITE
90. *Charles Robert Cockerell: East front for Cambridge University Library, first competition, 1829; and (Fig.91) second competition east front, 1830, the one moment, perhaps, when Cockerell was tempted to use a grand Roman Corinthian portico.*

ABOVE
92. *Cockerell: 'Thermal' design for Cambridge University Library, 1835–6.*

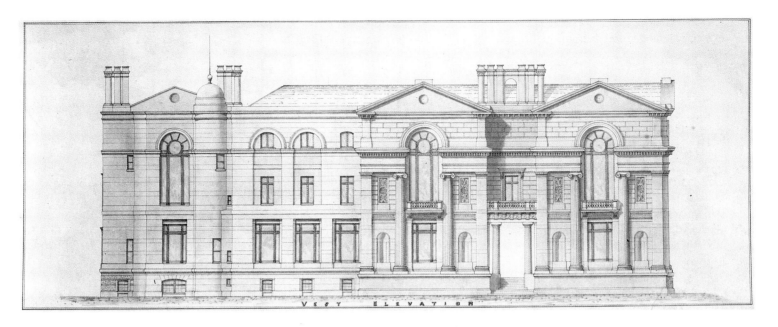

V E S T   E L E V A T I O N

93. Charles Robert Cockerell: West elevation for Cambridge University Library, final scheme, c.1837, a synthesis of ideas showing the arrival of architectural genius in Cockerell.

a scheme only briefly entertained. One might also infer that he had been studying Jean-Nicolas-Louis Durand's *Précis et leçons*, in which similarly small-scale and sparsely presented images were used in the exploration of Classical planning and form. Another drawing, in which Cockerell compared the section of the proposed University Library with that of the Chambre des Députés in Paris, confirms that he was interested in French precedents at this time.[21] It is also worth noting that Cockerell's use of superimposed columnar screens inside the central court of the 'thermal' scheme is not dissimilar to the use of columns inside the Basilica at Pompeii. Not only was the Basilica newly excavated at the time of Cockerell's visit, it had also been compared by his friend and correspondent Franz Christian Gau in (or shortly after) 1829 to the Chambre des Députés.[22]

Having been finally selected as architect for Cambridge University Library in 1836, Cockerell spent four months refining his designs yet further. The unpedimented decastyle Ionic portico was retained for the east front, but the building presented four complex and entirely different elevations around its outer boundary.[23] In a brilliant move, the elevations were to be tied together by a powerful entablature which ran continuously around the east and south fronts. On the west front, the entablature was present only in conjunction with the two pedimented sections below which stood an order of columns and antae (Fig.93). Where the entablature was lost, however, its presence was implied by the repetition of the lunettes which break into the attic above it. The lunettes insist on order, even where the functional demands of the building and differences in ground height seemed to make it unachievable. They also appear at the same level on the south front, the north end of the east front and across the north front, the austerity of which was complemented with massive Vanbrughian

linked chimney stacks. Thus, between 1829 and 1836, the design process of Cambridge University Library shows Cockerell developing a style of architecture in which a richly eclectic range of formal sources was combined with sculptural power in the handling of mass. A process which began with fairly conventional Greek Revival ideas, moved briefly to the possibilities of Roman templar form at the stage of the second competition and then beyond. Ideas abstracted from the Roman baths and the Pompeian basilica were combined with ideas taken from Palladio and other Italian sixteenth-century architects, from English Baroque and Neo-Palladian architecture and from contemporary French theory and practice. That the whole was much greater than the sum of its parts was due to the individual genius of the greatest English Neo-classical architect of the nineteenth century. That his style met with so little success in the competitions of the 1830s was due, as will be seen below, to the fact that the clientèle he encountered entertained different architectural ambitions.

The importance of the Institute of British Architects

Cockerell's exceptional talents were, of course, widely recognized by his peers. Even as a travelling student he had attracted the admiration of fellow students such as George Basevi, who wrote to his family in 1817 that 'to return as Cockerell did to Rome and, if possible, become as great a lion as he' would be 'the height of my ambition'.[24] Professional recognition came to Cockerell early, rather than late in his career. He was elected an Associate of the Royal Academy in 1829 and, in 1836, he became only the seventh architect to be elected Academician since the institution's foundation almost seventy years earlier. As in the cases of his living fellow academicians, Soane, Smirke, Wyatville and Wilkins, the institution's rules prohibited Cockerell from playing any major role in the most significant development of the architectural profession of the 1830s, the foundation of the Institute of British Architects (officially the Royal Institute of British Architects from 1866). The Institute was established with a range of objectives, perhaps foremost among them being the ambition to define the persona of the architect in nineteenth-century Britain and to defend him from the potential incursions of the rapidly growing surveying and engineering professions. In three important respects, however, the Institute was of fundamental importance to the developments occurring in English architecture at the time of its inception. One respect was the personalities and backgrounds of the figures principally involved in the foundation. Another was the way in which those figures sought to position the English profession internationally. The third was the nature of the debates, notably on historical issues, which the new Institute engendered.

The Institute of British Architects was founded during 1834 as a result of a series of meetings variously attended by a total of thirty-nine architects.[25] Some of these architects were established figures and members of the Architects' Club, one of several organizations which the new Institute was intended to unify into a single body. The majority, however, were men born around the turn of the century and thus on the cusp of their careers in the mid 1830s. A significant proportion of the architects (fourteen of the thirty-nine) are known previously to have visited Italy (and in some cases Greece of course), including Peter Robinson and Joseph Kay, the two most frequent chairmen of the meetings, Samuel Angell, Charles Barry, George Basevi, Edward Cresy, John Goldicutt, Joseph Gwilt, Ambrose Poynter and George Ledwell Taylor. The most important organizing force, however, was Thomas Leverton Donaldson, who was present at all but one of the meetings for which attendance can be ascertained and who hosted three sessions in his Bloomsbury house at a point when the reluctance of Kay and other senior members of the Architects' Club to join the new Institute might have rendered it stillborn.

Donaldson's commitment to the idea of a new professional body for architects was due in part to what he perceived to be shortcomings in what the Royal Academy had to offer. Although he had studied at the Academy (and, indeed, had won its Silver Medal for a measured drawing in 1816), he was aware of the more advanced footing on which architectural education was set in France and elsewhere in Europe in the early nineteenth century. In 1817 he had travelled to Paris to investigate how French students were taught under the aegis of the Académie des Beaux-Arts, reporting back on this matter in the *Annals of the Fine Arts* and founding an 'Architectural Students' Society', which pressed the Academy (with little success) for better facilities for student-architects. In Italy between 1818 and 1822, Donaldson had familiarized himself with fine arts academies in all the major cities he visited and

been elected an honorary member of the Accademia di S. Luca and of the academies of Florence, Venice and Milan (see Fig. 82). These experiences underpinned not just the dedicated service as Honorary Secretary he offered the Institute from its inception, but also the enthusiasm with which he undertook the additional role of Honorary Secretary for Foreign Correspondence. Perhaps because of the heavy administrative tasks which these responsibilities placed on him, Donaldson was joined as joint Honorary Secretary by Goldicutt, a man who shared both his French and Italian predilections. Goldicutt was, in fact, one of the few British architects in this period to have had direct experience of the French system, having worked in the atelier of Achille Leclère in 1815 and, according to some sources, competed for the monthly *Concours mensuels d'émulation* at the Ecole spéciale de l'Architecture.[26] Moreover, he too had secured honorary membership of the Accademia di S. Luca, when in Rome in 1818.

The fact that the principal moving forces behind the Institute took their lead from European academies in which the Classical tradition remained entrenched in the early nineteenth century, meant that the new body stood effectively in opposition to those who, for nationalistic or other reasons, wished to promote the Gothic Revival. As has been demonstrated elsewhere, the Institute retained something of this character throughout the nineteenth century, to the extent that Victorian Gothic Revivalists and later Arts and Crafts architects tended to be trained in offices beyond its immediate sphere of influence.[27] Moreover, although the Institute was set up partly as a result of dissatisfaction with the Royal Academy, it shared the older organization's orientation towards the historic European academies and benefited from coeval developments at the Academy. Soane's lectures, none of which had been heard since 1820, were read anew by the Academy's secretary Henry Howard, the first series of six lectures in 1832, 1834 and 1836, the second series in 1833 and 1835. Thus the orthodoxy of Soane's view that young architects should commit themselves to the study of ancient architecture and its modern application in France was reaffirmed at the very moment that Pugin's polemics began to appear. Pugin's opposition to the idea that architectural students should travel to the Mediterranean should not be allowed to obscure the fact that the tradition of Academy Gold Medallists making that journey continued, in some cases with the support of its Travelling Studentship. As late as 1847, we find the returned Travelling Student, Henry Bayly Garling, reading a paper to the London Architectural Society 'On the Present State and Antiquities of Rome', in which Garling reported on excavations undertaken at the Baths of Caracalla which he had witnessed.[28] The Institute's own plans for a student travelling fund did not materialize, but Donaldson, in his address to the Opening Meeting held in June 1835, stated that one of its objectives was to facilitate travel by members and students through contact with foreign academies. The following year two of Charles Barry's pupils arrived at the academies in Rome and Florence with letters of introduction from Donaldson, doubtless the first of many over the ensuing decades.[29]

Donaldson and Goldicutt were both, in fact, quite explicit in their views that only the study of Classical antiquity could produce an appropriate architecture for England in the 1830s. Furthermore, although they reverenced ancient Greek architecture, it was in Rome that they thought the key to success lay. In an address read before a General Meeting of the fledgling Institute in February 1835, for example, Goldicutt spoke of what he imagined to be common experience among his audience:

> none of us can contemplate [the city of Rome] without feelings of the deepest Interest, at the same time that it will remind us of those early Studies, which formed the Ground work of our subsequent pursuits & which are no less dear to the Artist for the delight they then afforded him, than they have since proved how necessary they were to his eventual success.[30]

He went on to deliver a eulogy on the architecture of Rome of all periods, except for 'the absurdities of Borromini', before concluding: 'May we then shortly hope to see the purest Designs emanate from the Rising Generation which shall be the glorious reward hereafter to be reaped by, and the best inheritance of the British Architect'. Donaldson's views on the matter of Rome, which emerged most clearly in the obituary notice he prepared for his drowned friend Thomas Lee in 1838, also merit quoting at length.

> At the period when [Lee] entered upon his studies the Continent had been closed to us for some years & few of our students had visited Greece or Italy, so that the high Roman examples were known only through the inadequate medium of the illustrations of Palladio, Vignola & Desgodets – the more elaborate and trustworthy work of Taylor & Cresy had not appeared – and in Greek architecture, which had almost superseded the more florid style of Rome, the examples which had been executed in this Country, although distinguished by many points of merit, were applications of the style adopted with perhaps too little reference to our usages & climate ... This it appears to me has now been generally recognised, but we are falling into a contrary extreme and are adopting as our models the less refined productions of the Italian masters, instead of mounting, as they did, to a higher source, the ancient monuments of Rome, for our first principles & details. Perhaps we may be so happy as to see the time when, from a judicious combination in our public monuments of Greek proportions & Roman enrichment of the best period, may result a style which, from its individuality and character and peculiar propriety of adaptation, may be denominated 'the English'.[31]

What might be termed Donaldson's 'foreign policy' for the new Institute was designed in large measure to assist with the pursuit of these objectives. Although contemporary architects and architectural developments in Germany and other northern European countries were by no means overlooked, long-standing connections with France and Italy were set on a new and more formal footing by the election of Corresponding and Honorary Members. Thus among the sixteen foreign architects first elected to the Institute in May 1835, we find the names of Europe's most celebrated living architects Percier and Fontaine, von Klenze and Schinkel; also named are Gau (who presented the Institute with Volume 3 of *Les Ruines de Pompéi* in 1837), Auguste-Jean-Marie Guénepin, Louis-Hippolyte Lebas, Goldicutt's mentor Leclère and Donaldson's Neapolitan contacts Stefano and Louis-Sylvestre Gasse (see Fig.63) although the last named had died in 1833. To these names were added between 1835 and 1840 those of Jacques-Ignace Hittorff, Antoine-Laurent-Thomas Vaudoyer, Guillaume-Abel Blouet, Giuseppe Borsato, Sebastiano Ittar and Ferdinando Albertolli (many of whom were travel acquaintances of Donaldson's), of Jean-Tilman-François Suys (see Fig.65), of Jean-Nicolas Huyot, whose Palestrina *envoi* Donaldson had so admired, and of the Italians Giuseppe Valadier, Luigi Canina and Pietro Bianchi, who had assisted generations of British architectural students in Rome and Naples.[32] Letters from these men began to arrive in London: Guénepin, Lebas and Hittorff wrote about recent buildings in Paris and elsewhere in France, while Borsato sent a memorandum on copies of Vitruvius in the San Marco library at Venice, the second of a series of scholarly communications to be read by Donaldson at a General Meeting which involved Classical archaeology. Ittar reported on recent discoveries made at Catania's ancient theatre; Vaudoyer wrote describing Percier's *envoi* restoration of Trajan's Column; Bianchi sent some drawings of excavations he had made in the amphitheatre at Pozzuoli; and Canina reported on the excavations made around the Porta Maggiore in Rome in the late 1830s. These must have been exactly the sort of communications Donaldson hoped to elicit, and all were enthusiastically conveyed to the body of London architects.

One archaeological issue above all others preoccupied the Institute in its early days: the question of polychromy in ancient art and architecture. One of the first sub-committees set up by the Institute was the 'Polychrome Committee' of 1836, asked to consider the question with specific regard to the Elgin Marbles. Donaldson was the official record-keeper, and the other architect-members were Cockerell, Samuel Angell and Joseph Scoles, the latter two being survivors of the group of British students which had discovered colour on metopes belonging to Greek temple 'C' at Selinunte.[33] These men were joined by the sculptor Richard Westmacott, the painter Charles Eastlake and the antiquarian diplomat William Richard Hamilton, who had served as secretary to the Earl of Elgin in Athens. Michael Faraday was included, in order to provide advice on chemical issues.

The debate on polychromy during the 1830s was, of course, one which took place on a Europe-wide basis.[34] In a sense, the British were returning to a topic they had had much to do with initiating in the early nineteenth century. A number of architect-travellers, including Wilkins, Cockerell and Joseph Woods, had noted traces of colour on Greek temples and, as has been seen in Chapter 3, deliberated on colour in Roman architecture in relation to its use at Pompeii. Donaldson himself had begun an essay outlining a system for the use of colour in ancient architecture as early as 1820 and had discussed the matter with Hittorff, probably in Paris in the summer of 1822 on his way back to London. Reaching Sicily with Karl Zanth in 1823, Hittorff had an opportunity to study the Selinunte metopes in the company of Angell, prior to commencing his own excavations which led to the uncovering of the 'Temple of Empedocles' (Temple 'B'). While the British reported their discoveries dispassionately enough, Angell in *Sculptured Metopes* of 1826 and William Kinnard in his new edition of Stuart's and Revett's *The Antiquities of Athens* (1825–30), bitter disputes on the subject had sprung up in France and in Germany. Central to the debate were the relative positions of Hittorff and the Professor of Archaeology at the Bibliothèque Royale in Paris, Désiré Raoul Rochette, the latter effectively arguing on behalf of Antoine-Chrysostome Quatremère de Quincy and the established aesthetic ideas of the Académie des Beaux-Arts. Hittorff, by 1830 (when his thoughts were published in the *Annali dell'Instituto di Corrispondenza Archeologica*, among other places), was pushed to the extreme view that even the stone 'ground' of Greek temples had been coloured yellow and that every element of architectural elaboration had been brightly painted. Raoul Rochette was prepared only to concede that the ancients had applied colour in panels and that the colour was, in a sense, therefore independent of the architecture. Important contributions to this debate were made by others during the 1820s: the Dane Peter Oluf Brønsted, for example, was among the first arguing that cella walls had been painted, and the German Gottfried Semper suggested that colour symbolized the organic decorations originally hung on the structural framework of a temple and thus had formal and social, not merely aesthetic value.

The new Institute of British Architects provided a public forum in which these contending ideas could be aired in London. Thus, in the first volume of the Institute's *Transactions*, Donaldson presented a critique of the argument between Hittorff and Raoul Rochette, together with translated extracts from the Prussian Franz Kugler's *Über die Polychromie der griechischen Architektur und Skulptur und ihre Grenzen*, which had appeared in 1835 in support of Raoul Rochette. Letters read on the subject included one in 1836 from Ittar, expounding his theories about polychromy on Greek temples in Sicily, insofar as they differed from Hittorff's interpretations.[35] The climax came, however, when first Hittorff and then Zanth visited the Institute's Grosvenor Street headquarters. Hittorff's visit took place on 29 May 1837, when he was in London to inspect the Elgin Marbles for a second time. He displayed his restoration drawings of the 'Temple of Empedocles' at a General Meeting, the text of his paper being delivered in translation by Donaldson. The following year Zanth displayed his 'highly finished Drawings of Buildings in Sicily' in Grosvenor Street, but as his visit took place in September during the Institute's summer recess, there was no formal meeting.[36]

Without doubt many British architects of the 1830s were deeply concerned with the detail of the ongoing debate on polychromy: the origin of colour in architecture; the extent of colour on the monuments of the Periclean age; the questions as to whether colour had degenerated during the Hellenistic period and whether the Romans had inherited a debased form of decoration or developed their own system. From the point of view of the history of nineteenth-century architecture, however, these matters of academic dispute are perhaps of less importance than the effect they had on contemporary design. Hittorff himself was later to admit that his investigations had had less to do with purely archaeological objectives than with finding 'elements of use in my professional career',[37] and the paper arguments he had with Raoul Rochette were played out in stone and paint in the new Parisian churches of Notre Dame de Lorette and St Vincent-de-Paul from the mid 1820s to the mid 1840s.

Architecture: domestic and monumental

When Franz Christian Gau succeeded the deceased François Mazois as author of *Les Ruines de Pompéi* some twenty pages into volume three, a significant change occurred in the tenor of the book's text. Almost immediately Pompeii was compared with modern buildings and towns, and, like his friend and fellow Cologne native Hittorff, Gau stated that he saw himself engaged not in an archaeological exercise of 'futile curiosity' but in a process of discovery which would 'clarify' and 'direct' nineteenth-century architectural practice. More specifically, Gau suggested that the example of Pompeii would encourage French designers to return to vigorous colours, based on black and red grounds, in place of 'powdery' tints currently fashionable.[38] The polychromatic schemes of Notre Dame de Lorette and St Vincent-de-Paul stand as a sign of almost coeval architectural response to that call in Paris. In England where, as has just been seen, the polychromy debate was also exercising architectural minds, similar issues were being played out.

The excitement of the uncovering of so much Roman domestic architecture in the first thirty years of the nineteenth century, coupled to the strength of vision of the town prior to its destruction created by architects and writers, inevitably made the idea of Pompeian recreations attractive to the English. At the same time, however, the impracticality of Roman domestic planning and environmental conditions for nineteenth-century English circumstances was clearly apparent. Joseph Woods summed up the dilemma well when he wrote of Pompeian house plans: 'One cannot see this arrangement without longing to produce something of the same

94. John Goldicutt:
Elevation of a wall for
Gundimore, Hampshire,
1818–19, decorated in
Pompeian style.

effect, consistently [sic] with our customs and our climate, but it is, I am afraid impossible.'[39] Occasional attempts were made to suggest that Pompeian dwellings suited to modern northern European living could be devised, as in the case of a room based on sources from the Villa of Diomedes in George Smith's *Cabinet-Maker and Upholsterer's Guide* of 1826, or the 'Pompeian Suburban Villa' among the plates in Richard Brown's *Domestic Architecture* of 1842. On the whole, however, English architects, like their French counterparts, found outlets for Pompeian enthusiasm in interior arrangements and colour schemes. Goldicutt's 1825 publication of *Specimens of Ancient Decorations from Pompeii*, for example, was specifically intended 'to assist the Artist in the interior decoration of houses, as well in what regards figure as colour [sic]'.[40] The architect himself tried to practise what he preached, attempting to create 'authentic' Roman interiors in his designs of 1818–19 for W. S. Rose at Gundimore in Hampshire, using large areas of yellow with small inset paintings from models in his own *Specimens* and illusionistic Pompeian foliage over the picture rails (Fig.94). In 1823 Goldicutt tried out these ideas, unsuccessfully, in the more public context of proposed new buildings at King's College, Cambridge.[41] Goldicutt was hardly alone with his ambitions for a style of interior decoration based on Roman precedents, however. In an album compiled by Alexander Roos, topographical and other drawings made at Pompeii around 1830 mingle with design proposals for Pompeian interiors, at least one of which was carried out.[42]

It is, of course, notoriously difficult to draw general conclusions about historical interior design. This is especially so when dealing with colour schemes which, because of their

strong character, were more likely to have offended and thus to have been removed by later generations. Recent research, however, has suggested that the use of Pompeian red, in particular, for English libraries, picture galleries and dining rooms was much more common in the 1820s and 1830s than the current evidence might suggest.[43] Moreover, the repertoire of Roman interior design used in England extended beyond the use of Pompeian colour to embrace marbling, bronzing and, as Goldicutt suggested, the inclusion of Roman figurative decoration on walls, such as the famous dancers from the House of the Dancers at Pompeii. All of these elements, backed by scientific research on Roman pigments and used in an archaeological manner quite different from the formal eclecticism and light palette of Robert Adam and his followers, can be seen most clearly today in some of the rooms of Soane's houses in Lincoln's Inn Fields and at Pitzhanger.[44]

More serviceable than Roman wall and ceiling decoration in modern England, perhaps, were Roman mosaics, which Goldicutt also recommended as models. When he was at Pompeii, Joseph Woods had commented on his familiarity with *opus sectile* patterns which he considered to have been a source for later eighteenth-century ornament, but it was in the early nineteenth century that Roman mosaics began to be deployed for floors of large, often public spaces, a usage which would continue throughout the Victorian period. A good early example is the floor of the saloon (effectively the atrium) of Barry's Reform Club of 1838–41, appropriately enough in view of the Roman interests of some of the Club's founders (Pl.xv). Here, the 'meander' pattern (the continuous swastika motif) could have come from a number of places in Pompeii, from the surround of the Temple of Apollo for example, while the 'Solomon's Knot' is another motif commonly found in Roman mosaics.

The Reform Club stands as a pivotal work in Barry's development of a revived *cinquecento* manner for Victorian architecture and, with the exception of its mosaic floor and atrium, it hardly belongs with the Antique Roman interests which are of concern in this book. It was in public architecture such as this, however, that the appropriateness of the various styles of Classical architecture for modern usage was most evidently questioned in the 1830s. Furthermore, just as British archaeological interest in ancient Rome after 1815 was stimulated by the excavations and clearances undertaken by the French during the Napoleonic era, so, it can be argued, English public and monumental architecture of the 1820s and 1830s was stimulated by the literalism with which Napoleon's architects had restated Roman building types, especially the triumphal arch and the temple.

Napoleon's architectural ambitions for Paris focused on what Pierre-Louis Baltard termed '*le forum Napoléon*', the area encompassing the Louvre and Tuileries, the Rue de Rivoli and the Place Vendôme, the Place de la Concorde, and the axes to the Madeleine northwards and the Chambre des Députés southwards.[45] A recent study has fully explored the political and artistic subtleties which lay behind the Arc du Carrousel and the Colonne Vendôme, monuments which have been dismissed as crass symbols far too quickly by later twentieth-century historians, perhaps mistrustful of the role of art as propaganda (Fig.95). It has been shown that the success of Napoleon and his ministers in developing a symbolism, first of Augustan Imperialism and then, as military events moved on, of Trajanic Imperialism, was due in large part to the receptiveness of the French people, accustomed to thinking of themselves as heirs to the Romans as a result of Revolutionary and even earlier political ideology and historiography. Moreover, when they are examined closely, the iconography and intrinsic sculptural merits of the Arc du Carrousel and the Colonne Vendôme can be read as asserting the historical significance and artistic qualities of their own moment, not the often assumed decline of Neo-classicism into unimaginativeness. In this sense, the Napoleonic monuments are no more copies of Roman structures than the statues of Antonio Canova are copies of Antique prototypes.

This background offers an important context for the English development of Roman ideas in the post-Napoleonic era, and in the chapters which follow it will be seen that design decisions taken by English architects were often made with an awareness of the development of the Roman temple form seen in, for example, the Madeleine, the Chambre des Députés and the Bourse in Paris. The 'Roman moment' was initiated in England, however, by the quite different form and symbol of the triumphal arches erected for George IV, partly in emulation of the Arc du Carrousel and the Arc de Triomphe. John

95. The Arc du Carrousel, Paris, by Charles Percier and Pierre Fontaine, 1806–7.

Nash's Marble Arch and Decimus Burton's Arch at Constitution Hill were conceived as complementary structures in 1825 and begun in 1827 (Fig.96 and Pl.xvi). Neither was completed as intended and both have subsequently been moved from their original locations. The Marble Arch was designed to stand in the forecourt between Buckingham Palace and The Mall, while Burton's Arch formed, in conjunction with the same architect's Ionic screen which had been begun in 1822, the gateway between the west end of the Palace grounds and Hyde Park across Piccadilly.[46] These arches represent, of course, a conscious attempt to aggrandize the image of a little-loved monarch, partly through associating him with the military successes which the country had recently enjoyed. To aid this process, the Marble Arch was helpfully referred to in *The Times* in 1826 as 'the Waterloo Monument' but, had the sculptural programme devised that year by the King himself in association with Nash and John Flaxman been carried out, the structure would have fulfilled a wider symbolic purpose, representing Waterloo and the army on its east and north façades but also Trafalgar and the navy on its west and south sides, all surmounted, of course, by George IV on horseback (see Fig.96). Burton's arch, meanwhile, was to be given iconography of mixed military and civil character in an 1826 development of the design (see Pl.xvi). Below a quadriga driven by Britannia Triumphans was a frieze in which ancient Greek figures mingled with modern British soldiers. The freestanding female allegorical figures, to be executed by the Hennings, included personifications of History and Astronomy.

As has been seen in previous chapters, neither Nash nor Burton had visited Rome themselves but both were busy com-

96. J. C. F. Rossi(?): Plaster model of the Marble Arch by John Nash, c.1826, showing the Arch, which stood between Buckingham Palace and the Mall, in its intended state of completion.

a pagan Emperor who had died while engaged in a hostile military campaign on British soil! Another respect in which Nash looked directly to Rome, rather than to Paris, was in the material with which his arch was constructed. A key characteristic of the architecture of the Arc du Carrousel was the use of the distinctive pink Languedoc marble for its columns, left over from the Grand Trianon at Versailles, which embued the 'Roman' monument with an indigenous French quality. (They also turned a symbol of private luxury into a focus of national pride, although whether this was consciously done or not is unknown.) For his part Nash, having initially proposed the use of indigenous Bath stone for his arch, suddenly decided in 1826 that it should be clad in Italian marble in the manner of an original Roman arch. The mason Joseph Browne, who had already been working at Carrara on the acquisition of marble for Buckingham Palace and for the statuary of the arch since November 1825, was told by Nash in early 1826 to extend his order to include sufficient *ravaccione* (a greyish marble quarried at Monte Sagro just east of Carrara) to clad the entire monument.

By the end of the eighteenth century the triumphal arch had a significant history of use in European urban contexts, serving such practical functions as gateways into towns and cities. In the early years of the nineteenth century, Napoleonic arches in Paris, Milan and Madrid represented a newly literal restatement of the original symbolic function of the building type. In Britain, by contrast, the numerous schemes to embed the arch in the urban fabric of the metropolis and produce royal processional routes, conceived from John Gwynn in 1766 to John Soane in 1817, had all remained on paper or, at best, had led to the erection of temporary structures.[48] The arch had remained an architectural symbol of personal vanity or local power located in the context of country houses and their grounds, an improper usage censured by Soane in his first Royal Academy lecture (not to mention by Alexander Pope in his 'Epistle to Lord Burlington' a century earlier). It was not until the 1820s that the idea of the arch as a public monument was finally realized; and with the Marble Arch in particular, London suddenly exceeded even Paris by the literalness of Nash's design.

The intended symbolism of the Marble Arch and the Constitution Hill Arch may have fallen flat in the face of an irredeemably unpopular monarch. The structures may have become embroiled in the wider problems surrounding royal expenditure and financial mismanagement by Nash in particular, and formed a subject of biting caricature; but they have, nonetheless, another significance. The triumphal arch was a specifically Roman building type, with no obvious parallel and certainly no architectural precedent in Greek architecture. The appearance of such structures, especially the Marble Arch with its gleaming *ravaccione* revetments, 'finished' in 1833 to a revised design by Edward Blore made after consultation with James Pennethorne, brought into the metropolis and to an

piling collections of casts and models of antiquities in the mid 1820s. The arches may be read as one response to the evident fascination which Rome evidently held for these architects and, in Burton's case, as a shift from the Greek ideas of his Hyde Park Screen to the Roman arch. Although Nash had seen the Arc du Carrousel during a visit to Paris in 1814 and the dimensions of his Marble Arch are close to those of Percier's and Fontaine's monument, he also looked to the original Roman sources, famously telling the Duke of Wellington that his arch was 'a plagiarism of the Arch of Constantine'.[47] The architect was being deliberately misleading here, of course, in that he knew full well that the Marble Arch design (which had neither the famous roundels nor the attic pilasters of the Arch of Constantine) was modelled far more closely on that of Septimius Severus and had, moreover, capitals based on casts he had ordered of the Corinthian order inside the Pantheon. It is probable that he thought the Duke would prefer the association with the Christian Emperor Constantine to that with

audience already familiar with the imagery of ancient Rome through the media described in earlier chapters here a more explicit physical reminder of ancient Rome than any other building type could have done. They prepared the way for architects who had been steeped in that imagery themselves to conceive of the possibility of further such literal Roman monuments. Perhaps the most extraordinary example of this came in 1832, when John Goldicutt proposed to the government that Trafalgar Square (the idea for which dated back to 1822) should be filled with an edifice modelled on the Colosseum (Figs 97 and 98). The 'London Amphitheatre' was intended to 'concentrate the Scientific Bodies of the Metropolis and to provide suitable accommodation for the encouragement of Infant Societies'.[49] The external form of the Colosseum, which 'will ever be beautiful and consistent when a distribution of plan unites with its utility and convenience', was clearly enough stated in the superimposed arches with their controlling orders of this hypothetical design. The direct connection with ancient Rome was insisted upon, however, in Goldicutt's 'title page' for the project, where a delightful vignette of the Colosseum itself was juxtaposed with the head and trident of Britannia and the head and arms of the new King William IV in the guise of an emperor on a Roman coin. Although this scheme came to nothing, it gained widespread exposure through its display at the Royal Academy in 1837.

In the chapters which follow, attention will be focused on four examples where literal Roman ideas such as Goldicutt's left the page and became built realities. Birmingham Town Hall, The Fitzwilliam Museum in Cambridge, the Royal Exchange in London and St George's Hall in Liverpool have been selected for particular reasons other than their identifiability as English Roman monuments: all four buildings re-

97. John Goldicutt: Cover sheet for 'The London Amphitheatre' design, 1832.

98. John Goldicutt: Longitudinal elevation for 'The London Amphitheatre' in Trafalgar Square, 1832.

sulted from competitions in which their designs were selected from a range of stylistic possibilities. There is good, or reasonable, drawn and documentary evidence for reconstructing these competitions which, moreover, were spread across the decade of the 1830s. Only one of these buildings, the Royal Exchange, was metropolitan and thus, in a sense, 'national', although the particular circumstances of the City of London and its government played a central role in the decisions which were taken. Moreover, the Exchange represents, with the possible exception of the National Gallery, the largest London commission of the 1830s other than the Palace of Westminster. Two of the buildings, Birmingham Town Hall and St George's Hall in Liverpool, represent the civic aspirations of burgeoning provincial towns in the Midlands and north of England. The competitions and commissions stand at either end of the decade but, in some senses, operated symbiotically. The fourth example, the Fitzwilliam Museum,

emerged in the quite different milieu of an English university, an academic context distanced from the more immediate politicized spheres of the other three commissions. In many respects, then, the buildings selected represent a cross-section of English society in the 1830s and, as none of them was finished in that decade, into the 1840s. Other buildings where the revival of Roman forms can be seen might equally have been chosen, such as Charles Dyer's Victoria Rooms in Clifton of 1839–41 (Fig.99).[50] A final reason for the selection of the four chosen examples lies, however, in the belief that they are buildings of a quality to merit this kind of detailed consideration. Indeed, it could be argued that some, if not all of them, are better Neo-classical public buildings than their less misunderstood Greek Revival counterparts, the British Museum, University College London and the National Gallery. Far from representing the dog-ends of Neo-classicism, they are in fact its English architectural climax.

Chapter 6
Birmingham Town Hall

They are high in feeling – Roman quite – and will be immortal in their great struggle. (Benjamin Robert Haydon, describing the Reformers in Birmingham on 19 June 1832)[1]

The commission for a Town Hall in Birmingham came about as a result of a number of political, social and cultural factors in the later 1820s and early 1830s (Fig.100). Birmingham's council remained manorial in its constitution until 1838, the power to implement changes in the urban fabric resting with local street 'Commissioners', appointed under Act of Parliament. The first such Act had been passed in 1769, and by the 1820s it had become necessary to introduce a fifth Act 'for better paving, lighting, watching, cleansing, and otherwise improving' the burgeoning Midlands industrial town.[2] The Act, passed in 1828, empowered the Commissioners to erect a number of public buildings, including a Town Hall to accommodate at least 3000 people for rate-payers' and other public meetings, or for judicial activities. The Act also embodied a direct response to the Governors of the Birmingham General Hospital. They had requested a public auditorium in which their increasingly popular triennial fund-raising music festivals could be held, and they duly received the right to place an organ inside the Hall and to take managerial control of the building for the duration of the festival. Furthermore, contemporary parliamentary discussion about extension of the franchise to the industrial towns of Birmingham, Manchester and Leeds suggests that the Commissioners saw the Town Hall as a potential forum for political debate and activity, although this was hardly envisaged in the Act itself. The Commissioners appointed in 1828 had many tasks to accomplish and did not especially prioritize the new Town Hall. The building quickly emerged, however, as the symbol of Birmingham's political and cultural aspirations in the 1830s, a point well illustrated by the choice of an image of its projected form to stand as the architectural embodiment of the town's character on the map of 1834 prepared by J. Dower (Fig.101).

The minutes and other papers of the Town Hall Committee do not survive in the Birmingham archives, so the story of the competition for the building, its design and construction has to be pieced together from the minutes of the Commissioners themselves (to whom the Town Hall Committee, as a subcommittee, reported) and from other alternative sources. A provisional Town Hall Committee, appointed by the new Commissioners at their second meeting, held in July 1828,

returned within two weeks with the recommendation of the purchase of a site on the corner of the newly-named Waterloo Street (running west from the area around St Philip's Church) and Bennett's Hill, at the southern end of New Hall Street (see Fig.101). When, a year later and the protestations of the Hospital Musical Committee notwithstanding, the Commissioners and the owner of the land refused to compromise on a price per square yard for the site, the Committee was forced to abandon this plan and seek alternatives. Its attention focused instead on the area of high ground next to Christ Church, at the west end of Waterloo Street. A plan dated July 1830 envisaged a building occupying part of a triangular piece of land between Hill Street and Pinfold Street.[3] In August, however, the Commissioners accepted a different recommendation from the Committee of a site diagonally opposite to the north-west, bounded by Paradise Street to the south and Congreve Street to the east and offering the attractive possibility of the Town Hall as the focal point at the top of New Street (Fig.102).[4] The adoption of this site must effectively have been determined in advance of the August meeting, since five of the Commissioners (William Phipson, Joseph Walker, Charles Shaw, William Beale and Edward Thomason), all of whom were also members of the Town Hall Committee, had taken advantage of a recent sale of the Colmore estates to purchase the freehold of the land between this intended site and Edmund Street to the north; purchases which they subsequently offered to sell on to the Commissioners for no profit. Not only does this indicate that the present-day Chamberlain Square has its origins in the earliest ambitions of the Commissioners to create an open urban area to the north of the new Town Hall, it also shows the willingness of Birmingham inhabitants to give private support to such a civic venture. On the latter point, it is worth noting further that the speed with which the Committee was able to proceed with purchase of the site was due to the generosity of eleven citizens (including two further Town Hall Committee members, but also six local women) in lending the Commissioners £1000 each until they could levy the six pence in the pound rate allowed for funding the erection of the Town Hall under the 1828 Act.

The rules for the national competition held to secure a design for the Town Hall and advertised in *The Times* in December 1830 were drawn up by the Committee and not ratified in the Commissioners' minutes, so their precise terms can no longer be determined. Evidently competitors had the re-

markably short period of only about a month in which to prepare their designs. From the Yorkshire architect Joseph Aloysius Hansom's 1834 *A Statement of Facts Relative to the Birmingham Town Hall*, it emerges that a personal visit to Birmingham was necessary, or at least expedient.[5] Hansom, and his partner Edward Welch, travelled to the town in January 1831 to discuss the town's expectations with two solicitors, John Arnold and William Haines, who were issuing the instructions for the competition in their capacity as Clerks to the Commissioners. On 28 February the Commissioners noted that seventy entries had been received and, as the Town Hall Committee had 'not themselves come to any conclusive opinion as to the relative merits of the numerous designs combining a display of great and varied talent', they resolved that the Committee should be asked to reduce their number to a minimum of ten in advance of the next Commission meeting. On 5 April, the Commissioners asked that the ten designs which the Committee had selected should be further reduced to three, noting that several of the ten had utilized more of Paradise Street than could be permitted and implicitly criticizing the Committee for leaving the written instructions unclear on this matter. It might be inferred that all three of the final selection were in this category, for, after having been chosen on 2 May, they were each to be sent back to their architects to be redrawn with a view to closer 'adaptation' to the site. At this point, the anonymity of the finalists was certainly abandoned, because the firm of Thomas Rickman and Henry Hutchinson and the architect John Fallows both wrote to the Committee during May insisting that their designs (numbered 40 and 32 respectively) did not encroach further onto Paradise Street than was permitted.[6] When the Commissioners voted on the three finalists on 6 June 1831, Rickman and Hutchinson were awarded the third premium of £40, and Fallows the second of £60. The first premium of £100, however, together

100. *Birmingham Town Hall, designed by Joseph Aloysius Hansom, Edward Welch and Charles Edge from 1831, viewed from the south-east across present-day Victoria Square.*

OPPOSITE
101. *J. Dower: Map of Birmingham, 1834, with the new Town Hall as an icon of the town.*

TOWN HALL.

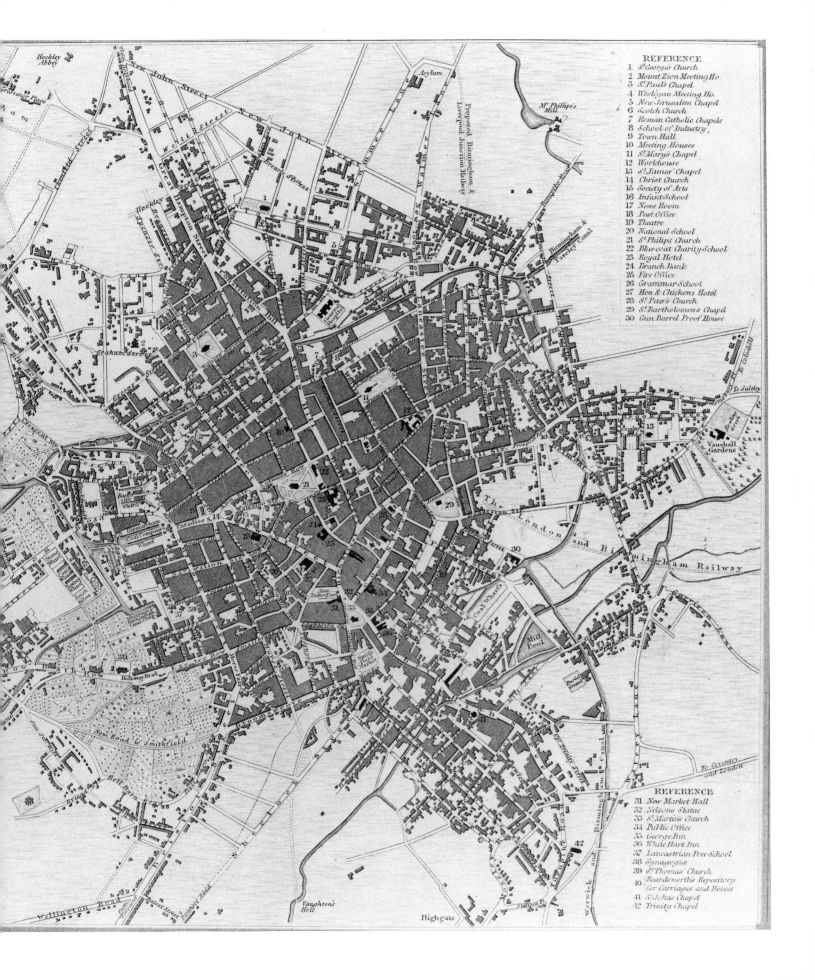

REFERENCE

1. St George's Church
2. Mount Zion Meeting Ho.
3. St Paul's Chapel
4. Wesleyan Meeting Ho.
5. New Jerusalem Chapel
6. Scotch Church
7. Roman Catholic Chapels
8. School of Industry
9. Town Hall
10. Meeting Houses
11. St Mary's Chapel
12. Workhouse
13. St James' Chapel
14. Christ Church
15. Society of Arts
16. Infant School
17. News Room
18. Post Office
19. Theatre
20. National School
21. St Philips Church
22. Blue-coat Charity School
23. Royal Hotel
24. Branch Bank
25. Fire Office
26. Grammar School
27. Hen & Chickens Hotel
28. St Peter's Church
29. St Bartholomew's Chapel
30. Gun Barrel Proof House

REFERENCE

31. New Market Hall
32. Nelsons Statue
33. St Martin's Church
34. Public Office
35. George Inn
36. White Hart Inn
37. Lancastrian Free School
38. Synagogue
39. St Thomas Church
40. Beardsworth's Repository for Carriages and Horses
41. St Johns Chapel
42. Trinity Chapel

with immediate appointment as architects, went to Hansom and Welch. A complicating factor in the otherwise straightforward story told by the minutes is that, in his 1834 *Statement*, Hansom recorded that Charles Barry, rather than Fallows, had been the third finalist, but that Barry's redrawing had been overlooked in favour of that of Fallows.[7] Whilst there is no evidence to corroborate this story, there was certainly a contemporary feeling in Birmingham that Barry's entry would win.[8]

The fortunate survival in the Birmingham archives of sets of drawings by Fallows and Rickman (Hutchinson, although the Birmingham principal of the practice, died in 1831 after a debilitating illness) makes possible further analysis of the terms of the competition. Both architects submitted a block plan of their proposals for the site, plans of the ground and gallery storeys (two of the latter in the case of Fallows), elevations to Paradise Street and Congreve Street, a transverse section (north to south), a longitudinal section (east to west), and an

exterior perspective of the proposed building drawn from New Street in the south-east. These drawings presumably represent the common requirement from competitors, possibly with the addition of the rear (west) elevation and an interior perspective of the great Hall viewed from the north end, which survive in the Fallows set. Because Fallows had introduced a basement (for the storage of moveable staging envisaged by the 1828 Act) and small mezzanine floors, his set also included plans of those levels. From these drawings the relatively simple functional requirements of the building emerge. There was to be a hall of 140 × 65 ft, 65 ft high, capable of accommodating at least 3000 people, in part on public galleries at the south end and along the east and west sides. At the north end there was to be an orchestra gallery, where an organ would also be situated. At least one room was to be provided for committee meetings, together with rooms for retiring and refreshment. Domestic accommodation was required for a caretaker.

The competition designs of Rickman and Fallows shed interesting light on the stylistic questions facing architects of public buildings such as Birmingham Town Hall at the beginning of the 1830s, especially when considered alongside four sheets of drawings which have been associated with Barry's involvement in this project. Alfred Barry later described his father's proposal for the Town Hall as a 'Greek design, of great massiveness and grandeur … the only design of the kind among those sent in by the competing architects', while Matthew Digby Wyatt recalled of the drawing which Barry exhibited at the Royal Academy in 1832 that it was a 'noble scheme for a Doric temple of grandeur, and at the same time of so much simplicity'.[9] A perspective of a hexastyle Doric temple from the Richardson Collection, now in Los Angeles, appears to represent Barry's competition entry (Fig.103). A slightly foreshortened version of the Athenian Theseion, adapted to the demands of site and function by its placement on a podium and its introduced windows, this design represents perhaps the most archaeologically literal statement of a Greek temple it is possible to imagine in a modern context. Three other sheets, however, preserved in the archives at Birmingham, present sketches in which Barry evidently experimented with stylistic alternatives. One (Fig.104) has two proposals pasted onto it: the upper for a building with a Tuscan portico overlooking Paradise Street and a pilastered façade to Congreve Street; the lower with Paradise and Congreve Streets elevations in an Italianate idiom, close to that which Barry was developing at the same moment for the rear (south) front of his Travellers' Club in London. A second sheet (Fig.105) has a plan, section and two elevations for a tall Corinthian temple with double-depth hexastyle portico,

while the third has elevational and sectional details inscribed 'Birmingham Town Hall' and evidently related to the Tuscan scheme.[10] Since this third sheet is watermarked 1832 (and the paper is identical with the other two sheets, all clearly having been detached from an album in which they were pages 22, 50 and 74 respectively), it cannot be assumed that these design ideas date from the time of the competition in early 1831. Instead, they may be experiments with the range of formal possibilities for a building of this type on this site which postdate the competition and represent an exercise in learning from a professional disappointment on Barry's part. In this context it should be noted that the drawing of Barry's Greek Doric scheme reverses the building in relation to the site, and was thus probably a version of the architect's competition perspective prepared for engraving, so that he could salvage some capital from the process. What is of greatest significance here, however, is that the four distinctly different characters of these designs indicate that, within the overall formal language of Classicism, this was a time when no one specific idiom was dominant in public architecture.

Further support for this reading of the evidence can be found in the two premiated designs by Rickman and Fallows. Rickman's design (Fig.106) was for a typical 1820s English Greek Revival public building, strikingly similar in fact to Francis Goodwin's Town Hall in Manchester of 1822–4 (also situated, incidentally, at the intersection of two town-centre streets). On a high podium of horizontally-striated rustication, Rickman set a hexastyle Erechtheion Ionic portico over the Paradise Street entrance and six further unpedimented Ionic columns along the Congreve Street elevation. The order continued inside the building, where Ionic columns were used to

104. Charles Barry:
Perspective and elevations
of Tuscan and Italianate
alternatives for Birmingham
Town Hall, 1832 or later.

support the front of the galleries in the concert hall. The design of Fallows, by contrast, was of an entirely different nature (Fig.107). He produced a plan in which the central hall was surrounded by four corner 'pavilions', all except that to the north-west housing staircases to the galleries. Hexastyle porticoes also projected from the rectangular body of the building to Paradise and Congreve Streets, the former leading to a vestibule set between a pair of committee rooms (matched by a pair of refreshment rooms at the north end) and the latter leading directly into the concert hall through a deep recess. More remarkable than this restless plan was the formal character of Fallows's design. The gallery level was treated as a piano nobile, its Corinthian porticoes linked around the rest of the south and east façades by pilasters. This whole system was then set upon a matching Tuscan order at ground level. The high attic proposed by Fallows terminated in a louvered central vent and cupola. The design seems to anticipate the plastic character of much later nineteenth-century and Edwardian

Classical public architecture, an impression which is further sustained by the considerable use of sculptural decoration inside.[11]

As has been seen, however, it was not the archaeologically Greek design of Barry, the Greek Revival design of Rickman, nor the quasi-Baroque design of Fallows which was selected by the Commissioners for the Town Hall, but the design of Hansom and Welch. Regrettably, none of the competition designs by these architects survive, so historians must depend on their not always consistent written accounts and on the building itself.[12] It is clear that, although working in partnership, the two architects decided to enter separate designs in order to maximize their chances of success, and that it was Hansom's scheme which the Committee placed on the final shortlist of three. From the outset, Hansom looked not to the precedents offered by Greece, nor to the Renaissance, but (as he and Welch both stated) specifically to the Temple of 'Jupiter Stator' (Castor and Pollux) in the Roman Forum.[13] In the competition entry, however, Hansom had used only the flank of the temple on its high podium, presumably forming an unpedimented frontage to Paradise Street accommodating the public access spaces of the building. The narrrower hall projected northwards behind, like the stem of an inverted capital letter T. Unlike Fallows and Rickman, Hansom admitted that his design had indeed encroached on more of the site than the Commissioners envisaged and that he had been forced to redraw during May 1831. From his description it would seem that the encroachment which concerned the Commissioners lay in the direction of Congreve Street, as a result of which Hansom contracted the T plan into a rectangular shape and reduced the width of its west side to a single corridor rather than a double one (see the parts of the plan tinted blue on Pl.xviiA).[14] Through this process the design became what Welch referred to as a 'simple Corinthian temple (after the example of Jupiter Stator), mounted on an elevated rustic basement'.

Welch, perhaps piqued by Hansom's statement that his partner had not become involved with the building before January 1833, when financial difficulties began to arise, took the opportunity in his own publication to say that the revised design was a restatement of an idea jointly conceived by the partnership in the late 1820s as a proposal for the new Fishmongers' Hall in London. A bitter exchange ensued in the press on this matter.[15] In an arrogant and insulting letter, Hansom said the Birmingham design was his in the same sense as St Paul's Cathedral was Christopher Wren's, and that Welch's role had been no greater than 'what a junior clerk would have done if beside me'. He observed that the competition for Fishmongers' Hall had taken place a year later than that for Birmingham Town Hall (in fact the London competition was announced within three months of the conclusion of the Birmingham process). An aggrieved Welch retorted that the architects had prepared for the Fishmongers' Hall competition well in advance of its actually being an-

106. Thomas Rickman: Perspective of competition entry for Birmingham Town Hall, 1831. This image has been computer-enhanced to overcome the poor condition of the drawing.

nounced (it was indeed clear from 1827 that a new building would be necessary as a result of the rebuilding of London Bridge). Welch added that it was he who had proposed 'a temple mounted on an elevated basement' to Hansom, an idea Hansom sketched out and subsequently used for Birmingham Town Hall. The fact that Hansom, by his own confession, prepared his initial competition design in just four days and that he was able to make major alterations to the design in a month does suggest some usage of earlier material, and this lends further weight to the identification of an anonymous lithographed 'Design Proposal for Fishmongers' Hall' as the sketch described by Welch (Fig.108).[16] In the lithograph, a Corinthian hexastyle temple with thirteen columns in its flank sits on a double-height platform, the upper level of which has pairs of baseless Doric columns set *in antis*. Thus Hansom and Welch had evidently begun to make literal use of Roman archaeological precedents a year or two before the Birmingham competition, the Roman forms superimposed on the Greek – a nice metaphor for the supersedence of the latter by the former which was about to occur when their Roman temple met with clients keen to adopt it. A similar development can be seen occurring in a design of 1827 for a monument in The Mall to the Duke of York, which has been attributed to William Wilkins.[17]

According to Hansom, his design attracted fifty-four votes in favour and only three against in the final stage of the competition, from which it can be inferred that the Commissioners had a strong preference for architecture of the nature he was proposing. Both Rickman and Fallows had Birmingham offices and their designs, along with those of another Birmingham architect, Charles Edge, had formed the Commissioners' shortlist in 1829 for the job of improving the town's Public Office building. Fallows's estimate of £16,000 for the Town Hall, moreover, was an attractive (if extremely opti-

mistic) £1000 less than the budget specified. The young architects from outside the town, Barry and Hansom, were offering something different and less provincial, however, in the explicitly templar forms of their designs. Even when the triangular Hill Street/Pinfold Street site was under consideration, the Commissioners had envisaged a rectangular Town Hall building, and Hansom's contraction of his plan into rectangular form for the Paradise Street/Congreve Street site might be seen as a reaction to the positive public reception Barry's Greek Doric temple had received. What presumably attracted the Commissioners, however, was the specifically Roman character of Hansom's scheme, and perhaps the way it harmonized with the Corinthian portico of the Society of Arts on New Street, built, ironically enough, to the designs of Rickman and Hutchinson in 1828 (see Fig.102). Hansom's and Welch's Town Hall had a pedimented octastyle Corinthian portico facing south over Paradise Street and a peristyle of thirteen columns running northwards along the Congreve Street flank of the cella, the whole set on a rusticated podium (Fig.109).[18] As the lower part of this drawing shows, the west elevation of the podium, which was tightly hemmed in by Paradise Street houses, was not given such magnificent treatment by Hansom and Welch, with its asymmetrical arrangement of doors and windows. The walls above were initially intended to be rendered brick, although in the autumn of 1832 the Committee agreed to the architects' request that stone should be deployed on the west front. As Fig.109 and other visual sources indicate, the west peristyle of thirteen columns was therefore set in place, rising above the roofs of the neighbouring Paradise Street houses. The north end, similarly hard against other buildings, had no portico and was pilastered.

In order to produce their version of the Temple of Castor and Pollux, Hansom and Welch, neither of whom is known to have visited Rome, must have depended on published sources. Given the widespread British interest in the archaeological activities going on in Rome over the previous fifteen years, they are unlikely to have settled for outdated surveys and reconstructions of the temple, such as those offered by Andrea Palladio or Antoine Desgodetz. The placement of thirteen columns in the flank might suggest that they had looked at Auguste Caristie's reconstruction of the temple published in 1821 (see Fig.66), although the intercolumniation of the order coupled to the length of the site would have been the principal factors determining this number. It is far more likely, of course, that the architects looked to Taylor's and Cresy's *The Architectural Antiquities of Rome*, a source published within the previous decade, containing information on the recent excavations made at the temple and providing minutely detailed measurements in English feet and inches. There are, indeed, proportional relationships between the surveys published by Taylor and Cresy and Hansom's and Welch's design. The height of the Birmingham podium is 23 ft, its columns and entablature 45 ft, and its pediment 15 ft to the apex: a total

107. Edward Fallows:
Perspective of competition
entry for Birmingham Town
Hall, 1831.

108. Joseph Aloysius
Hansom and Edward Welch:
Lithograph of perspective of
design for Fishmongers' Hall,
London, late 1820s.

109. Charles Edge: Copy of a drawing of the elevations of Birmingham Town Hall. The upper image shows the east front of the Town Hall as left by Hansom, Welch and Foster in 1834 (except that they had provided a double-arched arcade at the south end, not the single arch shown here). The lower image shows the inconsequential basement of the building on the west side, where it was tightly hemmed in by surrounding properties.

height of 83 ft.[19] Taylor's and Cresy's equivalent measurements are 22 ft 3 in 8 lines for the podium, and 61 ft 3 in for the columns and entablature: a total of 83 ft 6 in and 8 lines. The principal difference in dimension between the two buildings, therefore, is the height of the columns and entablatures, the Birmingham order being scaled down to almost exactly three-quarters of the height of its Roman model. The order at Birmingham was closely modelled on that of the Roman prototype, except that much of its decorative detail was removed in order to reduce carving costs (Fig.110). Thus the fluting and astragal of the column are identical, as are the acanthus leaves and famous interlocking spirals of the capital (see Fig.44). There, however, the richness ends at Birmingham. The caulicoli, echinus and abacus have none of the sculptural enrichments of the Roman temple, nor do the mouldings of the entablature, though they are all present in the right places, along with the dentils and modillions.

The almost exact coincidence in the respective heights of the ancient and modern podia draws attention to a further aspect of Hansom's and Welch's design which suggests the use of Taylor's and Cresy's *The Architectural Antiquities of Rome*. The latters' elevation of the newly excavated piers below the surviving three columns of the Temple showed the pitted character of the travertine blocks, an effect reproduced by Hansom's and Welch's choice of Anglesea 'marble' (actually a very white carboniferous limestone from Sir Richard Bulkley's Penmon quarries) for the Birmingham podium (Fig.111). Moreover, the Taylor and Cresy detail shows more clearly than any other published source the *opus incertum* bracing arches which linked the piers together (Fig.112), a feature Hansom and Welch appear to have seized upon when deciding on arched perforations in the podium as the means of access to Birmingham Town Hall (see Fig.1). The limitations of the site meant, of course, that Hansom and Welch had to provide access to levels

Nº 1   Elevation to Congreve Street

Birmingham Town Hall.
Copy april 1841.

Elevation of the Basement towards the Area.

above the ground floor within the body of the building. Even had they chosen to do so, they could not have made use of the recent discovery that the podium of the Temple of Castor and Pollux had been accessed at the front by steps leading to the sides of its podium. Taylor and Cresy had illustrated these steps (and also hypothesized erroneously that they had led to a mid-point platform which could also have been approached by a frontal flight of steps). It is noteworthy that Charles Barry, once freed from the practical problems of the actual site in Birmingham, toyed with just such a lateral approach to the podium in his Corinthian scheme (see Fig.105), perhaps exploring the very same Roman model which had evidently served Hansom and Welch so well at the second stage of the competition.

In the absence of any specific comments as to why it should have been Hansom's scheme which was ultimately successful in the competition for Birmingham Town Hall, the more general context of the town and its leading personalities at the time ought to be considered. The Chairman of the Birmingham Street Commissioners from 1824 to 1836 was Paul Moon James, a banker, public-spirited Liberal and the driving force behind Birmingham's civic improvement schemes, including the provision of the Town Hall.[20] The Commissioners over whom James presided were largely Birmingham entrepreneurs, such as Charles Shaw, a brassfounder turned manufacturer and merchant and one of the five who personally purchased land north of the Town Hall site on behalf of the Commissioners. Men like these selected the Roman temple in the summer of 1831, evidently as an appropriate architectural image around which their developing town could continue to grow. By the following spring, however, the image had taken on the character of an overtly political symbol: the first brick was laid on 27 April 1832, just one month before the clamour for the Great Reform Bill in Birmingham led to the town becoming the site of the biggest national public demonstrations.

The key figure in the history of Birmingham at this time was Thomas Attwood, a former High Bailiff and Chairman of the Commissioners and, like the current Chairman, James, a banker by profession. Although Attwood was a Tory, he had become an active campaigner for reform of national trade laws and fiscal policy in the post-Napoleonic period. In 1830 he was the principal founder of the 'Birmingham Political Union for the Protection of Public Rights', an organization which shortly became a local and national focus for dissent over parliamentary rotten boroughs and the under-representation of the populace in the Commons.[21] On 3 October 1831 the Union held the first of its great public meetings at New Hall Hill, some 12 acres of open ground just to the north-west of the town centre (see Fig.101). This site was in the acoustically beneficial shape of an amphitheatre, but it was also symbolically appropriate in that it had been the location of Radical demonstrations in 1819. The support of Attwood and the Birmingham Political Union was a major source of encour-

agement to the Prime Minister, Earl Grey, as he pushed the Reform Bill through a recalcitrant House of Lords in April 1832. When it became clear, however, that the Tories planned to destroy the Bill at the Committee stage, Attwood organized another mass meeting on New Hall Hill to coincide with the first sitting of the Committee on 7 May 1832. The aim was to gain popular support through a petition for the creation of fifty new peers prepared to accept electoral reform. This event was commemorated in a drawing by Henry Harris, composed from his eye-witness experience of the three successive meetings in that month and published as a lithograph (Fig.113). The huge crowd of 7 May (modern estimates have halved contemporary estimates, but the number is still put at 100,000) can be seen covering the hill as it slopes down from the portico of the Mount Zion Meeting House in Graham Street (no.2 on Fig.101). The temporary rostrum, with a banner bearing the word 'Order', can be seen towards the top left corner of

110. The order of Birmingham Town Hall. This capital was one of the few still surviving in good condition by the 1990s, although damaged stonework, mismatching repairs and protective lead capping can all be seen above.

the print, while the speakers approach in two carriages in the centre ground with Attwood, in his trademark fur-collared coat, silhouetted in profile against a white banner, in the second carriage. The procession is led by a band and there are, of course, numerous banners. Some bear the names of branches of the Union set up in Birmingham's satellite towns, others salute Attwood personally as 'Father of Unions', while still others carry the mottoes of the Union: 'The Safety of the King & of the People'; 'The Constitution – Nothing Less, Nothing More'.

Two days after this meeting, Grey's government resigned, following William IV's refusal to create all fifty of the necessary new peers. Attwood and the Union, strengthened by the Birmingham middle classes who now flooded to join their cause, held a meeting on New Hall Hill and, on 13 May, prepared a 'Solemn Declaration against the Duke of Wellington', in which they pledged to use every legal means at their disposal to obstruct the Duke in forming an alternative administration. On 16 May, Attwood was at home at Harborne, 4 miles south of Birmingham, anticipating arrest on a warrant which Wellington had had prepared for him. Instead, news arrived that Wellington had been unable to form a government and that Grey had therefore returned as Prime Minister. Attwood and his supporters processed in triumph to Birmingham, where a crowd estimated at 40,000 gathered for an impromptu meeting on New Hall Hill. With the passage of the Bill apparently assured, Attwood led a deputation to London, where he met Grey and received the Freedom of the City of London in a ceremony held at the Mansion House. The citation, prepared by the great historian of Greece, George Grote, saluted him for teaching 'the people to combine for a great public purpose, without breaking any of the salutary restraints of law, and without violating any of their obli-

gations as private citizens'.[22] When Attwood arrived back in Birmingham, having been fêted at every stopping point on the road from London, the crowds waiting to greet him were so large that his carriage was unable to reach the Bullring. The horses having taken fright and their harnesses broken, the carriage was drawn by hand to the Hen and Chickens Hotel (no.27 on Fig.101), from the balcony of which Attwood addressed the people. It almost goes without saying that, later in 1832, Attwood was elected as one of Birmingham's first two Members of Parliament, along with Joshua Scholefield, a Birmingham Street Commissioner since January 1831. Ballads in Attwood's praise were hawked through the streets, pint mugs made with the effigy of his head and shoulders, and a profile portrait of him with the accoutrements of the Union published (Fig.114).

111. George Ledwell Taylor and Edward Cresy: Detail of the travertine piers and arched support in the newly excavated podium of the Temple of Castor and Pollux (see Fig.46), from 'The Architectural Antiquities of Rome', 1822.

112. The Temple of Castor and Pollux, Rome, from the north-east.

The importance of these events in Birmingham on the national stage is debatable, some modern opinion holding that 'theirs was a local triumph … which through the peculiar lens of provincial conditions got magnified into national pretensions'.[23] To a contemporary like Edward Bulwer-Lytton, however, writing in his 1833 social commentary *England and the English*, 'the tone of Birmingham liberalism' filled upper class drawing rooms and demonstrated that political principles travelled from the base to the apex of society, the reverse of social principles.[24] Moreover, to the artist Benjamin Robert Haydon, looking to establish himself in the tradition of history painting, it was sufficiently evident that history had been made in Birmingham in May 1832 for him to travel there from London for ten days in June. Haydon wrote to Attwood that the New Hall Hill meeting of 7 May must have been 'imposing beyond expression', and thought that a 'grand Historical Picture commemorating the scene' would give 'an immense impulse to the art'.[25] A subscription was started for 'Haydon's Grand Picture of the Sublime Scene at New Hall Hill', the artist sketched portraits of sixteen of the leading Reformers (including both chalk and oil portraits of Attwood) and began on the oil sketch, now in Birmingham City Art Gallery, for the full-scale work. At Attwood's modest suggestion, Haydon chose to depict the moment on 7 May when

the minister Hugh Hutton uttered a spontaneous prayer, rather than Attwood's own speech. The artist, who later heard Hutton's powerful preaching himself, may have considered the prayer 'the finest thing in history', but it was Attwood who was the most 'wonderful man, with a strong, natural, native understanding. His features are cut, carved, & vigorous; his forehead high, white, & shining; his hair grows out, up, elastically like Alexander's.'[26]

To Haydon, Attwood may have appeared like the great Macedonian King, but it was in Roman learning, English history and contemporary politics that the Birmingham man was steeped. In terms of ancient history, Attwood's grammar school education had left him well versed in Latin literature and with an heroic admiration for the philosopher-emperor, Marcus Aurelius, after whom he had named both his second and third sons. Attwood also had English historical heroes, especially in the seventeenth-century parliamentary reformers John Hampden and John Pym. Hampden, who led resistance to Charles I's reintroduction of ship-money and the extension of the tax to inland counties, was one of the five impeached Members of Parliament who escaped arrest in 1642 thanks to protection in the City of London, dying a year later in the field near Oxford during a Civil War skirmish with Prince Rupert's cavalry. A Hampden Club had been formed in Birm-

113. Lithograph produced by Henry Harris after witnessing the three mass meetings held on New Hall Hill by the Birmingham Political Union during the passage of the Great Reform Bill in May 1832.

ingham in 1815, to campaign against the Corn Laws, although it was far too radical for the Tory Attwood to have become involved with it at that time.[27] It had been the Hampden Club which had organized the first demonstrations on New Hall Hill in 1819, and interest in Hampden in 1831 must have been heightened by the appearance that year of Lord Nugent's *Some Memorials of John Hampden, His Party, and His Times*, brilliantly reviewed in December by Thomas Babington Macaulay. Meanwhile, Attwood's contemporary role-model was the Marquis Lafayette, who had commanded the French National Guard during the 1830 Revolution, who helped install the July Monarchy of Louis-Philippe, and with whom Attwood corresponded in early 1832 on the Polish question.

All three of these streams of reference, ancient Roman, Civil War English and Revolutionary French, informed the beliefs and the rhetoric with which Attwood inspired the Birmingham people. At the New Hall Hill meeting held on 3 October 1831, for example, he quoted Lafayette in saying that 'for a nation to be free it was sufficient that she wills it'.[28] The example of the Civil War heroes was so close to his thinking about nineteenth-century events that it formed a central part of his speech at the great New Hall Hill meeting of 7 May: 'When the immortal Hampden hoisted the standard of Liberty in England, he adopted as his motto the words "Vestigia nulla retrorsum", or in English, the words "No retreat". Now this is our motto in the peaceful and legal contest in which we are engaged.'[29] It was natural, moreover, that his speech at the Mansion House on the occasion that he received the Freedom of London should have made reference to the 'first city of the world [which has] always been foremost in the fight of liberty. I will recall to your minds its history, its noble stand against the tyrant John, and that time when its Trainbands marched to defend the persons of a Hampden and a Pym.' In the same speech, Attwood's description of his actions during the past few days and months had something of the spirit of Marcus Curtius, who defended Rome by leaping into the abyss which had opened in the middle of the Forum (see Fig.3): 'when I saw the foundations of society loosening and breaking under our feet … when I felt the incipient heavings of a political earthquake that I knew would disorganise and crush all the institutions of this powerful Empire, – then I though it right to step forward and stand between the People and Rebellion.'[30]

Although Roman analogies could hardly be, and were not as potent a force in Attwood's campaign for political reform as the examples of the English Civil War and contemporary European revolutions, there is no doubt that Haydon's perception of the Birmingham Reformers as 'Roman quite', quoted as an epigraph at the head of this chapter, was a reflection of the Roman iconography which the Union successfully deployed. Foremost in this regard was the *fasces*, the bundle of rods carried by the lictors when accompanying the kings of ancient Rome as a symbol of the justice they could dispense.

According to Livy, the *fasces* were passed to the noble Lucius Junius Brutus after he had expelled King Tarquinius Superbus in the late sixth century BC and become the first of two Consuls in the Roman Republic (see Figs 114 and 3 again). The *fasces* did not merely appear in portraits of the Birmingham leader. They were physically made and carried, certainly in the procession which greeted Attwood on his return from London and possibly at the New Hall Hill meetings too, because a huge bundle of rods appears in Henry Harris's drawing, on the left at the top of the steps leading to the speakers' platform (see Fig.113). However, the *fasces* of 'King Tom', as William Cobbett called Attwood, did not have the protruding axe blade of the Roman symbol, perhaps a reflection of the peaceful means through which Attwood hoped reform could be achieved. Moreover, although a conversation held between Haydon and Joshua Scholefield led the former to comment that 'strong Republican feelings' in Birmingham resulted from the town's trading connections with America, Attwood's political goal was a reformed constitutional monarchy, as the Union motto 'The Safety of the King & of the People' showed.[31] Once this had been achieved, this modern hero reverted to the quiet life. It could hardly be more appropriate that he is commemorated today in Birmingham, reclining informally near his orange box on the steps of Chamberlain Square literally in the shadow of the Town Hall (Fig.115).

These were the contexts which helped make the new Town Hall such a popular emblem with the people of Birmingham during the 1830s, despite the financial difficulties into which the project soon ran and the fact that they had to pay an extra six pence in the pound rate for it. So many residents wished to visit the building site that a system of tickets giving access at limited times had to be introduced. In 1837, the Commissioners wrote that 'it is only by completing the Hall on the plan of the original Temple after which it was designed that they shall act in accordance with that increasing pride and satisfaction with which the inhabitants as well as strangers view this noble Building, and render it worthy the correct taste of the age, and the public spirit of the Town.'[32] In fact, then, the building might be read as the complete antithesis of Leo von Klenze's exactly contemporary and similarly templar Walhalla near Regensburg, which has been described as a 'Romantic rejection of contemporary experience, permitting no contact with nineteenth century urban realities'.[33] To a larger extent than its French sibling, Pierre Vignon's great peristylar Church of the Madeleine in Paris, the Town Hall was a temple to the collective and democratic endeavour of the Birmingham people, central to the town's civic life from its opening until 1989, when the City of Birmingham Symphony Orchestra moved to a new auditorium (Fig.116).

Having won the competitition to design the Town Hall, Hansom entered enthusiastically into Birmingham current affairs, allying himself with his friend Attwood's movement, attending some of the New Hall Hill meetings, playing a lead-

LEFT
114. W. Green and James B. Allen: Portrait of Thomas Attwood with the accoutrements and mottoes of the Birmingham Political Union, 1832.

ABOVE
115. Siobhan Coppinger and Fiona Peever: Installation sculpture of Thomas Attwood, Chamberlain Square, Birmingham, 1993. Attwood reclines in the shadow of the Town Hall.

ing role in the Birmingham branch of the Operative Builders' Union and almost being arrested for sedition himself.[34] For the architect, however, the excitement of the Reform cause was soon to turn to anxiety, as a result of the way in which the Town Hall building project was arranged. The Commissioners accepted a tender of £16,648 from the firm of Thomas and Kendall but, perhaps because this was £6000 less than the next lowest tender, capped their own contribution at £17,000 and required the architects to stand surety for any additional expenditure as well as to cover part of the expense of labour on their own credit.[35] The costs had indeed been seriously underestimated, the introduction of the Anglesea 'marble' for the west façade further increased them and the Commissioners were unwilling to countenance a reduction in interior detailing. Bankruptcy ensued for Hansom and Welch in 1834, and to their chagrin the Liverpool Surveyor, John Foster, doubtless known to them through their own work in that town, put himself forward free of charge and oversaw completion of their work between May and December of that year. In 1835, however, the Commissioners turned to the local architect, Charles Edge, for plans for extending the building. The following year Edge designed the small recess for the organ which can be seen in blue projecting from the centre of the north front on Pl.xviia. The exterior of the projection was given four antae (doubled around the corners), with windows in between. With the extra space provided by this extension, Edge redesigned the gallery for the orchestra and choir inside

the Hall. He also extended the length of the side galleries and reduced the depth of the south gallery, the frontages of which, with their ironwork lyres, were a remodelling of Hansom's design which had lyres on inset panels.[36]

In 1846, after at least six years of discussion, during which plans had been drawn up, Edge was finally asked to make more major alterations to the building, opening a new street 14 yd wide around its west and north sides and completing those two fronts in a manner consistent with the east and south fronts (the parts marked in red on Pl.xviia). The 'Specification for Completion' of the Town Hall and the contract drawings are dated 1848 and 1849.[37] They show that Edge doubled the width of the corridor on the west side of the building, thus removing the asymmetry from the plan left by Hansom and Welch. The new west and north sides of the podium, which he ashlared in Anglesea stone, were given arched openings to bring them into overall harmony with the existing east and south faces, but Edge, in a development which shows that he did not fully appreciate the Roman character of Hansom's and Welch's design, introduced the Renaissance feature of balustrades below windows around the north end.[38] At that end, Edge also extended the east and west peristyles by two columns and introduced an octastyle portico.[39] In order to observe correct intercolumniation around the cella, it was then necessary to introduce an additional column either side of the organ recess. These two inner columns of the north portico, still there when the ivory model now in the City Museum and Art Gallery was made in 1889, were removed in 1891 when stone staircases giving access to the roof space were erected in the angles of the organ recess. The capitals of the corner pilasters of the cella also disappeared in the late nineteenth century. The phase of work undertaken by Edge between 1848 and 1852 included the excavation of a large new

116. Print of a Banquet held at Birmingham Town Hall to celebrate the visit of Prince Albert in 1855.

design of belated Edwardian Baroque character and repainted the interior. Hansom's and Welch's Roman coffering was thus lost, but Allom did include Roman *fasces*, standards and armour in the spectacular cartouches which still survive in the four corners of the cove.

With Birmingham Town Hall, both as conceived and as built, English public architecture moved on to a new footing. The extent to which this was so may be seen from an event which occurred after the competition and which briefly threatened to throw the project off course. The Commissioners required the young and relatively inexperienced Hansom and Welch to 'consult some architect of acknowledged reputation' as to the detail of the design.[40] They chose John Soane, the septuagenarian doyen of the profession, and went to London to obtain Soane's advice. Soane, his admiration for Roman architecture notwithstanding, can hardly have approved of a design which made quite such literal use of the temple. Moreover, in his sixth Royal Academy lecture, he had railed against porticoes set on high podia with perforations – just what was proposed for Birmingham.[41] However, he confined himself to recommending that Hansom and Welch should change their Corinthian order from that of the Temple of Castor and Pollux in the Forum to that of the round Temple at Tivoli which he loved so much. Now, the Tivoli order is one of the smallest of all surviving Roman Corinthian orders, the height and diameter of the columns being less than half the size of those of the Temple of Castor and Pollux.[42] Its experimental Republican Roman Corinthian capitals, combined with an Ionic frieze, may have been well-suited to the circular form of the Tivoli Temple and its semi-rural situation. These features, moreover, had no doubt made it appropriate for picturesque 'quotation' by Soane on an awkward corner of the Bank of England and against the Bank's low screen wall in the first decade of the century. The Tivoli example, however, would have been a wholly inappropriate precedent for a large rectangular building with a peristyle, placed on a high podium and intended to function as the principal ceremonial edifice of a burgeoning Midlands town in the 1830s. The urban character and mature Augustan order of the Temple of Castor and Pollux were what was required. The Commissioners, no doubt unsure about Soane's advice, took a third opinion from John Foster. Despite Foster's own preference for Greek Revival forms, he immediately recommended that Hansom and Welch should revert to their original proposal to use the Temple of Castor and Pollux as their model. Soane's response, in other words, had betrayed the ideology of an architect trained in the highly eclectic spirit of later eighteenth-century Italy. He had failed to grasp the generative point of a design conceived by an architect inspired by younger men who had experienced Roman architecture afresh in the post-Napoleonic period, men like his own pupil George Basevi, whose design for the Fitzwilliam Museum in Cambridge forms the subject of the next chapter of this book.

116. Print of a Banquet held at Birmingham Town Hall to celebrate the visit of Prince Albert in 1855.

room below the Great Hall and further alterations to the orchestra and audience galleries.

The interior of the Town Hall seen on the occasion of Prince Albert's visit to Birmingham in 1855 (Fig.116) embodies these changes, including Edge's distinctive bracket lights projecting from below the windows. The decoration of the Hall, too, had twice been changed since Hansom's and Welch's time. The Corinthian pilasters (again drawn from the example of the Temple of Castor and Pollux), the coved square coffers and the more elaborate pattern of three ceiling roses with border panels all belonged to their design, but they had left these plaster elements tinted in a light, neutral colour. In the mid 1840s, the Council employed John Gregory Crace to redecorate the interior. Blue, white, cream and chocolate colours were used; the borders of the coffers received an Antique continuous key pattern and the ceiling patterns of pseudo-Roman arabesques (Pompeian sources for this type of decoration can be seen in Fig.141). The changes made by Crace are evident on an elevation for the interior walls and coffers produced by a Mr Ingram in 1855 (Pl.xviib). Ingram, however, introduced a more richly coloured scheme, in line with the growing understanding of ancient polychromy in English architectural circles. The walls now simulated Sienna marble and, in line with the theory of Jacques-Ignace Hittorff, a yellow ground was used for the crimson coffers with their white and gold rosettes. The pilasters were polished to resemble enamel and their capitals bronzed. Ingram also painted the frieze with Greek anthemions, having apparently mistaken them for an ornament from the Temple of Castor. This scheme was reiterated in the redecoration undertaken by John Taylor in 1891, in which Pompeian red was introduced. In 1927, however, Sir Charles Allom replaced the ceiling with a plasterwork

Chapter 7
The Fitzwilliam Museum, Cambridge

At a time when our University is so actively exerting itself to keep pace with the spirit of improvement which pervades the whole country, we cannot but hail with satisfaction and delight the auspicious commencement of this noble work. (Gilbert Ainslie, Vice-Chancellor of the University of Cambridge, on laying the foundation stone of the Fitzwilliam Museum, 2 November 1837)[1]

Richard, Viscount Fitzwilliam, died in 1816, leaving his art collections and books to the University of Cambridge together with a substantial endowment with which a museum to house them was to be built.[2] The culture of the University in the early nineteenth century has already been touched on in earlier chapters of this book. It had produced the 'Cambridge Hellenists' at the turn of the century and gone on to foster many of the finest Roman topographers and historians of the third and fourth decades, among them Sir William Gell, Richard Burgess, Julius Hare, Thomas Babington Macaulay and Christopher Wordsworth Junior. Moreover, the scholars who were associated with the Classics tripos after its establishment in 1822 were not academically isolated from contemporary antiquarian developments in Rome. A number had been able to travel there in the years after 1815, and some were early members of the Instituto di Corrispondenza Archeologica (see Appendix B).

These are the contexts in which Classical architecture flourished in early nineteenth-century Cambridge.[3] William Wilkins's Downing College, where building began in 1807, introduced scholarly Greek Revival architecture to the University, while in 1829 Charles Robert Cockerell began the design process of the University Library, instrumental in the establishment of his own rich and eclectic Classical style. Had the clause of Fitzwilliam's will requiring construction of a new building been acted upon sooner, either of these architects might have been leading contenders for the commission and their styles adopted. Indeed, it was Wilkins who fitted up the Perse Grammar School in 1816 to provide temporary housing for the Fitzwilliam collections. Also, in 1818, he produced a plan to build the Museum in association with the possible expansion of King's College. This scheme had been forwarded for approval by the University's Senate before one of the colleges involved, Catharine Hall, withdrew from negotiations over the release of some of its land. Even the arch-Greek Revivalist Wilkins, however, thought William John Bankes's extraordinary 1820 plan to demolish Gonville and Caius College and build the Museum as a replica of the Parthenon,

minus its sculptural decoration, 'out of harmony with the neighbouring buildings' (Fig.117).[4]

It was, in fact, the inability of the initial Syndicate, set up in 1816, to find a suitable site and then, having purchased land on Trumpington Street south of Peterhouse, to buy out its eight lessees, which delayed the whole project until the mid 1830s when the Perse trustees asked for the return of their premises. In July 1834, therefore, a new Syndicate, set up to manage the project, placed an advertisement in Cambridge and London newspapers inviting architects to send in designs for the Fitzwilliam Museum. Prospective competitors were given very little information, except an intimation that the building to be erected in the centre of the site for a sum not exceeding £40,000 represented the first stage of the projected museum buildings. Plans of the site and other particulars could be seen on application to the Vice-Chancellor in Cambridge or to a Mr Parker in the Strand in London, but unfortunately no copies of these documents appear to have survived. It is clear, however, that accommodation was required for Fitzwilliam's substantial library, numismatic and applied arts collections, as well as for a large number of paintings, the Viscount's bequest to the University having been supplemented by another 300 works from Daniel Mesman. Four months were allowed for preparation of designs, but within a few weeks the Syndics must have received requests for clarification on particular points, because they issued a supplementary instruction that while accommodation for the Curator might eventually be included in an extension to the rear or sides of the building, the first phase need not contain such a residence.[5] The Syndics also extended the deadline for submission of designs to April 1835.

By the mid 1830s, many of the architects who had visited the Mediterranean in the post-Napoleonic years were in the process of establishing themselves as professionals. It is no surprise, therefore, that among the twenty-seven entrants for a competition in a situation where Classicism was likely to be sympathetically received are to be found the names of George Basevi, Arthur Hakewill, James Pennethorne, Ambrose Poynter, Lewis Vulliamy and a Mr Taylor (conceivably George Ledwell Taylor, who was endeavouring to forge a career in practice at this time). In addition, entries from Charles Heathcote Tatham and Wilkins were representative of those who had travelled at the turn of the century. William Bardwell, describing himself as educated in the same office as Cockerell

THE WESTERN SIDE OF THE MAIN STREET OF CAMBRIDGE COMPRISING A LENGTH OF ABOVT 1540 FEET AS IT WOVLD APPEAR IF CAIVS COLLEGE WERE REMOVED AND SEVERAL SVGGESTED IMPROVEMENTS CARRIED INTO EFFECT.

117. William John Bankes: Detail of a lithograph of Bankes's scheme for a replica of the Parthenon to serve as the Fitzwilliam Museum, Cambridge, on the site of Gonville and Caius College, published in 1824.

and Decimus Burton (two architects not otherwise known to have had pupillage in common), had certainly studied in Paris (perhaps under François Debret), where he had also worked for two years on the construction of Pierre Fontaine's Chapelle Expiatoire (1816–21). Another constituency of entrant included those who, like Basevi and Poynter, were founder-members of the Institute of British Architects: Thomas Bellamy, Charles Fowler and William Chadwick Mylne (here one might also include William Southcote Inman, who became a Fellow of the Institute in 1835). Among local Cambridge or East Anglian architects were evidently Philip Barnes, William McIntosh Brookes and James Walter. Thomas Rickman represented the established provincial architect, with a reputation in the University for his New Court at St John's College of 1827–31. Rickman's former pupil, Samuel Charles Fripp, was now a fellow competitor. The other architects known to have entered were Henry Duesbury, John Thomas Hitchcock, Edward Lapidge, Anthony Salvin, and two men named Cheffins and Thomas. The University appears not to have stipulated any standard format for submissions, since twenty-one architects entered using their proper names, four using Latin mottoes, and two symbols. Inman, Rickman and Taylor each submitted three different schemes and Vulliamy four, one of them consisting of a model in addition to the drawings. The entries of Bardwell and Wilkins comprised solely models. In the majority of cases, however, standard plans, elevations and sections were no doubt provided. Perspectives were clearly submitted by some entrants, both of the exterior of the proposed building from the south-east and of major interior spaces.

The records of the votes taken on 29 October 1835 on the various designs submitted, coupled to the survival of a few of the drawings or descriptions of drawings related to the competition, enable some idea to emerge of the design issues involved. All members of the University Senate were invited to participate in a two-stage voting system, first expressing their preference for four schemes and then singling out one. In the first round a total of 628 votes was cast by 157 members of the Senate. Remarkably, no fewer than 140 (90 per cent) of these men voted for Basevi, followed by 105 for Poynter and 102 for Lapidge. Bardwell had 65 votes, Rickman's scheme 'A' received 44 and Pennethorne's 27. In the second round, out of the 175 members who voted, Basevi again received the resounding endorsement of 131. Bardwell now had 31 votes, Poynter had dropped back to 9 and Lapidge to 4.[6] In one sense, the Fitzwilliam Museum competition was the most democratic of all those held in the 1830s, in that the outcome was determined by the ballot of so large a group of individuals. On the other hand, the scale of the vote in favour of Basevi (and indeed in favour of Poynter and Lapidge at the first stage) clearly points to the likelihood that the six months during which the designs had been on display in the Pitt Press (now known as the Pitt Building) were ones in which much discussion had taken place among Senate members and a sort of consensus had emerged.

Basevi's design, which will be examined in greater detail below, offered Cambridge a new form of Classicism, with its powerful Roman portico fronting a building elevated on a podium (Pl.xviii). Bardwell described his fourth-placed model in a letter of April 1836 as having a cupola, a type of architectural feature in which he said Cambridge was deficient, and it was thus surely a Classical design.[7] Of Lapidge's third-placed design nothing is known, although the architect is known to have been a typical Regency designer, able to turn his hand to different styles as required. As has been seen, his support fell away to a mere four members of Senate in the second round. The greatest mystery, perhaps, surrounds the nature of the design by Poynter which took the second highest number of votes at the first stage. His Mediterranean travels and detailed Pompeian studies notwithstanding, Poynter had turned to working in Tudor Gothic style in the 1820s when building St Katharine's Hospital and Chapel in

Regent's Park. It must be unlikely, however, that his proposals for the Fitzwilliam Museum took this form: Rickman's Gothic entry (Fig.118), the work of the architect best known in Cambridge for practising that style, received only four votes, and the dramatic decline in votes for Poynter in the second round scarcely suggests that he had the support of a Gothic party. While it is unlikely, therefore, that members of the Senate voted with any enthusiasm for Gothic designs, architects other than Rickman certainly made Gothic proposals. Salvin's entry, for example, known from a tracing by John Loughborough Pearson, was a Gothic design with a tall tower and spire (significantly, it received just ten votes at the first stage).[8] Moreover, in a letter written in August 1835, when the drawings were still on display in the Pitt Press, the parliamentarian and architectural amateur Sir Edward Cust referred to them as 'Classical (so called) or Gothic', bemoaning the fact that only one was 'adapted to the Italian School, and that one might perhaps be considered as too close an imitation of Inigo Jones projected Palace at Whitehall'. Cust backed his argument that Italian architecture was best suited to the functional and aesthetic demands of a picture gallery by offering an elevation for the Museum of his own devising.[9]

Rickman's three entries represent the range of stylistic possibilities of the 1830s, or perhaps the stylistic uncertainties of the moment. His design 'B' (see Fig.118) was a skilful pictorial manipulation of those late Gothic elements he himself had done much to popularize in the 1820s.[10] The preposterous impracticality of the tower, however, was matched by the unsuitability of the plan for the function it was intended to serve, seen most obviously in the fact that no provision was made for bookcases in the vast Medievalizing hall which was intended to serve as the library. With design 'C' (Fig.119), Rickman attempted to catch the eye of the Cambridge Greek Revival lobby, using Greek Doric porticoes and a figurative frieze outside, and Greek Ionic colonnades for the galleries inside. Surmounting the building was a huge tholos containing the library. In a gesture towards Roman detailing, however, the Corinthian order of the circular peristyle was a simplified version of that of the Temple of Castor and Pollux in the Forum. This scheme was striking but never likely to succeed and, in fact, it received the support of only three members of Senate in the first stage of voting. It was Rickman's design 'A' (Fig.120) which attracted a quarter of the Cambridge Dons at that stage. This proposal was for a Roman public building, its penetrating Corinthian portico modelled, like Robert Adam's at Osterley, on the Portico of Octavia in Rome. Indeed, it has been suggested that the three coloured perspectives which survive from this scheme, certainly in a different hand from those of schemes 'B' and 'C', were drawn by Rickman's chief draftsman J. A. Bell, who had returned from Rome himself only the year previously.[11] Perhaps the fact that this scheme was given the alpha denotation may be taken to imply that Rickman considered it the most serious contender,

although the plan, which placed four ranges around an open courtyard, would surely have occupied far greater depth of site than the University possessed.

Similarly Roman in its forms but impractical in its functioning was the entry of J. J. Hitchcock (Figs 121 and 122). Hitchcock proposed a double-depth octastyle Ionic portico on a high, laterally approached podium, and wings linked to the central block by caryatid porticoes. Behind the front was a great rotunda against the inner walls of which a pair of staircases curved up to the first floor. The presence of the rotunda, however, created redundant spaces which this architect was unable to resolve, where it was juxtaposed with the west room of the library (in fact the whole of the ground floor was given

119. Thomas Rickman:
Perspective of competition
entry C for the Fitzwilliam
Museum, 1834–5.

120. Thomas Rickman:
Perspective of competition
entry A for the Fitzwilliam
Museum, 1834–5.

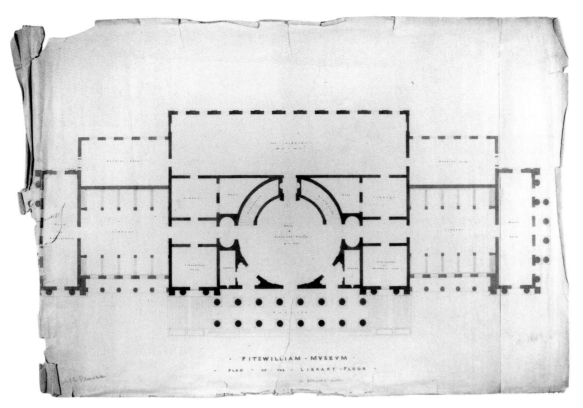

121. J.J. Hitchcock: Plan of competition entry for the Fitzwilliam Museum, 1834–5.

122. J.J. Hitchcock, Perspective of competition entry for the Fitzwilliam Museum, 1834–5.

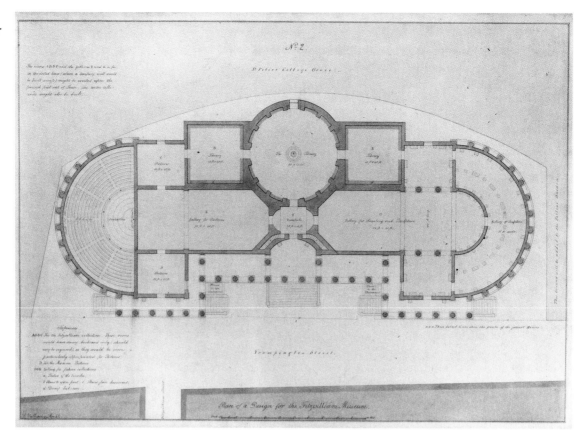

123. Lewis Vulliamy: Plan of competition entry no.2 for the Fitzwilliam Museum, 1834–5.

124. Lewis Vulliamy: East elevation and longitudinal section of competition entry no.2 for the Fitzwilliam Museum, 1834–5.

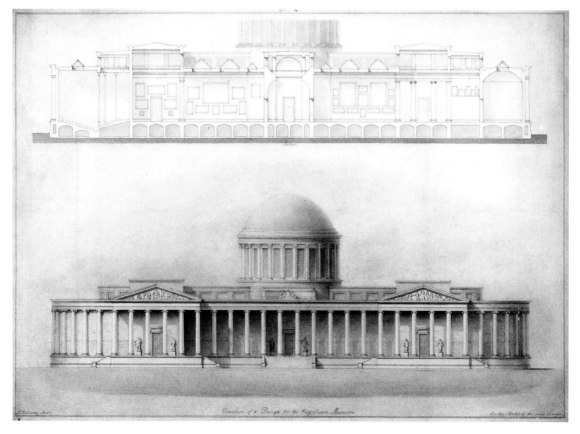

over to the library). There were further indeterminate spaces on the first floor. On grounds of practicability, therefore, the design was never likely to succeed and it can have received only 4 or 1 votes, or none at all (unless Hitchcock was the anonymous architect whose motto was '*Exitus acta probat*', in which case he received 21 votes). The circular entrance hall was nonetheless an impressive feature, horizontally rusticated below and with coupled Corinthian columns at first-floor level. The shallow coffered dome would have provided an unexpected feature, since it did not project above the roofline outside. The principal picture gallery was to have been tunnel-vaulted with deep penetrations in the vault to admit light.

The four entries of Lewis Vulliamy were quite the opposite of Hitchcock's, in that they display a superb control of planning. Vulliamy might be thought of as the closest fellow competitor of Basevi in terms of his age (he was three years older), his educational and his travel experiences (a pupil of Robert Smirke, he had visited Italy as the Royal Academy's Travelling

Student between 1818 and 1821). Three of Vulliamy's submissions were variants of a single scheme, but the fourth was substantially different. Of design no.1, only a sheet with the east elevation and longitudinal section survives. Design no.2 has an identical sheet but also a plan (Figs 123 and 124). Moreover, it was accompanied by a model and thus probably represented Vulliamy's preferred option. The plan shows a brilliant use of curvature at both the south end (where the architect proposed an odeon) and the north (a sculpture gallery). On the west, where the site projected, Vulliamy placed a circular library. The single-storey exterior was unified by a continuous Ionic order, colonnaded across the east front and, after paired hexastyle porticoes, attached around the semi-circular south and north ends. In design no.1 the lateral porticoes were reduced to two columns *in antis*, and a hexastyle portico was introduced centrally. Both designs had a dome of tall hemispherical shape over the library, the dome placed on a drum with attached peristyle in the case of design no.2. In design no.4, which

125. *Lewis Vulliamy: East elevation and longitudinal section of competition entry 3 for the Fitzwilliam Museum, 1834–5.*

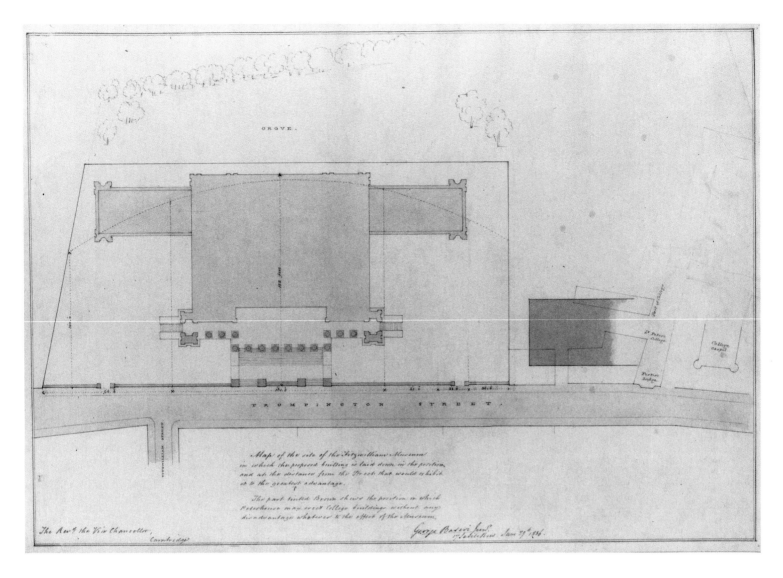

126. *George Basevi: Site plan for the Fitzwilliam Museum, 29 June 1836.*

survives in plan only, Vulliamy abandoned the idea of the unifying order in favour of a grander central portico. A dominant central portico is also a feature of design no.3, but in this quite differently conceptualized scheme the architect eliminated all curvature from the outline of the building (Fig.125). The dome now stood over a central square hall with the theatre to the west of it. Subsidiary octagonal cupolas were introduced over lateral picture galleries and the cross axis was terminated by belvederes.

Vulliamy's designs, all of which are clearly thought out with regard to the provision of space and beautifully drawn up, attracted only ten votes at the first stage, six going to design no.2 with its model. A possible reason for the low esteem in which these eminently buildable designs were held lies in the nature of the architectural ideas, which have a decidedly later eighteenth-century character. Reminiscences of semiprivate country-house sculpture galleries and other such spaces, some with small-scale Pantheon domes, might perhaps

have put off Cambridge academics who, on the basis of their enthusiastic endorsement of Basevi's design, were evidently looking for a powerful Roman public building for their new museum. Even Vulliamy's inclusion of a great drum, like that of James Gandon's Four Courts building in Dublin, did not attract them. In this context it is noteworthy that older architects who entered the competition did not fare well in general. Wilkins's model received just ten votes, while Tatham got only one. Tatham, who had slipped out of practice (and into debt) by 1835, is likely to have entered the design for the museum he had submitted voluntarily to the University in 1827.[12] If that was indeed the case, then his hypothetical design will hardly have embodied the brief stipulated by the University in 1834. Tatham's elevation was based on the archaeological source of the Corinthian Library of Hadrian in Athens (with the addition of a small tetrastyle portico). However, its unfenestrated and rusticated walls gave it something of the brutality of his mausoleum at Trentham, a work designed

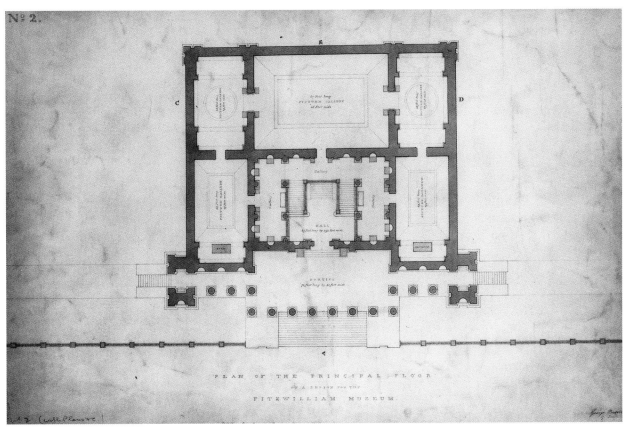

127. *George Basevi:
Competition plan of
principal floor of the
Fitzwilliam Museum,
1834–5.*

128. *George Basevi:
Competition east elevation
of the Fitzwilliam Museum,
1834–5.*

129. Paolo Brognoli: Frontispiece of 'Nuovo Guida di Brescia', published in 1826 and a possible source of information for George Basevi on the Flavian Capitolium at Brescia.

two decades previously and perhaps inspired by French Revolutionary design. Other entries which may have smacked of slightly outdated architecture also fell by the wayside. In his design, Henry Duesbury used elements of Soane's distinctive language, basing his elevation on the Lothbury front of the Bank of England but adding a porte-cochère which resembled the loggia in front of 13 Lincoln's Inn Fields.[13] William Inman was another architect who may have deployed Soanean ideas in at least one of his three competition entries (he was a pupil of Soane's late eighteenth-century pupil Thomas Chawner, and also a Royal Academy student).

While the Soane idiom itself did not meet with any success in the competition for the Fitzwilliam Museum, it was nevertheless the Soane office that produced the winning architect. George Basevi had studied at Lincoln's Inn Fields from 1810 to 1816, where he had doubtless imbibed Soane's insistence on the importance of Antique precedents. However, as has been seen in Part I of this book, the Rome he had reached in 1816 was in neither physical nor conceptual terms the same as the Rome which Soane had visited forty years before. Basevi returned equipped to produce a more literally Roman architecture than his master, who had already been politely ignored when asked to comment on the literal version of the Temple of Castor and Pollux which Hansom and Welch were proposing for Birmingham Town Hall. Moreover, like Hansom and Welch, though in the very different circumstances of a University, Basevi found hugely enthusiastic patronage for his ideas.

Basevi's approach to the awkward site, in contrast to the curvature deployed by Vulliamy, was to fill the central part with a cubic building. At its north and south extremities the

site had a depth of 100 ft from east to west, with the elliptical bow projecting to a maximum 60 ft further westwards. The outline can be seen on a plan prepared by Basevi in 1836 (Fig.126). By the time this plan was prepared, however, the architect was persuading the Syndicate to negotiate with Peterhouse to extend the maximum depth of site further to the west, so that the building would be placed 'at the distance from the street that would exhibit to the greatest advantage'.[14] When the 1836 site plan is compared with the plans and east elevation Basevi had submitted in the competition the previous year, it is evident that he had modified his initial concept, which had been a direct approach to the principal entrance between large retaining stylobates which projected out to meet Trumpington Street (Figs 127 and 128). The dominant feature of the design from the outset, however, was the octastyle portico, with its lateral extensions of two columns brilliantly offsetting the fact that the building faced the relatively narrow Trumpington Street and would never be seen front-on from a distance. While Basevi might have derived this idea generically from Robert Smirke's design for the British Museum, it is possible that he had a specifically Roman archaeological source in mind. Robert Willis commented that the design was 'said to have been suggested, at least so far as the arrangement of the portico is concerned, by the remains of a Roman building discovered at Brescia in 1820'.[15] As a member of the 1835 Fitzwilliam Museum Syndicate, Willis was ostensibly well placed to know this. The Vespasianic Capitolium at Brescia, however, had not been excavated until shortly after Basevi had returned from Italy (from 1822, in fact) and, in any case, it cannot be established with certainty that the architect had visited Brescia during his travels in northern Italy. Moreover, the publication of a report and plan of the Roman remains in the *Annali dell'Instituto di Corrispondenza Archeologica*, to which Willis referred, did not occur until 1839, well after the frontispiece of the Fitzwilliam Museum was conceived. Finally, Willis and Basevi are likely to have discussed the design of the building when they were seated adjacently at the banquet held in Pembroke College Hall to celebrate the laying of the first stone and, although Willis composed his account of the building late in life, he would surely have recalled if Basevi had mentioned explicitly so specific a source.[16] It is perfectly possible, however, that information about the excavation had circulated among members of the Instituto in Cambridge prior to 1839. Moreover, a part-plan and a perspective were available respectively in Giovanni Labus's *Antichi Monumenti Scoperti in Brescia* of 1823 and Paolo Brognoli's *Nuovo Guida di Brescia* of 1826 (Fig.129), and Basevi could have had access to either of these sources.

Whether or not Basevi's inspired use of a laterally extended portico came from the Roman Capitolium at Brescia, it is certain that dominant elements of the principal elevation were drawn from specific Roman precedents. The column shafts, capitals, plain frieze and cornice of the Corinthian order

chosen by Basevi are all similar to those of the Pantheon, while the architect appears to have taken the soffit under the architrave from the Hadrianeum (Fig.130). In 1837, the sculptor William Grinsell Nicholl agreed to 'carve in Portland stone the Corinthian Column and Pilaster Capitals for the outside of the Fitzwilliam Museum in the style of the Pantheon Portico at Rome as exhibited by your designs'.[17] The transverse section of the competition entry (Fig.131) shows that the architect initially intended the portico to have a coffered arch within it spanning the central three intercolumniations in a manner similar to reconstructions of the Pantheon, not the flat coffered ceiling as built. Basevi retained this idea for some time, because there are detailed construction drawings in the Museum's library showing how the arch was to be turned in brick. At the competition stage, the side and rear external elevations of the building were to have tall windows set below relieving arches at ground level and blind walls with a trio of niches above (Fig.132). As built, however, the north, south and west elevations of the Museum received ground-floor windows crowned with entablatures and central pediments derived from the upper part of the Arch of Hadrian, which had appeared in Willey Reveley's third volume of Stuart's and Revett's *The Antiquities of Athens* in 1795 (Fig.133). The drawings on which this variation appears are consistent in format with Basevi's competition entries, but they are not signed

or numbered in the same way. They also show the 4½ ft extension to the height of the attic over the Entrance Hall, introduced by Basevi in early 1837 after his appointment as architect. Basevi explained this change by saying that the height of the attic in his original 'geometrical elevation' was only intended as an indication of a feature which would have to be worked out 'in the Perspective', from which it may be inferred that, unlike Rickman, he had included no eye-catching exterior perspective among his competition drawings.[18] The comparison of the two south elevations shows the modification made by Basevi to the front podium and steps to the portico, once the site had been extended and the pile moved westward. After the competition, the architect also removed the anachronistic festoons which hung between the paired pilasters, and visually strengthened the attic above the entablature around the building. These changes were presumably introduced once it became clear that the University had no immediate intention to add wings to the building, since they make it even less clear how the wings hypothesized on Basevi's site plan (see Fig.126) could have been attached.

Basevi's competition drawings show his initial intentions for the interior of the Museum (Fig.134 and see Fig.131). Entry from the portico was by four steps into a relatively small hall, 32½ × 27 ft. To left and right were flights rising to the first floor with simple balustrades, while straight in front was a

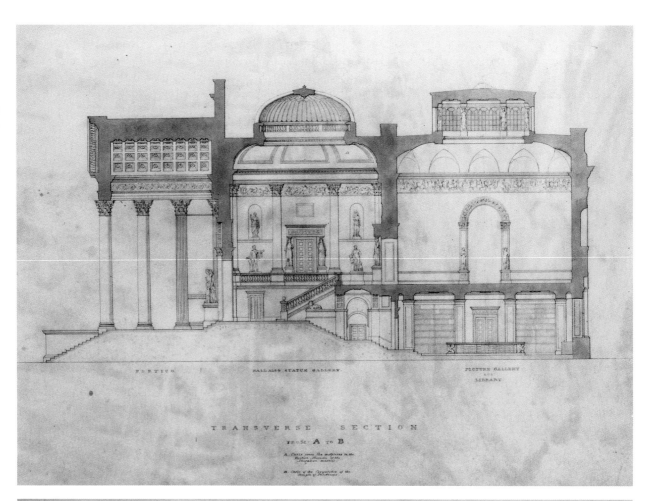

131. George Basevi:
*Competition transverse
section of the Fitzwilliam
Museum, 1834–5.*

132. George Basevi:
*Competition south elevation
of the Fitzwilliam Museum,
Cambridge, 1834–5.*

TRANSVERSE SECTION
FROM A TO B

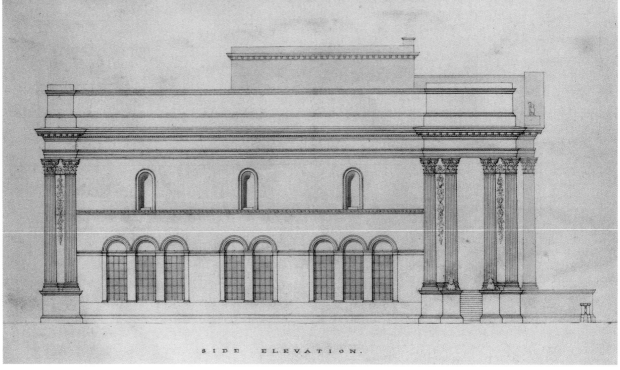

SIDE ELEVATION.

single flight of steps leading down into the Library, which occupied the whole of the west side of the building. From a lobby outside the Library, access could be gained to the medals, coins and bronzes gallery to the south, or Etruscan vases and other terracottas to the north. At first-floor level the Hall was more spacious, because it incorporated the areas above the ground-level Keeper's Office and Porter's Room (right image on Fig.134). Basevi planned for one large and four subsidiary galleries at first-floor level, the principal room having a coved rectangular lantern and the subsidiary spaces domes and barrel vaults on piers.

The perspective drawing of the Hall (left on Fig.134) is misleading, in that it is taken not 'from the Entrance Door', as the architect indicated, but from an impossible viewpoint halfway up the inner face of the entrance wall. By this means the architect distracted attention from the small distance of 13 ft which lay between door and foot of stairs. The space of the Hall was broken up at first-floor level by a grid of columns arranged on a Greek cross pattern: pairs were attached to all four inner walls, while the north and south pairs dividing off the stair area from the upper landings were freestanding. The columns, which Basevi proposed should be built in Bath stone, were to be of the same Pantheon Corinthian order as the columns of the portico. From the inner entablature sprung a coved ceiling and domical skylight, with a simple balustrade and a surround enriched with eagles and decorative carving. The capitals of the first-floor columns, corner piers and paired pilasters on the east and west walls were linked by a figurative

frieze. Basevi evidently intended from the outset that this frieze should consist of plaster casts of the Phigaleian marbles in the British Museum, purchased after their discovery at Bassae by Cockerell and his travelling companions. In 1837 Basevi persuaded the Syndics to buy casts of the Phigaleian marbles, and in the same year they bought casts of the Elgin marbles, already envisaged by the architect for the frieze of the principal picture gallery in his competition drawings. Basevi's Entrance Hall included further pieces of decorative frieze over the three doorcases flanked by caryatids which opened into the picture galleries, but otherwise the upper walls were interrupted only by twelve simple round-headed niches for statues. The landings over the Keeper's Office and Porter's Room had ceilings of large single coffers with central rosettes, while the floor of the Hall comprised a pattern of stone octagons inset with small diamond-shaped pieces of marble.

In its overall conception, therefore, the Fitzwilliam Museum as selected in 1835 by Cambridge academics was essentially a very Roman building.[19] Whether or not the disposition of the frontispiece depended on the newly discovered Flavian Capitolium at Brescia, it was certainly the Pantheon from which Basevi had drawn many of the details of his design: the order, both for the exterior and for the Entrance Hall, the arch beneath the portico, perhaps even the idea of a single lantern over the Hall like an oculus. The most obvious architectural feature to have been drawn from a 'Greek' monument came, in fact, from the Arch erected at Athens by Hadrian in about

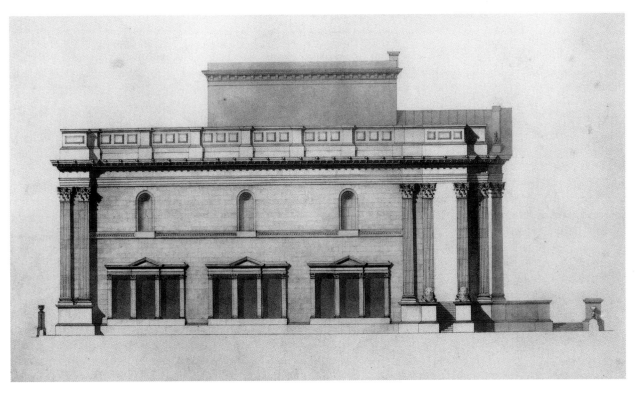

133. George Basevi: Remodelled south elevation of the Fitzwilliam Museum, probably dating from February 1837.

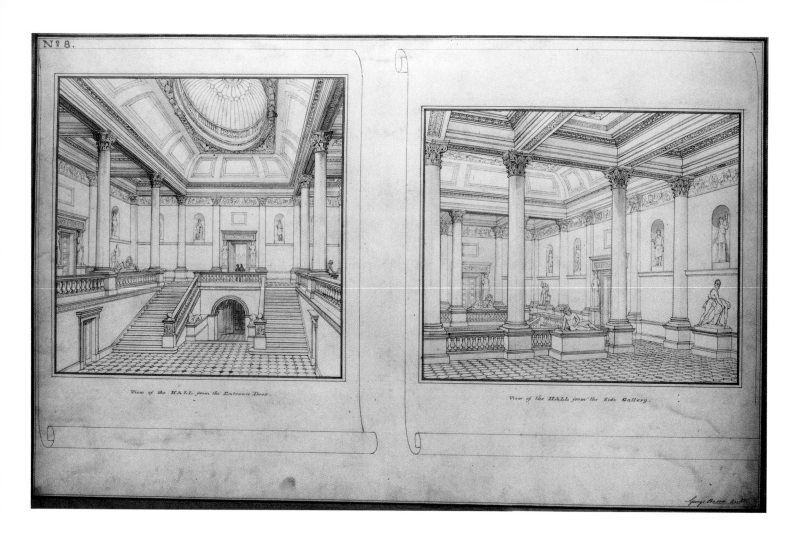

134. George Basevi:
Competition perspectives
for the Entrance Hall of
the Fitzwilliam Museum,
1834–5.

AD 131. Furthermore, although in 1843 Basevi specified that the columns of the lower galleries should be of the Greek Doric order, drawings in his own hand in the Museum's library confirm that it was he who introduced the bases and transformed the order to its present Roman Doric form. The proposed use of casts of the marbles from Bassae and from the Parthenon for the friezes around the Hall and Picture Gallery was, of course, an explicitly Grecian element in the design, but one which was counterbalanced in the competition drawings by copies of famous Graeco-Roman statues which everyone knew were to be seen in the great Italian museums: Niobe from the Uffizi and the Farnese Hercules flanking the principal entrance, for example, or the Apollo Belvedere and the Capitoline Dying Gladiator in the Hall. One further respect in which Basevi looked to Greek architecture was in his perception that Greek temples always enjoyed elevated positions, but even in comparing the situation of the Greek temple favourably with that of the Pantheon he qualified his criticism of the latter by acknowledging that it had been 'injured by its present low position and the vicinity of the other buildings'.[20] It is also worth bearing in mind that Basevi had made careful

studies of temple buildings in Rome, the podia of which had been cleared by the French (see Fig.36).

For a public building which the architect must have considered to be his *magnum opus*, it was never likely that Basevi would simply settle for putting into effect the design with which he had secured the commission. In February 1837, having persuaded the Syndics to alter the shape and extent of the site so that the effects of the building could be fully appreciated, Basevi made the first material changes in recommending the use of Portland Stone for the entire exterior in place of Bath stone for the east front and white brick for the others. The move towards the English equivalent of white marble for the exterior was matched by the first enrichment of the interior, as the austerity of the Baths columns in the Entrance Hall gave way to scagliola columns and a marble floor. Then, in May 1837 the Syndicate accepted a new design for the Entrance Hall in which Basevi had made major revisions (Fig.135). Evidently concerned about the level of light which the single lantern would admit, the architect now planned for three small glass cupolas over the central space. The upper landings were given a trio of transverse tunnel

vaults, each with a thermal window opening to north or south and fenestrated in the Diocletian manner. This drawing shows that Basevi was making other alterations to his design ideas, though still within the vocabulary of ancient Roman architecture. An example of this is the substitution of polygonal coffers, derived from the Basilica of Maxentius, for the Pantheon's square coffers in the arch which Basevi still intended for the vault below the portico of the Museum.

Construction of the shell of the Fitzwilliam Museum commenced in the spring of 1837 and was completed early in 1841. The external decorative features were all carved by William Nicholl, including the pedimental group representing the nine muses (to a design by Charles Eastlake) and the four lions guarding the north and south steps up to the portico. For the frieze between the capitals of the two blocks which terminate the principal elevation, Basevi realized that he needed something more forceful than the chimeras envisaged in his competition design. He therefore introduced two pairs of winged lions, similar to the griffins on the famous frieze of the Temple of Antoninus and Faustina at Rome, which he had drawn at close quarters when at Rome (Figs 130 and 136). While the

builders turned to the plasterwork of the ceiling below the portico during 1841–2, Basevi developed the ideas regarding the interior of the Museum, which he presented to the Syndicate in May 1843. In the case of the Entrance Hall there was to be a considerable enrichment of the forms, largely achieved through the use of scagliola not just for the columns but for the balustrades of stairs and landings, for the lower walls and the upper walls up to dado level. The steps themselves were to be of veined marble, and the tunnel vaults of highly enriched plasterwork with space left in the centre for fresco or oil painting.[21] The doorcases of the principal picture gallery were to be enriched with scagliola. One of Basevi's drawings shows his intentions for the rich colours of these doorcases: red marble and 'verd antique' for the dado, set between black and grey granite with gold bronzing, pink 'Egyptian Granite' for the columns and pilasters, 'Sienna Marble', 'Yellow Antique' and a bronzed laurel frieze for the entablature (Pl.xixa). When in Rome in 1819, following his visits both to Greece and to Pompeii, Basevi had told Soane that Classical polychromy 'must have been exquisite, the ancients seem to have left nothing unpainted'.[22] By the late 1830s, as has been seen

135. George Basevi: Remodelled transverse section of the Fitzwilliam Museum, probably dating from May 1837.

136. George Basevi: Study of the frieze of the Temple of Antoninus and Faustina, Rome, 1816–19. The relief panels on the east front of the Fitzwilliam Museum (see Fig.130) appear to have been derived from this source.

137. Charles Robert Cockerell: Design for the entablature and architrave soffit in the Entrance Hall of the Fitzwilliam Museum, 1847. The order, shown faintly in pencil here, has been altered to an early Greek type from that of the Roman Pantheon intended by George Basevi.

in earlier chapters, the topic had become a source of furious debate in France and elsewhere in northern Europe. Basevi, as a Fellow of the Institute of British Architects in London, is likely to have been party to the presentations on the subject made to that new professional body by Jacques-Ignace Hittorff in 1837 or by Karl Zanth the following year. The increasing strength of the black, red and gold colours Basevi proposed for the interiors of the Fitzwilliam Museum surely represents a response to this most topical of issues concerning Classical architecture.

On 16 October 1845, when carrying out an inspection of the belfry in the west tower of Ely Cathedral, George Basevi missed his footing. Having his hands in his greatcoat pockets, the architect was unable to catch hold of anything to save himself and so fell to his death on the floor of the nave below. Faced with this disaster, in December 1845 the Fitzwilliam Museum Syndics invited Charles Robert Cockerell to take over as architect 'with instructions to adhere as closely as may be to Mr Basevi's designs in carrying on the work to its completion'.[23] Three months later Cockerell, after a close examination of Basevi's surviving drawings, advanced new proposals for finishing the building. The ground-floor rooms both on the north and south side had been left wholly unfitted by Basevi. Cockerell, having considered using both these spaces for a pair of libraries, elected to place the library solely on the south side. The fireplace, bookcases and other detailing of what is today the Founder's Library were all designed by Cockerell, as shown by drawings in the Museum's library signed and dated from his office at the Bank of England, where he had succeeded Soane as official architect. The other major space concerning which Cockerell had to make decisions was the Entrance Hall, evidently still a brick shell in early 1846.[24] The dead architect would doubtless have approved when Cockerell persuaded the University to accept Scottish red granite in place of scagliola as the material for the columns of the Hall but, by 1847, Cockerell had changed Basevi's order as well (Fig.137). Thus, instead of the mature Roman Corinthian order of the Pantheon, the Hall today has a bronzed Greek order modelled on that of the Choragic Monument of Lysicrates of about 334 BC (though without the distinctive tongue-like leaves which link the flutes of the column to the acanthus leaves on the Athenian structure). Early Greek Corinthian orders, with central caulicoli which curve and touch at mid-point in the capital well below the corner volutes, were a particular favourite of Cockerell's, which he had used, for example, at the Bristol Philosophical and Literary Institution as early as 1821–3.[25] The architect's enthusiasm for this type of order may well relate to the fact that it was characteristic of what is perhaps the oldest known Corinthian column, that in the cella of the late fifth-century BC Temple of Apollo Epicurius at Bassae, the discovery of which he had himself been party to. Perhaps Cockerell felt it appropriate to use this order at Cambridge, because Basevi

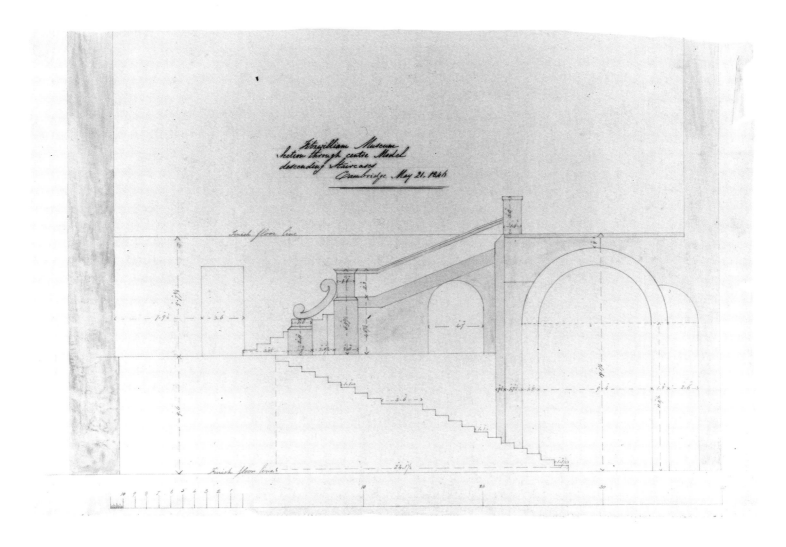

Fitzwilliam Museum
Section through centre Model
descending Staircases
Cambridge May 21. 1846

Finish floor line

Finish floor lines

himself had incorporated casts of the frieze of that Temple around the Hall, but there is no denying that it introduced an explicitly Greek architectural element to Basevi's essentially Roman atrium.

In the other design ideas introduced by Cockerell to the Entrance Hall of the Museum, he moved further away from Basevi's Antique sources. Perceiving the problem of accommodating the pair of rising staircases in the relatively confined space of the Hall, Cockerell's solution was to reverse the existing plan, placing a single rising flight in the centre of the space and a pair of stairways descending either side to the ground-floor library and galleries. The central stair thus became a much more architectonic feature in its own right, like that in William Kent's atrium at Holkham Hall or that in the vestibule of the Laurentian Library in Florence. Indeed, there is reason to suppose that it was Michelangelo's work at S. Lorenzo that Cockerell had in the back of his mind, since his design for the central stair incorporated the massive inverted Ionic volutes which Michelangelo transformed to serve as lids to the Medici tombs in the same church's New Sacristy (Fig.

138). In the decorative articulation of the Hall Cockerell also introduced complicated elements drawn from Renaissance precedents (Fig.139). Finally, he abandoned Basevi's tripledomed skylight for one large central lantern with rich plasterwork and caryatid figures around, and proposed glass painted with elaborate floral patterns for the thermal windows.

By the end of 1847, the cost of building the Museum had already reached over £90,000, more than double the amount stipulated in the 1835 competition. The Syndicate decided to suspend the decorative completion of the interiors and to move the collections in. It was not until 1870, seven years after the death of Cockerell, that the University turned to the matter of completing the Entrance Hall, the upper walls of which still consisted of exposed brickwork. In June of that year, detailed proposals were received from Matthew Digby Wyatt, accompanied by drawings which survive in the Museum's library.[26] Wyatt's ideas, involving the excessively bold proposal to create extra space in the Hall by means of a coffered apse backing out into the portico, were not taken up. A year later, a newly appointed Syndicate turned to Edward Barry,

138. Charles Robert Cockerell: Elevation of central stair for the Entrance Hall of the Fitzwilliam Museum, 1846.

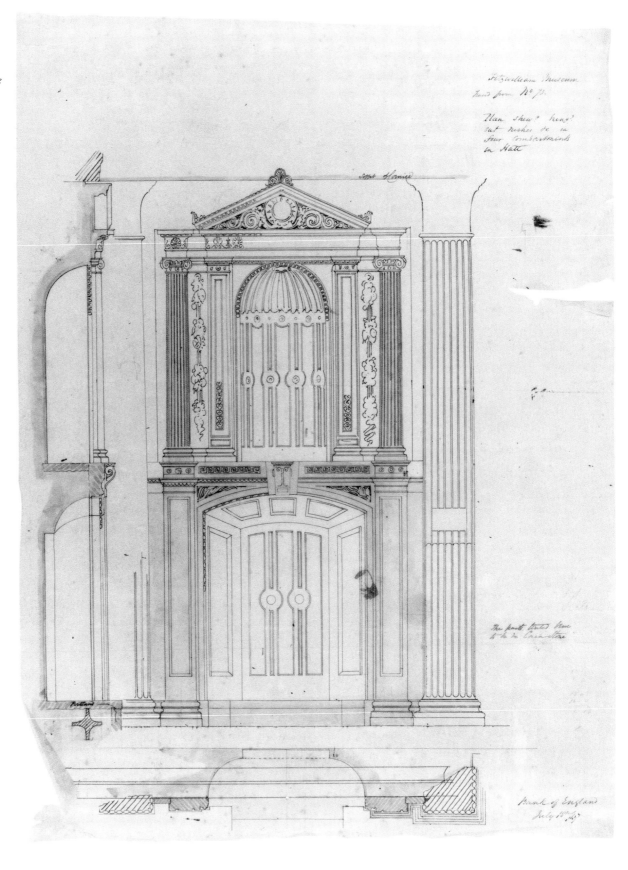

and it was that architect who, in the marvellous words of one recent authority, 'transformed the whole space by unleashing into it a rich cascade of sumptuous marbles, a molten polychromy of chocolate, ox-blood and amber' (Fig.140).[27] This High Victorian Classical effect was a far cry from the design of Basevi, to which the Syndics indicated that they wished to return in its essentials, but Barry met their concerns by reverting to paired rising flights of stairs and lowering the floor level of the Hall by 2 ft, thus increasing the sense of space by increasing the volume. Intelligently conscious of the first architect's intentions, Barry also revived Basevi's plan to place caryatids either side of the doorway leading from the hall to the principal picture gallery.[28] Finally, he designed the pavement 'of Roman mosaic in small tesserae'.[29] It is apparent that for this Barry looked back to some of the source books which would have been available to Basevi. The motifs in the prominent positions at the foot of the stairs, for example, have surely been taken from John Goldicutt's 1825 *Specimens of Ancient Decorations from Pompeii*, although with green and red colours reversed at the centre and some other modifications to the arrow corners of the border (Figs 140 and 141).

In 1817 Basevi had written modestly from Rome to his sister: 'How little I know of architecture … I stare at the Pantheon and the buildings in the Forum like an idiot, my eyes and mouth open.'[30] By the time of his premature death nearly three decades later, the architect had graced England with a building which brilliantly synthesized forms taken from those very same Roman edifices and which provided a generation of Cambridge intellectuals with a monument perfectly symbolizing their academic immersion in Roman archaeology and history. Moreover, as the Vice-Chancellor's comment made at the time the first stone was laid and quoted as an epigraph at the head of this chapter indicates, the Cambridge academics who chose this design by such a large majority thought of the building as a part of their University's contribution to the national 'spirit of improvement' of the 1830s.

Chapter 8
The Royal Exchange, London

It is only ignorance and stupidity that can be insensible to our commercial triumphs – that can fail to exult in these glories,

'Beyond all Greek, beyond all Roman fame',

that have been purchased to us by the enterprise of mercantile speculation. A fitting thing then is it, that a building, consecrated to such noble purposes should at its inauguration be honoured by the presence of our Royalty. (Leader in *The Pictorial Times* on the opening of the Royal Exchange, 1844)[1]

On 10 January 1838 the second Royal Exchange in London, built by Edward Jerman after the Great Fire, itself fell victim to a spectacular conflagration. For the second time since the destruction of the Palace of Westminster three and a half years previously, the capital city faced the difficulties inherent in rebuilding one of its major public buildings. The events which occurred between the announcement of an open competition for the design of the new Exchange in March 1839 and the laying of the first stone of its superstructure by the Consort of the young Queen Victoria in January 1842 are remembered by architectural historians chiefly for two reasons: the apparently directionless, even disreputable manner in which the competition was conducted, and the way that the process concluded with London receiving a building held to be devoid of merit and meaning instead of what all might agree, with the benefit of hindsight, would have been a masterpiece by Charles Robert Cockerell. In the light of the broader contexts suggested in this book, however, the early Victorian Royal Exchange should be reappraised. There is more to be said, both about the aesthetic aspects of the process through which William Tite's design finally came to be selected and about the political and social circumstances surrounding the design of a significant public monument in the City of London, a place with a very particular form of self-government (Fig.142).

Responsibility for matters connected with the estate of Sir Thomas Gresham, founder of the Royal Exchange in the sixteenth century, rested jointly with the Corporation of London and the Company of Mercers.[2] After the 1838 fire, the Common Council of the City set up a Special Royal Exchange Committee comprising the Lord Mayor, 10 Aldermen (including 4 Members of Parliament) and 29 Commoners. This Committee in turn delegated 12 of its members to meet with the Mercers in order to secure a new Exchange building. For its part, the Court of the Company of Mercers appointed its Master and 11 other members to form a Joint Committee with the 12 City representatives. In practice much of the work was done by ad hoc sub-committees and deputations. The structure thus created was labyrinthine, generally involving, on the City side alone, three levels of report and vote-taking.[3] A major factor in the conduct of the rebuilding was certainly the number of individuals involved, their desire to proceed democratically and the consequent frequency with which motions and amendments were proposed and voted on in committee. However, three principles were clearly established at the outset. First, it was determined that the Exchange should be rebuilt on a larger scale than its predecessor, thereby satisfying the opportunistic requests made by London merchants since the fire for a 'piazza enlarged' in which they could mingle.[4] The extra space required for this was to be created by clearance of the buildings around Sweetings Alley at the east end of the site and by incorporation of a small building between Cornhill and Threadneedle Street at the west end (Fig.143). Second, the streets around the new Exchange were to be improved, both for vehicular access and 'to render the building in all respects worthy of this great metropolis'.[5] Third, the 'Bank Buildings' designed by Robert Taylor in the 1760s, which occupied a triangular piece of land between Threadneedle Street and Cornhill to the west of the site, were to be demolished to create a new open space in the heart of the City (Fig.144). Before it could contemplate architectural matters, however, the Joint Committee had to attend to the practicalities of the displacement of freeholders caused by the scheme, the prosecution of the Act of Parliament necessary to effect it, and the raising of funds. To rebuild the Exchange, the Corporation and the Mercers' Company agreed to add in equal measure from their own funds to the £45,000 insurance money they received in order to bring the total sum up to £150,000. The identical amount required for the metropolitan improvements around the new building was secured through the agreement of the Treasury to lend the Committee the capital, a loan which was to be repaid through custom duties on coal and wine entering London in the 1850s. There was a price for the City to pay for this assistance, however, in the form of the Treasury's subsequent insistence on a right of veto over the plans for the new building. The dispute which ensued delayed the process of rebuilding and raises important questions about the relationship between the City and Westminster, which will be returned to later.

In March 1839 the Committee finally printed its 'Resolu-

142. *The Royal Exchange, London, by William Tite, 1839–44, viewed from the south-west.*

OPPOSITE
143. *George Smith: Site plan for the Royal Exchange, 9 October 1838.*

144. *James Henry Nixon: Print of Cornhill, London, in about 1834. The triangular profile of the Bank Buildings masks the view of the side of the second Royal Exchange. The new King William Street can be seen leading down to the Monument and London Bridge to the right.*

tions and Instructions to Architects'.[6] There was to be an open and anonymous competition lasting four months. Entrants were given a lithographed plan of the awkwardly shaped site (with the condemned Bank Buildings shown in outline) and a list of the accommodation required in the new building, essentially comprising three suites of rooms for Lloyds, the Royal Exchange and the London Assurance companies. For the merchants to meet there was to be the part-covered part-open court, made traditional by the preceding Elizabethan and Restoration buildings, and additional revenue to the Gresham funds was to be provided by shops. The plans, elevations and sections required were to be tinted only in Indian brown ink, and angles for the two perspectives permitted were indicated, the exterior one being from a point south-west of the proposed building. If these rules were largely derived from those for the Palace of Westminster competition, there was one very striking departure: it was specified that the building should be 'of the Grecian, Roman, or Italian style of architecture'.[7] From these conditions, and from the 1838 'Act for improving the Site of the Royal Exchange … and the Avenues adjoining thereto', architects entering the competition knew

that the City still viewed its public architecture as Classical in style and intended that the new building should be oblong or trapezoidal in plan. They also knew that its western elevation was to be the principal one, forming the monumental centre-piece of a newly emerging urban zone, already bounded on the north side by the Bank of England but now to be extended to include the area before the Mansion House. That space had itself recently been linked to the Monument and to London Bridge by King William Street, and was the proposed City site for an equestrian statue of the Duke of Wellington (see Fig.144). To most architectural minds in 1839, these formal and functional factors would have suggested the precedent of a Roman Forum, where temples, administrative buildings and heroic monuments were drawn into a unified civic space. Moreover, there were strong symbolic reasons for the Exchange and the surrounding area of the City to be considered in these terms. The building had served for generations as the City's rostrum for the pronouncement of important state affairs and as the locus for public celebrations or demonstrations. In living memory the 1802 Peace of Amiens (Fig.145) and the 1814 abdication of Napoleon had

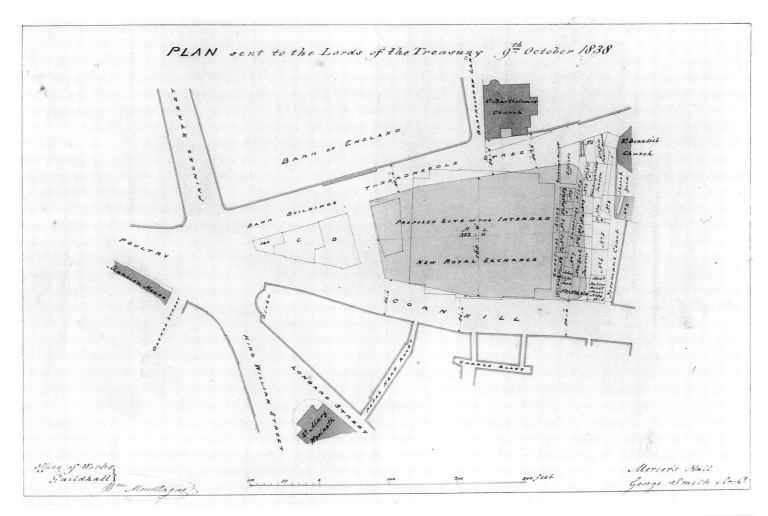

PLAN *sent to the Lords of the Treasury* 9th *October* 1838

PRINCES STREET

BANK OF ENGLAND

St Bartholomew Church

BARTHOLOMEW LANE

St Benedict Church

THREADNEEDLE STREET

BANK BUILDINGS

Church yard

C   D

PROPOSED SITE of the INTENDED
A O L
302 : O
NEW ROYAL EXCHANGE

POULTRY

Mansion House

CORNHILL

KING WILLIAM STREET

LOMBARD STREET

POPES HEAD ALLEY

CHANGE ALLEY

St Mary Woolnoth

Office of Works
Guildhall
Wm Mountague

10 50   0   100   200   300 feet

Mercer's Hall
George Smith Archt

Text below the image (engraving captions):
Escort of the City Volunteers. / Mayor's State Coach. — Sheriff. — Sword Bearer of the City. — The Rt Honble the Lord Mayor. — Mace Bearer of the City. — City Marshal. — Richmond Herald. — Norroy King of Arms. — Windsor Herald. — Trumpeters. — Major Genl of the Horse Guards. — Horse Guards. — Ward Beadle. — Serjeant Trumpeter. — Musicians of the Band. — Marshals { Knight Marshal } Marshals. — Chester Herald. — Lancaster Herald.

Published in the Art Directs June 1st 1803 by P.W Tomkins 49 New Bond Street London.

145. Print of the Royal Proclamation of the Peace of Amiens at the Royal Exchange in 1802. The Exchange was, and remains, the 'rostrum' of the City of London where important State announcements are made.

OPPOSITE

146. Thomas Leverton Donaldson: Competition first-floor plan for the Royal Exchange, 1839.

been announced there, the fiftieth Jubilee of George III had been celebrated with illuminations and fireworks outside the Mansion House in 1809 and George IV had come to the Exchange to be proclaimed King in 1820. The Royal or Imperial imagery of the Exchange was further supported by John Spiller's replacement version of Grinling Gibbons's statue of Charles II 'in the Garb and Habit of a Roman Caesar', which stood at the centre of Jerman's court and remained miraculously unscathed amid the debris of the 1838 fire.[8] But the area around the Exchange was also the centre of Whig foment at the time of the Reform Bill, with the protest meeting of merchants, bankers and traders organized in October 1831 by George Grote being held outside the Mansion House.[9] These are essential contexts which should be borne in mind when the characters of the various designs submitted in the competition and the nature of the eventual building are discussed here.

When the competition closed in August 1839, a total of thirty-eight entries had been received. In addition to the fourteen competitors previously identified, four further names may be associated with the new Exchange, including those of John Goldicutt and Harvey Lonsdale Elmes.[10] Having put the drawings on public display, the Committee decided to elect three architects as professional referees. Charles Barry, fresh from success in the competition for the Palace of Westminster, was an obvious choice but, when he declined to serve, Philip Hardwick (the architect placed first in the ballot) was joined by the third and fourth choices Sir Robert Smirke and Joseph Gwilt. In Smirke the Committee had the middle-aged arch-Greek Revivalist, but in Gwilt and Hardwick it had two men who had been in Rome between 1816 and 1819. As the author of *Notitia Architectonica Italiana*, Gwilt had shown an interest in Medieval and Renaissance Italy to counterbalance the overwhelmingly archaeological character of post-Napoleonic Rome, whilst Hardwick, whose great Greek Doric Euston Arch was nearing completion in 1839, had earlier in the 1830s signalled his willingness to draw on unfashionable sources by producing the remarkable Wren-School façade of Goldsmiths' Hall in the City. On inspecting the drawings, however, the referees found themselves unable to recommend any, both on aesthetic grounds and on practical grounds of cost and constructability. The Committee therefore asked them to select a 'First Class' of five entries which had met the functional and financial conditions of the competition and a 'Second Class' of up to three designs which had failed to satisfy the practical concerns but which were 'of peculiar merit'.[11] When, on 21

October 1839, the referees duly reported, they found that they could recommend no five 'practical, advisable and ... durable' designs which could be built without much alteration. However, they arranged in order of preference, 'referable to them as works of external art', five entries which could be constructed within budget: those of William Grellier, the Hamburg architect Alexis de Chateauneuf (working with Arthur Mee), Sydney Smirke, Thomas Henry Wyatt and David Brandon, and James Pennethorne. In the Second Class they agreed to name three 'works of very clever artists, who have produced pieces of composition in which ... stability ... and other essential matters, have been sacrificed to grand architectural features': these were the designs of Thomas Leverton Donaldson, Henry Beckley Richardson (providing a front for his master, Cockerell) and Sir John Soane's former pupil David Mocatta.[12]

The principal question raised by the competition at this stage concerned the relationship between the architectural appearance of the new Exchange and the practicalities of its function, construction and cost. The papers of Gwilt, which closely document the judgement procedure he followed, show an aesthetic preference for the designs of Donaldson, Mocatta and in particular (given Gwilt's Italianate interests) the 'very extraordinary and fine composition and drawing' of Richardson. In weighing aesthetic quality against practical function, Gwilt began to favour the former.[13] Moreover, a transcript of the notes kept by Smirke and concurred with by Hardwick shows that they, too, gave detailed consideration to the qualities and defects of Donaldson, Richardson and Mocatta.[14] For its part, the Committee was obliged as a matter of honour to award the three prizes respectively to Grellier, Chateauneuf and Mee, and Sydney Smirke, since these candidates had adhered to the Instructions to Architects. The Committee's maladroit attempts to move forward from the unfortunate outcome of the competition led to the resignation as referees first of Robert Smirke, then of Hardwick and Gwilt before, in November 1839, the Mercers' Company Surveyor George Smith was asked to work out costings for all eight selected schemes.[15] The instruction given to Smith, however, was that the designs of Donaldson, Cockerell (his authorship of the design now acknowledged) and Mocatta were the 'best and most splendid' and that one of them should be selected for construction if it could be found to be practicable.[16] Moreover, even after these three designs had eventually been discounted, one of the Mercers on the Committee, Robert Sutton Junior, argued that the architects should be compensated because their work had been 'declared far superior to those for which the 1st, 2nd and 3rd premiums had been awarded'.[17] In the light of this, the architectural character of the designs for which the referees and Committee alike had expressed their admiration should be considered next.

The designs of Donaldson and Grellier are represented by the survival of their actual competition drawings and, in

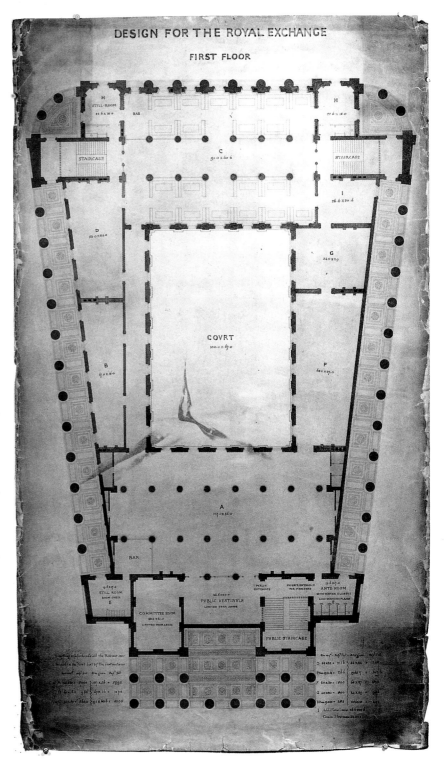

Donaldson's case, by a lithograph, published after the competition but no doubt reproducing his competition exterior perspective. Cockerell's entry is represented by at least one competition drawing and some sketches; that of Sydney Smirke by rough sketches alone; and that of Pennethorne by

a coloured perspective drawing made for the 1840 Royal Academy exhibition. Of Mocatta's design it is known only that it had a very large portico and pediments, a court which somewhat resembled Jerman's and that it was considered handsome despite a plan which Gwilt liked but Robert Smirke found incomprehensible. Chateauneuf's and Mee's scheme had a three-storeyed arcade, for which they substituted a version of the Florentine Loggia dei Lanzi when later issuing a lithograph of the external perspective.[18] No record survives of the design of Wyatt and Brandon. What can be ascertained from this evidence is that, with the exception of the 'Italian' design of Chateauneuf and Mee, the architects selected had mostly opted for the Committee's invitation to propose buildings in the 'Roman' style, since what we have are all versions of great Corinthian monuments of essentially Roman character. The most favoured design, that of Donaldson, was the work of a man at a turning point in his career. At the time of the competition Donaldson was in his early forties, a little younger than Hardwick (with whom he had overlapped at Rome in 1818–19), and in May 1839 he stepped down as principal founding Honorary Secretary of the Institute of British Architects in order to concentrate on its foreign correspondence and, presumably, on developing his career as a practitioner. In the preceding three years his French friends from the Académie de France à Rome had been working on the design of major public structures in Paris: Jean-Baptiste-Cicéron Lesueur on the reconstruction of the Hôtel de Ville and

Guillaume-Abel Blouet on the attic of the Arc de Triomphe. It is clear that France was in Donaldson's mind at this moment, for in a letter to the Exchange Committee, sent in April 1839 under the cover of the Institute, he asked the Committee whether 'there will be any objection to the principal or entrance floor being raised upon a flight of steps, like the Bourse at Paris'.[19] In the same letter, a question as to whether a tower would be strictly necessary in the new building may be interpreted as an interest in removing a traditional feature of the Exchange for which Antique precedent would be hard to find. These contexts no doubt lie behind Donaldson's decision to reach for Roman prototypes for a major public building in London, intended to be his *magnum opus*. It seems clear that his great west portico was modelled, like Basevi's at the Fitzwilliam Museum, on that of the Pantheon (Figs. 146–8). This source is suggested by a number of features: the depth of the portico (though Donaldson reduced the Pantheon's three rows of columns to two, compensating for this by introducing additional columns in the second and seventh positions of the second rank); the arched central recess framing the entrance doorway (from which George Ledwell Taylor and Edward Cresy had inferred that the central 'nave' of the portico had been vaulted); the unfluted granite columns without pedestals; and perhaps the frieze inscription, with its reference to Gresham as originator of the building. The scale of the order is naturally adapted to the specific context, but the overall dimensions are similar despite Donaldson's contraction of the

Pantheon's column diameters, intercolumniations, portico height and width. In a further skilful development he transferred the Pantheon's lateral niched recesses outside the portico in order to provide linkage to the north and south sides of his proposed Exchange. One would be able to pass beneath the Still Room or an anteroom straight into side peristyles with shops, before exiting the arcade at curved north-east or south-east corners (Pl.xx). The stylobate was another feature used by Donaldson to unify the west portico with the Threadneedle Street and Cornhill elevations. It continues around the building in the manner of a rectangular temple, rather than the circular drum of the Pantheon, of course, but Donaldson's choice of six steps might be seen as a further feature derived from restorations of the Pantheon.

The longitudinal section of Donaldson's design (Fig.149), taken together with the plan of the principal storey, shows how the portico is a prelude to the implantation of the temple idea for the major spaces of the building. The 'cella', set back behind a splendid barrel-vaulted public vestibule, is turned through 90 degrees and given a basilical section to become the Lloyds Subscription Room (A on Fig.149). Corresponding with the Corinthian capitals around the room is a rich Roman frieze of heavy foliage and mermaid or merman figures. The framed paintings indicated by Donaldson appear to be of the Queen, flanked by a merchant in Italian Renaissance dress and a toga-clad Roman. At the same level but at the east end of the court is the second large room of the complex (C), this time of single height and with Ionic colonnades. The ground floor below the mezzanine at this east end has fluted Doric columns, their baseless character the only explicitly Grecian element in the entire design. Donaldson's section also shows his treatment of the central court: a noble Roman Doric peristyle (the theme announced by the portion of frieze which appears over the great Roman gates of the west elevation) surmounted by Ionic pilasters defining bays with late fifteenth-century Italian windows.[20] In the attic above, small windows on all sides but the west alternate with reliefs of seguent griffins, taken from the Temple of Antoninus and Faustina (see Fig.136). Instead of the candelabra of the Roman temple's frieze, however, Donaldson has inserted the grasshopper of Sir Thomas Gresham's famous crest between the griffins.

Donaldson's clever adaptation of the forms of Roman temples filled almost the entire site allotted for the new Exchange building, with only a tiny south-west corner of the portico steps extending beyond its boundaries. The design suggested a modern building of Roman character to match Parisian counterparts of the Napoleonic period such as Bernard Poyet's river front of the Chambre des Députés and, of course, Alexandre-Théodore Brongniart's Bourse. However, there is little evidence of Beaux-Arts planning skill in Donaldson's handling of the difficult site. The double-height peristyles along the Cornhill and Threadneedle Street elevations left him seriously short of space on the north and south sides of the

design for the shops at ground level and the not insignificant rooms (B, D, F and G) above. Those on the north side, in particular, where a corridor linked the great west and east rooms, took on especially infelicitous trapezoidal shapes. The impracticability of the smaller shops and the dearth of fireplaces and chimneys in the design were aspects commented on by Robert Smirke, though not before he had noted the beauty of the drawings, the handsomeness of the exterior and the suitability of the design in terms of the surrounding streetscape.

The competition entry of Richardson and Cockerell can be assessed with less clarity than that of Donaldson, because sketches and presentation drawings exist relating to the design at various stages of a process which, for Cockerell, went on for ten months. One should start, however, with the only draw-

148. George Ledwell Taylor and Edward Cresy: Elevation of the Pantheon, Rome, and section of the portico, from 'The Architectural Antiquities of Rome', published in 1821.

149. Thomas Leverton
Donaldson: Competition
longitudinal section for the
Royal Exchange, 1839.

ing which was definitely submitted in competition in August 1839, the longitudinal section of the Exchange design viewed from the Cornhill side (Fig.150).[21] Among Cockerell's sketch elevations is one which relates quite closely to the west front of this section, as well as to its more developed tower form and central high balustraded attic; and an early plan sketch for the principal floor is probably also coincident with the design at this stage (Figs 151 and 152). By contrast to Donaldson, Richardson and Cockerell placed both the large rooms for Lloyds at the east end of the site, separated by an ingenious cross arcade at ground level. The arcade was the site for the majority of the shops in the design and was, perhaps, an allusion to Sweetings Alley (the street which was to be lost through its incorporation into the enlarged site for the Exchange). The situation of these major rooms at the east end of the site caused the architects to think in terms of an important entrance from Cornhill into the centre of the court. At the west end, the court was accessed by a deep single passageway under small offices for the Royal Exchange and London Assurance Companies, rather belying the power of the frontispiece. It is not possible to ascertain from the visual evidence whether or not the Cornhill or Threadneedle Street façades were intended to have colonnades: the elevation suggests that they were but, as the columns appear almost attached and on a podium in the same way as those of the west front, it is hard to imagine how shops additional to those in the arcade could have been accommodated behind. It is also difficult to say to what extent the subsidiary Doric order, hinted at in the suggestion of triglyfs in the elevation and apparently supporting a shallow west front balcony in the section, formed part of the 1839 competition entry. Certainly the full integration of this subsidiary Doric order, praised by Cockerell's biographer for its brilliant uniting of court, exterior and urban context (in the way it related to the height of Soane's screen wall at the Bank of England), had not yet developed in the design, since the

competition section (see Fig.150) shows that an Ionic order without pedestals was used around the court.[22] As has been seen above, it was Donaldson's competition entry which quite emphatically linked the Doric order of the court to the west elevation of the building, a point Cockerell may have taken note of when later revising his design.

The sketched west elevation for the 1839 competition entry of Richardson and Cockerell suggests that the sources Cockerell would describe six months later were already present. Foremost among these was Andrea Palladio's prefectorial Loggia del Capitaniato in the Piazza dei Signori at Vicenza. Curiously, however, Cockerell cited this building as the source for his giant Corinthian and subsidiary Doric orders when the precedent actually has neither. The principal order in Palladio's building, which is attached, has a distinctly Composite character and the arches of the loggia spring from imposts, which Cockerell evidently deemed to be Doric. In Palladio's design the Doric frieze is present only in pairs of triglyfs, used as corbels to entablature-like window-sills on the floor above, a mannerism entirely different from Cockerell's intention to bind his building together with a continuous Doric frieze at first-floor level. Although Cockerell had visited Vicenza in 1816, there is no evidence that he paid particular attention to the Capitaniato. As the building was not illustrated by Palladio in *I quattro libri*, it is likely that the British architect's source was Ottavio Bertotti Scamozzi's *Le fabbriche e i disegni di Andrea Palladio*, which does describe the minor Doric order under the loggia on the backs of the piers and also envisaged the building extended from its actual three to a hypothetical seven bays. However, Cockerell also specified three Antique prototypes for Corinthian columns supporting broken-forward entablatures: the Library of Hadrian in Athens, the frontispiece of the Forum of Nerva (the Forum Transitorium) in Rome and the triumphal arches of the same city. Cockerell thought of the Hadrianic building as a stoa or marketplace (an appropriate

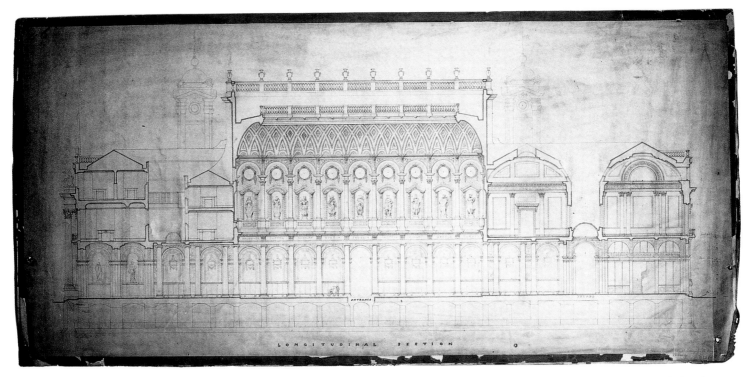

150. Charles Robert Cockerell: Competition longitudinal section for the Royal Exchange. This is the only drawing to survive which was certainly submitted by Cockerell (albeit under the cover of his pupil Henry Richardson) in the 1839 competition.

151. Charles Robert Cockerell: Sketch for the west elevation for the Royal Exchange competition, 1839.

symbolism, perhaps, for the Exchange) and of the forum as part of a Temple of Nerva, but, in their surviving and hypothetically restored states, neither had the penetrations of the triumphal arch. If the idea of the extended arch was central to Cockerell's thinking, however, it had not been fully worked out at the moment of the 1839 competition. In the elevation (see Fig.151) only a single arched opening was intended and horizontality of the triumphal arch was countered by a rather underplayed pediment between two small obelisks with finials at the centre of the attic. Set well back from this frontispiece rose the broken pediment of the attic around the central court, a huge thermal window cut into it. Examination of the section (see Fig.150) shows that this window could have lit nothing but the void between the coving around the court and the attic designed to hide it. Below the elongated diamonds of the cove were bays divided by Corinthian pilasters. Statues of monarchs stood in alternately segmental and triangular broken-pedimented niches surmounted, except on the east side, by circular windows with swags, set into diapered wall surfaces rising to foliage-filled spandrels.

On the basis of Richardson's and Cockerell's section, the only drawing certainly submitted to the Committee and to public scrutiny in 1839, it is hard to reach definitive conclusions. That the architects, perhaps through their joint operation, might have failed to integrate their eclectic range of

sources fully, seems to be suggested by the fact that the submitted section is much less worked up than, for example, Donaldson's equivalent and other drawings, which took full advantage of the invitation to shade given in the instructions (see Fig.149). In his notes, Robert Smirke commented on the apparent haste with which the Richardson/Cockerell scheme had been prepared. Moreover, the orthogonal nature of the elevation sketch shows a misalignment of central pediment and apex of attic above which, if presented in the competition west elevation, might have indicated to the Committee a failure to come to terms with the awkward shape of the site. Gwilt, in fact, noticed inconsistency between the plan and other drawings, though in what respect is unknown. Furthermore Smirke, in addition to criticizing the inconvenience of the shops and other rooms and the impracticability of the decoration, voiced a serious concern in pointing out that the 86-ft high coved walls around the court would produce a damp and gloomy effect at ground level within it. Cockerell noted that this dimension was almost identical to its equivalent in the Paris Bourse which he had visited in 1824, and one might wonder whether the cove was partly inspired by the cupolas covering the loggias around the principal space of the Bourse.

Unlike Donaldson and Cockerell, the first-class first prize-winner of the 1839 competition, William Grellier, is not

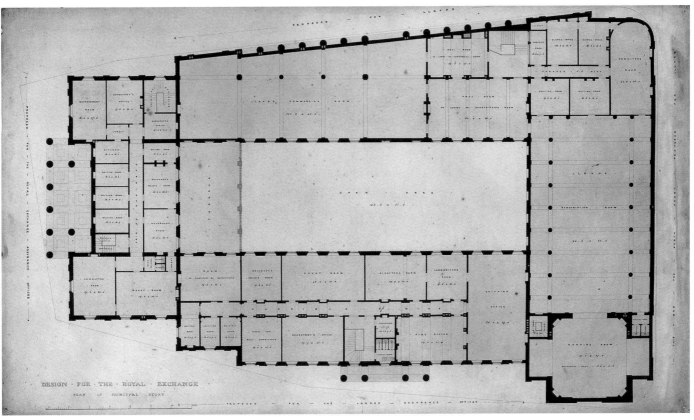

DESIGN · FOR · THE · ROYAL · EXCHANGE
PLAN · OF · PRINCIPAL · STORY

THE ROYAL EXCHANGE, LONDON

199

known to have enjoyed the benefits of Mediterranean travel, although he had entered the Royal Academy Schools in 1824 and won both the silver and the gold medals – the latter in 1829 for a British Senate House design. His Exchange entry (Fig.153) had something of the austerity of Donaldson's approach, with its unfluted giant Corinthian order (here from the Temple of Castor and Pollux) and plain entablature, but there is little else temple-like or archaeological about the design. Each of the four sides was treated quite distinctly: an attached giant Corinthian order along Threadneedle Street, a central entrance with a tetrastyle portico on Cornhill, a severe Italianate east front. Grellier's elevations were quite Palladian in form, with their rusticated ground floors, pedimented windows at piano nobile level, and attics above with surmounting balustrades. A former pupil of the Mercers' Company surveyor, George Smith, Grellier's approach to the complexities of the building's functional requirements appears, in fact, to have been laudably pragmatic. He treated the plan as a series of interlocking rectangles around the court (Fig.154). This enabled him to avoid awkwardly shaped offices along the south side of the building altogether, whilst the trapezoidal shape of the Lloyds Commercial Room was cleverly concealed by a screen of two piers and two columns. The central court was long and narrow, its elevational treatment again Italianate, featuring Tuscan arcades with alternating triangular and segmental windows above. Like Richardson and Cockerell, Grellier chose to situate the Lloyds Subscription Room at the east end of the site, where it does not enjoy good access. In the perspective view (see Fig.153) Grellier strangely played down the enormous square tower which featured at the south-east corner of his design and which would certainly have been a dominant factor in the view from this point to the south-west. It is almost as though the perspective was offering the Committee a more Antique alternative to the asymmetrical power of the full design.

Placed third in the first class was Sydney Smirke, whose ideas for the Exchange can be judged only from very preliminary sketches. These show that he intended to force a huge dipteral temple onto the site, leaving the cella open as the central court and a considerable portion of the site vacant (Fig.155). Given the way in which Smirke's aesthetic had been moulded by his older brother, it is very striking that almost all potential Grecian elements of such a design were suppressed in favour of Roman. The decastyle Corinthian portico (the 4 ft 8-in diameter of the columns made them larger than Donaldson's) was approached by a flight of steps to the central six bays, between podium returns. The relative narrowness of this central flight was to be emphasized by projecting stylobates bearing figurative statuary in front of the third and eighth columns. The three central intercolumniations, however, were open right through to the court, in the manner of the Portico of Octavia at Rome, famously introduced to Britain by Robert Adam at Osterley. The temple was to be raised on a podium 10 ft in height, each of the eighteen columns in the Cornhill flank standing on a rusticated pedestal.[23] Two small sketches on the right of Fig.155 show slightly more inventive alternative elevations for the east façade. Smirke's design, if indeed his competition entry was a version of these sketches, was probably the most literal version of a Roman temple and also demonstrated the problems inherent in being overly literal. The columns mark out a grid plan for the west end of the building, but the whole scheme begins to peter out as it progresses east to where the major rooms were to be situated.

Last placed of the five candidates in the first class was James Pennethorne, whose design is known only from a full-colour perspective shown at the Royal Academy in 1840 (Pl.XXI). The fact that the angle of view is more or less that required for the external perspective in the competition suggests that this vibrant image, although not seen by Committee or public in 1839, does represent the western aspect of the architect's entry. As Pennethorne's biographer has remarked, the frontal design was largely 'an essay in the style of the early Roman Empire which he had so admired in Italy'.[24] The deep portico's high podium and grand sweep of steps between retaining stylobates with four statues recall Pennethorne's own image of the 'Graecostasis' in his 1825 Forum restoration (see Fig.77). That this precedent was in his mind is further suggested by the flight of steps which appears to cut through the podium to the right side of the portico. As has been seen in Chapters 2 and 4, the lateral steps to the podium of the Temple of Castor and Pollux had been discovered in the excavations of 1816–18 and, although it is now known that the Temple had a rostrum at the front, the restoration of Taylor and Cresy had included both lateral and frontal steps in the manner evidently employed by Pennethorne (see Figs 46 and 47). However, the architect was not as systematically Roman as some of his fellow competitors. The order used appears to be a version of the very early Corinthian of the Monument of Lysicrates in Athens and the shallow triangularity of the pediment is a further Grecian feature. Moreover, Pennethorne introduced a huge tower just behind his portico, an element no doubt intended to complement City church towers such as St Bartholomew-by-the-Exchange, St Michael Cornhill (both included in Pennethorne's perspective) and especially, given the character of the design, Nicholas Hawksmoor's St Mary Woolnoth. It is possible, however, that Rome was again in the architect's mind, since there is a similarity between the mass of the tower and that of the Torre delle Milizie surmounting the Forum of Trajan, popularly said (regardless of its Medieval date) to have been the edifice from which Nero watched Rome burn. Of Pennethorne's plan for the Exchange nothing can be said, except that its largely unfenestrated walls must have created difficulties with internal light arrangements. It was also commented by George Smith that Pennethorne had made very little provision for shops and, despite the splendour

of his aesthetic ideas, the scheme was probably never seriously considered by the Committee because of its impracticability.[25]

In February 1840 the Committee met to discuss Smith's assessment of all eight premiated schemes for the new building. Significantly, the three architects of the best 'designs', Donaldson, Cockerell and Mocatta, had all co-operated and provided detailed estimates. Grellier and Smirke had half-heartedly offered some general figures and the other three had declined to produce further information, whereupon the Committee removed all five first-class schemes from further consideration. In Smith's view, the eight schemes had all been seriously underestimated, the last thing the Committee had hoped to hear. However, his views on the merits of the three best designs and their authors did offer a way forward. He found that Donaldson's scheme 'will never answer internally or externally' and had nothing positive to say about Mocatta's; but Cockerell's, although spoiled in his opinion by the cove overhanging the courtyard, could be erected 'as a Creditable Building to the country and convenient to the public', and he added that the Committee would not find 'a more honourable or competent man than the architect of this plan'.[26] Despite the support of the City men Richard Taylor and Henry Elmes, Donaldson was then discounted, closely followed by Mocatta. However, there was little enthusiasm for Cockerell either, now that he was the sole survivor by default. Although the Committee voted not to exclude him altogether, a motion to adopt the external form of his design with internal rearrangements to be managed by Smith was immediately amended by a resolution asking Cockerell to resubmit in limited competition with five other architects, namely the three original referees, Charles Barry and William Tite (President of the Architectural Society). Although Tite had previously declined to become involved with the Exchange competition when asked by the Committee to assist Smith with his report, he now accepted. Since Hardwick, Robert Smirke, Gwilt and Barry all refused

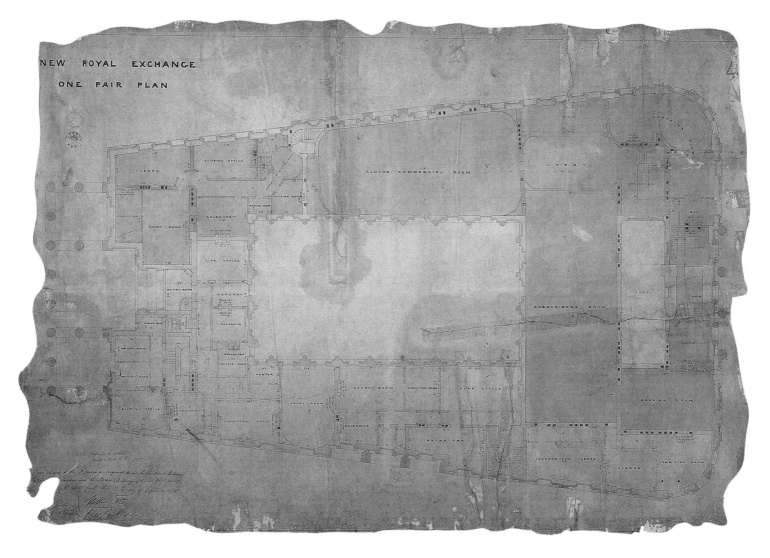

NEW ROYAL EXCHANGE
ONE PAIR PLAN

156. William Tite: Contract Plan 4 of the Royal Exchange, 1840.

to participate, the Committee was left with a limited competition between Tite and Cockerell.

In late April and early May 1840 Tite and Cockerell submitted their drawings and descriptions, then appeared before the Committee to give two-hour explanations of the designs. Although Tite's drawings for this competition do not survive, the design must have corresponded closely to that of the building finally erected except in the depth of the west portico, which was increased after Tite's plans had been accepted. His plan suggests that he had solved with considerable skill the problem of fitting the diverse functions of the building into its awkward profile (Fig.156). The case of Cockerell's design, however, is complicated and can be chronicled only tentatively. Later in 1840 the architect published lithographed perspectives of the west front and internal court of the Exchange together with a ground plan, images which must be presumed to represent what he regarded as his ultimate design. The published views were intended to impress upon the public the splendour of a rejected scheme and they do not cor-

respond exactly with the presentation and sketch drawings which survive. It is probable, however, that they do relate closely to the designs shown to the Committee in the spring of 1840. The development of the west elevation away from the meagre pediment of the 1839 competition version (see Fig.151) and towards a much more integrated use of the triumphal arch and the other sources specified by the architect at this time can be read in a sequence of sketches; these sketches terminate in one which, with a watermark of 1840, must have postdated the initial competition and formed the basis of the perspective which Cockerell probably showed the Committee at the second stage (Fig.157).[27] The lithographed perspective inside the court of the Exchange published by Cockerell can also be related to one of the surviving presentation drawings (Fig. 158).[28] This longitudinal section, viewed from the Cornhill side, is a development of the 1839 competition section (see Fig.150) in which the Roman Doric order replaced the Ionic around the court, small thermal windows divided by short pilaster strips replaced the circular openings and the lozenged

coving was reduced in height. At the east end, Cockerell reduced the vaulting of the two major rooms, tentatively pencilling in the revisions. It is possible that this drawing, despite its somewhat unfinished appearance, represents the actual longitudinal section shown in the competition of 1840, because Cockerell did apologize to the Committee for the imperfect state of his drawings. From Cockerell's descriptions and the Committee's deliberations, it is clear that the revised scheme had retained the coving round the court, a row of three-quarter columns along the Cornhill flank (visible, in fact, in the perspective) and pilasters along the north side.[29] However, at this crucial moment Cockerell was evidently racked with uncertainty, for he also submitted two further sections which he said might serve if the Committee disliked the cove in his preferred scheme.[30] This makes his claim to have been short of time to produce finished drawings seem a little disingenuous, as does the fact that he had prepared a large model in support of his design but in contravention of the rules of the 1839 competition. It has been suggested that, had Tite not objected, the Committee would have taken the model into consideration and might have been swayed in Cockerell's favour. The reason, however, that the model was not visited officially was that most individual Committee members stated they had already seen it privately.

The Committee's reflections on the designs before it are instructive. Strongly in favour of Cockerell was John Horsley Palmer of the Mercers' Company, a former Governor of the Bank of England for whom Cockerell had succeeded Soane as official architect. The counter-motion for the acceptance of Tite was put by two City men, Thomas Corney and Jacob Cope, the latter of whom had been heavily involved in the entire process of securing a new Exchange, attending all but two of the Committee's fifty-one meetings between 1838 and 1840. When the discussion entered into detail, it appeared that Cockerell's design was in breach of important conditions which needed to be met: the northern edge of his proposed building was 6 ft closer to the Bank of England than could be permitted under the terms of the Act and it was observed that he had provided fewer shops than the number requested, with a consequent loss of revenue.[31] Tite, by contrast, had not only satisfied the Committee in terms of the income it could expect from tenants, but had also secured a precise quotation from the reputable firm of Grissell and Peto for his design to be built well within budget (Cockerell having only a general tender from Messrs Hicks).

Important though these practical and financial matters were, however, it would be a mistake to think that aesthetic issues did not form a significant part of the Committee's deliberations. In their statements both architects had commented on the style of their designs, referring to contemporary architectural developments in Paris. Tite said that he had eschewed 'elaborate' and 'picturesque' forms believing that, as at the new Bourse, only 'plain grandeur and elegant simplicity' would be consistent with 'the purposes and uses of this building, or its

157. Charles Robert Cockerell: Perspective of the west front of the Royal Exchange, prepared for the second competition, 1840. This was one of Cockerell's greatest designs, but the Chairman of the selection committee at the time considered its 'florid' style inappropriate for England.

situation in the very heart of the City of London'. He stressed
that his portico would, at a width of 90 ft and a height to its
apex of 74½ ft, be 'very superior in dimensions to any in the
country, and not very inferior to any in the world' and that
its entablature would continue round the building to give an
effect of unbroken mass in which English architecture was
deficient. Cockerell, too, said that the 49-ft high Corinthian
order, governing all façades except the east in his design,
would satisfy the 'fashionable amateurs of the day … who
consider the unbroken line, in imitation of the temples of
Greece and some of the palaces of Rome, to be the grand
nostrum of architectural beauty'. However, whilst stating that
'the European family [had] agreed to adopt' a taste depending
on 'a travelled reflection and experience, and comparison of
antient [sic] and modern works', he implicitly criticized the
Roman literalism of post-Napoleonic public buildings, saying
that 'the pomp of steps … largely indulged in by our elegant
neighbours at Paris … are inconsistent with the rapid movements and convenience of a commercial people'.[32] It was,
however, precisely to the 'modern' features of Cockerell's design that there were strong objections in the Committee. The
City men Corney, Cope, Robert Obbard and Jonathan Prior
all disliked the four corner towers, whilst the Master of the
Mercers' Company, Nathaniel Clarke, criticized the cove over
the central court. Instead, the aesthetic preference was predominantly for Tite's design and specifically for the great
Roman portico which, as Tite had hinted, provided a recog-

nizable symbol for the City immediately comparable with
contemporary national and international examples as well as
with the ancient world. A comparative plan in the Mercers'
Company archives, possibly drawn by Smith, suggests that the
Committee examined the two porticoes from the point of
view of their urban setting, and dimensional comparison was
certainly made between Tite's portico and those of Robert
Smirke at the nearby General Post Office (see Fig.89) and
James Gibbs at St Martin-in-the-Fields.[33] The Chairman of the
Committee, Richard Lambert Jones, summed up the debate:
Cockerell's design (which he had in fact voted to exclude at
the time of the first competition), in his opinion, fell short of
the mark on practical and functional grounds. He reminded
the Committee of Smirke's view that Cockerell's court would
be dark and airless; he pointed out that ninety-two steps
would have to be negotiated in order to reach the upper floor
of the building and he noted the shortfall in revenue to be
expected from the shops. The secretary also minuted Jones as
making a striking comment on Cockerell's aesthetic: 'Objects
to the style [of] architecture as applicable in this country – no
cases [of] florid architecture – may do in the climate [of]
Italy'.[34] In the vote which ensued, Tite's design was selected
by a majority of two to one. Of the other ten City men
present, eight followed Jones in voting for Tite, including
those most closely involved with the project during the previous two years: Cope, Elmes and William Richardson. Only
Richard Taylor, originally a supporter of Donaldson, had

attended meetings as conscientiously as these men, and he abstained. Tite also had the support of the Master of the Mercers' Company and three of his colleagues. However, the remaining six mercers who voted were against Tite, including Robert Sutton Junior, still feeling perhaps that justice demanded preference be given to Cockerell as remaining prizewinner from the second class in the first competition.

At the end of the entire competition process the City men outnumbered the mercers and largely followed the lead provided by Lambert Jones in selecting Tite's design. Unanimously elected Chairman at the first meeting of the Joint Committee in January 1838, the Common Councilman for the ward of Cripplegate (Without) was in fact the dominant personality from the outset in the efforts of the Gresham Trustees to secure a new Royal Exchange. Lambert Jones attended every Committee meeting and led every sub-committee and deputation for which records exist. It was he who promulgated the three fundamental principles on which expansion, reorientation and urban redefinition of the new Exchange was to be based. It was also Lambert Jones who read out the proposals for the 'Instructions to Architects' which the appointed subcommittee, meeting on 14 March 1839, endorsed as the rules for the first competition. The idea that the new building should be generically Classical thus almost certainly originated with Lambert Jones, giving an indication of his overall stylistic and symbolic preferences. However, it is possible to narrow down his architectural beliefs a little further. He certainly valued the judgement, if not the explicit Greek Revivalism, of Robert Smirke, whom he nominated to serve as a referee and whose opinions on the site and the competition drawings he introduced at various stages of the process. As Chairman of the Bridge House Estates Committee, Lambert Jones was already well acquainted with Smirke, the designer of street façades for the new approaches to London Bridge. The Royal Exchange Committee papers also show that, in December 1839, the Chairman used his casting vote to send the design of Grellier forward for Smith's consideration alongside those of Donaldson, Cockerell and Mocatta. Taken together with his disparagement of Cockerell's 'florid' style, this might be interpreted as a sign that Lambert Jones wished the new building to have a character of Antique austerity, and his ultimate strong preference for Tite would seem to confirm this.

There are other, less explicit but perhaps no less significant reasons, however, why Lambert Jones might have determined on Tite's design in 1840. The two men knew each other quite well, not just, as the cynical pointed out, through their joint employment by the Eastern Railway Company, but also as Whig City Councilmen, Lambert Jones having represented his ward since 1819 and Tite Aldgate between 1832 and 1836. Lambert Jones's political career was one of tireless devotion to the improvement of the facilities of the City. His approach to modernizing the City's infrastructure showed some recklessness with regard to its historic fabric, but no more so than that

of Baron Haussmann in Paris a generation later. Lambert Jones was not an uncultured man, to judge from his Fellowship of the Society of Antiquaries and his dedicated service over nineteen years to the committee of what became the Guildhall Library, effectively founded by him in 1824. The commitment he showed to the City cannot be divorced from the historical insularity of City attitudes within the metropolis more generally, and there is no doubt that the rebuilding of the Royal Exchange was an intensely political matter for the Committee and its Chairman, in which its governmental independence needed to be reasserted. The background to this situation can be gauged from the example of the ceremonial events which accompanied the Proclamation of the Peace of Amiens at the Exchange in 1802 (see Fig.145). The procession on that occasion, having proceeded from St James's Palace to Charing Cross, came to a halt at the closed gates of Temple Bar. Blue Mantle Pursuivant of Arms was required to enter the City alone to ask permission from the Lord Mayor for the procession to continue to the Exchange for the final reading of George III's Proclamation. The permission was granted, but not to the Officers of Westminster, who had to retire at this point. The legendary lack of trust between the City and the Court, dating back at least to the City's protection of the Five Members at the outset of the Civil War, had received fresh impetus at the time of the Reform Bill when, as has been seen in Chapter 6, the hero of the Birmingham Political Union, Thomas Attwood, had been made a Freeman at the Mansion House. Although a supporter of much City-led legislation, Wellington's implacable opposition to the Bill gave rise to such fears for his safety that he did not attend the opening of London Bridge in 1831 and, as a result, William IV peevishly refused the traditional invitation to attend the inaugural banquet of the incoming Lord Mayor at the Mansion House in November 1832.[35]

This is the background against which the Committee's otherwise inexplicably outraged response should be judged, when the Chancellor of the Exchequer, Thomas Spring-Rice, tried to assert a right of veto over the site of the Bank Buildings and the plan of the new Exchange. A meeting on 3 November 1838 attended by Lambert Jones, Cope, Taylor, twelve other Councilmen (including three who, like Jones and Cope, ultimately voted for Tite) and a single Alderman unanimously agreed a resolution that the Parliamentary Act did not permit the legislature to interfere with the building of the Royal Exchange, the plan for which could therefore not be subject to approval by the Lords of the Treasury. The following month Jones led a deputation to meet Viscount Melbourne on this matter and, not satisfied with the Prime Minister's response, the Committee retained legal counsel to take their grievance to the Queen's Bench. Taylor was especially vitriolic about a Chancellor otherwise well known for his Whig affability, saying that his intervention displayed 'the petty insolence of an ill-bred banker's clerk, anxious to show his

NEW ROYAL EXCHANGE :
SECTION OF PORTICO FROM NORTH TO SOUTH.

No. 15

159. William Tite: Section of the portico of the Royal Exchange, 1840.

consequence by making you wait'.[36] It is important to recall that this disagreement was about a point of principle, not at that stage any specific design for the new building. When a compromise was finally struck in March 1839 it was that the Committee would submit plans and estimates to the Treasury, but only for approval of their financial probity. The Treasury, for its part, would not 'force on the Corporation or the Gresham Trustees the adoption of any Plan which they have not themselves previously approved'.[37]

Viewed from this perspective, the explicit Roman forms utilized by Tite might be seen as bearing considerable meaning, particularly when opposed to what has been identified as the 'note of continental baroque despotism' the Committee might have perceived in Cockerell's 'Late-Imperial' design.[38] For the principal elevation of his 1840 competition entry Tite had evidently drawn ideas from the design of the previously successful Donaldson, particular similarities being the portico extending to all but one bay on either side and the stylobate. When, in 1841, Tite responded to criticism, increasing the depth of the portico and introducing the arched central recess,

Donaldson's model of the Pantheon was even more obviously implanted (Fig.159). The allusion was recognized at the time, of course, *The Penny Sunday Times* issue accompanying the opening of the building by the Queen in 1844, commenting that the architect had derived his portico by reducing the 'majestic original' of the Pantheon by a proportion of one-fifth. Tite, along with most other students of Roman architecture, would probably have subscribed to the view upheld by Taylor and Cresy that the surviving Pantheon was that built by Agrippa as a late Republican work and only restored by successive emperors.[39] In other modifications Tite increased the Roman character of the portico by closing in the frontal steps through the introduction of projecting stylobates and by placing tablets on the attics bearing the inscription 'S.P.Q.L.' (for *Senatus Populusque Londiniensis*). The sculptural embellishment on the inner wall of the portico has been interpreted by architectural historians almost always as a derivative of baroque carving as well as an early sign, alongside Hardwick's Goldsmiths' Hall, of a tendency to decorative excess in later Victorian Classicism. It might indeed be seen as a response to

160. George Ledwell Taylor and Edward Cresy: Lithographic detail of one of the sculptural swags in the portico of the Pantheon, Rome, from 'The Architectural Antiquities of Rome', 1821.

the decorative carving of St Paul's Cathedral, a building on which Tite surely reflected during the design process, not least because a drawing of 1840 by Smith in the Mercers' Company Archives shows that the Committee made comparison of his portico with that of Wren's Great Model on the matter of depth.[40] It is also possible that the carving was introduced at the contract drawing stage after the 1840 competition in deference to Cockerell's defeated design. However, such decoration was not thought of as exclusively modern in the early nineteenth century. During the 1820s, images of Roman architectural decoration were disseminated which, thanks to the deep shading possible in the new print medium of lithography, have the appearance of high relief. Taylor's and Cresy's representation of the Pantheon includes just such an image, showing the swags on the back wall of the portico which are, in reality, carved in very low relief (Fig.160). Tite was evidently familiar with this approach to Roman architectural decoration, because he owned a copy of John Jenkins's and William Hosking's lithographed *A Selection of Architectural and other Ornament: Greek, Roman and Italian* of 1827 (now in the British Architectural Library).

In the Spring of 1841 a new Roman context emerged for the site of the Exchange. In excavating the ground for the foundations of the new building, the workmen discovered that the west wall of Jerman's Exchange had been founded on the remains of a Romano-British building. Archaeological finds both here and elsewhere on the site included coins of the Imperial era and numerous other artefacts. The antiquarian Charles Roach Smith, perhaps the greatest nineteenth-century student of Roman London, was quickly into the field, publishing a letter on the subject in *Archaeologia* in 1842. The antiquarian interests of Roach Smith were soon to clash with the developmental ambitions of Lambert Jones and Tite, leading

to acrimonious exchanges over many years. Tite, however, was far from unenthused by the discoveries, as his report to the Committee after the initial discovery shows, and he was later to publish *A Descriptive Catalogue of the Antiquities found in the Excavations at the New Royal Exchange*.[41] The sense that the new building was rising on land once occupied by actual Roman edifices might well have been behind the architect's decision in 1844 to propose Roman decorative work for the court. Two forms of decoration were envisaged. The first was a series of encaustic paintings for the ceilings of the ambulatory around the court, Tite justifying the technique to the Committee by its durable deployment in Roman bath buildings and by modern exemplars such as the Munich Glyptothek and the Madeleine in Paris.[42] Second was the idea for a mosaic pavement for the open centre of the court (Pl.xixb). The tessellated pavement design, with a meander border and other Antique motifs, was the design of Henry Pether and was executed in Vauxhall by the Singer company. It is surely significant that, only two years previously, Owen Jones had published ten chromolithographic plates of ancient tessellated pavements, prefaced by an essay by F. O. Ward on their style and on the new technologies which were emerging for their manufacture. Unfortunately, the speed with which the Exchange pavement was laid (so that the Queen could stand upon it for the important ceremony of naming the new building in October of that year) meant that it soon began to disintegrate, and the pavement had to be wholly removed only weeks after the opening ceremony, a cause of great derision in *The Times* which pointed out that the Romans' own mosaic pavements were capable of surviving in near perfect condition over fifteen hundred years. Frederick Sang's encaustic paintings lasted little longer, disappearing beneath layers of soot and being removed finally in 1889–90.

Much less easily dislodged than the painted and mosaic

161. Jules Arnout: Print of the Bank of England and the Royal Exchange, London, c.1850.

162. Print of the Peace Illuminations at the Royal Exchange, London, celebrating the end of the Crimean War, from the 'Illustrated Times', 10 May 1856.

decoration, however, was the notion, strengthened by the Roman archaeological finds on the site, that the Exchange was the focal building in the modern 'forum' of London. The site of this modern forum lay, like its Roman predecessor, to the north of the ancient Via Decumana, but it had migrated some 200 m westwards. As far back as 1700 the philosopher John Toland had called London the 'new Rome in the west', its centre being the Bank of England (a repository 'like the Temple of Saturn') and the Mansion House an official residence of the Mayor as a Consul. The City sheriffs were Praetors, the Common Council was a popular assembly and the Court of Aldermen were the Senators.[43] In 1839 and 1840 the competitors for the new Exchange did not specifically talk in terms of producing a 'forum', but Cockerell did describe the building as 'the greatest commercial mart and metropolitan Exchange of the World [in] the one of the most antient [sic] and certainly the most wealthy city of the universe' and, in his 1858 architectural history of the Bank of England, he was to define the Bank's urban setting precisely in relation to its ancient history.[44] It is worth noting, moreover, that the perspective views of at least three competitors (see Pls xx, xxi and Fig.157) show the equestrian statue of Wellington – originally proposed for a position in front of Mansion House in the 1830s (see Fig.144) and commissioned from Sir Francis Chantrey in February 1839 – transferred to a more commanding spot before the Exchange. The three architects concerned (Donaldson, Cockerell and Pennethorne) are unlikely to have known how Chantrey intended to treat the figure, but all had been to Rome in the post-Napoleonic period, had an eye for envisioning the city in its ancient state and depicted the modern saviour of Britain in military guise; in Donaldson's case, with his horse rearing in a manner akin to Jacques-Louis David's celebrated image of Napoleon crosing the Great St Bernard Pass. Chantrey's figure, finished after his death and erected in 1844, although cast from cannon captured at Waterloo, is actually less martial, celebrating Wellington's political support for City-instigated legislation for urban improvement.

The early nineteenth-century excavations of the Forum in Rome, coupled with the academic and popular images of the Forum which had been disseminated in the 1820s and 1830s, had surely increased the public vision of the urban nature of the ancient city's governmental centre. Cockerell had produced a design for the Royal Exchange in which the Forum motif of the Triumphal Arch might have been recognized, but Tite's building certainly presented a Roman temple front to the new urban space – arguably a more powerful termination to what had now become '*the* central focus of the entire City of London'.[45] In this regard an informative comparison can be made between the image of this area of the City as drawn in the mid 1830s (see Fig.144) and that as drawn by Jules Arnout in about 1850 (Fig.161), thought worthy of joint publication in London and Paris. The crowded modern townscape of the former had given way to the grandeur and expansiveness of

an Antique administrative centre in the latter, bordered by the Bank of England to the north and the Mansion House (more temple-like since the removal of its high attics in 1794 and 1843) to the south. The easterly aspect was dominated now not so much by the bowed façade of the Globe Fire Office as by the portico of the new Exchange.

Public comment on the competitions for and building of the new Exchange was certainly mixed, with a considerable amount of adverse criticism both of the procedures of the Committee and the designs themselves.[46] Cockerell drew support from various quarters in the press though significantly, in view of Lambert Jones's later comments, his 1839 design was said in *The Spectator* to be 'too showy for its purpose, and overstepping the bounds of pure taste'.[47] The quasi-Venetian High Renaissance sculptural enrichment seen in, for example, Sydney Smirke's Carlton Club was to come a decade after Barry had definitively established the Italianate Revival using more austere models from sixteenth-century Rome at the Reform Club, a building exactly contemporary with the Exchange competition and explicitly referred to by Tite as a good example of unbroken mass and line. In this sense, the rich plasticity in design which Cockerell had established when working on Cambridge University Library and which he deployed again for the Royal Exchange competitions might well be judged to have been premature for an audience still steeped in the Napoleonic regalvanization of the Roman world. Certainly the public soon began to play its role in the Roman allusion, especially once Tite had overcome the problem of his shallow portico. The press accompanying the opening ceremony in October 1844 eulogized British merchants, 'beyond all Greek, beyond all Roman fame', as seen in the epigraph to this chapter, and their 'magnificent' new building with its Pantheon frontispiece, its coffered vaults after the manner of Roman palaces and its mosaic pavement 'after the best Roman examples'.[48] Moreover, the building quickly resumed its function as the site for major civic ceremonials. The reorientation of the Exchange and the creation of the new urban space to the west meant that far greater crowds could gather than before, as can be seen from the number which assembled before the illuminated building in 1856 to celebrate the cessation of the Crimean War (Fig.162).

The opprobrium heaped on Tite and the sense of deprivation felt by architectural historians at the 'loss' of Cockerell's building have perhaps obscured the real significance of the Royal Exchange affair. Cockerell's design, richly eclectic in its range of Classical sources, was ahead of its time, prefiguring the quality of much later Victorian and Edwardian Classical architecture. Tite's Exchange, its west elevation recalling Donaldson's thwarted winning competition entry, succeeded in providing Lambert Jones and his Committee of City men with a quite literal version of the Roman temple which suited their symbolic purposes, both for the individual building and for the new urban context of the London Forum they envisaged.

THE ROYAL EXCHANGE, LONDON

Chapter 9
St George's Hall, Liverpool

That noble pile of Building, which it is the pride and honour of
the Senate and People of Liverpool to call their own. (James Elmes,
describing St George's Hall in 1855)[1]

In March 1839, the same month that the Royal Exchange Committee in London announced the competition to design its replacement building, an advertisement appeared in *The Times* inviting architects to submit designs in an anonymous and open competition for a new building in Liverpool to house the town's triennial music festival and other such public events. The competition for St George's Hall, as the Liverpool building was to be known, attracted a larger number of entrants than the Exchange and concluded sooner, with the premiation in July 1839 of the 25-year-old Harvey Lonsdale Elmes.[2] Liverpool Town Council had provided the Company set up to secure the building with a trapezoidal piece of land on the central site where the Old Infirmary had stood, extending southwards from the corner of Lime Street and Shaw's Brow (Fig.163).[3] The St George's Hall Company Committee had been even more explicit than the Exchange Committee in determining that its building should be of ancient 'Grecian or Roman character', and Elmes's winning design proposed a rectangular structure, the principal (south) façade dominated by a peristyle of fourteen fluted Ionic columns raised on a high podium with entrances at either end.[4] The east elevation, overlooking the screen of Lime Street Station with its attached columns, comprised a portico of six Ionic columns *in antis*, raised over rusticated basement piers. The Town Council intended to use the Old Infirmary site as a civic zone which would include new Assize Courts as well as St George's Hall and had obtained a Parliamentary Improvement Act for this purpose in 1837. Two months before the result of the competition for the Hall was announced, the Council's Finance Committee finalized specifications for a competition for the Assize Courts. The site was a rectangle at right angles to that for St George's Hall (see Fig.163) and it was again stipulated that the 'character of the Building is to be of Grecian or Roman Architecture', the intention being that the two buildings should 'connect' architecturally in a manner bringing credit upon Liverpool.[5] When, in April 1840, the Council opened the sealed envelope containing the name of the architect whose design had been placed first by its sub-committee, it was found that Elmes had been selected again, this time from a field of eighty-six competitors.[6] Elmes had proposed a Greek Doric hexastyle portico fronting an east façade with

peristyles of four columns leading either side to solid pavilion-like corners.

Victory in the competitions did not bring with it commitment to build the winner's designs, and criticism in the press of the impracticalities of Elmes's Assize Courts probably lay behind the Corporation's decision to set up a Law Courts Committee and hand its own Surveyor, Joseph Franklin, the task of preparing a more practicable design. However, at the same meeting in August 1840 that Franklin presented the Committee with 'an entire new design' of either Ionic or Doric character, a letter from Elmes was read, complaining about the procedures. He had only learned of the Council's actions from a conversation with Alderman Hardman Earle, having had no communication with the Council since April, and petitioned for the opportunity to develop his winning scheme for the Assize Courts himself.[7] The Committee acceded to this request and when, on 8 October 1840, Elmes returned with two new sets of designs for the Courts, Franklin generously backed him and he was appointed. The Committee sent its new architect away to draw up proposals, not just for the Assize Courts but for Daily Courts it intended to build on a site now extended to include Islington Market further north. Elmes was also to show how these buildings might relate to St George's Hall. Two weeks later he returned with five plans for placing the three buildings on the Old Infirmary and Islington Market site, including the possibility of maintaining St George's Hall as a separate edifice on the site intended for the Assize Courts and combining the two Court buildings on the site intended for the Hall.[8] Since Elmes's proposals also included the possibility of combining the Assize Courts and St George's Hall into a single edifice, the Law Courts Committee decided to call a joint meeting with the Committee of St George's Hall Company. This meeting took place on 27 October, when it was determined that Hall and Assize Courts should be combined on the site intended for the latter. The St George's Hall Company agreed to return the land the Council had ceded it so that the Daily Courts could be built in that vicinity. (Elmes's designs for a Daily Courts building with a great dome or an octagonal drum modelled on the Tower of the Winds reached a quite advanced state before the scheme was abandoned in 1843.) The St George's Hall Company also agreed to turn its capital over to the Law Courts Committee and, in January 1841, that Committee took control of the entire building.

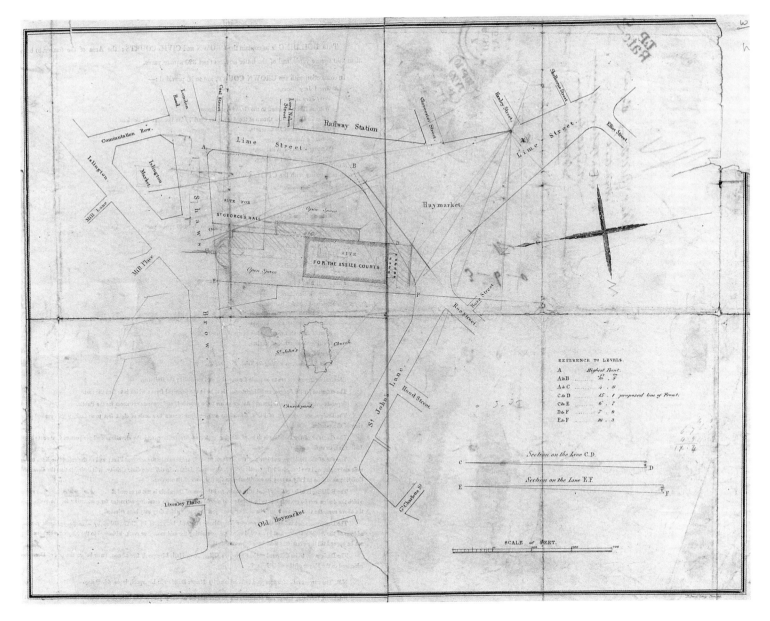

In the six months from November 1840 to April 1841 Elmes developed his combined design for the Hall and Assize Courts (Pl.XXII). The architect had transformed the conservative Greek Revivalism of his two competition entries into the hugely powerful Corinthian monument universally recognized by historians as a masterpiece of nineteenth-century Classical design. Insofar as it departs from British Greek Revival traditions, however, the character of the building has generally been interpreted by architectural historians in terms of contemporary European, specifically German and French architectural theory and practice.[9] It is true that in 1844 Elmes expressed the desire to contribute his 'unit' towards helping Britain 'rival her Continental neighbours in producing original and beautiful works, equally adapted to climate, materials, and habits of the people'.[10] However, at the time St George's

Hall was conceived, Elmes had no first-hand knowledge of architecture outside Britain. The building can be understood, in fact, precisely as its architect wished: as a magnificent component of nineteenth-century European Classicism, nonetheless rooted in the general context of British architectural developments of the 1830s and in the particular context of the town of Liverpool. As such, it represents the climactic point of the literal interpretation of Antiquity in England, and more specifically of Roman Antiquity, which has been the subject of this book.

The long-standing belief that Elmes drew inspiration for his design directly from the work of Karl Friedrich Schinkel, especially from the Prussian architect's Altes Museum in Berlin, was challenged some time ago when it was pointed out that the Englishman's visit to Belgium, Germany and Austria

163. Site plan for St George's Hall and Assize Courts, Liverpool, annotated by Harvey Lonsdale Elmes, 1839–40.

(which in any case took place in 1842 when St George's Hall was already under construction and its external form had been determined in all but detail) did not extend to Berlin.[11] Since then, studies have focused instead on the British sources available to a young architect working in the late 1830s. Elmes' education largely took place in a London where the leading figures were the Greek Revivalists Robert Smirke and William Wilkins. When he was a boy, his architect-father argued in lectures, delivered in London and Birmingham, that 'no remains of architecture or sculpture are to be found in Greece but what are canons of art, while Rome possesses more to corrupt the taste of the young architect than all its excellencies can counterbalance'.[12] By 1827, however, when Harvey Lonsdale was a teenager, James Elmes had changed his position so greatly that he could conceptualize London as 'the ROME of modern history', citing Augustus's famous comment that he found Rome a city of brick and left it one of marble, adding 'the reign and regency of George the Fourth has scarcely done less'.[13] As a student at the Royal Academy in the early 1830s, the younger Elmes is likely to have heard Soane's lectures read by Henry Howard, and therefore may have absorbed Soane's views on the primacy of the ancient Graeco-Roman and modern French worlds as exemplars for contemporary Europe. It should be recalled, moreover, that throughout the period of the Liverpool competitions and after he had secured the commission Elmes lived in London, where he was closely associated with leading architectural figures of the metropolis. Charles Robert Cockerell was evidently his guiding light at this time, Elmes's competition design for St George's Hall having been shown to be a paraphrase of one of his mentor's 1829–30 designs for Cambridge University Library.[14] Cockerell's 'Idea for the Frontispiece of a Publick Building in England', published in 1843, was so admired by Elmes that he persuaded the Law Courts Committee to commission it for the south pediment of St George's Hall. After Elmes's premature death in 1847, Cockerell wrote of his 'admired friend' in touchingly personal terms to Robert Rawlinson (then in charge of the construction of St George's Hall), saying that 'no one could appreciate more highly [than I] his splendid and rare talents', and it was to Cockerell that the task of completing the building would ultimately fall.[15] Further scholarly suggestions have been that Elmes's competition design for the Assize Courts was a Greek Doric version of George Basevi's Fitzwilliam Museum and that the distinctive arrangement of St George's Hall in its final state, with temple portico to the south and square piers along part of the east longitudinal axis, was derived generically from Wilkins's Grange Park, which Elmes might have known as a child living in Hampshire near to the house.[16] Another context which might be noted is the probability that Elmes and Charles Barry felt sufficient admiration for one another to have exchanged ideas: Barry's unlikely 1842 Greek Doric design for London Law Courts in Lincoln's Inn Fields was effectively a replica, albeit without

the attic, of Elmes's by then abortive Liverpool Assize Courts competition entry, shown at the Royal Academy in 1841.[17] In turn, the plain high attic at St George's Hall, although directly derived by Elmes from his own Assize Courts competition design, is as likely to have been justified in relation to Barry's Royal Institution in Liverpool's rival town, Manchester (a building Elmes can only have known from drawings or prints, since he did not visit Manchester until 1846), as it was by the often cited Prussian source.

Given that Elmes's competition designs for both St George's Hall and the Assize Courts can be read as relatively unambitious Greek Revival ideas, the question to be asked is how he progressed during late 1840 and early 1841 to the magnificent, combined building that we see today. The answer lies partly in the design logic of bringing the two original schemes together. In one version of his Assize Courts designs, Elmes had conceived the two courtrooms at the centre of the plan almost as a single rectangular space with D-ends, but separated in the middle by the judges' benches and retiring rooms.[18] An early sketch plan for the combined building shows how he returned to this idea, splitting up the two courtrooms, pushing them further apart, transferring the judicial benches to their semi-circular ends and interposing the Concert Hall between them (Fig.164). The only reservation expressed by the Committee about this disposition of Crown and Civil Courts at opposite ends of the Hall – that the judges would have difficulty in conferring – was set aside after Elmes consulted with two judges who saw no difficulty in walking one hundred yards in the event of a meeting being necessary. In its independent state, the Hall itself had been intended to have apsidal ends (that to the west for the orchestra and that to the east, with a moveable partition and balconies, to serve as a Concert Room).[19] In the combined version, the Hall was initially to be a simple rectangular space, its apses effectively having become detached to serve as the courtrooms. However, the apsidal form of the Concert Room was to reappear when, in April 1841, Elmes was asked by the Committee to increase the capacity of the Concert Room in the combined building, situated at the north end on a level higher than the Hall and courtrooms. His solution was to add a semi-circular projection to the previously flat north end of the early sketch plan (see Fig.164). (It is clear that this idea was an addition to the preliminary plan on Elmes's part, not just from the way that there was insufficient room for the semi-circle on the sheet of paper but from the fact that it is applied off-centre to the north wall of the building, evidently an error resulting from haste.) A further respect in which the combined plan can be seen as a development from Elmes's competition designs is the arrangement of the peristyles. The juxtaposition of an unpedimented façade of fourteen Ionic columns with pedimented end porticoes was, as has been seen above, the principal characteristic of Elmes's competition design for St George's Hall, and this basic idea remained in his thoughts when preparing the five

164. Harvey Lonsdale Elmes:
Plan and perspective for
St George's Hall, Liverpool,
drawn before April 1841.

options for the site in October 1840 and subsequently when designing the combined building. One of his elevations for the east side of the combined building proposed an extension of the Ionic order along its entire length, perhaps the idea rejected by the Committee, when in February 1841 it selected the Corinthian alternative offered by Elmes.[20] In the combined building the Doric order of the Assize Courts competition entry disappeared altogether, except in the internal articulation of the north entrance hall. However, in addition to the high central attic over the Assize Courts, which became the attic over the Concert Hall, the blocky corner 'pavilions' became features of the west elevation of the combined building (see Fig.164).

It might appear, then, that the design of St George's Hall represents nothing more than the logical fusion of ideas conceived by Elmes for separate Hall and Assize Courts buildings. But this mechanical process alone cannot explain the charac-

ter with which Elmes invested the combined building in the spring of 1841, nor the subsequent development of its external details and interior form. For the competitions he had produced designs which were meant to catch the eye of Liverpudlians familiar with the 1820s academic Greek Revivalism of their erstwhile Corporation Surveyor, John Foster Junior, a language in which Elmes was as competent as he was in that of the Gothic Revival (which he used at the same time in designing the Liverpool Collegiate Institution). Once confirmed as architect of the combined St George's Hall, however, Elmes's imagination was freed to respond to the archaeological spirit of post-Napoleonic Europe and to the British architectural manifestations of it which had occurred during the 1830s. The precedent of the Corinthian temple on a high platform, nowhere in evidence in the competition designs, made an immediate appearance once Elmes had received the commission. The order, which Elmes finalized for the building in June

1844, shows him to have been working hard at his Roman textbooks (Fig.165). The architect discussed the applicability to St George's Hall of the orders of the Temple of Castor and of the Pantheon with his father (finding fault in the proportions of Wren's Corinthian capitals in the process). There was widespread agreement, when St George's Hall was under construction, that Elmes had used the order of the Temple of Castor, but modern archaeological opinion bears out Elmes Senior's recollection that his son's capitals were 'designed and adapted for their situation and height … from the best examples of the order'.[21] The square-cut upper termination of the fluting is a typical feature of the order in the late Republican era, seen for example in the round temple at Tivoli or the Basilica at Pompeii, the former illustrated by George Ledwell Taylor and Edward Cresy, the latter in considerable detail by Thomas Leverton Donaldson. The capital itself is of a normal Imperial Roman type, but the variation of the abacus flowers suggests observation of a source such as the Temple of Hercules Victor in the Forum Boarium. Taylor and Cresy had included a plate which showed five of the flower variants of

this temple's capitals and they commented on this aspect of the design in their text, disapprovingly in fact, as they considered that consistency should outweigh variety.[22] In the entablature of St George's Hall the modillions are again of the late Republican type and only the particular form of egg and dart suggests the use of an Athenian source. This analysis suggests that, as Rawlinson noted, Elmes's admiration for Greek detail was outweighed by his sense of its inapplicability in Britain, given the character of indigenous stone and of local environmental conditions.[23] As Elmes's father stated, the order of St George's Hall was designed in relation to the site and height of the building, and the architect determined at an early stage how to handle the temple front at the south end, towards which the land sloped appreciably. Elmes's first thought about the south end of an independent St George's Hall on the site originally intended for the Assize Courts had been to deploy a hexastyle portico with four attached columns behind *in antis*, approached from St John's Lane by a double flight of frontal steps.[24] In the combined building, however, he introduced the quite different idea of a double-depth octa-

style portico on a high podium, approached only by flights of steps to the sides, the whole set on a high platform (Fig.166).[25] Although access to the south end of the building was to be provided through a doorway at ground level in the platform, it is important to realize that Elmes was more concerned with the magnificent architectural effect of an elevation towering over New Haymarket and seen in conjunction with the east façade which, as he told Rawlinson, was always intended to be the principal one.

It was, in fact, the view of St George's Hall from the southeast which dominated Elmes's thinking about the building in its urban context and suggests how steeped he was in the scenographic effects of Roman civic spaces which had fascinated Cockerell, James Pennethorne and others since 1815. When conceiving the combined building, Elmes once again took up the plan issued in connection with the Assize Courts competition (see Fig.163) and used his pencil to rule sightlines across New Haymarket from a point on the corner of Lime Street with what was then Hanley Street. The precise positions and forms of the south and east porticoes, and even

the rounded north end of the building, can be read in terms of their effects from the perspective of these sight-lines. This point, or a point close to it in the middle of Lime Street, which brought the façades of the railway station and proposed Daily Courts into play, was that from which Elmes's perspective views (not to mention virtually all contemporary topographical views) were taken (Fig.167). It is remarkable to note how closely the spectral but distinctive form of St George's Hall seen from the south-easterly viewpoint resembles the conjoined 'Graecostasis' and 'Curia' (Temples of Castor and 'of Augustus') shown on the left of Pennethorne's restoration of the Roman Forum of the mid 1820s (see Fig.77). Pennethorne had brought both versions of his Forum restoration back to England and, as it had secured his election to the Accademia di S. Luca, he must have been proud of it. As seen in Chapter 4, the work was not displayed at the Royal Academy and is not known to have been engraved, but it remained in the architect's family until the 1980s and there is no reason why it should not have been known in London architectural circles when Elmes was a student or subsequently.

167. Harvey Lonsdale Elmes:
Perspective for St George's
Hall and the proposed
domed Daily Courts build-
ing, Liverpool, drawn by
1843. The façade of Lime
Street Station on the right
completes the assemblage
of buildings around this
Forum-like space.

By the spring of 1842 the site of the Hall had been excavated and Contract A, for the construction of vaulted brick
foundations, as sublimely cavernous as any Roman substruc-
ture, was in progress. Elmes's design for the superstructure was
sufficiently settled for him to be hard at work on the contract
drawings for the shell and for a model of the building to be
sent to the Committee. It was at this point that the architect
was persuaded to join a leading Liverpool politician and Law
Courts Committee member, William Earle, and his party of
three for a visit to southern Germany and Austria. The itinerary took the group through Belgium and up the Rhine
to Frankfurt, then on to Munich by way of Würzburg and
Nuremberg, along the northern edge of the Alps from Salz-
burg to Innsbruck and back to Frankfurt through Augsburg,
Stuttgart and Heidelberg. Of this journey James Elmes later
recorded that his son had studied Leo von Klenze's Walhalla
near Regensburg and the Munich Glyptothek, together with
other Classical buildings in the Bavarian capital 'with a math-
ematician's eye', suggesting only that Elmes's travels served
to sharpen his appreciation of Germano-Greek proportions
and details. From Earle's account we learn further that he accompanied Elmes into the roof space of the late sixteenth-
century Michaelskirche at Munich, because Elmes 'had formed

the design of having a roof constructed of brick over St
George's Hall'.[26] Thus, although in January 1842 Elmes had
told the Committee that he was 'leaving the whole of the interior fittings and finishings to be more maturely considered',
it is clear that he was already thinking at least about the disposition of the grandest internal space, the Concert Hall.[27]
The church in Munich offered an example of a modern brick-
vaulted interior to be studied when the opportunity arose, but
his father specifically recorded that what Elmes wished to
achieve in Liverpool was a vault 'in the Roman manner', and
that in pursuit of this objective he had made detailed studies
of Soane's hollow pot constructions at the Bank of England
and of the vaults of commercial buildings at London docks,
where James Elmes was Surveyor.[28]

The development of the internal disposition and articulation of St George's Hall from the early plan (see Fig.164)
towards the presentation version which must be close to
Elmes's ultimate intentions (Fig.168) cannot be chronicled with
certainty, because the relevant drawings which survive are un-
dated and Elmes's verbal communications with the Committee
from 1842 to 1844 were largely concerned with ongoing con-
tracts for the shell and exterior carved detail of the building.
It would probably be incorrect, however, to think that the key

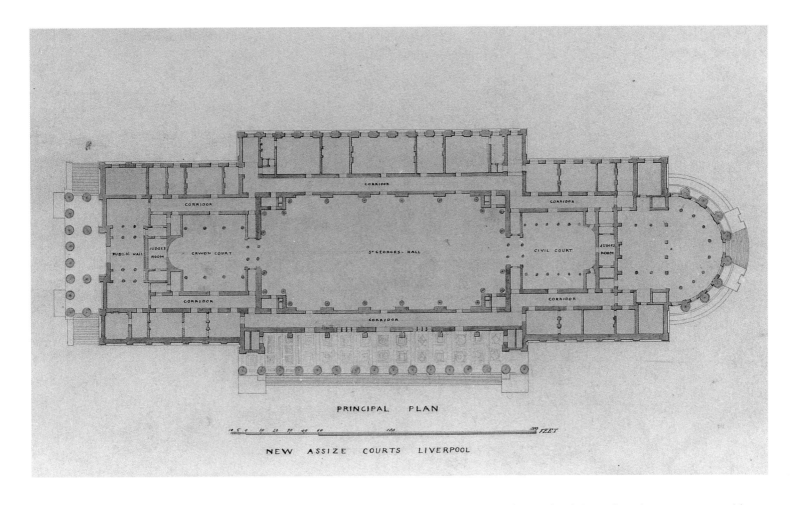

PRINCIPAL PLAN

NEW ASSIZE COURTS LIVERPOOL

168. Harvey Lonsdale Elmes: Plan of St George's Hall, Liverpool, after July 1844.

phase of planning which led to the introduction of twenty-four columns around the interior of the Concert Hall, along with the implications those columns hold for the vault, took place as late as 1844, as has been thought hitherto. It is true that Elmes first raised the question of the columns with the Committee early that year, but this was to ask whether he might be permitted to change the material from which they were to be made, since he had received a good offer from a quarry in Aberdeen to supply granite, and granite, being a durable material, would best support the load (presumably of the intended vault) which the columns would have to bear.[29] In all likelihood, then, the development of the 'Roman manner' in the interior had accompanied or flowed from the development of the same concept in the exterior. To begin with, Elmes probably thought of the Concert Hall in the combined design more or less directly in terms of his competition design, where it had shallow pilasters defining bays, each with a coffered barrel vault no doubt intended for construction in plaster.[30] In April 1841, however, he told the Committee that 'the adoption of so enriched an order of Architecture as the Corinthian for the exterior [requires] a correspondent feeling to be displayed in the interior', an indication that the plasticity of the Hall was to be increased, and, as has been seen above, the idea of a brick vault certainly pre-dated the architect's 1842 visit to Germany.[31] The vault may have begun its life as a simple barrel, spanning from wall to wall, but the specifications for the contract to build the shell, which was let in April 1843, suggest that Elmes was then in the process of re-thinking its form and structure, since most of the supporting brickwork, apart from two major cross walls and the north and south recesses, was to be 'constructed hereafter as will be directed by the architect'.[32] In fact, in the very same month that the superstructure contract was let, Elmes submitted a memorandum of alterations to the Committee which included changes to the great vaulted ceiling and the various works connected with it.[33] It seems certain, then, that by October 1843, when he submitted a further plan of the interior to the Committee for its consideration, Elmes was committed to the idea of what he thought of as a Roman vault springing from columns freestanding against each of the twelve piers (Pl. XXIIIa).

Underpinning this process of design was Elmes's study of planning principles for major Roman public buildings, such as the Basilica of Maxentius and the Roman bath complexes. In the early 1840s the young architect was not long out of his studentship and his father later observed that academic

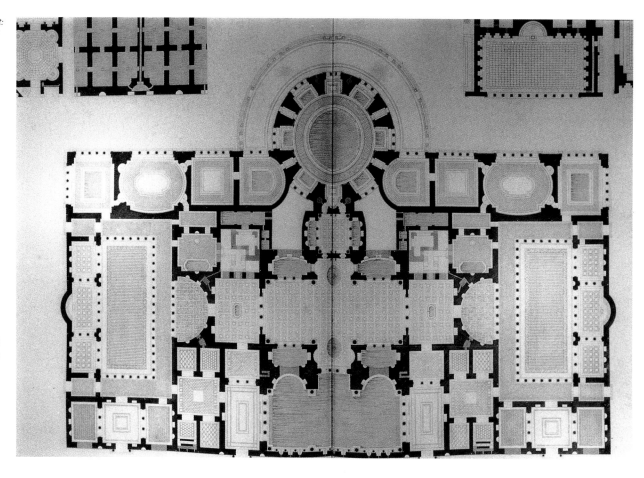

exercises had prepared his son for the combination of disparate functions into a single monumental whole, a process best exemplified in the ancient world by Roman bath complexes. Elmes's own 1837 Royal Academy Gold Medal competition design for a National Museum bears this out, showing him to have been fully capable of manipulating Antique elements in the grandiose eighteenth-century manner reminiscent of Marie-Joseph Peyre and Soane, the latter of whom informed early nineteenth-century students in his seventh Royal Academy lecture that 'in the general combination of the plans of buildings of every kind the artist will receive most effectual and powerful assistance in the knowledge to be obtained from the remains of the Baths'.[34] There is no doubt that Elmes's imagination was fired by Roman exemplars and that he would have travelled to Rome himself whilst working on St George's Hall, but for his developing tuberculosis. Five months before his death he told Rawlinson that he had been advised against his desire to travel to Italy, 'as my enthusiasm for art would induce me possibly to neglect my health, by over-exerting myself among the innumerable wonders of the "Eternal City"', and in lieu of travel he had carried on with the academic study of architecture 'unceasingly and earnestly' (as another contemporary put it) throughout the entire process of designing St George's Hall.[35] Among the sources he studied

was surely Guillaume-Abel Blouet's *Restauration des Thermes d'Anthonin Caracalla à Rome* (Fig.169). Lord Burlington's *Fabbriche antiche* (c.1736–40) and Charles Cameron's *The Baths of the Romans* (1772) were English works on the baths to which Elmes might have referred, but Blouet's work was more topical, having been published in 1828. Indeed, Blouet's survey and restoration of the Baths of Caracalla, presenting the results of new excavations made in 1824, became the only early nineteenth-century French *envoi* to reach printed form, thanks to the support of Antoine-Chrysostome Quatremère de Quincy. As discussed in Chapter 4, the published work departed from the strict guidelines of the *envois*, however, in that it included a plate showing a perspectival reconstruction of the Frigidarium, enlivened by groups of historical figures (Fig.170). This image served a double purpose, for whilst it made it very clear how late Roman vaults sprung from columns against the wall, the presence of human figures also suggested that this was an architecture of living relevance. Many years later, with St George's Hall approaching its completion, Cockerell's assistant John Goodchild was to produce a wonderful *capriccio* of the Concert Hall which provides a modern counterpart to the scene depicted by Blouet (Pl.xxiv). It has been suggested that it was Cockerell, in fact, who directed Elmes's attention towards Blouet's work, not least because he produced his own restored perspective of the Frigidarium of the Baths of Caracalla, inspired by that of Blouet, to illustrate his lectures as Professor of Architecture at the Royal Academy.[36] But it cannot be assumed that this was the case, as Cockerell's drawing (finished by his assistant Jackson) dates from 1845, and Blouet was in any case already a well-known figure in England, where, as a friend of Thomas Leverton Donaldson's, he had been elected an Honorary Member of the Institute of British Architects in 1837. Moreover, in his fourth Royal Academy Lecture of 1843, Cockerell spoke of the great central spaces of Roman baths and basilicas, saying: 'The interest excited amongst the French students recently … promises that this admirable feature of ancient architecture will be reproduced in Europe before many years pass'.[37] Cockerell referred to Blouet but not to St George's Hall, suggesting that he was not party to Elmes's design intentions at this point.

Elmes had possibly already drawn on Blouet in early 1842, when he remodelled the north end of his building so that the semi-circular projection was fully integrated with the body in the manner of the Caldarium of the Baths, rather than simply added on as it had been when first conceived (see Fig.164).[38] Indeed, he had also experimented with this device in his 1837 Royal Academy Gold Medal design. However, what seems to have caught his attention more than the formal northeast to south-west progression from the open-air swimming pool to the circular Caldarium was the central cross-vaulted Frigidarium (thought by Blouet to be a Cella Tepidaria or Spheristerium), with its screens of paired columns at either end leading through rectangular vestibules (which Blouet called Frigidaria) and semi-circular exedrae to twin palastrae (peristyles). Elmes's most fully developed plan for St George's Hall shows that he had not only modelled his Concert Hall on the Caracalla Frigidarium but had also set up a similar sense of cross-axis, using screens of paired columns between Hall and courtrooms (see Fig.168). The columns within the courtrooms, which were introduced in 1844, were intended to create an architectural linkage of their own by lying in the same plane as those of the South Hall and north entrance hall.[39] For functional reasons, however, the Committee asked Elmes to set those in the Crown Court slightly further from the side walls than those in the Civil Court and, once the link was lost, Elmes remodelled the entrance halls.[40] The architect clung on, however, to the axial linkage between the Concert Hall and the two courtrooms, evidently deeply inspired by Blouet's restoration. In his perspective (see Fig.170) Blouet had placed an entablature with two standing statues over paired columns *in antis* at the ends of the Frigidarium. Behind the statues was the void of the rectangular vestibules, their terminating walls given painted architectural decoration. The lunette above the void of the Frigidarium had a tripartite thermal window. A series of drawings show how Elmes attempted to emulate this form within the contexts of the functions of St George's Hall and the environment of Liver-

pool.[41] In an early scheme, the shape of the Caracalla thermal window became the void between Hall and courtroom, the lunette above having a small rectangular window (Fig.171). Realizing the need for more light, however, Elmes experimented and eventually opened a much larger semi-circle of the upper lunette to be glazed and returned to the Caracalla precedent of a semi-circular void over the entablature, effectively the arrangement seen in Pl.xxiv, except that Elmes intended the glazing of the upper lunette to have radial bars.[42] In Blouet's perspective, the view from the centre of the Frigidarium penetrated right through to the slight apse of the Ephebeum on the outer periphery of the central block. One of the longitudinal sections shows that the figure Blouet proposed at the terminal point of this axis to the west was the Farnese Hercules, the most famous statue to have been excavated from the site, whilst that at the east was a Minerva, perhaps also from the Farnese Collection in Naples or the Minerva Giustiniani, a centrepiece of Pius VII's Vatican

OPPOSITE

*171. Harvey Lonsdale Elmes:
Elevation for the north end
of the Concert Hall in St
George's Hall, Liverpool,
mid 1840s.*

Braccio Nuovo. There is a correspondence here with Elmes' conception of the axis through his own building. In late 1846 he wrote to Rawlinson:

I hope, when you 'contemplated the finished structure' that there was *no organ* at the *end*, but that you stood on the Judges' Platform in one Court, your eye glancing along the ranges of ruddy columns on either side, in all the richness and strong colour of a fore-ground; then reposing for an instant on the lofty arched opening communicating with the Hall, whose broad and richly-coffered soffite throws a shadow upon the grey columns beneath, and forms the middle distance, it pierces the atmosphere of the great Hall, passes the corresponding opening into the other Court, without distinguishing a particle of the detail, from the great distance, and finally rests upon the further Judge's Throne.[43]

In this remarkable passage, the strength and wisdom of the judges are symbolically interlinked like Hercules and Minerva in Blouet's Baths of Caracalla, just as St George's Hall represents a built sibling of Blouet's vision of the whole Roman building. The sense of pictorial composition in the way Elmes described the light and spatial recession of the interior, how-ever, suggests that he had not entirely lost sight of Piranesian imagery of Roman ruins which he had never been able to see in actuality for himself.

The strength of Elmes's vision of his building as a modern version of a mighty Roman enfilade was such that he spent much of 1845 countering the arguments of S. S. Wesley, brought in by the Committee as a musical expert, that the organ should be placed at the end of St George's Hall, there-by obstructing the axial concept. In early 1847 Elmes made one final attempt to delay implementation of the Committee's decision to insert the organ at the north end of the Concert Hall, only to be rebuked by the Council which told its Law Courts Committee that the musical function of the Hall 'should not be made subservient to architectural ornament'.[44] Elmes, however, had not been as naïve about the matter of the organ as this statement has led modern historians to believe. His preference, accepted by the Committee before Wesley's views were known, was to place it to one side of the Hall, but he had also proffered a clever alternative design in which it was to be placed at the end with a split case, so that the view into the Civil Court and the window above were not impeded.[45]

In terms of the internal 'architectural ornament' of St George's Hall, more specifically, it is difficult to know pre-cisely what Elmes intended, partly because relatively few drawings survive from early 1847 when he was preparing the contract for the completion of the building and partly because much of what was executed reflects Cockerell's later alter-ations. However, Pl.xxiiia, which probably post-dates the 1844 introduction of Aberdeen granite for the columns of the Hall, shows some of the detail the architect had in mind at that fairly advanced stage. The coffers of the barrel vault were rectangular and figurative scenes were hinted at in pencil in the row just above the spandrels, an indication of the 'fresco'

Rawlinson said Elmes intended to introduce to the Concert Hall's walls and ceiling.[46] It is significant that Blouet had also filled the coffers of his reconstructed Caracalla Frigidarium with such scenes, although in his case the groined vault and polygonal shape of the coffers reflected the precedents he took from the surviving examples of the Baths of Diocletian (the Church of S. Maria degli Angeli) and the Basilica of Max-entius. For the spandrels, Elmes proposed the introduction of the caduceus motif, symbol of Mercury, messenger of the gods, though an alternative was contemplated between the fourth and fifth bays to the north (right). Over the central arch the architect proposed the inscription '*Deus Nobis Haec Otia Fecit*' ('Our God Gave Us This Leisure'). Restrained Roman devices and details such as these are to be found in those Elmes sketches and working drawings for interior articulation which do survive.

When, in the autumn of 1847, Elmes left England for Jamaica in a fruitless attempt to recover his health, he must have felt confident that his vision for St George's Hall was in the final stages of realization. The shell of the building was complete, the roofs were on all but the central part and he had even made alterations to the top of the attic, the appearance of the skyline being 'not so satisfactory as I could have desired' as a result of the 'unexpected vistas' caused by demo-lition of houses in Lime Street.[47] In the interior all of the columns were in place except those of the north entrance hall, and the Concert Hall was almost ready for the centring needed to erect the vault. He had left drawings for the finish-ing contract which, although incomplete, did provide a block plan showing the 'arrangements of the Terraces and steps' for all but the north end of the building, plans of all floors, plans and sections of all the principal rooms, foyers and staircases and some drawings of architectural and ornamental details at one-eighth of the actual size.[48] His mentor Cockerell had offered to provide advice on matters of architectural taste and detail, while a London friend named Meredith had agreed to complete the finishings contract specifications with Raw-linson, who was also to superintend the construction work. However, the completion of St George's Hall over the next seven years actually took place under other circumstances. After Elmes's departure and subsequent death, Rawlinson sub-mitted the draft specifications for the finishings contract to the Committee and continued to plan the structure of the brick vault and to strengthen the floor for its erection. He was unable, however, to control the building contractor, whose dilatory behaviour meant that the roof timbers were exposed to the elements for too long and became liable to rot. The Committee therefore determined that the Corporation Sur-veyor, John Weightman, should be required to superintend completion of the building. Although Weightman was to con-sult with 'some eminent architect from time to time', the Com-mittee began to think about reducing costs by, for example, purchasing gas lamps for the Concert Hall in London rather

than having them specially designed.[49] Perhaps it was in response to these developments that the Chairman, John Buck Lloyd, took the opportunity of a visit to London in March 1849 to arrange for Cockerell to provide architectural advice for a series of one-off fees. Less than three weeks later, Cockerell arrived in Liverpool and went over the building with the Committee. A week after that he had redesigned the south front.

With the exception of the two innermost columns (which were fluted by Weightman in 1848, despite Elmes's wish that they remain plain) and the placement of the pedimental sculpture executed by William Nicholl, showing Britannia overseeing domestic production and the country's role in world affairs, the south portico was completed by early 1849.[50] However, the platform on which the superstructure stands was not and, although Elmes clearly left his instructions for how this area was to be handled, there may have been some problems for Cockerell to resolve. Elmes intended that there should be access through the doorway in the platform facing St John's Lane (see Fig.166) to a ground-level vestibule (which still survives at ground level underneath the portico) and from there to the south sub-hall and the pair of staircases which rise to the principal floor east and west of the South Hall. Cockerell, however, decided that direct access to the portico and South Hall was required from street level, necessitating wholesale rebuilding of the recently completed podium and redesign of the lower platform.[51] In a remarkably insensitive intervention for someone who had in all likelihood encouraged Elmes in his design ideas during the preceding decade, Cockerell replaced Elmes's podium with flights of steps which surround the entire portico (see Pl.xxii), and opened up access to the terrace at the foot of the portico by building bifurcated steps rising east and west from St John's Lane across the front of the platform. The power of Elmes's superimposed platform, podium and portico was dissipated by both devices. The portico steps have the visual effect of countering its verticality, partly because they wholly surround the columns (to which Cockerell gave no compensatory pedestals) and partly because the steps, built as a stylobate in proportion to the order, were too steep for anthropometric convenience, necessitating doubling of the treads and risers to the centre of the portico to match those Elmes had designed for comfortable lateral access. The loss of energy caused by the spreading effect of the portico was further exacerbated by the bifurcated flights in the platform below which, for reasons of security, were given railings and gateposts consisting of truncated Aberdeen granite columns removed from the Concert Hall when the organ was installed. The bifurcated flights, 'like the bow legs of an unfortunate cripple', and the 'complication of the upper steps' were the subject of a stinging attack by the railway entrepreneur and Committee member, Henry Booth, in 1857, and over the following two years the platform was built out to its present position, obliterating the bifurcated flights.[52] Cockerell's portico steps, however, have remained in place.

It was not until 1851 that Cockerell was officially appointed architect of St George's Hall and, until that time, construction continued under the supervision of Weightman. It seems likely that the Corporation Surveyor did make design contributions of his own, because he persuaded the Committee to purchase over twenty architectural works, 'absolutely necessary for example and reference'.[53] The books included histori-

cal publications, such as copies of Vitruvius and Antoine Desgodetz, and modern European works by Jean-Nicolas-Louis Durand, Paul Letarouilly, Schinkel and von Klenze. Among the modern British works, naturally enough, were Charles Heathcote Tatham's studies of ancient ornament, Taylor and Cresy on Roman antiquities and Donaldson's *Examples of Doorways*, presumably the 1833 volume on ancient buildings in Greece and Italy. Once Cockerell assumed overall control, however, he began to apply his own outstanding working vocabulary of Classical form.

As the development of his designs for Cambridge University Library, his competition entries for the Royal Exchange and his development of Basevi's Fitzwilliam Museum designs showed, Cockerell's vision of modern Classicism drew more on the full chronological range of possibilities than on reinterpretations of Antique usage alone. An early indication of what was to come inside St George's Hall and its Concert Room lay in the Renaissance feature of stone balustrades which he had introduced outside to the platform at the south end of the building. The balustrade reappeared in the balconies of the Hall, replacing Elmes's metal fences and advancing across the front of the piers to meet the columns (Pl. xxiiib).[54] Cockerell's longitudinal section of the Hall was dated 15 November 1851 and makes a striking comparison with Elmes's equivalent image (see Pl.xxiiia). The older architect used colour, as well as form, to give added plasticity to the interior. At pedestal level greeny-grey and red stone facings alternate. The walls above, which Elmes had proposed to inset with simple yellow disks, now had green panels with small blue insets just below the balconies of green marble with yellow balusters. In the spandrels above, Cockerell introduced huge angel figures (derived perhaps from the Stanza della Segnatura in the Vatican, or even from the Angel Choir of Lincoln Cathedral). Finally, Elmes's simple coffered vault gave way to a busy pattern of square and rectangular coffers, featuring the caduceus and fasces. A drawing of the vault by Cockerell prepared slightly earlier in 1851 laid out the iconography of the arms in octagonal surrounds and of the coffers in the arches at either end of the Hall.[55] Additional work in the Hall included the introduction of lamps hanging from rostra which project from the summit of each arch and the enriching of the doors into their present almost Celtic form, incorporating the banner 'S.P.Q.L.', for '*Senatus Populusque Liverpudliensis*' (see Fig.174). Cockerell also commissioned Alfred Stevens to bring the floor into play through a spectacular Minton tile design on an appropriately marine theme.

It would be incorrect to think that Elmes left no information about his intentions for the smaller Concert Room at the north end of the building, since two sheets of sketches showing this interior still survive. Elmes intended the body of the semi-circular room to have four tiers of seating, like a Classical theatre, and Corinthian pilasters around the hemicycle. The stage area, with a large organ below a lunette window, was given square-coffered shallow barrel vaults, springing from the entablature over pairs of Corinthian columns.[56] However, the interior which today represents one of the building's great glories is entirely the work of Cockerell.[57] In some of its features it parallels Hector Lefuel's exactly contemporary small theatre at Fontainebleau. Certainly the analogies which can be drawn between the richness of the Concert Room interior, where Cockerell had an almost entirely free hand, and Second Empire design in France indicate the extent to which Elmes's more strictly Antique language had been superseded.

Cockerell's alterations and additions to the building notwithstanding, St George's Hall stands as a testimony to the vision of Roman Antiquity in Britain during the second quarter of the nineteenth century, which that architect had ironically done much to create with his restoration of the Forum. In that respect, the men of Liverpool who were responsible for the commission and for oversight of the design and building procedure played a role of equal significance. Some of the individuals are commemorated by statues in the building: Henry Booth in the north entrance hall and Jonathan Brooks (carved in Rome by the Liverpool sculptor Benjamin Spence) in the Concert Hall for example. Brooks, Cambridge educated and Archdeacon of Liverpool, was a man of immense local influence. When he died in 1855, sixty thousand attended his funeral in the largest demonstration of civic grief since the funeral of William Huskisson, Liverpool's Member of Parliament and Prime Minister George Canning's President of the Board of Trade, who was run down by a locomotive at the opening of the Liverpool and Manchester Railway in 1830. Although the decision to form a company to erect St George's Hall was taken partly because of objections to the performance of oratorios in Liverpool churches, Brooks was an enthusiastic Chairman of the company's Committee up to the point at which it relinquished its responsibilities to the council's Law Courts Committee. Indeed, it was Brooks who chaired the joint meeting of the two Committees at which the decision was taken to accept Elmes's proposal for a monumental combined Hall and Assize Courts building.[58] Also among those at the meeting were, for the St George's Hall Company, Booth and its Deputy Chairman (the former Mayor) Hardman Earle, and for the Council William Currie, William Earle and Hugh Hornby (all three also recent Mayors, and Currie and Hornby members of the Finance Committee sub-committee which judged the Assize Courts competition in 1840). The Earle family emerged as leading supporters of Elmes and his ambitions. Hardman, a London and Liverpool broker educated at Charterhouse, was responsible for keeping Elmes's interest in Liverpool alive when the Law Courts Committee favoured giving the commission to the Corporation Surveyor Franklin. In 1846 he commissioned Elmes to design his Italianate house, Allerton Tower. A staunch Liberal and modernizer, who supported George Stephenson's ambitions for the Liverpool-Manchester Railway and became a Director

of the company, Hardman Earle later received a baronetcy from William Ewart Gladstone.[59] His son William, although never formally chairman of the Law Courts Committee, was a key member for most of the 1840s and, as a close personal friend, took Elmes abroad for his only view of European architecture in 1842 and wept when reporting the architect's death to the Committee in 1848. Other influential figures in the genesis of St George's Hall were the Committee's chairmen Hugh Hornby (1840), Henry Lawrence (1842–4) and John Buck Lloyd (from 1845), this last, as has been seen, being instrumental in ensuring a full role for Cockerell after the death of Elmes.[60] The great Victorian Liverpool Liberal politician, James Picton, himself trained as an architect, was elected to the Council in 1849 and joined the Law Courts Committee the following year.

The men who led the way in the commission for St George's Hall were largely the leading politicians of the Whig party, which had gained a majority on the Liverpool Town Council in the elections of 1835 following the passage of the Reform-inspired Municipal Corporations Act. However, the fact that there was no discernible change of policy towards the Hall, once the moderate Tory faction regained control of the Council in 1841, suggests that a common sense of civic identity outweighed any party political symbolism in the architectural choices that were made. Liverpool merchants, whatever their internal differences, were in favour of aggrandizing Liverpool, and it is no surprise to note that the modern buildings with which Elmes visually compared his proposals for St George's Hall to impress the Committee were those of a rival city and town, Smirke's General Post Office and Wilkins's University in London, and the Birmingham Town Hall (see Figs 89 and 100).[61] Individuals like Brooks, Booth and Hardman Earle were educated to value the political and enterprising achievements of their contemporaries in terms of Classical history, a process seen at work slightly earlier in the artist Samuel Austin's watercolour *Carthage: Aeneas at the Court of Dido*, exhibited in London in 1827, which features four contemporary Liverpool buildings and the original design for the St James Cemetery Chapel by the artist's friend and fellow Liverpool academician, Greek Revivalist John Foster.[62] By the 1830s, however, the paradigm sought by those dominating Liverpudlian cultural life was changing from that of Athens to that of Rome, as witnessed by the terms of both the St George's Hall and the Assize Courts competitions which distinguished between Greek and Roman styles and indicated that the latter would be equally acceptable. Foster himself, indeed, had signalled this change in one of his last works, the screen of Lime Street Station of 1835–6 opposite St George's Hall, which featured triumphal arch motifs and, accordingly, the Corinthian order. Whilst this changing evaluation of ancient Rome was no doubt underpinned by the general development of Roman archaeology and reconstruction, which had occurred in the previous years, there were more specific reasons. One, as has just been indicated, was Liverpool's role in the development of the railway, commonly described in the 1830s and 1840s (including by Booth) as an achievement which equalled or even surpassed Roman engineering prowess.[63] A second was the intention to create a new civic space surrounded by important public buildings in the Classical idiom, which led those charged with decision-making more readily to the precedent of the Roman Forum than to that of the Athenian Agora, of which comparatively little was known.

Although Elmes visualized his work on the plateau outside Lime Street Station in a manner akin to images of the Roman Forum, such as Pennethorne's reconstruction (see Fig.167), the term 'Forum' does not occur in his dealings with the Committee or correspondence with Rawlinson. Rawlinson did, however, write to Elmes of St George's Hall as a 'temple-like structure to pleasure the "merchant princes"', adding that the architect was achieving effects which 'the ancients knew and studied, hence the majestic, awe-inspiring ruins of the faded empires, Egypt, Greece, and Rome – the learned, the refined,

the mighty!'.[64] When, in 1855, Elmes's own father called the building the 'pride and honour of the Senate and People of Liverpool', he was drawing attention to the fact that St George's Hall was intended not just a place for the bourgeoisie, as seen in Goodchild's interior view (see Pl.xxiv) or at the inaugurating oratorio, but also for the common people, who were visiting the site in such numbers by 1849 that the Committee had to draw up restrictive rules so that the workmen were not hindered.[65] After its completion the Hall quickly became a venue for such Liverpudlian celebrations as the Christmas entertainment given to their workers by the cigar manufacturers Cope, Brothers and Co. in 1864 (Fig. 172).[66] By that time, the improvements committee of the town's Architectural and Archaeological Society had suggested that the proposed construction of Salt Water Baths on the site of St John's Village offered 'the opportunity of attaining an effective architectural combination quite unequalled in this country', by means of a screen linking the Hall and Baths. This arrangement 'like the Forum and the Baths of ancient Rome, would minister alike to the convenience and grandeur

of this important town'.[67] No doubt inspired by this idea, in September 1854 Henry Sumners published a perspective in the *Liverpool Mercury* showing St George's Hall as the focal point of a grandiose Forum stretching to the west, an image which coincided with Joseph Boult's history of the Hall in the same paper. The process of fulfilling the Forum vision began in 1856, with the competition to design a Free Public Library (now the William Brown Museum) on Shaw's Brow, just to the north-west of St George's Hall. Behind the decision-making were the Liberal Member of Parliament, William Brown, Picton and Weightman. Although no style was stipulated, of the sixteeen finalists all except two presented Classical designs in line with the spirit of St George's Hall (the exceptions were one attempt in 'Byzantine' idiom and one in 'Romanesque'). Thomas Allom's winning design, modified by Weightman (and now remodelled), used the Corinthian order of the Temple of Castor and Pollux (simplified as at Birmingham Town Hall), and placed the south portico on a frontal podium, as Elmes had intended for his south portico.[68] The pattern established by the outcome of this competition, which took no account of the contemporary rise of Ruskinian High Victorian Gothic, was continued along Shaw's Brow by Cornelius Sherlock's and Henry Vale's Walker Art Gallery (1874–7), by Sherlock's Picton Reading Room (1875–9) and by the Sessions House by Francis and George Holme (1882–4), producing from a rambling townscape the finest assemblage of Neo-classical buildings in England (Fig.173).[69] When one adds the honorific Wellington Column, erected by Andrew Lawson by 1863, it is clear that Picton (who saw St George's Hall as 'Roman in the style and order selected') was justified in saying in 1875 that 'the esplanade in front of St George's Hall might be called the Forum of Liverpool'.[70]

In 1844 Elmes had written to Rawlinson that 'Architecture, as a noble science and beautiful art, in the highest sense of those terms, exists unfortunately at present only in ruins, or in history and imagination.'[71] Eleven years later, when Goodchild's perspective of the completed interior of St George's Hall was shown at the Royal Academy (see Pl.xxiv), one writer commented that 'a growing feeling is spreading amongst architects that the building is almost the only

173. Comparative elevations of Shaw's Brow / William Brown Street, Liverpool, in 1850 and 1950, showing the transformation of the townscape to the north of St George's Hall in England's grandest assemblage of Classical architecture.

After W. Herdman

1850   SHAW'S BROW (now William Brown Street)   SITE CHOSEN FOR THE CENTRAL LIBRARIES

After A. P. Tankard

TECHNICAL COLLEGE AND MUSEUMS   BROWN LIBRARY   PICTON REFERENCE LIBRARY   WALKER ART GALLERY

1950   WILLIAM BROWN STREET (formerly Shaw's Brow)   FACADE OF THE CENTRAL LIBRARIES

174. St George's Hall, Liverpool, by Harvey Lonsdale Elmes, completed by Charles Robert Cockerell: The Concert Hall, with statues from right to left of Sir William Brown, Sir Robert Peel and George Stephenson.

modern erection that will confer lasting fame on the art of the century'.[72] The words 'lasting fame', used to describe an early-Victorian Classical building, along with Goodchild's visual reference to long-standing conventions for depicting vaulted Roman ruins whilst showing a new building under construction and in use, suggests the extent to which the English of the mid nineteenth century could display their achievements through the exemplar of ancient Rome. Elmes, as a contemporary remarked, had 'never ascended the Acropolis at Athens, or contemplated the splendour of the Roman Coliseum', but the strength of his imagination and the sense of history it was possible for him to develop in England during the 1830s enabled him to forge from remote ruins a building to match the aspirations of its self-confident patrons.[73] This vision of modernity expressed within an historical framework is beautifully encapsulated in a view inside the Concert Hall, looking south-west beyond the statues of Sir William Brown and Sir Robert Peel to the only Victorian hero to appear dressed in a toga (Fig.174), for this figure, dividers and notebook in hand like a stylus and tablet, carved in Rome 'to look like an Archimedes' by the Liverpool-bred sculptor John Gibson,[74] is none other than George Stephenson, pioneer of the locomotive engine.

Epilogue

In some respects the 'Roman moment' in public architecture which closed the history of the hegemony of English Neoclassicism ended with the careers of the architects who had designed its most characteristic monuments. Harvey Lonsdale Elmes died in 1847, two years after George Basevi was killed in Ely Cathedral. Joseph Hansom's work at Birmingham had bankrupted him, through no fault of his own. He found himself a new role as an architectural journalist and inventor, only later returning to architecture when circumstances had changed entirely. William Tite's introduction to the politics of the City of London proved intoxicating. He gradually withdrew from practice, becoming the Liberal Member of Parliament for Bath in 1855 (though assuming the Presidency of the Royal Institute of British Architects in the 1860s).

In truth, the tradition of travel to Italy and of archaeological study of antiquities as fundamental underpinning factors of architectural design in England had run its course by the 1840s. In 1843 Welby Pugin wished to 'circumscribe' the limits of travelling architectural students to English and northern European cathedrals, while three years later *The Builder* received a provocative letter from students:

> on the eve of completing their term of apprenticeship, relative to the next step they should take [and inquiring] if we do not consider (as they do) that it is waste of time to go to Greece and Rome, and that their proper course is to confine themselves to the study of mediaeval art in France, Belgium, and Germany.[1]

The editorial in *The Builder*, probably written by George Godwin, did not, in fact, agree, but the number of architectural students travelling to Italy had already begun to dwindle in the 1830s, with the most talented (Gilbert Scott, William Butterfield and Benjamin Woodward, for example) following their pupillage by sketching trips around Britain or northern Europe. The strength of Pugin's attacks on the Neo-classical tradition was doubtless an influential factor in this. Another was probably the fact that John Soane had failed to give any of his lectures at the Royal Academy throughout the 1820s, while from 1832 to 1836 they were merely read on behalf of the octogenarian professor by the Academy's secretary, Henry Howard. Students can hardly have been inspired by this demise in Neo-classical pedagogy, and, moreover, the 1835 decision that the new Palace of Westminster should be a 'Gothic' building probably meant more to young architects in the middle of training than it did to those already in practice. As the

case of the Roman moment itself showed, innovations in design tended to follow a generation after the innovations in education and study which had laid the foundations for them.

In one respect, the apparently antithetical Roman and Gothic Revivals were related to one another. It is not unreasonable to consider the phase of Gothic Revivalism initiated by Pugin as in itself an 'archaeological' phenomenon, in which Medieval precedents were in some ways drawn upon as literally as a Roman precedent was at Birmingham Town Hall. Moreover, travel continued to underpin the study of source material, and, while Pugin argued against any contact with the Mediterranean, men such as the antiquarian Henry Gally Knight and the Secretary of the Ecclesiological Society, Benjamin Webb, specifically looked to Italy as a source of early Christian and Gothic design. It is John Ruskin who was most closely associated with this approach, of course, but it is worth noting that many of the British architects who travelled to Italy in the twenty years after 1815 had already applied similar archaeological standards to surveying Medieval buildings to those they applied to Roman ruins, even though they had no aesthetic predilection for Romanesque or Gothic design. The greatest exponents here were none other than the authors of *The Architectural Antiquities of Rome*, George Ledwell Taylor and Edward Cresy, who in 1829 also published finely measured surveys of the four buildings around the Campo at Pisa in *Architecture of the Middle Ages in Italy*.

The archaeological literalism of all three of the Greek, Roman and Gothic Revivals finds a further parallel in a fourth new idiom used in English public architecture during the first half of the nineteenth century, even though this did not draw on an 'ancient' architecture for its inspiration. Charles Barry, through his loyal friend from their time together in Italy, John Lewis Wolfe, was keen to deny that his Italianate (Renaissance Revival) buildings were overtly dependent on certain prototypes, but most historians today would hardly discuss Barry's Travellers' Club in Pall Mall or Athenaeum in Manchester without reference to Raphael's Palazzo Pandolfini in Florence, or Sydney Smirke's Carlton Club without reference to Jacopo Sansovino's S. Marco Library in Venice.[2] What this idiom offered, which the Neo-classical could not, however, was precisely the sort of flexibility needed for the increasingly large-scale public architecture of rapidly growing cities and governmental administration – a situation foreseen by Franz Christian Gau and by Thomas Leverton Donaldson in their

175. Thomas Allom: An imaginative view of Rome, c.1860, in which restored ancient buildings such as the Mausoleum of Hadrian mix with modern Roman buildings such as St Peter's. On the left, ramshackle houses overhanging the Tiber add a picturesque touch.

deliberations on Roman civic buildings and spaces inspired by the Forum at Pompeii, and reflected by the subsequent development of public architecture in London, Paris and other European cities.[3]

Interest in the ruined architecture of ancient Rome did not disappear, however, in the changing architectural climate of the 1840s and 1850s. Indeed, although no study has been made of the subject, the arrival of the European railway system probably enabled architects not otherwise inclined to do so to visit Rome, although Greece remained a journey for only the most committed of travellers. Taylor's travels in Europe during the 1850s and 1860s were largely made by train and therefore under altogether different circumstances than in 1818–19. Some architects maintained an interest in the archaeological discoveries of Roman Italy, an interest reflected in the academic deliberations of the Institute of British Architects and in, for example, the impressive restoration of the Roman Capitol and Fora including the city as far as Diocletian's Baths beyond, made from a perspective high on the Palatine Hill, which was shown at the Royal Academy in 1858 by the architect Arthur Ashpitel.[4] In the face of a Victorian architecture he called an 'omnium gatherum' of 'shreds and patches … without rhyme or reason', Taylor returned to Rome in 1857–8 determined to rekindle enthusiasm for the archaeology of the

city.[5] His paper, 'The Stones of Ancient Rome, and of Etruria', was read at the Institute and published in 1859. It embodied the results of the excavations and topographical discoveries which had taken place in the forty years since his first visit. There was evidently sufficient demand for a new edition of *The Architectural Antiquities of Rome* to be brought out in 1874, though Taylor had died the previous year and it fell to his son to see the revised work through the press.

The great porticoes of Huddersfield Railway Station by James Pritchett, opened in 1850, and of Birkenhead Town Hall by Christopher Obee Ellison, 1883–7, or the Elmes-like colonnade of Cuthbert Brodrick's Leeds Town Hall, 1853–8, represent built counterparts of these continuing interests in ancient Roman architecture. In some of these examples the high podia associated with Roman temples were used as an appropriate way of aggrandizing what was often a town's most significant civic edifice. All, however, possess other features clearly not drawn from the Neo-classicist's vocabulary. The use of Antiquity by Victorian architects belonged with their eclecticism, and elements drawn from Renaissance or even Baroque sources were happily introduced. It is this eclecticism, in which a visionary response to the ancient world mingles with Renaissance architecture, that is so well illustrated in Charles Robert Cockerell's 'Professor's Dream', prepared for his Royal Academy lectures in 1848, or in Thomas Allom's 'Imaginative View of Rome' of *c.*1860 (Fig.175).[6] Pompeii, too, continued to capture the imagination of the Victorians (there were at least twelve new editions of Edward Bulwer-Lytton's *The Last Days of Pompeii* during the reign of Victoria and it was twice staged as a dramatic spectacle). Ambrose Poynter's studies of Pompeian houses bore fruit in the work of his son, Edward Poynter, well known as one of the leading painters working with Classical subject material in the second half of the century. Poynter actually designed a Pompeian interior decorative scheme for the Earl of Wharncliffe at Wortley Hall, Yorkshire, in 1882–3. No doubt his sources included his father's pioneering studies, and he certainly owned a copy of Sir William Gell's *Pompeiana* (now in the library of the Warburg Institute in London).

These examples do not, of course, counter the hegemonic status accorded by historians to High Victorian Gothic and Progressive Eclectic architecture in the second half of the nineteenth century, but they do point to the dangers inherent in seeing the Regency and Victorian dilemmas of style as indicative of indecisiveness, shallowness and a lack of clear direction against which only the Gothic tradition, with its high principles, stands out. They suggest that British culture supported and enjoyed a kind of architectural pluralism which, in many ways, was to remain true of the twentieth century as well. In other words, the diversity of nineteenth-century design can be read as both positive and as a fore-runner of our own reluctance to be bound into any single approach. This book has attempted a reappraisal of just one of those diverse forms of architecture, one which has hitherto been much misunderstood, even maligned. The 'Roman moment' occurred at the end of a Neo-classical tradition of British architectural travel to Italy stretching back to the middle of the eighteenth century. Its monuments reflect the remarkable progress of Roman archaeology in the early nineteenth century and the equally extraordinary vision of Roman buildings and cities that archaeology inspired among architectural students, but they also reflect the symbolic value placed upon Roman civilization by the Englishmen who selected them as designs and paid for their construction.

Appendix A
British architects in Italy, 1740–1840

Professional architects and architectural students (those who were clearly amateurs have been omitted) are listed below in the chronological order of their visits to Italy, as far as this can be ascertained. For travellers up to 1800, readers may consult the relevant entries in Ingamells, and annotations have therefore been kept to a minimum. For architects travelling 1800–1840 more notes have been provided, with the particular purposes of supplementing information given in Colvin and of demonstrating that the pattern of residence in the quarter of Rome around Piazza di Spagna was resumed. Lines of asterisks denote an interruption to the otherwise continuous presence of British architects in Italy. The symbol † identifies architectural students who died before returning to Britain.

1740
George Mercer[1]

1740–42
Robert Taylor

1742–51
Nicholas Revett

1742–51
James Stuart

1747–54
Matthew Brettingham Junior

1750
George Mercer (second visit)

1750–53
Stephen Riou

1750–55
William Chambers

1755
James Paine Senior

1755
Willis[2]

1755–7
Robert Adam

1755–8
William Mylne (travelling with his brother Robert)

1755–9
Robert Mylne

1756–9
Mills[3]

1759–64
George Dance the Younger

1760–63
James Adam

1760–63
George Richardson (travelling in the entourage of James Adam)

1761–7
John Baxter

?1762–8
James Wyatt

Early to mid 1760s?
Thomas Collins Overton[4]

1766–7?
William Newton

1766–70
James Paine Junior

1768–9?
Charles Cameron

1768–70
William Kirby

1769
?Graham Myres

1769
Richard Norris

1769–76
Thomas Harrison

1770–72
James Lewis

1770–72
Michael Shanahan

1770–78
Thomas O'Brien

1774–5?
James Paine Junior (second visit)

1774–5
†Edward Stevens

1774–7
Christopher Ebdon

?1774–9
John Henderson

1775
Theodosius Keene

1776–9
Thomas Hardwick

1778–80
John Soane

1778–82
Robert Furze Brettingham

1783–4
Alexander Nasmyth

1784–8
Willey Reveley

1785–6
Thomas Johnson

1786
?John Thomas Groves

1786–98
Thomas O'Brien (second visit)

1787–8
George Saunders

1789–90
Samuel Bunce

?1790
John Craig

?1790–91
John Thomas Groves (possible second visit)

1790–94
George Hadfield[5]

1791–3
James Playfair

1791–6
Francis Sandys

early 1790s?
George Gibson the Younger[6]

1793–4
Robert Golden

1794–6
Charles Heathcote Tatham

1794–7
Joseph Michael Gandy

* * * * * * * * * * * * * *

1801–3
William Wilkins Junior

1802–3
George Tappen

1802–4
Joseph Kay[7]

1802–4
Thomas Martyr (travelling with Joseph Kay)

1802–5
Robert Smirke Junior[8]

pre-1807?
John Newman[9]

* * * * * * * * * * * * * *

1811–13
John Peter Gandy
(later Gandy-Deering)

c.1811–13
Archibald Simpson

1814–15
Thomas Allason

1815–16
John Foster Junior

1815–17
Charles Robert Cockerell

1816
Thomas Cundy Senior

1816
Thomas Cundy Junior (travelling with his father)

1816
Joseph Gwilt

1816
Peter Robinson

1816–17
J. Buxton[10]

1816–17
James Hakewill

1816–19
George Basevi[11]

1816–19
John Goldicutt[12]

1816–19
Richard Sharp (travelling with Joseph Woods)

1816–19
Matthew Evan Thomas

1816–19
Joseph Woods (travelling with Richard Sharp)[13]

1817–19
George Ledwell Taylor[14]

1817–19
Edward Cresy (travelling with George Ledwell Taylor)

1817–19
William Kinnard

1817–20
Charles Barry

1817–20
William Purser (travelling as draftsman to John Sanders)

1817–20
John Sanders

1818–19
†Henry Graham[15]

1818–19
Philip Hardwick

1818–19
Henry William Inwood

1818–21
John Bond

1818–21
Lewis Vulliamy

1818–22
Thomas Leverton Donaldson[16]

1819
John Peter Gandy (second visit)[17]

1819
Thomas Jeans

1819–21
William Wesley Jenkins[18]

1819–21
Ambrose Poynter[19]

1819–21
John Lewis Wolfe[20]

1820
Lewis Wyatt

1820–
Samuel Paterson (travelling with John Davies)

1820–23?
John Davies[21]

c.1820–22
William Booth

1820–24
Henry Parke

1821–2
Charles Tyrell

1821–3
Samuel Angell

1821–3
†William Harris[22]

1821–5
Frederick Catherwood

c.1822
Joseph Bonomi Junior[23]

c.1822
Richard Bridgens

?1822
Richard Brown

1822–6
Joseph Scoles

1823–4[24]
Charles Mathews

1823–4?
Arthur Mee

1823–5
William Hosking (travelling with John Jenkins)

1823–5
John Jenkins

c.1824–6
Charles Parker[25]

1824–6
James Pennethorne

1824–6
Sydney Smirke[26]

1825
George Wightwick[27]

1825–6
Joseph Woods (second visit)

1827–30
Charles Mathews (second visit)

c.1827–30
†Henry Palmer[28]

1828
Thomas Lee[29]

c.1828–9
Robert Wetten[30]

c.1828–32
Samuel Loat

1829
Henry Goodridge

1829
Henry Roberts

late 1820s
Francis Arundale[31]

late 1820s – c.1831
J. B. Atkinson[32]

c.1830
Marriott Field

c.1830
John Hayward[33]

1830
Arthur William Hakewill[34]

1830
David Mocatta

c.1831
Richard Smirke Martyr

c.1831
David Rhind[35]

c.1831
Thomas Scandrett[36]

c.1832
John Henry Hakewill[37]

1832
S. J. Walker[38]

1832
Owen Jones

1833
Sampson Kempthorne[39]

–1833
J. A. Bell[40]

1834
Ewan Christian

mid 1830s
William Shoubridge[41]

c.1836
Francis Nash[42]

c.1836
Charles Parish (travelling with Francis Nash)

1837
Thomas Henry Wyatt[43]

–1837
Edward I'Anson Junior

c.1837
John Johnson

c.1838
Robert Lacon Sibley

c.1839
James Thomson[44]

Appendix B
British Members of the Instituto di Corrispondenza Archeologica 1829–36

This Appendix lists Associate, Honorary, Ordinary and Corresponding members of the Instituto in Rome who were British, or who appear to have been British. The list of members for the opening year of the Institute, 1829, is transcribed from the *Bullettino* of that year, pp.iii–xv. The names of members elected in the five years from 1831 have then been extracted from the *Bullettino*. Although this publication was issued monthly, new members are listed below simply under the year of election, generally with their class of membership. Places of residence are also given, where indicated.

1829–30
(1) ASSOCIATI
Duke of Bedford (London)
William Betham (London)
H. Bunbury (London)
Lord Burghersh, British Minister Plenipotentiary to the Court of
  Tuscany (Florence)
Thomas Burgon (London)
Edward Cheny (London)
Keppel Craven (Naples)
General Sir Rufane Dunkin (London)
Marquis Douro (London)
Colonel Fitzclarence (London)
Hon. Henry Edward Fox (London)
William Fraser (London)
Bartle Frere (London)
Rt Hon. Charles Grant (London)
Greville, Secretary of the Privy Council (London)
Lord Haddington (London)
George Hamilton (London)
Tarrick Hamilton (London)
Revd J. C. Hare (Rome)
Graves Haughton (London)
Revd Edward Hautrey (London)
Hawkins (London)
Henderson (London)
Godfrey Higgins (London)
Lord Holland (London)
Thomas Hope (London)
Dr Jenks (London)
Henry Gally Knight (London)
Charles King, Prefect of the Natural History section of the British
  Museum (London)
Lord Lovaine (London)
Mr Morier, British Ambassador to the Court of Persia (London)
Viscount Newark (London)
William Ouseley (London)
Gore Ouseley (London)
Phillip Pusey (London)
James Ruddol Todd (London)
Earl of Shrewsbury (Rome)
Mrs Marianna Starke (Sorrento)
Alexander Thomson (Edinburgh)

George Warrender MP (London)
Revd [sic, but perhaps Richard] Westmacott (London)
Countess of Westmoreland (Rome)
Revd Wisemann, Rector of English College (Rome)

(2) HONORARY
Duke of Buckingham (London)
Marquis of Northampton (Rome)

(3) ORDINARY
Revd Richard Burgess (of St John's College, Cambridge, but in Rome)
C. R. Cockerell (London)
Edward Dodwell (Rome)
Fox, British Minister designate in Buenos Aires (then in Italy)
Sir William Gell (Rome)
Captain Leake (London)
James Millingen (London)
Revd Dr George Frederick Nott (Canon of Winchester, but in Rome)

(4) CORRESPONDING
None

1831
Lord Aberdeen
Hon. C. B. Bathurst
Trinity College and the University of Cambridge (as institutional
  subscribers)
Charles McFarlane
J. W. Head (Oxford)
Michael Jones
Revd Professor Lee
J. B. S. Morrit
Sir J. O. Newport, Bt
The Society of Dilettanti (as institutional subscriber)
John L. Stoddart
Sir Vesey Fitzgerald
Howard Vyse

1832
None

1833
Julius Hare (Cambridge)
Mr Wordsworth (Cambridge)

1834
Lord Pembroke (then in Rome, Honorary Member)
Dr [Thomas] Arnold, Rector of Rugby School (Ordinary Member)
Lord Stanhope (then in Rome, Honorary Member)

1835
Professor Robert Consword (Cambridge, Associate Member)
Mr Pashley (Cambridge, Associate Member)

Mr Milnes (Corresponding Member)

P. L. [sic] Donaldson, Secretary of the Institute of British Architects
(Ordinary Member)

Mr Wilkinson (Ordinary Member)

Nicholas Carlisle, Secretary of the Society of Antiquaries
(Corresponding Member)

Mr Hawkins, Keeper of the British Museum (Corresponding Member)

1836

James Ingram (Associate Member)

Mr Trevelyan (Associate Member)

Mr Witham (Associate Member)

Appendix C
British architectural pupillage 1740–1840

Names in square brackets indicate important architects who did not travel to Italy.

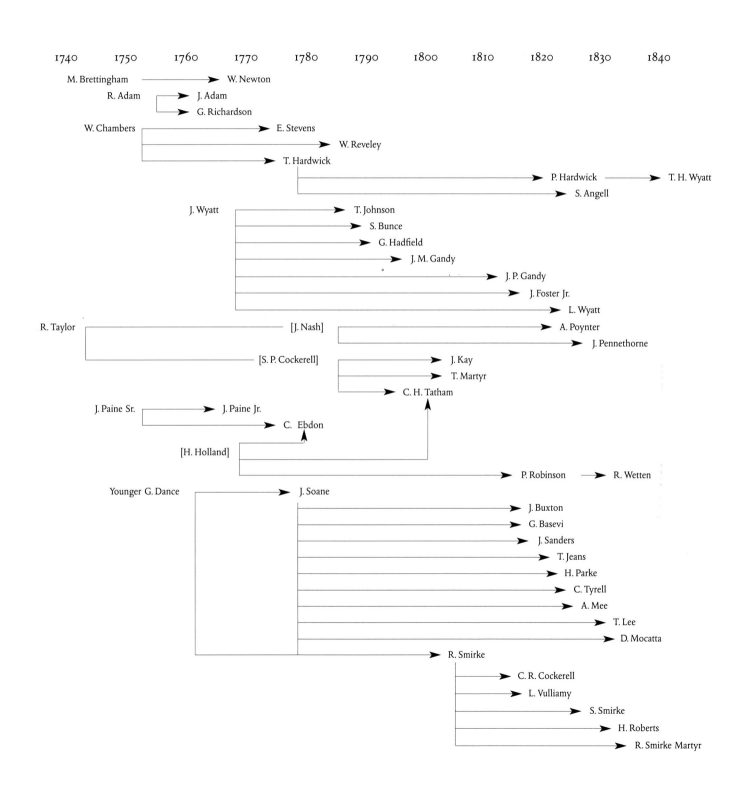

Notes

See the abbreviations listed on p.17 for a guide to shorter entries in the notes.

Introduction

1. On this point see R. Middleton and D. Watkin, *Neoclassical and 19th Century Architecture*, I, p.78: 'English architects were less troubled by theory and ideas than their French counterparts and their powers of invention were further stimulated by the growth of the Picturesque tradition'. For surveys of English architectural theory in this period see J. Mordaunt Crook, *The Dilemma of Style: Architectural Ideas from the Picturesque to the Post-Modern*, Chs 1, 2, 4, 7; and H.-W. Kruft, *A History of Architectural Theory from Vitruvius to the Present*, Ch.19.

2. I, p.310.

3. p.75.

4. J. Summerson, 'L'Architettura Neoclassica in Inghilterra', in *Bollettino del Centro Internazionale di Studi di Architettura Andrea Palladio*, p.259.

5. Hitchcock, op.cit., I, p.303.

6. For a recent study see P. Ayres, *Classical Culture and the Idea of Rome in Eighteenth-Century England*.

7. The only two studies of British travel to Italy in the early nineteenth century to counterbalance the huge quantity of literature on the eighteenth are J. Hale's introductory essay to *The Italian Journal of Samuel Rogers*, pp.56–99, and C. Brand, *Italy and the English Romantics: The Italianate Fashion in Early Nineteenth-Century England*.

8. Richard Colt Hoare, quoted in Brand, op.cit., p.160.

9. N. Vance, *The Victorians and Ancient Rome*.

10. The story of Curtius was also illustrated by John Martin in the Frontispiece to the 1829 edn of *Forget Me Not*, one of the most popular magazines of the day, which reached as many as 10,000 impressions. See M. Campbell, *John Martin: Visionary Printmaker*, p.165.

11. I, pp.vi–vii.

12. 'Stages of the Revolution', in *The Quarterly Review*, 47, July 1832, p.588.

13. The 'Italian' style appears to have been self-consciously chosen by the 'noble and distinguished Travellers and Diplomatists' who founded the Club because 'Grecian architecture is beginning to lose our favour'. See W. Leeds, *Studies and Examples of the Modern School of English Architecture: The Travellers' Club House*, pp.14, 18–24, 29; and D. Watkin, 'The Travellers' Club and the Grand Tour: Correcting Raphael…', in *The British Art Journal*, pp.56–62.

14. R. Rosenblum, *Transformations in Late Eighteenth Century Art*, p.3.

15. It might be argued in fact that, as a 'national' monument, the Walhalla lacked the functional civic value of the English examples discussed in Part II of this book.

16. M. Crinson and J. Lubbock, *Architecture: Art or Profession? Three Hundred Years of Architectural Education in Britain*, p.23; H. Colvin, 'What we mean by Amateur', in G. Worsley, ed., *The Role of the Amateur Architect: Papers given at the Georgian Group Symposium 1993*, pp.4–6.

17. Quoted in D. Walker and C. McWilliam, 'Cairness, Aberdeenshire', in *Country Life*, p.248.

18. pp.14–15.

19. K. Garlick, et al., eds, *The Diary of Joseph Farington*, VI, p.2083. For a recent account of precisely what membership of the Club involved, see F. Salmon, 'Charles Heathcote Tatham and the Accademia di S. Luca, Rome', in *The Burlington Magazine*, pp.85–92. On the institutionalization of travel and 'travel fraternity', see E. Kaufman, 'Architecture and Travel in the Age of British Eclecticism', in E. Blau and E. Kaufman, eds, *Architecture and its Image*, pp.59, 79.

20. In one recent survey, however, it is Neo-Palladianism which is seen as extending forward into the period generally called Neo-classical. See G. Worsley, *Classical Architecture in Britain: The Heroic Age*.

21. See E. McParland, 'Sir Thomas Hewett and the New Junta for Architecture', in Worsley, op.cit., pp.21–6; R. Hewlings, 'Chiswick House and Gardens: Appearance and Meaning', in T. Barnard and J. Clark, eds, *Lord Burlington: Architecture, Art and Life*, pp.1–149; and J. Harris, 'The Transformation of Lord Burlington: From the Palladio and Jones of his Time to the New Vitruvius', in D. Arnold, ed., *The Georgian Villa*, pp.41–7.

Chapter 1 The later eighteenth-century background

1. BAL, Gandy Family/1/Letter 31.

2. A. Oppé, 'Memoirs of Thomas Jones', in *The Walpole Society*, p.53.

3. *London and Westminster Improved*, pp.65–6.

4. J. Paine, *Plans, Elevations and Sections of Noblemen and Gentlemen's Houses*, Preface. Ironically, Paine's own son was in Italy at this moment, and he himself had gone to some lengths to gain leave from his official position as Clerk of the Works at Newmarket in order to 'make the tour of Italy' ten years earlier. See P. Leach, *James Paine*, p.26.

5. For a recent study which also stresses this point, see N. Llewellyn, 'Those Loose and Immodest Pieces: Italian Art and the British Point of View', in S. West, ed., *Italian Culture in Northern Europe in the Eighteenth Century*, p.75.

6. Fleming, p.140 (see also p.149); L. Stainton, 'Hayward's List: British Visitors to Rome 1753–1775, *The Walpole Society*, p.10.

7. Fleming, p.227. For the costs of Grand Tours generally see J. Black, *The British Abroad: The Grand Tour in the Eighteenth Century*, p.103.

8. Fleming, Fig.88 and p.281.

9. D. Watkin, *Athenian Stuart: Pioneer of the Greek Revival*, p.14; BAL, SMK 1/12.

10. Ingamells, p.808.

11. J. Kenworthy-Browne, 'Matthew Brettingham's Rome Account Book 1747–1754', in *The Walpole Society*, p.40.

12. The Academy's intention to increase the sum to £100 notwithstanding, the painter James Irvine reported from Rome that Hadfield had still only received £60. See British Library, Add. Ms. 36946, fol.191.

13. P. de la Ruffinière du Prey, 'John Soane's Architectural Education 1753–1780', Ph.D Dissertation, p.89.

14. BAL, MyFam/4/8–43.

15. M. McCarthy, 'Art Education and the Grand Tour', in M. Barasch and L. Sandler, eds, *Art the Ape of Nature: Studies in Honor of H. W. Janson*, pp.489–90.

16. Charles Heathcote Tatham received 5 guineas for a design for Ickworth from Frederick Hervey, Earl of Bristol and Bishop of Derry (Ms. Tatham Autobiography, pp.13 and 16). See also D. Stillman, 'Chimney-pieces for the English Market: A Thriving Business in Late Eighteenth-Century Rome', in *The Art Bulletin*, pp.85–94.

17. YCBA, Ms. Riou Itineral Remarks.

18. V&A, PDP, D.1479.8; British Library, Add. Ms. 45545.

19. See E. Chaney, 'Inigo Jones in Naples', in *The Evolution of the Grand Tour: Anglo-Italian Cultural Relations since the Renaissance*, pp.168–202.

20. James Stuart, Nicholas Revett, Matthew Brettingham Junior, Stephen Riou and Willey Reveley appear to have been the only five British architects to have reached Greece in the second half of the century. With the exception of Reveley's, all of these expeditions were complete by 1755. The next student visitors were probably William Wilkins and Robert Smirke in the first years of the nineteenth century.

21. R. Wood, *The Ruins of Palmyra, otherwise Tedmor in the Desart*, pp.(a)r–v.

22. BAL, Gandy Family/1/Letter 20; BAL, SMK 1/14.

23. BAL, SMK/1/26; YCBA, B1977.14.611 and 612.

24. See F. Salmon, 'British Architects, Italian Fine Arts Academies and the Foundation of the RIBA, 1816–43', in *Architectural History*, pp.81 and 104, n.23.

25. For full accounts of British architects' involvement in the *concorsi* see D. Stillman, 'British Architects and Italian Architectural Competitions, 1758–80', in *Journal of the Society of Architectural Historians*, pp.43–66; and F. Salmon, 'An Unaccountable Enemy: Joseph Michael Gandy and the Accademia di San Luca in Rome', in *The Georgian Group Journal*, pp.25–36.

26. BAL, MyFam/4/34.

27. For a summary of what this entailed see Salmon, 'British Architects, Italian Fine Arts Academies', pp.82–3.

28. J. Summerson, *Architecture in Britain 1530–1830*, p.383.

29. For a summary see F. Salmon, 'Charles Heathcote Tatham and the Accademia di S. Luca, Rome', in *The Burlington Magazine*, p.92.

30. Accademia Nazionale di S. Luca, Ms. Congregazioni, 53, fol.113v; 52, fol.140v (Piranesi was elected one of two *Assistenti alle Liti* for 1769–70); 53, fol.56v (Piranesi was one of two *Pacieri* and *Ceremonieri* for 1775–6, although it appears that he attended no meetings during his tenure of these offices).

31. See P. Marconi, et al., *I disegni di architettura dell' Archivio storico dell' Accademia di San Luca*, nos 2159–63.

32. See Stillman, 'British Architects and Italian Architectural Competitions', pp.57–60.

33. The seminal article remains J. Harris, 'Le Geay, Piranesi and International Neo-classicism in Rome 1740–1750', in D. Fraser, et al., eds, *Essays in the History of Architecture Presented to Rudolf Wittkower*, pp.189–96.

34. See J.-M. Pérouse de Montclos, *Les Prix de Rome: Concours de l'Académie royale d'architecture au XVIIIe siècle*, pp.48–55.

35. For a full analysis see J. Barrier, 'Chambers in France and Italy', in J. Harris and M. Snodin, eds, *Sir William Chambers: Architect to George III*, pp.19–33.

36. For illustrations of the Caffè and the Piazza see A. Wilton and I. Bignamini, eds, *Grand Tour: The Lure of Italy in the Eighteenth Century*, nos 71, 73, 74 on pp.114–17.

37. See B. Ford, 'The Grand Tour', in *Apollo*, pp.396–7.

38. Harris, op.cit., pp.190, 192.

39. See W. Herrmann, 'Antoine Desgodets and the Académie royale d'Architecture', in *The Art Bulletin*, pp.23–53.

40. The exceptions to this are the famous Temple of 'Vesta' at Tivoli (A. Desgodetz, *Les Edifices antiques de Rome dessinés et mesurés très exactement*, p.89) and the Arch of Titus (ibid., pp.178–9), which Desgodetz showed with its Medieval encumbrances.

41. BAL, MyFam/4/55 (partly published in translation in C. Gotch, 'The Missing Years of Robert Mylne', in *The Architectural Review*, p.182). The rare erection of the scaffolding is omitted from the latest history of the monument (S. Sande, 'History of Excavation and Research', in I. Nielsen and B. Poulsen, eds, *The Temple of Castor and Pollux, I: Lavori e Studi di Archeologia Pubblicati dalla Soprintendenza di Roma*, pp.5–29.

42. M. Wilson Jones, 'Designing the Roman Corinthian Capital', *Papers of the British School at Rome*, Appendix 1 on p.142 and p.110, n.21.

43. Fleming, pp.170–71, 217; Harris and Savage, pp.72–81.

44. Fowler Collection, John Work Garrett Library, Johns Hopkins University, Baltimore. The monuments covered are the Pantheon, the Temple of Antoninus and Faustina, the Arch of Titus, the Theatre of Marcellus, the Forum Transitorium, the Basilica of Maxentius, the Temple of Venus and Rome, Trajan's Column, the Arches of Constantine and Septimius Severus and the round temple at Tivoli. In addition there are details of the Temples of Saturn and of Vespasian.

45. RIBA DC, H1/2, fol.92r–v. See M. Wilson Jones, 'Designing the Roman Corinthian Order', in *Journal of Roman Archaeology*, Appendix, p.67.

46. See P. de la Ruffinière du Prey, 'Soane and Hardwick in Rome: A Neo-Classical Partnership', in *Architectural History*, pp.51–67.

47. A. Braham, *The Architecture of the French Enlightenment*, p.90; Harris and Savage, pp.73 and 89, n.19. Peyre subsequently published plans of the Baths of Diocletian and of Caracalla in his 1765 *Œuvres d'Architecture*, though they lack measurements.

48. Ingamells, p.169; V&A, PDP, E.1444, 1445, 1456, 1457–1914; RIBA DC, Hardwick Album 7, fols 52–3. Copies such as these, whether or not they changed hands for money, testify less to indolence or dishonesty on the part of the students, as has been suggested, than to pragmatism in the face of the economic and practical problems involved in endeavouring to make such surveys themselves.

49. For the complete story see F. Salmon, 'Charles Cameron and Nero's Domus Aurea: una piccola esplorazione', in *Architectural History*, pp.69–93; and Harris and Savage, pp.136–9.

50. T. Hardwick, 'Observations on the Remains of the Amphitheatre of Flavius Vespasian at Rome, as it was in the Year 1777', in *Archaeologia*, p.370.

51. See R. Ridley, 'To Protect the Monuments: The Papal Antiquarian (1534–1870), in *Xenia Antiqua*, pp.117–54.

52. C. Pietrangeli, *Scavi e scoperte di antichità sotto il Pontificato di Pio VI*, and Wilton and Bignamini, op.cit., pp.203–5.

53. G. Carletti and L. Mirri, *Le antiche camere delle Terme di Tito e le loro pitture*.

54. D. Watkin, *Sir John Soane: Enlightenment Thought and the Royal Academy Lectures*, p.525; P. de la Ruffinière du Prey, 'John Soane's Architectural Education', pp.167–8, 173–7.

55. See C. Parslow, *Rediscovering Antiquity: Karl Weber and the Excavation of Herculaneum, Pompeii, and Stabiae*.

56. See ibid., p.58, for Bellicard's manuscript plan. See also pp.49–55 for Pierre Bardet de Villeneuve's plans of the Basilica and discussion of its form.

57. See J. Mordaunt Crook, *The Greek Revival: Neo-Classical Attitudes in British Architecture 1760–1870*, pp.13–17; and Harris and Savage, pp.439–50.

58. R. Wood, *The Ruins of Palmyra*, p.(a)r. Stuart's words were 'accuracy and fidelity'. See J. Stuart and N. Revett, *The Antiquities of Athens*, I, 1762, p.vii.

59. Wood, ibid., p.35; Stuart and Revett, ibid., p.vi. See Harris and Savage, pp.49–55, 491–5.

60. It should also be noted that Wood did not provide actual state views in support of all his restorations. In the case of the Temple of the Sun at Palmyra, for example, nineteen restorations of different parts of the complex are supported by a single topographical plate.

61. Some of Adam's 'actual state' views followed Desgodetz in presenting buildings stripped back to their surviving antique elements. For the creative licence taken by Adam at Split see I. Gordon Brown, *Monumental Reputation: Robert Adam & the Emperor's Palace*, pp.34–9.

62. One exception to this is Pl.41 in Wood's *The Ruins of Balbec*, a bizarre illustration showing the octastyle temple in perspective and restored but standing amidst its own debris.

63. Watkin, *Sir John Soane*, pp.373, 622.

64. P. Petrini, *Memorie Prenestine*, p.9; [D. Hemsoll and E. Caplin], *Palestrina: The Temple of Fortune as an Inspiration to Architects*, 1989, p.14. Joseph Kay, who visited Palestrina a decade after Hadfield, commented that 'there seems enough of the Remains to be traced on the spot to make out pretty satisfactorily the great lines of the plan & general levels of

the principal steps of the Building but the detail of the super-structure must for the greater part be left to be imagined' (BM, Add. Ms. 45545, fols.21–2.

65. SM, Adam vol.28, fol.1 (illustrated in, for example, D. Stillman, *English Neo-classical Architecture*, I, pp.52–3).

66. Scottish Record Office, GD18/4843.

67. Fleming, p.217.

68. There is an extensive literature on this point. See, especially, D. Stillman, 'Robert Adam and Piranesi', in Fraser, et al., eds, op.cit., pp.197–206; A. Tait, 'Reading the Ruins: Robert Adam and Piranesi in Rome', in *Architectural History*, pp.524–33; Harris and Savage, pp.72–81; T. McCormick, *Charles-Louis Clérisseau and the Genesis of Neo-Classicism*; J. Wilton-Ely, *Piranesi as Architect and Designer*, pp.22–5, 41; A. Tait, *Robert Adam: Drawings and Imagination*, Chs 1–2.

69. See P. de la Ruffinière du Prey, *John Soane: The Making of an Architect*, p.131.

70. For example SM, Adam vol.56, no.103, featuring the Arch of Constantine, but semi-submerged in a lake.

71. Scottish Record Office, GD18/4833.

72. E. Kaufman, 'Architecture and Travel in the Age of British Eclecticism', in E. Blau and E. Kaufman, eds, *Architecture and its Image*, p.70.

73. W. Newton, *The Architecture of M. Vitruvius Pollio*. See also Harris and Savage, pp.464–6. On Pl.24 of vol.I, Newton's Fig.47 offers a small perspective view of a Roman street scene, with triumphal arch and a temple-like structure seen beyond a proscenium, a rare English attempt to visualize a Roman streetscape in this period.

74. Pierpont Morgan Library, New York, 1954.14.

75. SM, 45/3/2, like its companion plan and elevation of the Temple itself (45/3/4), was prepared as an illustration to Soane's Royal Academy lectures. The plan is based, however, on memoranda taken by Soane on 5 January 1779 (see SM, Soane Italian Sketches 1779, fol.11r) and, although the elevation is dated 4 November 1779 when Soane was back at Rome, it presumably represents a neat drawing up from the architect's own notes.

76. For the importance of Hardwick's drawings as perhaps the most faithful record of the discovery see H. Joyce, 'The Ancient Frescoes from the Villa Negroni and their Influence in the Eighteenth and Nineteenth Centuries', in *The Art Bulletin*, pp.433–4.

77. See I. Bristow, *Architectural Colour in British Interiors 1615–1840*, pp.81, 83–96.

78. The plasterwork of the Saloon was finished some twenty years after Adam's first design for the room, in which the niches were to have vertical fluting with horizontal bands of decoration. See L. Harris, *Robert Adam and Kedleston*, pp.58–9.

79. See D. Stillman, *The Decorative Work of Robert Adam*, pp.32–9 for Adam's use of antique sources.

80. For the theme in literature see L. Goldstein, *Ruins and Empire: The Evolution of a Theme in Augustan and Romantic Literature*. For a recent architectural exhibition on the subject see 'Visions of Ruin: Architectural Fantasies and Designs for Garden Follies', Sir John Soane's Museum, 1999.

81. Shown in the 1996–7 Grand Tour exhibition. See Wilton and Bignamini, op.cit., p.298. The appearance of a scale in *palmi romani* on the base argues against the suggestion that Chichi used Desgodetz's measurements. For a comprehensive account of later eighteenth- and nineteenth-century cork models, focusing on the superb collection mostly by Carl May at Aschaffenburg, Germany, see W. Helmberger and V. Kockel, 'Rom über die Alpen tragen', in W. Helmberger and V. Kockel, eds, *Rom über die Alpen tragen: Fürsten sammeln antike Architektur – die Aschaffenburger Korkmodelle*, pp.1–24.

82. S. Rowland Pierce, 'Thomas Jenkins in Rome', in *The Antiquaries Journal*, p.222 (and see n.50 above).

83. M. Richardson, 'Model Architecture', in *Country Life*, pp.224–7.

84. BAL, DA 1/1/i(r) and i(v).

85. V&A, PDP, D.1479.1.

86. Ingamells, p.895; 'A catalogue of the capital, truly valuable and interesting collection […] of that distinguished artist and civil engineer, the Athenian Reveley', Christies, 11 and 12 May 1801, lots 54–70. Some of these casts came from objects in the Museo Pio-Clementino, but there were also casts of the Temples of Antoninus and Faustina, Vespasian (including the cornice and architrave), Castor, 'Neptune', and of the Pantheon (three modillions). Lots 69 and 70 are Soane's Museum casts M45 and M47. In the same year Soane bought ten lots at the sale of the 2nd Earl of Bessborough's collections, mostly cinerary urns, including one which had appeared as Pl.5 in Piranesi's *Vasi, Candelabri* of 1778.

87. Fleming, pp.227–8, 362.

88. V&A, PDP, D.1479.4 and 24.

89. C. H. Tatham, *Etchings Representing the Best Examples of Ornamental Architecture, Drawn from the Originals in Rome and other Parts of Italy during the Years 1794, 1795 and 1796*, p.4.

90. See P. Andrew, 'Jacob More: Biography and a Checklist of Works', in *The Walpole Society*, pp.140–3.

91. See B. Lukacher, 'Joseph Michael Gandy: The Poetical Representation and Mythography of Architecture', Ph.D Dissertation, Figs 11–14, 19; RIBA DC, J3/24–29.

92. See Salmon, 'An Unaccountable Enemy', p.27, where I suggest that Gandy might have drawn on memory of the triumphal arch design with which he had won the gold medal at the Royal Academy five years previously.

93. See W. Oechslin, 'Pyramide et Sphère: Notes sur l'Architecture Révolutionnaire du XVIIIe Siècle et ses Sources Italiennes', in *Gazette des Beaux-Arts*, pp.201–38; H. Rosenau, 'The Engravings of the *Grands Prix* of the French Academy of Architecture', in *Architectural History*, Pls 118–19 on pp.167–8.

Chapter 2 The British and Roman archaeology after Napoleon

1. J. Woods, *Letters of an Architect from France, Italy and Greece*, II, p.162.

2. BAL, Gandy Family/1, summarized in Ingamells, pp.388–9.

3. C. Pietrangeli, 'Archaeological Excavations in Italy 1750–1850', in *The Age of Neo-Classicism*, 1972, p.xlix.

4. The full story is told in R. Ridley, *The Eagle and the Spade: Archaeology in Rome during the Napoleonic Era*.

5. BAL, SMK 1/41; BAL, PeJ/1/3, January 1825.

6. Ridley, *The Eagle and the Spade*, p.253.

7. The history of the Academy and its lists of members are given in C. Pietrangeli and A. Diotallevi, 'La Pontificia Accademia Romana di Archeologia: Note Storiche', in *Memorie della Pontificia Accademia Romana di Archeologia*, pp.5–92. John Foster (1765–1843) was not the Liverpool architect of that name. A 'Count' William Hawks le Grice and a 'Mons' John England, elected in 1832 and 1833 respectively, may be presumed to have been British.

8. See E. Clay and M. Frederiksen, *Sir William Gell in Italy: Letters to the Society of Dilettanti 1831–1835*, pp.26–9.

9. R. Ridley, 'The Founding of the German Archaeological Institute: Unpublished Documents', in *Mitteilungen des Deutschen Archäologischen Instituts Römische Abteilung*, pp.275–94.

10. Gell's account was reproduced in English in his *Topography of Rome and its Vicinity*. See also J. Ward-Perkins, 'Veii: The Historical Topography of the Ancient City', in *Papers of the British School at Rome*, pp.1–2, 82–4 for the pioneering importance of Gell's work.

11. *Bullettino degli Annali dell'Instituto di Corrispondenza Archeologica*, 1830, p.154; 1831, p.118.

12. K. Grenville, *The Private Diary of Richard, Duke of Buckingham and Chandos*, III, pp.57–70.

13. Burgess, *The Topography and Antiquities of Rome*, I, pp.vii, ix, xiii.

14. ibid., I, p.ix; Ridley, *The Eagle and the Spade*, p.xxiii.

15. Burgess, op.cit., I, p.356.

16. ibid., I, pp.218, 414. In fact Burgess placed the Domus Aurea on the site of the Domus Transitoria.

17. G. Darley, *John Soane: An Accidental Romantic*, p.255.

18. M. Richardson, 'Learning in the Soane Office', in N. Bingham, ed., *The Education of the Architect: Proceedings of the 22nd Annual Symposium of the Society of Architectural Historians of Great Britain*, pp.15–21.

19. SM, Basevi Transcript, pp.168, 264; G. Wightwick, *Hints to Young Architects*, p.24.

20. G. L. Taylor, *The Autobiography of an Octogenarian Architect*, I, p.iv.

21. SM, Basevi Transcript, p.205.

22. D. Watkin, *Sir John Soane: Enlightenment Thought and the Royal Academy Lectures*.

23. ibid., pp.531, 661.

24. Wightwick, *Hints to Young Architects*, pp.18, 23–4.

25. E. Strong, 'Istituti stranieri in Roma', in *Annales Institutorum*, pp.22–3, pp.169–72.

26. R. Rodd, *Rome of the Renaissance and To-day*, pp.25–6; F. Salmon, 'British Architects, Italian Fine Arts Academies and the Foundation of the RIBA, 1816–43', in *Architectural History*, p.104, n.25.

27. The first committee, established in 1823, comprised J. B. Lane, Joseph Severn, Richard Westmacott Junior, Richard Evans, Kirkupp, John Gibson and Charles Eastlake as secretary. Among other early members were: William Etty, Richard James Wyatt, a Rennie (perhaps the later Sir John), a Bonomi (probably Joseph Junior) and William Theed the Younger. See D. Robertson, *Sir Charles Eastlake and the Victorian Art World*, pp.22–3.

28. Woods, op.cit., II, pp.147–9.

29. Quoted in C. Brand, *Italy and the English Romantics*, p.140.

30. SM, Basevi Transcript, p.176.

31. Watkin, op.cit., pp.162, 314, 512, 531–2, 661.

32. SM, Basevi Transcript, pp.112, 214–15.

33. G. Wightwick, 'Sketches by a Travelling Architect', in *Library of the Fine Arts*, pp.29, 117.

34. pp.19–20.

35. Transcribed and discussed in F. Salmon, 'Storming the Campo Vaccino: British Architects and the Antique Buildings of Rome after Waterloo', in *Architectural History*, pp.146–75.

36. ibid., p.153.

37. BAL, SMK 1/43.

38. I, p.87.

39. SM, Basevi Transcript, p.214.

40. *The Builder*, 16, 1858, pp.773–4. I am indebted to Professor Joe Mordaunt Crook for this reference.

41. V&A, PDP, E.4087–1918, fols 7r–8v; Taylor and Cresy, II, p.1.

42. M. Wilson Jones. 'Designing the Roman Corinthian Capital', *Papers of the British School at Rome*, Appendix 1 on p.142.

43. Taylor and Cresy, II, p.20.

44. J. Jenkins and W. Hosking, *A Selection of Architectural and other Ornament: Greek, Roman and Italian, Drawn from the Originals in Various Museums and Buildings in Italy*, p.1.

45. Taylor, op.cit., II, p.251.

46. SM, Basevi Transcript, pp.313–16.

47. SM, AL Case 155, fol.67. The sentence about the temple being dilapidated does not appear in the copy of the 1819 version (SM, AL Case 156, fol.67).

48. SM, Basevi Transcript, p.95.

49. BAL, PeJ/1/3, 22 February 1825.

50. BAL, SMK 3/2.

51. BAL, PeJ/1/3, 9 January 1825.

52. N. Bingham, 'Architecture at the Royal Academy Schools, 1768–1836', in N. Bingham, ed., *The Education of the Architect*, pp.6–7.

53. Watkin, op.cit., pp.531, 579. For similar complaints see J. Elmes, *Lectures on Architecture*, p.397.

54. SM, Basevi Transcript, p.121; BAL, PeJ/1/3 (22 February 1825).

55. Elmes, op.cit., p.254; RIBA DC, Wolfe Journal with Sketches 6, p.3; SM, Letter from Wyatt to Soane of 1834 accompanying an illustrated catalogue of his casts.

56. Taylor and Cresy, II, p.9; BAL, PeJ/1/3.

57. In 1835 Angell offered three casts of Roman monuments to the new Institute of British Architects to form the nucleus of a collection (BAL, RIBA LC 1/1/2).

58. Elmes, op.cit., p.254.

59. Burton's casts included: the Temple of Mars Ultor (5 pieces of details); the Pantheon (possibly 6 pieces, including a portico capital); the Temple of Vespasian (6 pieces, including part of the cornice and architrave but evidently not the famous frieze); Trajan's Forum (4 pieces) and Column (5 pieces); the Temple of Castor and Pollux (11 pieces, all details); the Temple of Antoninus and Faustina (10 pieces); the Temple of Hercules Victor (3 pieces); part of the cornice of the Arch of Septimius Severus and four details from Hadrian's Villa at Tivoli. In 1838 Burton ordered a further 17 casts from Rome, mostly ornamental but including a portion of frieze from the Forum of Trajan. Many of these casts are now in storage at the Victoria & Albert Museum. I am much indebted to Professor Dana Arnold for sharing her research on Burton's cast collection with me. For a full list, see her *Re-presenting the Metropolis: Architecture, Urban Experience and Social Life in London 1800–1840*, pp.130–37 (see also pp.112–15).

60. See V. Kockel, 'Rom über die Alpen tragen', in W. Helmberger and V. Kockel, eds, *Rom über die Alpen tragen: Fürsten sammeln antike Architektur – die Aschaffenburger Korkmodelle*, pp.15–16; *Louis-François Cassas 1756–1827*, exh.cat. pp.242–6.

61. See G. Cuisset, 'Jean-Pierre and François Fouquet, Artistes Modeleurs', in *Gazette des Beaux-Arts*, p.237, for discussion of the fact that Soane paid only £100 for Cresy's collection.

62. M. Richardson, 'Model Architecture', in *Country Life*, pp.224–5. The persistent idea that the model was made to measurements taken by Taylor and Cresy follows an error made by the first Curator of Soane's Museum, George Bailey, in 1837.

Chapter 3 Pompeii in the Napoleonic and Restoration periods

1. T. L. Donaldson, *Pompeii, Illustrated with Picturesque Views*, I, p.2.

2. II.4.1–12 (property of Julia Felix); VIII.2.39 (House of Emperor Joseph II). In this last case, however, plans made by Soane in 1779 show that the house was not backfilled immediately after the Emperor's departure in 1769 (*pace* Mazois, II, p.73). See SM, Soane Italian Sketches, 1779, fol.25v.

3. Donaldson, op.cit., II, p.3.

4. See D. Romanelli, *Viaggio a Pompei a Pesto e di ritorno ad Ercolano*, with Pozzuoli included in the 1817 edn; A. de Jorio, *Notizie su gli scavi di Ercolano*.

5. VIII.2.1 (Championnet I) and 3 (Championnet II).

6. BAL, SMK 1/26.

7. For Pompeii under the French generally, see G. Fiorelli, ed., *Pompeianarum Antiquitatum Historia*; E. Corti, *The Destruction and Resurrection of Pompeii and Herculaneum*, pp.160–76; W. Leppmann, *Pompeii in Fact and Fiction*, pp.114–20; *Envois*, 1981, pp.25–37.

8. VI.2.4 (also called the House of Actaeon in the early nineteenth century on the basis of a painting in the peristyle).

9. The copy (of the third edition) in the British Library was presented by Bonucci to Désiré Raoul-Rochette, author of *Pompéi: choix d'édifices inédits*, 1828–, with drawings by Jules-Frédéric Bouchet of the House of the Tragic Poet (VI.8.3–6).

10. See Romanelli, op.cit., p.35; F. Mazois, 'Considérations sur la forme et la distribution des théâtres antiques', in J.-B. Levée, ed., *Théâtre complet des Latins*, I, p.xlix.

11. For Antoine Bibent's plan of Pompeii see *Envois*, 1981, p.29, Fig.24. It is important to note that Mazois's equivalent 'General Plan' only appeared at the end of the fourth volume of *Les Ruines de Pompéi* in

1838, incorporating the excavations made in the eleven years since the author's death.

12. VI.7.23; VI.6.1; VI.8.3–6; VI.12.2.

13. Mazois, III, p.71. The first three fascicules of vol.3 appear to have been printed prior to the death of Mazois.

14. Yale University, Beinecke Library, Osborn Ms. D.293 and Osborn File 13.381.

15. W. Gell and J. P. Gandy, *Pompeiana: The Topography, Edifices and Ornaments of Pompeii*, p.xvi. Gandy was at Smyrna in May 1812 and said he intended to return to England in February 1813 (SM, Correspondence Cupboard, Division III.G.2). John Soane Junior met Gandy at Naples in December 1819. See A. Bolton, *The Portrait of Sir John Soane, R.A.*, p.286.

16. Leppmann, op.cit., pp.120–1.

17. *Envois*, 1981, pp.4, 41, 51. The work of British architects is noted, though by no means comprehensively, in H. van der Poel, *Corpus Topographicum Pompeianum*, IV (Bibliography) and V (Cartography), and their published works in L. Garcia y Garcia, *Nova Biblioteca Pompeiana: 250 anni di bibliografia archeologica*, 2 vols, 1998.

18. *Envois*, 1981, p.36.

19. BAL, SMK 1/15. Smirke again asked his father to pursue this application after arriving in Naples in April 1803 (BAL, SMK 1/16).

20. BAL, SMK 1/26.

21. J. Woods, *Letters of an Architect*, II, p.208.

22. RIBA DC, Poynter Transcript, p.70

23. G. L. Taylor, *The Autobiography of an Octogenarian Architect*, I, p.146. Taylor claimed, at this late stage in life, to have 'visited Pompeii frequently, and to have obtained permission to draw' earlier in 1818 (p.88), but his sketchbook (V&A, PDP, E4087–1918, fol.17r) accounts for all ten days his party spent in Naples, and includes just a single visit to Pompeii on 16 April.

24. BAL, SMK 2/4.

25. H. Eschebach, *Die städtebauliche Entwicklung des antiken Pompeji*, p.72 lists a version of this plan in the Public Library of Cleveland, Ohio, as the first plan of Pompeii to be drawn by the British.

26. VI.2.22 (RIBA DC, Donaldson Album Greek and Roman, fol.50v).

27. [W. Clarke], *Pompeii: Its Past and Present State; Its Public and Private Buildings etc., Compiled in Part from the Great Work of M. Mazois; the Museo Borbonico; the Publications of Sir W. Gell, and T. L. Donaldson*. These two volumes first appeared anonymously, though 'numerous observations' made on site by the architect William Clarke were acknowledged. For the second edition of 1846, however, the title was extended to read *But Chiefly from the MS. Journals and Drawings of William Clarke Esq., Architect*.

28. RIBA DC, H6/1 (a sketchbook of Cockerell's purchased in Naples on 17 April 1815); BAL, COC: Add./1/29 (giving the date of his arrival in Rome as 28 July).

29. Mazois, I, p.34, n.4 and p.36, n.4; II, p.99, n.1; IV, p.60, n.1. See also F. Mazois, 'Considérations sur la forme et la distribution des théâtres antiques', in Levée, ed., *Théâtre Complet des Latins*, I, pp.xlix–lxvi.

30. Mazois, III, p.39, n.1; F. Salmon, 'British Architects, Italian Fine Arts Academies and the Foundation of the RIBA, 1816–43', in *Architectural History*, p.100.

31. RIBA DC, J6/36, 37, 42, 44–50.

32. VI.1.7 and 24–6.

33. VI.3.7. In 1821 Henry Parke also drew a plan of this house RIBA DC, W5/43/18). These plans are not noted in the standard monograph, E. de Albentiis, 'La casa dell'Accademia di Musica (VI 3,7–25–26) e le Tabernae', ch.3 of *Le Insulae 3 e 4 della Regio VI di Pompei*, pp.57–110. Indeed, the historiography of the building offered there does not extend beyond the actual period of excavation, as described by Fiorelli, op.cit.

34. VI.3.5 and 6.

35. RIBA DC, W5/43/12 (VI.1.6). See *Pompei: pitture e mosaici*, IV, p.7, Fig.3.

36. G. Tappen, *Professional Observations on the Architecture of the Principal Ancient and Modern Buildings in France and Italy*, p.252.

37. For a Forum plan drawn slightly earlier in 1816, see *Envois*, 1981, p.41. Ms. 180 in the Bibliothèque d'Art et d'Archéologie in Paris, in which this plan appears, has previously been attributed to John Peter Gandy but is, in fact, in the hand of Gell. This document, Gell's preparatory work for the first volume of *Pompeiana*, is discussed in a recent paper by Hélène Dessales to be published in the proceedings of a 1999 colloquium held at Grenoble on the subject 'Mois du Patrimoine Ecrit'.

38. Illustrated in *Envois*, 1981, p.23, Fig.19.

39. *Envois*, 1981, p.119.

40. Donaldson, op.cit., I, following p.52. The 1827 plan is credited to Donaldson and William Wesley Jenkins. Since the former had left Italy in 1822 and the latter was a competitor for the new buildings at King's College, Cambridge in 1823, either a return visit to Pompeii by one or other might be inferred. Note that Donaldson's plan follows the depiction of the Forum on Bibent's general plan, with the addition of English measurements.

41. See K. Ohr, *Die Basilika in Pompeji*, pp.51–67, Pls 34–7, 61, and L. Richardson, *Pompeii: An Architectural History*, pp.95–9.

42. Mazois, III, pp.29, 59.

43. Donaldson, op.cit., II. pp.51–2.

44. Mazois, III, p.65.

45. Woods, op.cit., II, p.373; RIBA DC, Y3/63, Pompeii 19/1; 11/5 and 6.

46. Donaldson, op.cit., II, p.55. Parke's sketch for the mosaic from the Temple of Apollo made in situ is RIBA DC, W5/43/24. For other versions see RIBA DC, Roos Album, nos 22 and 42. For an 1830 sheet of mosaics by David Mocatta neatly prepared in the same way as Parke's, see RIBA DC, V9/48/1.

47. Woods, op.cit., II, p.360 (and Woods's notes on the Basilica on RIBA DC, Y3/63, Pompeii 8/7v). Woods also dated Pompeian buildings by their construction, apparently believing for reasons which remain unclear that the *opus incertum* of the Small Theatre indicated that it preceded the earthquake of AD 62, whilst the presence of *reticulatum* in the discharging arch of the Great Theatre showed it belonged to 'the latter part of the reign of Augustus' (RIBA DC, Y3/63, Pompeii 2(2) and 3(1).

48. Mazois, II, p.4, n.1. Strangely he did not mention the Golden House, perhaps because he still believed it to be part of the Baths or Palace complex of 'Titus', nor did he mention the domestic but Imperial buildings on the Palatine Hill.

49. RIBA DC, Y3/63, Pompeii 21; RIBA DC, J6/13–15; RIBA DC, Roos Album, nos 45, 69.

50. RIBA DC, Poynter Transcript, p.1.

51. RIBA DC, Poynter Portfolio, no.16 (descriptive notes); nos 8, 11 (House of Pansa); no.7 (House of Championnet I, see Parke's RIBA DC, W5/43/15 and 16 respectively); no.9 (the tablinum of House E); nos 6, 12, 19 (House of the Vestals).

52. Woods, op.cit., II, pp.370–71.

Chapter 4 The vision of Rome after 1815

1. 'Sketches by a Travelling Architect', in *Library of the Fine Arts*, p.112.

2. See M. Liversidge and C. Edwards, *Imagining Rome: British Artists and Rome in the Nineteenth Century*, pp.87–91, 94–6.

3. For an extended account of this system see P. Pinon and F.-X. Amprimoz, *Les Envois de Rome (1778–1968): Architecture et Archéologie*. The third section of this book (pp.385–440) is a full catalogue of the *envois*.

4. The *envois* have been the subject of four major exhibitions held in Paris, Naples, Rome, Athens (and Houston) in 1981, 1982–3, 1985–6, 1992. Pompeii subjects are included in *Envois*, 1981, and city of Rome subjects in *Envois*, 1985 and 1992.

5. R. Burgess, *The Topography and Antiquities of Rome*, I, p.266; B. Bergdoll, *Léon Vaudoyer: Historicism in the Service of Industry*, p.99, Fig.80.

6. For Coussin's work see *Envois*, 1992, pp.223–7; for Gasse see *Envois*, 1985, pp.113–19.

7. R. Ridley, *The Eagle and the Spade*, pp.182–7; *Envois*, 1985, pp.92–109, especially p.104.

8. For Leclère see *Envois*, 1992, pp.100–123; for Gauthier and Provost see *Envois*, 1985, pp.212–13 and pp.77–81 respectively.

9. See *Envois*, 1985, pp.83–7.

10. *Envois*, 1992, pp.xviii–xix; S. Sande, 'History of Excavation and Research', in I. Nielsen and B. Poulsen, eds, *The Temple of Castor and Pollux, I: Lavori e Studi di Archeologia Pubblicati dalla Soprintendenza di Roma*, pp.14–18.

11. According to Pinon and Amprimoz, op.cit., p.259, figures only appeared in the students' reconstructions 'towards the end of the nineteenth century'. They give Marcel Lambert's Acropolis restoration of 1877, with its crowded statuary as a forerunner (see *Envois*, 1982, p.257, Fig.110), but do not describe in detail the changes introduced to the rules by decree in 1871, which presumably permitted the inclusion of figures for the first time. Moreover, since Edmond Paulin's Baths of Diocletian restoration of 1880 seems to be the earliest *envoi* with a perspective (cut-away), as well as historical figures (see *Envois*, 1992, p.35, Fig.19), it might be assumed that permission to produce this type of image was also a change instituted in 1871. The earliest full restoration perspectives, albeit bird's-eye views, appear to have been those of the Tiber Island drawn by René Patouillard-Demoriane in 1900 (see *Envois*, 1992, pp.157–8). By 1897, however, the Académie was already regretting that 'picturesque' elements were replacing 'exactitude' in the *envois* (see *Envois*, 1982, p.152).

12. A. Nibby, *Del Foro Romano*, pp.59–67; F. Nardini (ed. A. Nibby), *Roma Antica*, 4th edn, II, pp.151–2. In his edition of Nardini, Nibby used a plan of the Forum oriented north-south drawn by Antonio de' Romanis (facing p.136). For a fuller account of topographical study of the Forum in this period, see R. Ridley, 'The Monuments of the Roman Forum: The Struggle for Identity', in *Xenia*, pp.71–90.

13. Piranesi had suggested the identification in *Le antichità romane*, I, p.34 and Pl.33; Fea took it up again and Valadier further established it after the 1813 and 1816–17 excavations in the 1818 *Raccolta*.

14. S. Piale, *Del Foro Romano – sua posizione e grandezza non bene intese dal Nardini e non ostante generalmente seguite da' Moderni*, pp.7–8, 13, 20. I owe a special debt to Professor Ronald Ridley for drawing Piale's little-recognized work to my attention.

15. S. Piale, *Della Basilica Giulia*, pp.16–19.

16. In L. Canina, *Descrizione storico del Foro Romano*, p.134 (although, on the key to the plan, Canina continued to call the building the Temple of 'Jupiter Tonans', p.171).

17. BAL, CoC: Add/2/10.

18. BM, Department of Greek and Roman Antiquities, Cockerell misc. drawings, items 3, 11, 12 and 15, in 1993.

19. BM, Department of Greek and Roman Antiquities, Cockerell misc. drawings, items 13 and 14, in 1993.

20. Gabinetto Nazionale delle Stampe, Rome, FC 36777. A facsimile illustration which accompanied Sydney Smirke's obituary of Cockerell in the *RIBA Proceedings* (Sessional Papers), 1863–4, was described as 'The First Study for Mr Cockerell's Restoration of the Roman Forum'. This 'first study', however, is closer to the second British Museum restoration and therefore probably represents an intermediate stage between Fig.74 and the image as engraved.

21. A. Graves, *The Royal Academy of Arts: A Complete Dictionary of Contributors and their Works from its Foundation in 1769 to 1904*, I, p.91. A preparatory pen, ink and watercolour sketch for this painting came onto the London market with Stair & Company in 2000. Cockerell's annotations included a quotation recording the battle between Caesar and Pompey from Lucan's *Pharsalia*.

22. J. Hodgson and F. Eaton, *The Royal Academy and its Members 1768–1830*. P. de la Ruffinière du Prey, *The Villas of Pliny from Antiquity to Posterity*, p.323, does not mention the 1819 Royal Academy gold medal competition, although notes that Cockerell displayed his own restoration of the villa during his fourth Royal Academy lecture in 1843 (see *The Athenaeum*, 798, p.134).

23. Sotheby's (New Bond Street, London) Sale, 30 April 1987, lot 561, p.120, quoting the original Royal Academy citation.

24. Burgess, op.cit., I, p.341. Burgess also included a plan of the Forum.

25. D. Watkin, *The Life and Work of C. R. Cockerell*, p.25 and Pl.8.

26. ibid., p.34.

27. See, for example, the version at Gainsborough's House, Sudbury, Suffolk, attributed to J. M. Gandy, or a copy by Cockerell's granddaughter now at Vassar College (information kindly supplied by Professor Brian Lukacher, who does not accept the attribution of the Gainsborough House painting to Gandy). See also R. Spiers, 'Cockerell's Restorations of Ancient Rome', in *The Architectural Review*, pp.123–8, apparently a study of drawings used by Cockerell in his Royal Academy lectures.

28. For a recent assessment of the importance of this work see C. Edwards, 'Translating Empire? Macaulay's Rome', in C. Edwards, ed., *Roman Presences*, pp.70–87. It is worth adding that, in 1819, Macaulay had won the Chancellor's Medal at Cambridge for his poem on the subject 'Pompeii' and that, in 1822, the set subject was 'Palmyra'.

29. BAL, PeJ/1/3, 23 January 1825.

30. BAL, PeJ/1/2, fol.3r. On 30 January Pennethorne told Nash not to show anyone his drawing of Trajan's Forum as it was not 'entirely [sic] my own', having been discussed with someone in London prior to his departure (BAL, PeJ/1/3).

31. BAL, PeJ/1/3, memorandum.

32. BAL, PeJ/1/3, 30 January 1825.

33. BAL, PeJ/1/3, 22 February 1825.

34. BAL, PeJ/1/2, fols 6r–v. In addition to Nibby's *Del Foro Romano*, the books were presumably the fourth edition of Nardini's *Roma Antica* and C. Fea, *Nuova descrizione di Roma antica e moderna*, 1820.

35. BAL, PeJ/1/3, memorandum; BAL, PeJ/1/4, 17 April 1825. Pennethorne told Nash that the drawing he had sent was 1 ft 6 in long, possibly corresponding with Fig.77 here, which is actually 1 ft 8 in wide. Figure 77 remained the property of his descendants until 1988. However, Pennethorne would surely have retained a copy (or copies) of his restoration for his own use in Rome, so it is impossible to be certain about which version has survived.

36. BAL, PeJ/1/3, memorandum.

37. This structure is considered today to have been an entrance hall of the Domus Tiberiana (see L. Richardson, *A New Topographical Dictionary of Ancient Rome*, pp.45–6). Taylor and Cresy, I, p.xi, were indeed perspicacious in identifying the remains as substructures of the Imperial Palace. The actual Curia, converted to use as the Church of S. Adriano in the seventh century, was not recognized until later in the nineteenth century. Pennethorne took it to be the 'Secretarium Senatus' (no.20 on his plan).

38. BAL, PeJ/1/3, memorandum. Since he knew from reading Martial that the Temple of Castor was situated near to the round Temple of Vesta, Pennethorne took the Church of S. Teodoro (no.5) to be the round temple and thus placed the Temple of Castor on the site of the Horrea Agrippina (no.4). The actual Temple of 'Vesta', the columns of which form a conspicuous feature of the Forum today, is a reconstruction of 1930, following the discovery of its precise site in late nineteenth-century excavations.

39. Ridley, *The Eagle and the Spade*, pp.239, 253. Nibby accepted this identification in *Del Foro Romano* (see Fig.67), presumably the authority taken by Pennethorne.

40. See T. L. Donaldson, *Architectura Numismatica*, pp.15–20, and Pl.5. Donaldson refers to Luigi Canina's *L'Architettura romana*, II, p.201 and Pl.LVII, for more information on the Temple of Concord. This agrees with the site suggested by Nibby in *Del Foro Romano*.

41. Richardson, op.cit., p.154, citing F. Coarelli, *Il Foro Romano*, pp.171–3.

42. BAL, PeJ/1/3, 14 March 1825.

43. See *Envois*, 1985, pp.2–14.

44. BAL, PeJ/1/3.

45. G. Tyack, *Sir James Pennethorne and the Making of Victorian London*, p.15.

46. BAL, PeJ/1/4, 11 May 1825.

47. A restoration of the interior of an ancient basilica, now in the Musée d'Orsay, drawn by Hittorff in 1831 is reproduced in A. Jacques, *Les Desseins d'Architecture du XIXe Siècle*, pp.28–9. For the importance of the perspective to Labrouste and Duban, see D. van Zanten, *Designing Paris: The Architecture of Duban, Labrouste, Duc and Vaudoyer*, 1987, pp.32–6. In discussing the scandal caused by Labrouste's *envoi* of the 'Basilica' (Temple of Hera I) at Paestum, scholars have concentrated on the social and theoretical issues raised by the drawings, but it is worth noting that Labrouste's very inclusion of a cut-away perspective was also an infringement of etiquette likely to have given offence to the Académie.

48. Illustrated in colour in D. van Zanten, 'The Harmony of Landscape, Architecture and Community: Schinkel's Encounter with Huyot, 1826', in J. Zukowsky, ed., *Karl Friedrich Schinkel: The Drama of Architecture*, p.84.

49. ibid., p.88. It is significant that it was one of Huyot's pupils, Jean-Amond Leveil, who was the author in 1836 of the first restoration of the entire Roman Forum since that of Caristie (see *Envois*, 1985), pp. 3–14). Leveil's work was partly published in the second edition of Charles Dezobry's *Rome au siècle d'Auguste*. Huyot's own *Forum Romanum* appeared posthumously.

50. See F. Salmon, 'British Architects, Italian Fine Arts Academies and the Foundation of the RIBA, 1816–43', in *Architectural History*, p.89.

51. BAL, RIBA LC I/3/23 (a letter of 1837, in which Blouet addresses Donaldson as 'Mon cher collègue et ami', speaks of Donaldson's 'bonne et franche amitié' and sends greetings from Madame Blouet to Donaldson's wife and daughter).

52. See Salmon, op.cit., pp.86–91.

53. P. Andrew, 'Jacob More: Biography and a Checklist of Works', in *The Walpole Society*, p.183 and illustration 129.

54. Richard, Abbé de Saint-Non, *Voyage pittoresque de Naples et de Sicile*, II, Pls 75, 75bis, 88, 80 respectively. See P. Lamers, *Il Viaggio nel sud dell' Abbé de Saint-Non*, 1992, pp.202–7.

55. Four preliminary sketches for the restoration of the *scenae frons* are RIBA DC, J10/24/1–4, watermarked 1824.

56. J. Woods, *Letters of an Architect*, II, p.364.

57. W. Gell and J. P. Gandy, *Pompeiana: The Topography, Edifices and Ornaments of Pompeii*, Pls 19, 36, 48, 51, 77. See also the sketched restoration of the House of Pansa attributed to Gell's working colleague Gandy (*Envois*, 1981, p.84).

58. W. Gell, *Pompeiana: The Topography, Edifices and Ornaments of Pompeii – The Result of Excavations since 1819*, I, Pl.21 and BM, Department of Greek and Roman Antiquities, Cockerell misc. drawings. The drawing can hardly be Cockerell's, however, as the Temple had not been excavated at the time of his visit to Pompeii.

59. ibid., II, Pls 36, 37. There is a very similar coloured actual state view in the Roos Album at the RIBA DC (but without the nineteenth-century protective roofs), reproduced in I. Bristow, *Architectural Colour in British Interiors 1615–1840*, Pl.189.

60. The Countess of Blessington, *An Idler in Italy*, II, p.130. An untraced 'Restoration of a House at Pompeii from Drawings made on the Spot' by Ambrose Poynter was shown at the Royal Academy in 1823. Graves, op.cit., III, p.196. At some stage Cockerell also made a 'Restoration of a Pompeian House', shown in 1863 after his death (see *RIBA Proceedings*, 1863–4).

61. See Liversidge and Edwards, eds, op.cit., for the latest study of this topic.

62. N. Vance, *The Victorians and Ancient Rome*, p.44 (and see pp.41–7).

63. YCBA, B1975.4.1203. I owe a substantial debt to the leading authority on Gandy, Professor Brian Lukacher, for sharing his thoughts on this (and on similar Gandy drawings) with me. He has drawn attention to the similarities between this drawing and the amphitheatre-like stage designs of Louis-Jean Desprez. The Getty Research Institute owns a large number of similar though less finished stage designs attributed to Gandy.

64. In fact the episode shown occurs during Scene one of the play.

65. See R. Hyde, *Panoramania! The Art and Entertainment of the 'All-Embracing' View*.

Chapter 5 Architecture in England in the 1830s

1. Review of T. Hope's *Historical Essay on Architecture*, in *The Quarterly Review*, 53, April 1835, p.370.

2. J. Bassin, *Architectural Competitions in Nineteenth-Century England*, p.19.

3. RIBA DC, J11/37/1–5 (sketches).

4. See M. Port, 'The New Houses of Parliament', in J. Mordaunt Crook and M. Port, *The History of the King's Works, VI, 1782–1851*, pp.573–6. See also M. Port, ed., *The Houses of Parliament*, esp. pp.20–52.

5. Bassin, op.cit., p.35; R. Quinault, 'Westminster and the Victorian Constitution', in *Transactions of the Royal Historical Society*, pp.79–104.

6. W. Rorabaugh, 'Politics and the Architectural Competition for the Houses of Parliament 1834–1837', in *Victorian Studies*, pp.155–75.

7. 58, p.77.

8. See especially J. Mordaunt Crook, *The Greek Revival*.

9. One might include here William Wilkins's National Gallery begun in 1834, although Wilkins was compelled for reasons of economy to reuse eight of the columns and capitals of Henry Holland's Carlton House, modelled on the order of the Temple of Castor and Pollux in Rome, to which he added a simplified version for the central portico. It should also be observed that the Greek idiom continued in use in the provinces in the 1830s, both for public buildings such as Worcester Shire Hall, Exeter Higher Market and Gravesend Town Hall, and for individual monuments and houses. Crook, in ibid., p.99, is thus correct in saying that the English Greek Revival continued into the 1840s.

10. V&A, PDP, D.1479.13. Since Tatham went on to say that the Theatre of Marcellus was a Greek building, or 'nearest to it' in Rome, however, quite what he meant by the term 'Greek' must remain a matter of conjecture.

11. D. Watkin, *Sir John Soane: Enlightenment Thought and the Royal Academy Lectures*, pp.106–7, 281.

12. R. Ackerman, ed., *Repository of Arts*, p.314.

13. F. Arundale, *The Edifices of Andrea Palladio*, Preface.

14. *The Quarterly Review*, 53, April 1835, pp.368–9.

15. D. Watkin, *The Triumph of the Classical: Cambridge Architecture 1804–1834*, p.8. See also D. Watkin, *The Life and Work of C. R. Cockerell*, and D. Watkin, 'Newly Discovered Drawings by C. R. Cockerell for Cambridge University Library', in *Architectural History*, pp.87–91, in which the author also notes that the Library represents 'a turning point in [Cockerell's] stylistic development' (p.87). For a full and well-illustrated account of the building see J. Olley, 'University Library', in *The Architects' Journal*, pp.34–63.

16. For a variant of this design and other drawings for the first competition see Watkin, 'Newly Discovered Drawings by C. R. Cockerell', Pls 44a–46b, 48a–b.

17. ibid., Pls 47a–b.

18. See also ibid., Pls 49a–51a.

19. Illustrated in ibid., Pl.51b.

20. See J. Harris, 'The Transformation of Lord Burlington', in D. Arnold, ed., *The Georgian Villa*, pp.46–7.

21. See Watkin, 'Newly Discovered Drawings by C. R. Cockerell', Pl.53a.

22. Mazois, III, pp.37–8.

23. See Watkin, 'Newly Discovered Drawings by C. R. Cockerell', Pls 54a–56b.

24. SM, Basevi Transcript, p.89.

25. See F. Salmon, 'British Architects, Italian Fine Arts Academies and the Foundation of the RIBA, 1816–43', *Architectural History*, pp.78–9, including a tabulated list of meetings and architects.

26. Anon., 'John Goldicutt and his Times', in *The Architectural Review*, p.322.

27. M. Crinson and J. Lubbock, *Architecture: Art or Profession?*, pp.38–42, 48–53.

28. BAL, LAS.4/3.

29. BAL, RIBA/MS.SP/4/1, fol.D(v) and see Salmon, op.cit., pp.95, 110, n.96.

30. BAL, RIBA/MS.SP/2.

31. BAL, RIBA/MS.SP/4/8.

32. For a full list see Salmon, op.cit., Appendix C.

33. S. Angell and W. Harris, *Sculptured Metopes Discovered Amongst the Ruins of the Temples of the Ancient City of Selinus in Sicily by William Harris and Samuel Angell in the Year 1823*.

34. For a succinct overview see R. Middleton, 'Hittorff's Polychrome Campaign', in R. Middleton, ed., *The Beaux-Arts and Nineteenth-Century French Architecture*, pp.175–88.

35. BAL, RIBA/LC/1/3/9.

36. BAL, RIBA Proceedings, 1, 1834–42.

37. See Middleton, op.cit., p.188.

38. Mazois, III, pp.28, 65.

39. *Letters of an Architect*, II, p.370.

40. p.1.

41. Colvin, p.413; J6/292–293 (King's College drawings).

42. RIBA DC, Album of Alexander Roos.

43. See I. Bristow, *Architectural Colour in British Interiors*, Chs 6, 7, esp. pp.187, 210.

44. For an analysis see ibid., pp.206–10.

45. E. Tollfree, 'Napoleon and the "New Rome": Rebuilding Imperial Rome in late Eighteenth and early Nineteenth-Century Paris', Ph.D Dissertation, p.170. Tollfree's work is an important reappraisal of the whole relationship between Napoleonic France and ancient Rome. See also V. Huet, 'Napoleon I: A New Augustus?', in C. Edwards, ed., *Roman Presences: Receptions of Rome in European Culture, 1789–1945*, pp.53–69.

46. For the most recent accounts see D. Arnold, 'The Arch at Constitution Hill', in *Apollo*, pp.129–33; and A. Saint, 'The Marble Arch', in *The Georgian Group Journal*, pp.75–93.

47. Saint, ibid., p.77.

48. Arnold, op.cit., p.53 lists schemes for an arch at Hyde Park Corner by the following: John Gwynn (1766); King George III (with William Chambers); Robert Adam (1778); Jeffry Wyatt [Wyatville] (1791); John Soane (1796); William Kinnard (1813); Soane (1817). See also S. Sawyer, 'Sir John Soane's Symbolic Westminster: The Apotheosis of George IV', in *Architectural History*, pp.54–76.

49. Goldicutt's drawings and descriptions are in RIBA DC, J6/328–339. The building was envisaged as the home of the Royal Academy, the Architectural Society and ten other such bodies.

50. Had this book extended to include the contextually somewhat different situation in Scotland, David Rhind's particularly fine Commercial Bank of Scotland in Edinburgh of 1844–6 might have been included, as might Archibald Simpson's Stracathro House, Tayside, of 1828. English country houses of this time with Roman elements include Thomas Hopper's 1834–40 reworking of John Webb's Amesbury, while Thomas Allom and F. H. Lockwood's Great Thornton Street Chapel at Hull of 1843 showed the idiom at use in religious architecture.

Chapter 6 Birmingham Town Hall

1. W. Hope, ed., *The Diary of Benjamin Robert Haydon*, 3, p.620.

2. The background is given in C. Gill, *History of Birmingham, I, Manor and Borough to 1865*. For the Town Hall, in particular, see pp.197–9, 323.

3. BCL, BCC Plan 209.

4. BCL, 'Proceedings of the Commissioners for Paving, Lighting, Watching, Cleansing and otherwise Improving the Town of Birmingham (1828–37)', 10 August 1830; BCL, BCC Plans 203 show the freeholders of this site at this time.

5. J. A. Hansom, *A Statement of Facts Relative to the Birmingham Town Hall with an Appeal to the Rate-Payers and Inhabitants of Birmingham*, pp.4–5.

6. BCL, BCC Plans 216 and BCC Plans 210.

7. Hansom, op.cit., p.5. Hansom also gave an indication of others he believed had competed: Francis Goodwin, Samuel Beazley and pupils of both Soane and Nash. Owen Jones showed a design for the Town Hall at the Royal Academy in 1831. However, the great majority of the seventy competitors at Birmingham remain unidentified.

8. See Gill, op.cit., p.324, citing the report of the competition in the local *Gazette*.

9. A. Barry, *The Life and Work of Sir Charles Barry*, p.73; M. Digby Wyatt, 'On the Architectural Career of the Late Sir Charles Barry', in *The Builder*, p.323.

10. BCL, Ms. 617/2/4.

11. See BCL, BCC Plans 210, Drawings 10–12, Fallows's sections and interior perspective.

12. Hansom, op.cit.; 'A Resident of Birmingham' [E. Welch], 'A Descriptive Account, Accompanied by Plans, Elevations, Sections etc. of the Birmingham New Town Hall', in *The Architectural Magazine and Journal*, pp.16–27. Birmingham Museum and Art Gallery has on loan from the Assay Office a watercolour of the Town Hall attributed to Henry Harris (2000 E 2) with an attached inscription indicating that it represents Hansom's and Welch's 'original competition design … presented by them to the late Charles Fiddian'. Although the perspective of the Town Hall is similar to that published in [Welch], op.cit., p.24, and Fiddian was the Commissioners' accountant from 1831, the urban and architectural contexts around the building suggest a much later date.

13. The architects' own words thus show that the attribution to them of a lithograph of an octastyle Greek Doric temple design possibly related to Birmingham Town Hall (BCL, Ms. 897, Pershouse Collection, I, 114) cannot be correct. Indeed, if Alfred Barry was right in thinking that his father was the only architect to submit such a scheme (see note 9, above), the lithograph might be associated rather with Barry's entry.

14. On this plan, all parts tinted blue belong to Hansom's design except for the 13-foot projection of three bays' width at the north end of the building, an addition by Charles Edge made in 1836–7.

15. See *The Architectural Magazine and Journal*, II, 1835, pp.238, 326.

16. P. Metcalf, *The Halls of the Fishmongers' Company: An Architectural History of a Riverside Site*, p.125.

17. See G. Worsley, *Architectural Drawings of the Regency Period 1790–1837*, p.43.

18. This drawing is a tracing of one bearing the names of Thomas and Kendall, the first builders of the Town Hall. It is identical with the east elevation published in [Welch], op.cit., p.21, except that it has only a single arched arcade across the south front instead of the double arches built. Although this is unusual, there are a few other nineteenth-century images which show the same variation.

19. See D. Evinson, 'Joseph Hansom', M.A. Dissertation, p.73.

20. Gill, op.cit., p.343.

21. See C. Flick, *The Birmingham Political Union and the Movements for Reform in Britain 1830–1839*; and D. Moss, *Thomas Attwood: The Biography of a Radical*.

22. C. Wakefield, *Life of Thomas Attwood*, pp.v, 225.

23. Flick, op.cit., p.13. Moss, op.cit., by contrast, accords events in Birmingham a central position on the national stage.

24. I, p.164.

25. Hope, ed., op.cit., 3, p.617.

26. ibid., pp.617, 619–20.

27. Moss, op.cit., p.53.

28. Wakefield, op.cit., p.176.

29. ibid., p.203. On the significance of Hampden and seventeenth-century political reform for early nineteenth-century radicals, see J. Epstein, *Radical Expression: Political Language, Ritual and Symbol in England 1790–1850*, pp.27, 153–4.

30. Wakefield, op.cit., pp.224, 221.

31. Hope, ed., op.cit., 3, p.621. Only after the King refused to create the

new peers, leading to Grey's resignation, did Attwood briefly agree that the Union medal, with the motto, should not be worn. See Moss, op.cit., p.217.

32. Gill, op.cit., p.326.
33. R. Rosenblum, *Transformations in Late Eighteenth Century Art*, p.138.
34. Evinson, 'Joseph Hansom', pp.83–5.
35. B. Walker, et al., *The Birmingham Town Hall 1834–1934*, p.17.
36. BCL, Ms. 1703/15/4/36, 10/36, 27/36, Edge's plans and north and east elevations for this alteration, dated August 1836 (a small window between a pair of louvered vents in the pediment above appears not to have been constructed); BCL, Ms. 1703/15/17/36 and 23/36, plans for the orchestra staging of the same date.
37. BCL, Ms. 1703/15/36/36 (the 'Specification', with thirteen drawings).
38. BCL, Ms. 1703/15/15/36. On the balustrade as a distinctive Renaissance invention (but with an account of the origin of the baluster in antique decorative sculpture) see P. Davies and D. Hemsoll, 'Renaissance Balusters and the Antique', in *Architectural History*, pp.1–23.
39. Edge also had to attend to the shafts and bases of twenty of the existing columns which had not yet been dressed. These are likely to have been the twelve comprising the west peristyle (behind the south front), the lower part of which had been hidden by the roofs of houses in Paradise Street, plus eight unidentifiable others.
40. Hansom, op.cit., p.6.
41. D. Watkin, *Sir John Soane: Enlightenment Thought and the Royal Academy Lectures*, pp.574–5. This did not prevent Soane, however, from preparing a drawing to see what James Gibbs's portico of St Martin-in-the-Fields would have looked like placed on a perforated podium. See ibid., Fig.87.
42. Soane surely recognized this. However, he had altered the proportional relationship between the two orders in showing them on the title page of his *Designs for Public and Private Buildings* of 1828, which illustrates the Castor and Pollux columns he had used for the Privy Council Office in Whitehall and those of the Temple at Tivoli at the Bank of England.

Chapter 7 The Fitzwilliam Museum, Cambridge

1. Quoted in R. Willis and J. Willis Clark, *The Architectural History of the University of Cambridge*, 3, p.212.
2. The point of departure for the architectural history of the Museum is ibid., pp.198–224. The authors' principal sources were Minutes of Syndicates (now CUL, U.A. Min.VI.1) and four files of correspondence, reports and plans (U.A. CUR 30.1–4).
3. See D. Watkin, *The Triumph of the Classical: Cambridge Architecture 1804–1834*.
4. R. Liscombe, *William Wilkins, 1778–1839*, pp.135–6.
5. The fourth drawing in Thomas Rickman's competition design 'A' set (RIBA DC, E1/34/1) indicates in outline the potential position of the Curator's House at the rear of the Museum, demonstrating that some competitors nonetheless thought it expedient to indicate this extension.
6. CUL, U.A. CUR 30.1, items 68d, 69.
7. CUL, U.A. CUR 30.1, item 77. An elevation for a large dome behind an octastyle Corinthian portico among the miscellaneous competition drawings in the Museum's library may relate to Bardwell's scheme.
8. J. Allibone, *Anthony Salvin: Pioneer of Gothic Revival Architecture*, pp.52–3.
9. CUL, U.A. CUR 30.1, item 68a. Cust's proposal for the Museum is illustrated in Watkin, *The Triumph of the Classical*, Pl.13.
10. For colour reproductions of Rickman's perspectives for designs 'B' and 'A', see G. Worsley, *Architectural Drawings of the Regency Period*, pp.50–51.
11. A. James, 'Rickman and the Fitzwilliam Competition', in *The Architectural Review*, p.271.
12. Illustrated in D. Watkin and C. Proudfoot, 'A Pioneer of English Neo-Classicism: C. H. Tatham', in *Country Life*, p.921, Fig.12.
13. RIBA DC, E1/39, illustrated in colour in Worsley, op.cit., p.51.
14. CUL, U.A. CUR 30.1, item 75d contains two other site plans. On the

first, presumably drawn in early 1836, Basevi moved the building west beyond the limit of the site by 10 ft and suggested a further 12 ft should be allowed for a circulation gap up to the new west boundary. In the second, prepared on October 1836, this gap was reduced to just 7 ft as the architect moved the building still further west in order to accommodate his redesigned approach to the portico.

15. Willis and Willis Clark, op.cit., 3, p.206.
16. CUL, U.A. CUR 30.1, item 117b.
17. CUL, U.A. CUR 30.1, item 93.
18. Willis and Willis Clark, op.cit., 3, pp.208–9.
19. Members of the 1834 and 1835 Syndicates who might be presumed to have played a leading part in the choice of Basevi are listed in Willis and Willis Clark, op.cit., 3, pp.203, 205–6. Among the 1835 Syndics was Charles Merivale, later author of numerous Roman histories.
20. Quoted in Watkin, *The Triumph of the Classical*, p.13.
21. Willis and Willis Clark, op.cit., 3, p.213.
22. SM, Basevi Transcript, p.322.
23. Willis and Willis Clark, op.cit., 3, p.215.
24. See Watkin, *The Life and Work of C. R. Cockerell*, pp.204, 236–7 and Pls 152–4.
25. There is also a design for a pilaster capital of this type of order among Cockerell's drawings for Cambridge University Library (CUL, Add. 6630, fol.8).
26. Fitzwilliam Museum Library, Ms. 591A. The perspective of Digby Wyatt's proposals for the hall is reproduced in Watkin, *The Triumph of the Classical*, Pl.25.
27. Watkin, ibid., p.14.
28. In 1836 Basevi had persuaded the Syndics to purchase from the *formatoro* Sarti two casts of caryatids from the Pandrosium which he had made from moulds in Paris, but Barry's caryatids were new sculptures in white marble (CUL, Min.VI.1, subsection IV, fol.140 and CUR 30.1, fol.80).
29. Willis and Willis Clark, op.cit., 3, p.221.
30. SM, Basevi Transcript, p.176.

Chapter 8 The Royal Exchange, London

1. 26 October, p.258.
2. A thorough historical account of the events from 1838 to the completion of the new Exchange, superseding all earlier ones, can be found by M. Port, 'Destruction, Competition and Rebuilding: The Royal Exchange 1838–1884', in A. Saunders, ed., *The Royal Exchange*, pp.279–305. Details of the competition which follow here naturally relate to Port's article, which should be read alongside the present account.
3. The Royal Exchange papers held in the Corporation of London Records Office on which this chapter is based, many of them drafts or document duplicates, have not been catalogued in modern times. References have therefore been provided below only for direct quotations.
4. CLRO: Royal Exchange and Gresham Trusts Committee, Draft Minutes 1838–45, Bundle 2, meeting of 26 February 1838.
5. CLRO: Royal Exchange and Gresham Trusts Committee Minutes, I, 20 January 1838 to 29 August 1839, fol.14.
6. Copies of the documents printed in association with the work of the Joint Committee are held at both the CLRO and the Mercers' Company, the latter set bound as 'Reports'.
7. See Port, op.cit., pp.283–5.
8. See K. Gibson, '"The Kingdom's Marble Chronicle": The Embellishment of the First and Second Buildings, 1600–1690', in A. Saunders, ed., *The Royal Exchange*, pp.152, 165. A statue of James II in Roman dress, also by Gibbons, stood in the line of monarchs in the second Exchange.
9. D. Kynaston, *The City of London: I – A World of its Own 1815–1890*, pp.96–7.

10. The fourteen previously identified entrants are: Henry Baddock; James Bunstone Bunning (competitor no.22); Alexis de Chateauneuf, with Arthur Mee (43); Cockerell, with Henry Beckley Richardson (46); Thomas Leverton Donaldson (50); Walter Long Bozzi Granville; William Grellier (36); David Mocatta (27); William Bonython Moffatt; John Davis Paine; James Pennethorne (51); Sydney Smirke (37); Francis Wigg, with G. Pownall; and Thomas Henry Wyatt with David Brandon (33). Goldicutt showed his Royal Exchange design at the Royal Academy in 1840 (and an anonymous article in *The Architectural Review* (31, 1912, p.323), very likely by a descendant, says that he submitted designs for the competition). The possible involvement of Elmes has been inferred from two sheets of drawings (RIBA DC, U12/3/1 and 2) with interesting sketched alternatives for a domed semi-circular peristyle or an octastyle Corinthian portico. These sketches do not prove that Elmes entered the competition, however, and, given his contemporary involvement with St George's Hall, Liverpool, it seems unlikely. Colvin, p.1071, identifies Frederick Wood as a competitor, and Thomas Drew is named as the author of design no.15 in a draft minute of 19 November 1839 (CLRO, Draft Minutes, loose paper). Three pencil drawings in the Getty Center ascribed to Charles Barry and John Lewis Wolfe (whose name appears on one) and catalogued as relating to the Exchange are Tudor in style and thus can hardly have anything to do with the 1839 competition.

11. CLRO: Draft Minutes, Bundle 1, meeting of 27 September 1839.

12. 'Royal Exchange: Report of Sir Robert Smirke, Mr Joseph Gwilt and Mr Philip Hardwick on the Designs and Plans', copy in CLRO.

13. Port, op.cit., p.287.

14. Smirke's notes are transcribed in the draft minutes of a meeting of the Committee held on 14 January 1840, CLRO: Draft Minutes, Bundle 5.

15. See Port, op.cit., pp.293–6. The Committee recognized that its own 'vacillation' was 'highly derogatory to a Public Body' and a source of 'dissatisfaction' to the competing architects, but was too unwieldy to help itself (CLRO: Minutes, II, 6 September 1839 to 19 October 1840, fol.138).

16. CLRO: Draft Minutes, Bundle 2, meeting of 29 November 1839.

17. CLRO: Draft Minutes, Bundle 1, meeting of 11 February 1840.

18. See Port, op.cit., p.289 and Fig.107.

19. CLRO: Royal Exchange and Gresham Trusts Committee, Papers, 1838–46, loose letter.

20. For the transverse section of Donaldson's court see S. Blutman, 'The Father of the Profession', in *RIBA Journal*, p.543.

21. The drawing bears Richardson's competitor no. 46, has a presentation border and bears the marks of having been pinned up in the same way as other competition entries.

22. D. Watkin, *The Life and Work of C. R. Cockerell*, p.211.

23. RIBA DC, J11/51/2.

24. G. Tyack, *Sir James Pennethorne and the Making of Victorian London*, p.40.

25. Port, op.cit., reproduces unpremiated competition entries by Bunning (Figs 104, 105) and Paine, who simply submitted his 1833 Royal Academy Gold Medal-winning design for a Royal Exchange (Fig.108). Moffatt's involvement is represented by RIBA DC, ARC 1A/1–3 and includes an idea for an octastyle west portico with a simplified order from the Temple of Castor and Pollux (see K. Esdaile, 'Battles Royal: No.1 – Some Great Architectural Controversies of the Past', in *The Architect and Building News*, p.49.

26. CLRO: Draft Minutes, Bundle 5, meeting of 3 February 1840.

27. The sequence of sketches leading to the final west elevation may read as follows: RIBA DC, J10/30/ Drawing 1, a close variant of the probable 1839 competition entry (Drawing 11 – Fig.151 here) in which Cockerell toyed with the idea of opening the bays either side of the central arched entrance; Drawing 8, a variant of the 1839 competition west elevation in which the balustrade was replaced by an attic with œil de bœuf windows; Drawing 10, in which the pediment was removed from the attic masking the central court and the central arch of the west elevation was definitively abandoned in favour of three trabeated entrances of equal height, framed by a subsidiary order (in the manner of Michelangelo's Capitoline Palaces); Drawing 2, where the entablature over the west columns was made continuous, thereby creating a frieze which could be used for an inscription; then Drawing 5 (watermarked 1840), which is closest to the perspective (Fig.157 here) and the published version (although the latter does not show the court attic). It should be noted, however, that at some stage in 1839 or 1840 Cockerell experimented with four distinctly different design ideas for the Exchange, represented by RIBA DC, J10/30/ Drawings 3, 4, 6 and 9.

28. RIBA DC, OS/5/2/4. Related to this section are two sketches, RIBA DC, J10/30/ Drawings 13 (see Watkin, op.cit., Pl.125) and 14. For the lithograph see ibid., Pl.124 or Port, op.cit., Fig.109.

29. The introduction of a giant order along the Cornhill elevation can be seen in presentation drawing RIBA DC, OS 5/2/1, but this design features a semi-circular colonnaded porch at the west end which does not relate to any of Cockerell's other design ideas.

30. The first of these alternative sections survives (RIBA DC, OS 5/2/3).

31. CLRO: Draft Minutes, Bundle 5, meeting of 7 May 1840.

32. Mercers' Company Archive: 'Reports', I.

33. Mercers' Company Archive: RE 6.2; CLRO: Draft Minutes, Bundle 5, meeting of 28 April 1840.

34. CLRO: Draft Minutes, Bundle 5, meeting of 7 May 1840.

35. R. Lambert Jones, *Reminiscences of the Public Life of Richard Lambert Jones*, p.49.

36. Port, op.cit., p.283.

37. CLRO: Minutes, I, 1 March 1839.

38. Port, op.cit., p.297.

39. Taylor and Cresy, I, pp.39–46.

40. Mercers' Company Archives, RE.19.2.

41. J. Hall, 'The Site of the Royal Exchange in the Roman Period'; and P. Marsden, 'The Excavation for the Third Exchange', both in A. Saunders, ed., *The Royal Exchange*, pp.3–10, 272–5 respectively.

42. C. Willsdon, 'The Mural Decoration at the Royal Exchange', in ibid., pp.311–13.

43. See P. Ayres, *Classical Culture and the Idea of Rome in Eighteenth-Century England*, pp.11–12.

44. Mercers' Company Archive, 'Reports', I; and see D. Abramson, 'C. R. Cockerell's "Architectural Progress of the Bank of England"', in *Architectural History*, pp.120–21. The term 'Forum Londinium', used to describe Cockerell's attitude to this space, quoted in A. Richardson, *Monumental Classic Architecture in Great Britain and Ireland*, p.79, appears to be Richardson's own.

45. I. Leith, 'The Sculpture of the Third Exchange', in A. Saunders, ed., *The Royal Exchange*, p.337.

46. See Port, op.cit., esp. pp.291–3, 298.

47. Port, op.cit., p.289.

48. See *Pictorial Times*, 26 October 1844; *Penny Sunday Times*, special issue; *Illustrated London News*, 2 November 1844; *Common Council Reports*, 1844, p.97.

Chapter 9 St George's Hall, Liverpool

1. BAL, ELM/i–iv, fol.75.

2. Of the seventy-four unsuccessful competitors only a few can be identified: the runner-up George Alexander, Edward Buckton Lamb, William Bonython Moffatt submitting much the same design as he did for the Royal Exchange, and Peter Ellis who published his design later in 1839. William Bardwell, David Mocatta and Owen Jones all showed designs for the building at the Royal Academy in 1840. A file of photographs relating to St George's Hall in the Binns Collection in Liverpool Central Library contains two further unattributed schemes, both for monumental Corinthian buildings.

3. The site plan illustrated here was actually issued on the reverse of the details of the Liverpool Assize Courts competition of 1839–40.

4. The best account of St George's Hall to date, which includes illustration of Elmes's competition drawings, can be found in J. Olley, 'St George's Hall Liverpool', in *The Architects' Journal*, I, pp.36–57 and II, pp.36–61. See also L. Knowles, *St George's Hall, Liverpool*.

5. LCL, Finance Committee Minutes, 1/2, 24 May 1839; Law Courts Committee Minutes 1/1(i), 9 August 1839.

6. LCL, Council Minutes II, 1/2, 22 April 1840. Other known competitors were Samuel Greig, who won the second premium, Charles Lang, John Lightfoot, Francis Wigg and G. Pownall, and John (or Thomas, both names are given) Davies. The perspective of entrant no.37 ('A.B.'), showing the building fronted by a decastyle Corinthian portico with a great flight of steps between projecting stylobates, was destroyed by World War II bombing of Liverpool. A newspaper reproduction, however, can be found in Liverpool Central Library's 'Collection of Illustrations, Photographs, Newspaper Cuttings etc.' of 1933, I, p.146. The following showed designs for the Assize Courts at the Royal Academy in 1841: G. Aitchison, J. J. Cole, J. Taylor Jr., G. Marr and E. H. Browne, J. T. Crew and H. Case.

7. LCL, Law Courts Committee Minutes 1/1, 6 August 1840. Elmes's complaint was justified, as the competition rules stated only that the winning design would not be built if it was found to exceed the £50,000 cost, whereas the sub-committee had later assumed the right to modify the design for other reasons. Franklin, moreover, had already tried to forestall the competition in 1839 by producing plans of his own, when only asked to prepare the brief.

8. See Olley, op.cit., I, pp.39–42, for a largely accurate illustrated account of Elmes's different schemes.

9. H.-R. Hitchcock, *Early Victorian Architecture in Britain*, I, p.310. See also N. Pevsner, *The Buildings of England: South Lancashire*, p.155.

10. [R. Rawlinson], *Correspondence Relative to St George's Hall Liverpool*, p.30.

11. See S. Bayley, 'A British Schinkel', in *Architectural Association Quarterly*, pp.28–32. Bayley points out, however, that Elmes might have known the Altes Museum from Schinkel's 'bleak' illustrations in *Sammlung architektonischer Entwürfe*, the plates of the museum having been published in 1825.

12. J. Elmes, *Lectures on Architecture*, p.234.

13. J. Elmes, *Metropolitan Improvements; or London in the Nineteenth Century*, pp.1, 2. In 1833, Elmes showed a drawing of the death of Pliny at Pompeii in the Royal Academy exhibition.

14. See Olley, op.cit., I, p.50 (Figs 3, 32).

15. [Rawlinson], op.cit., p.62.

16. See Olley, op.cit., I, p.50 and Figs 4, 33 for the Assize Courts and the Fitzwilliam Museum; see Bayley, op.cit., p.32, for St George's Hall and Grange Park. Bayley's comparison depends partly on the use of piers in the side elevations of the two buildings, but Wilkins actually used antae (directly emulating his archaeological source, the Choragic Monument of Thrasyllus in Athens), whereas Elmes's piers have full capitals.

17. For Barry's design see M. Port, 'The New Law Courts Competition, 1886–87', in *Architectural History*, p.76 and Fig.17a.

18. RIBA DC, w9/1/22.

19. RIBA DC, w9/1/8.

20. RIBA DC, u13/52; LCL, Law Courts Committee Minutes 1/1, 8 February 1841.

21. BAL, ELM/i–iv, fol.58.

22. Taylor and Cresy, II, p.31 and Pl.96.

23. [Rawlinson], op.cit., p.68.

24. RIBA DC, u13/29–30, see Olley, op.cit., I, Fig.5.

25. For a full account see F. Salmon and P. de Figueiredo, 'The South Front of St George's Hall, Liverpool', in *Architectural History*, pp.195–218.

26. BAL, ELM/i–iv, fols 51–2; *Sessional Papers of the Royal Institute of British Architects*, 1864. In the same papers, responding to Sydney Smirke's

memoir of Cockerell, William Tite said that he had seen the Munich church and recommended that Elmes should study it during his own visit as a potential source for St George's Hall. It is worth noting that the arch which terminates the barrel vault of the nave of the Michaelskirche where it meets the chancel is similar to the way Elmes handled the north and south ends of St George's Hall.

27. LCL, Law Courts Committee Minutes 1/1, 26 January 1842.

28. BAL, ELM/i–iv, fols 50–51.

29. See LCL, Law Courts Committee Minutes 1/1, 8 February 1844.

30. RIBA DC, w9/1/11.

31. LCL, Law Courts Committee Minutes 1/1, 7 April 1841. At this stage the Hall had 'small domes' to admit light on the east side (see Olley, op.cit., II, Fig.5).

32. LCL, 'Contract and Specification for the Erection of the Carcase of the Building', March 1843, p.14. A transverse section of the Hall for this contract does appear to show the vault spanning between the two wall plates, but it probably represents an intermediate stage between the independent St George's Hall interior design and the introduction of screens of columns at either end (RIBA DC, w9/1/31).

33. LCL, Law Courts Committee Minutes 1/1, 28 April 1843. In March 1843 Elmes had shown the Committee a sketch for alterations to the ends of the Hall, necessitating rebuilding of the foundations. In the memorandum he indicated that this alteration involved the introduction of two columns and the curving of the recesses.

34. RIBA DC, w9/2/1–3; D. Watkin, *Sir John Soane: Enlightenment Thought and the Royal Academy Lectures*, p.590. Cockerell made the same point in his diary in 1821, with reference to the planning of the Adam brothers (see D. Watkin, *The Life and Work of C. R. Cockerell*, p.60).

35. [Rawlinson], op.cit., p.46; J. Kilpin, 'The Late Mr Elmes and St George's Hall', in *Transactions of the Historic Society of Lancashire and Cheshire*, p.236.

36. Printed in *The Builder*, 62, 23 March 1889, reproduced in Olley, op.cit., I, Fig.36 and Knowles, op.cit., Fig.23.

37. See *The Athenaeum*, 796, 1843, p.89.

38. As suggested by Watkin, *The Life and Work of C. R. Cockerell*, p.241. One of Elmes's sketches of the projection does indeed have the Pantheon-type dome of the restored Caracalla Caldarium (RIBA DC, u13/17B verso). RIBA DC, u13/83 is Elmes's study for the change, which was made after Contract A for the foundations was in progress (LCL, Law Courts Committee Minutes 1/1, 26 January 1842).

39. LCL, Law Courts Committee Minutes 1/1, 12 July 1844.

40. LCL, Law Courts Committee Minutes 1/1, 21 June 1845 and 18 July 1845. A plan by Elmes for the South Hall close to its built form (RIBA DC, u13/121) is dated 8 February 1847.

41. RIBA DC, u13/77, 78, 84, 119, 120 and w9/1/29.

42. See, for example, RIBA DC, u13/120.

43. [Rawlinson], op.cit., pp.43–4.

44. LCL, Law Courts Committee Minutes 1/1, 3 February 1847.

45. LCL, Law Courts Committee Minutes 1/1, 8 January 1845 and RIBA DC, u13/84.

46. [Rawlinson], op.cit., p.7. RIBA DC, u13/75 and 79 show that Elmes also contemplated more elaborate figurative painted scenes for the walls behind the balconies.

47. LCL, Law Courts Committee Minutes 1/1, 9 July 1847.

48. LCL, Law Courts Committee Minutes 1/1, 26 August 1847.

49. LCL, Law Courts Committee Minutes 1/1, 5 and 27 April 1848.

50. See G. Stamp, 'Architectural Sculpture in Liverpool', in P. Curtis, ed., *Patronage and Practice: Sculpture on Merseyside*, pp.8–9.

51. See Salmon and de Figueiredo, op.cit.

52. A typescript of Booth's pamphlet survives in LCL, Collection of Illustrations, p.8.

53. LCL, Law Courts Committee Minutes 1/2, 30 August 1849. The books were listed on 1 October.

54. For Cockerell's work inside St George's Hall, see Watkin, *The Life and Work of C. R. Cockerell*, pp.239–41. For the balustrade as a Renaissance

invention see P. Davies and D. Hemsoll, 'Renaissance Balusters and the Antique', in *Architectural History*, pp.1–23.

55. V&A, PDP, E.2001–1909.

56. RIBA DC, U13/82 and 83.

57. Watkin, *The Life and Work of C. R. Cockerell*, pp.239–41.

58. LCL, Law Courts Committee Minutes 1/1, 27 October 1840.

59. See T. Algernon Earle, 'Earle of Allerton Tower', in *Transactions of the Historic Society of Lancashire and Cheshire*, pp.57–60; and R. Millington, *The House in the Park*, p.14.

60. Elmes appears to have worked for the families of two of these men. In about 1845 he designed a house for G.H. (probably George Hall) Lawrence and in 1847 said he was designing one for Mr Hornby [Rawlinson], op.cit., pp.48–9, perhaps related to a surviving sketch for Joshua Hornby (RIBA DC, U21 and the villa Druid's Cross at Woolton).

61. RIBA DC, U13/37–38.

62. Walker Art Gallery, Liverpool. Identification of these buildings has been made by Joseph Sharples of the Gallery. See also N. Vance, *The Victorians and Ancient Rome*, p.74.

63. See J. Delaine, 'The *Romanitas* of the railway station', in M. Biddiss and M. Wyke, eds, *The Uses and Abuses of Antiquity*, pp.145–52, citing Booth's *Account of the Liverpool and Manchester Railway* of 1830, among many other sources.

64. [Rawlinson], op.cit., pp.26–8.

65. BAL, ELM/i–iv, p.75; LCL, Law Courts Committee Minutes, 1/1, 23 March 1849.

66. The inaugurating concert was depicted in *The Illustrated London News*, 23 September 1854, p.277.

67. 'Report … from the Committee appointed at the Annual General Meeting in May 1852 for the purpose of promoting the Improvement of the Town', in *Proceedings of the Liverpool Architectural and Archaeological Society*, Session 1852–3 (1857), p.373.

68. See D. Brooks, *Thomas Allom (1804–1872)*, pp.79–81 and Fig.55.

69. M. Rivlin, 'A Nineteenth Century Classical Forum: William Brown Street, Liverpool', M.A. Dissertation. See also R. Jenkyns, *Dignity and Decadence: Victorian Art and the Classical Inheritance*, pp.6–9.

70. J. Picton, *Memorials of Liverpool*, II, pp.204, 208.

71. [Rawlinson], op.cit., p.34.

72. *The Athenaeum*, 2 June 1855, p.649.

73. Kilpin, op.cit., p.234.

74. See B. Read, 'From Basilica to Walhalla', in P. Curtis, ed., *Patronage and Practice: Sculpture on Merseyside*, p.34. The Hellenistic scientist and engineer, Archimedes, worked at Syracuse which, from the time of the First Punic War, allied itself with the Roman Republic.

Epilogue

1. A. W. N. Pugin, *An Apology for the Revival of Christian Architecture*, p.20; *The Builder*, 4, 1843, p.313.

2. See, most recently, D. Watkin, 'The Travellers' Club and the Grand Tour: Correcting Raphael…', in *The British Art Journal*, pp.56–62.

3. For the English case, see M. Port, *Imperial London: Civil Government Building in London 1850–1914*.

4. Ashpitel's restoration is illustrated with its topographical companion in M. Liversidge and C. Edwards, *Imagining Rome*, pp.115–16. This catalogue also contains a representative selection of Victorian paintings of Roman subjects.

5. G. L. Taylor, *The Autobiography of an Octogenarian Architect*, II, p.251.

6. See D. Watkin, *The Life and Work of C. R. Cockerell*, p.132 and Pl.16, for 'The Professor's Dream'. For colour reproduction, see *Der Traum von Raum: Gemalte Architektur aus 7 Jahrhundertern*, exh.cat., 1986, p.395.

Appendix A British architects in Italy, 1740–1840

1. Master Mason to the Board of Ordnance. An illustrated journal of tours of Italy, made by Mercer in 1740 and 1750, is in the Bodleian Library, Oxford (Ms. Top.gen.e.98).

2. Two Scottish architects of this name arrived in Rome in 1755 (Ingamells, p.1005).

3. See Ingamells, p.662.

4. An elevation of the façade of St Peter's, exhibited at the Free Society of Artists in the mid 1760s, suggests that Overton had been in Rome (see Colvin, p.716).

5. Hadfield had passed his childhood years (1764–79) in Florence, where his father kept an inn.

6. The younger Gibson is likely to have been born about 1770 (see Colvin, p.408) and thus to have travelled in the early 1790s. By the late 1790s he was taking pupils in London. Gibson's father was also an architect, said to have worked for Queen Caroline (died 1737) and to have visited Italy, arranging collections purchased there in his house in Lewisham (built 1771) where he lived until 1795.

7. Kay (and presumably Martyr, with whom he was travelling) lived in Piazza di Spagna (British Library, Ms. 45545, fol.1r).

8. In 1804 Smirke was living in Via Mario di Fiori, near Piazza di Spagna (BAL, SMK 2/2).

9. A drawing of the Temple of Vespasian, shown at the Royal Academy in 1807, suggests that Newman had recently visited Rome.

10. A pupil of Soane, Buxton evidently decided to abandon his architectural career while in Italy.

11. In 1817 Basevi was living in the Casa Cordelli, Piazza Rosa. He then moved to Piazza S. Carlo (1817–18) and, after his return from Greece, to Via della Croce (1818–19).

12. In 1818 Goldicutt was living in the Strada Gregoriana (Accademia Nazionale di S. Luca, Rome, vol.86, no.250). Goldicutt's putative second visit to Italy in 1832–3, unlikely because of his involvement at that time in the competition for Fishmongers' Hall, London, rests on the insecure attribution to him of a sketchbook at YCBA.

13. Woods lived first in Franz's German Lodging House in the Via Condotti, then in Piazza Trinità de' Monti (J. Woods, *Letters of an Architect*, I, p.330).

14. Taylor (and presumably Cresy) lived in Piazza di Spagna in 1817–18 (G. L. Taylor, *The Autobiography of an Octogenarian Architect*, I, p.87).

15. The 'ardent pursuit of improvement in his profession as an Architect' exposed Graham to 'the dissipating and corrupting air of foreign lands'. He died in Naples and is commemorated by a monument in the Protestant Cemetery in Rome (Colvin, p.420).

16. In 1822 Donaldson was living in Strada Gregoriana (Accademia Nazionale di S. Luca, Rome, vol.72, no.76).

17. Gandy returned to Naples in 1819, when he was met by John Soane Junior (A. Bolton, *The Portrait of Sir John Soane*, p.286).

18. Jenkins is known to have been in Athens in 1820, but he also visited Italy, probably in the autumn of 1819 (see T. L. Donaldson, *Pompeii*, I, Pls 6, 22).

19. In 1820–21 Poynter lived in Via Condotti (RIBA DC, Poynter Transcript, p.79).

20. In 1821 Wolfe was living in Piazza di Spagna (RIBA DC, Wolfe Journal with Sketches 6, fol.2), then in Via Gregoriana in 1821 (Archivio di Stato di Roma, Camerlengato I, Antichità e Belle Arti, Busta 42, Fasc. 231, item 1).

21. In entering the competition for Fishmongers' Hall, London, Davies reported having been in Italy for three years (see P. Metcalf, *The Halls of the Fishmongers' Company*, p.130). He visited again in 1858.

22. Harris (and presumably Samuel Angell) lived in Via del Tritone in 1822 (Archivio di Stato di Roma, Camerlengato I, Antichità e Belle Arti, Busta 43, Fasc. 260, item 4, no.5). In 1823 Harris and Angell discovered the coloured metopes of Temple C at Selinunte but Harris, 'from his extreme anxiety to complete the drawings there, remained too late in the Season – caught the fever & died at Palermo' (1825 letter from Selinunte of Sydney Smirke, BAL, SMK 3/3). Smirke reported that Harris, who is commemorated by a monument in the Protestant Cemetery in Rome, had become a legendary figure locally, known as 'Don Guglielmo'.

23. See V. W. von Hagen, *Frederick Catherwood Architect*.

24. Mathews was taken to Italy by Lord Blessington, a rare revival of this early eighteenth-century and seventeenth-century form of patronage of architectural travel. His second visit to Italy in 1827–30 was undertaken with a parental allowance.

25. Sydney Smirke reported the presence of 'Parker, an Architectural youth' in Rome in 1825 (BAL, SMK 3/2). In the third book of *Villa Rustica*, 1841, Charles Parker reported that he 'had again visited the continent to examine the structures there erected' (Preface).

26. Smirke lived in Via Frattina 1824–5 (BAL, SMK 1/41 to 1/43).

27. Wightwick lived in Via Frattina in 1825 (Wightwick, 'Sketches by a Travelling Architect', in *Library of the Fine Arts*, p.118).

28. Palmer, a silver medallist of the Royal Academy, died at Paris on his homeward journey from Italy (Colvin, pp.727–8).

29. Lee visited Italy on his honeymoon (BAL, RIBA/MS.SP/4/8).

30. Wetten prefaced his *Designs for Villas in the Italian Style* in Florence in 1829.

31. Arundale's *Edifices of Andrea Palladio* of 1832 suggests a visit to Italy just before that time. Arundale travelled in the Mediterranean for much of the 1830s, regularly sending drawings of Italian subjects for exhibition at the Royal Academy.

32. A 'fellow traveller' of Arundale's, according to the latter's Preface in *Edifices of Andrea Palladio*.

33. Hayward showed a drawing of the Temple of Juno at Agrigento at the Royal Academy in 1831.

34. Hakewill is referred to as a fellow-traveller on a drawing by David Mocatta (RIBA DC, v9/41).

35. See I. Gow, 'David Rhind: The Master of Mercantile Ornament', in R. Brown, ed., *The Architectural Outsiders*, p.155.

36. Scandrett's drawing of Pompeian fragments was exhibited at The Royal Academy in 1832.

37. Hakewill showed a drawing of a tomb on the Via Appia at the Royal Academy in 1833.

38. An 'architect' from Nottingham (see Fig.81).

39. Kempthorne's drawing of the Forum, made in 1833, was exhibited at the Royal Academy in 1835.

40. See A. James, 'Rickman and the Fitzwilliam Competition', in *The Architectural Review*, p.271.

41. The 1837 Royal Academy exhibition included a drawing of the Forum by Shoubridge.

42. Nash, travelling with a fellow student of Charles Barry named Parish (possibly Charles Parish), visited the Accademia delle Belle Arti in Florence in 1836 with a letter of introduction written on behalf of the Institute of British Architects by T. L. Donaldson. See F. Salmon, 'British Architects, Italian Fine Arts Academies and the Foundation of the RIBA', in *Architectural History*, p.95.

43. Wyatt's collection of travel sketches is YCBA, B1975.2.704.

44. Thomson displayed a drawing of the Capitol at Rome in the 1840 Royal Academy exhibition.

Bibliography

Manuscripts: UK

BIRMINGHAM

Central Library (City Archives)
'Proceedings of the Commissioners for Paving, Lighting, Watching, Cleansing and otherwise Improving the Town of Birmingham (1828–37)'
Ms. 897 (Pershouse Collection, 2 vols)

CAMBRIDGE

Fitzwilliam Museum Library
Ms. 591A (Matthew Digby Wyatt's proposals for completing the Fitzwilliam Museum)

University Library
U.A. Min.VI.1 and U.A. CUR 30.1–4 (Fitzwilliam Museum Syndicate papers)

EDINBURGH

Register House
GD/18 (Adam Letters)

LIVERPOOL

Central Library (Local History Division)
'Contract and Specification for the Erection of the Carcase [of St George's Hall]', March 1843
Council Minutes, 352, II, 1/1 and 1/2
Finance Committee Minutes 1/2
Law Courts Committee Minutes 352, 1/1(i), 1/1 and 1/2
'St George's Hall, Liverpool: Collection of Illustrations, Photographs, Newspaper Cuttings etc.', 2 vols, compiled in the Library, 1933

LONDON

British Architectural Library (RIBA)
(Entries in notes, prefixed BAL)
CHA 1/2–4 (William Chambers Royal Academy lectures draft)
CoC: Add./1– and Add./2– (C. R. Cockerell letters)
DA 1/1/i–xviii (letters of George Dance the Younger)
DoT/12– and 3/6 (passports and diplomas of T. L. Donaldson)
ELM/i–iv (James Elmes, memoir of Harvey Lonsdale Elmes)
Gandy Family (letters from J. M. Gandy to his family)
LAS.4/3 (Henry Bayly Garling, paper of 1847 'On the Present State and Antiquities of Rome')
MyFam (Mylne Family papers)
PeJ/1– (papers of James Pennethorne)
Poynter Transcript (transcript of Ambrose Poynter's Journal and Notes and extracts from his letters, 1821, by Robert Finch, held in the RIBA Drawings Collection)
ReW/1 (Willey Reveley travel journal)
RIBA LC 1/1/2 (letter from Samuel Angell to T. L. Donaldson)
RIBA LC 1/3/9 and 23 (letters from S. Ittar and G.-A. Blouet to T. L. Donaldson)

RIBA/Ms. SP/2 (address by J. Goldicutt)
RIBA/Ms. SP/4/8 (Memoir of Thomas Lee by T. L. Donaldson)
SaT/1 (Thomas Sandby Royal Academy lectures)
SMK/1, 2 and 3 (Robert and Sydney Smirke letters)
TaG/1/1/1 (licence for George Ledwell Taylor and Edward Cresy from Antonio Canova)

British Library
Add. Ms. 36493 (letters to George Cumberland)
Add. Ms. 36946
Add. Mss. 39780–92 (letters from John Flaxman and his wife)
Add. Ms. 45545 (journal and papers of Joseph Kay)

Corporation of London Records Office (Guildhall)
Royal Exchange and Gresham Trusts Committee, 281D: Draft Minutes 1838–45
Royal Exchange and Gresham Trusts Committee, 380C: Minutes, I and II 1838–47
Royal Exchange and Gresham Trusts Committee, 281D: Papers, 1838–46

Mercers' Company Archives
'Reports' of Royal Exchange Committee proceedings, 1838–47 (3 vols)
Misc. Mss. 25–27 (papers of Robert Sutton)
Misc. Mss. 40–42 (correspondence of John Horsley Palmer)

Sir John Soane's Museum
Architectural Library Soane Case 155, 156 (Royal Academy lecture texts)
Basevi Transcript (letters of George Basevi, transcribed by A. T. Bolton)
Correspondence Cupboard I, Division III.G.2 (letters from J. P. Gandy)

Victoria & Albert Museum (Department of Paintings, Drawings and Prints)
99.A.3 (letters and sketches to Henry Holland from Christopher Ebdon and C. H. Tatham)

OXFORD

Bodleian Library
Ms. Top.gen.e.98 (George Mercer Italian travel journal)

Manuscripts: Italy and USA

ROME

Accademia Nazionale di S. Luca
Ms. Congregazioni, vols 51–6, 59
Misc. papers, vols 68, 72, 76, 86, 88, 89, 90, 92, 95, 101, 102, 171

Archivio di Stato
Camerlengato I, Antichità et Belle Arti
Busta 42, Fasc. 231, item 1
Busta 43, Fasc. 260, item 4, no.5

NEW HAVEN, CONNECTICUT

Beinecke Library, Yale University, Osborn Ms. D.293 and File 13.381 (Gell letters)

Yale Center for British Art
Ambrose Poynter, 1820 diary
Ms. Riou: 'Itineral Remarks from Italy to the Archipelago and
    Constantinople by sea and thence by land through Romelia,
    Bulgaria, Servia and Hungary to Vienna, in the years 1753 and 1754'

UNLOCATED

Ms. Tatham Autobiography: copy of a typed transcription (in
    possession of Sir Howard Colvin)

Drawings: UK

BIRMINGHAM

Central Library (City Archives)
BCC Plans 201, 202, 203, 209, 210, 211, 216
Ms. 617/2/1–4 (drawings by Charles Barry)
Ms. 1703/15/1–36/36 (drawings by Charles Edge)

CAMBRIDGE

Fitzwilliam Museum Library
Uncatalogued design and working drawings for the Museum building

University Library
Add. 6630 and 9272 (C. R. Cockerell drawings for the University
    Library)

CHESTER

City Record Office
CR 73 (drawings by Thomas Harrison)

EDINBURGH

Penicuik House
'Sketch Book of Italian Views' by Robert Adam, Charles-Louis
    Clérisseau, et al.

LONDON

British Architectural Library (RIBA)
(Entries in notes prefixed RIBA DC)
L12 (Robert Adam, drawings of Hadrian's Villa, Tivoli)
Sketchbooks (8) and 1819 album of Charles Barry
Palmyra and Balbec drawings by Giovanni Battista Borra
W14/13 (Decimus Burton)
E2/11 (C. R. Cockerell, Pompeii Theatre)
H6/1 and 2 (sketchbooks by C. R. Cockerell)
J10/24/1–4 (C. R. Cockerell, sketches for Pompeii Theatre restoration)
J10/30 (C. R. Cockerell, sketches for the Royal Exchange)
OS 5/2/1–4 (C. R. Cockerell, design drawings for the Royal Exchange)
T. L. Donaldson: Album Greek and Roman
OS 5/4/1–7 (Donaldson, competition drawings for Royal Exchange)
OS 5/5 (Donaldson, Temple of Victory drawings)
E1/39 (Fitzwilliam Museum design by Henry Duesbury)
U13 and W9 (Harvey Lonsdale Elmes, drawings for St George's Hall,
    Liverpool)
U12/3/1–2 (Harvey Lonsdale Elmes sketches, possibly for the Royal
    Exchange)
U21 (drawing by Harvey Lonsdale Elmes for a house for Joshua
    Hornby)
J6 (drawings by John Goldicutt)
OS 5/14 (William Grellier, competition drawings for the Royal
    Exchange)
George Hadfield: drawings and restoration of the Sanctuary of Fortune,
    Palestrina

CC8/19 (Philip Hardwick drawing, and sketchbook)
H1 and AF6 (sketchbooks by Thomas Hardwick)
E3 (flat drawings by Thomas Hardwick)
Hardwick albums of drawings and tracings collected in Italy (7)
V9 (drawings by David Mocatta)
ARC 1A/1 and 1/1/2–3 (William Moffatt, designs for the Royal
    Exchange)
W5, (flat drawings, also albums (2) and sketchbooks (2) of Henry Parke)
Ambrose Poynter: Pompeii sketchbooks and portfolios of drawings of
    Rome (2), Sicily and Pompeii
E1/34 (Thomas Rickman, designs for the Fitzwilliam Museum)
Album of Alexander Roos
CC12 and J11/37/1–5 (Robert Smirke drawings)
Albums of drawings by Sydney Smirke (2)
J11/51/1–2 (Sydney Smirke, sketches for the Royal Exchange)
CC4 and Y30 (sketchbooks and drawings by James Stuart)
K4 (drawings by Charles Heathcote Tatham)
H6/8 (Sketchbook of Charles Wilde)
John Lewis Wolfe: journals with sketches (16) and volumes of sketches
    and measured drawings made with Charles Barry (2)
Y8 (John Lewis Wolfe drawings)
Y3 (Joseph Woods: Sicilian sketchbook, travel album and portfolio of
    Pompeian drawings, some copied from other architects, notably
    Richard Sharp)

British Museum (Department of Greek and Roman Antiquities)
Box 41b (five sketch- and notebooks of C. R. Cockerell)
Misc. box of 73 sheets (associated with travels of C. R. Cockerell)

Corporation of London Records Office
27.J.2, 4, 7, 8 and 9 (site plans for the Royal Exchange)

Mercers' Company Archives
RE 6.2 (George Smith, comparative plan of the Royal Exchange
    porticoes of W. Tite and C. R. Cockerell)
RE 19.2 (George Smith, comparative plan of the Royal Exchange
    portico with that of St Paul's Cathedral)
Contract plans for the Royal Exchange, 1841, by William Tite

Sir John Soane's Museum
Adam Volumes 4, 26, 28, 55, 56, 57 and misc. volume
45/7/5 (anon. plan of Forum, Pompeii)
44/2 (drawings by George Basevi)
44/7 (drawings by Charles Cameron)
Dance Cabinet (Italian drawings)
14/6/5 (drawing by J. M. Gandy)
Soane Architectural Library, misc. sketches 1780–82
45/3 (Soane Italian drawings, some redrawn for Royal Academy
    lectures)
Soane Italian sketches 1779
Soane Italian sketches and memoranda 1779
89/1 (drawings by John Soane Junior)
26/6/13 (copy of Edward Stevens's restoration of Pliny's Villa at
    Laurentinum)

Victoria & Albert Museum (Department of Prints, Drawings
    and Paintings)
5712 (William Chambers, Franco-Italian Album)
Chambers flat drawings
E.2000–1909, etc. (C. R. Cockerell, drawings for St George's Hall,
    Liverpool)
E.2114–1909 (C. R. Cockerell, drawing for Fitzwilliam Museum,
    Cambridge)
D.417–449.188 (album of drawings by Theodosius Keene)
E.1403/1696–1914 (albums of drawings by Richard Norris (2))
3859.1–57 (album of drawings by James Paine the Younger)
E.4087–1914 (sketchbook of George Ledwell Taylor)

Drawings: Italy and USA

ROME

Accademia Nazionale di S. Luca
Architectural Drawings 535–50, 581–611, 904–27, 1059–84, 2148–9, 2159–63, 2190

British School
Sketches in Italy by James Hakewill

BALTIMORE

John Work Garrett Library, Johns Hopkins University
NA311.H3 1777 (album of drawings by Thomas Hardwick)

LOS ANGELES

The Getty Research Institute
860602 (Charles Barry, design for Birmingham Town Hall)

NEW HAVEN, CONNECTICUT

Yale Center for British Art
B1975.4.1203 ('A Scene in Ancient Rome', by J. M. Gandy)
Drawings by Willey Reveley, including B1977.14.19455
B1975.2.780 (volume of drawings by Stephen Riou)
B1977.14.369–795 (volumes of drawings by Robert Smirke (4))
B1975.2–704 (album of drawings by Thomas Henry Wyatt, 1837)

NEW YORK

Cooper-Hewitt Museum
DP1901.39.271 and 1938.88.4049 (drawings by J. M. Gandy and R. Mylne)

Metropolitan Museum, Department of Prints and Illustrated Books
34.78.2 (58–65) (drawings by William Chambers)
34.78.2 (67–8 and 70–90) (drawings attributed to Thomas Hardwick)

Pierpont Morgan Library
1954.14 (Robert Adam Album) and 1961.39 (Adam sheet)

Books and articles

Square brackets denote here authors' names which do not appear on the publications' title pages but which are identifiable, and dates of first editions, where known.

D. Abramson, 'C. R. Cockerell's "Architectural Progress of the Bank of England"', in *Architectural History*, 37, 1994, pp.112–29

R. Ackerman, ed., *Repository of Arts*, 2nd series, 14, 1822

R. Adam, *Ruins of the Palace of the Emperor Diocletian at Spalatro in Dalmatia*, London, 1764

R. and J. Adam, *The Works in Architecture of Robert and James Adam*, 2 vols, London, 1773–9

The Age of Neo-Classicism, Royal Academy and Victoria & Albert Museum: London, 1972

T. Allason, *Picturesque Views of the Antiquities of Pola in Istria*, London, 1819

J. Allibone, *Anthony Salvin: Pioneer of Gothic Revival Architecture*, Cambridge, 1988

P. Andrew, 'Jacob More: Biography and a Checklist of Works', in *The Walpole Society*, 55, 1993, pp.105–96

S. Angell and W. Harris, *Sculptured Metopes Discovered Amongst the Ruins of the Temples of the Ancient City of Selinus in Sicily by William Harris and Samuel Angell in the Year 1823*, London, 1826

Anon. 'John Goldicutt and his Times', in *The Architectural Review*, 31, June 1912, pp.321–5

D. Arnold, 'The Arch at Constitution Hill', in *Apollo*, 138, September 1993, pp.129–33

——, 'George IV and the Metropolitan Improvements: The Creation of a Royal Image', in D. Arnold, ed., *Squanderous and Lavish Profusion: George IV, His Image and Patronage of Arts*, London, 1995, pp.51–6

——, ed., *The Georgian Villa*, 2nd edn, Stroud, 1998 [1996]

——, 'The Illusion of Grandeur? Antiquity, Grand Tourism and the Country House', in D. Arnold, et al., *The Georgian Country House: Architecture, Landscape and Society*, Stroud, 1998, pp.100–116

——, 'London Bridge and its Symbolic Identity in the Regency Metropolis: the Dialectic of Civic and National Pride', in *Art History*, 22/4, 1999, pp.79–100

——, *Re-presenting the Metropolis: Architecture, Urban Experience and Social Life in London 1800–1840*, Aldershot, 2000

T. Arnold, *History of Rome*, 3 vols, 5th edn, London, 1848 [1838–43]

F. Arundale, *The Edifices of Andrea Palladio*, London, 1832

T. Ashby, 'Thomas Jenkins in Rome', *Papers of the British School at Rome*, 6, 1913, pp.487–511

E. Atherstone, *The Last Days of Herculaneum and Abradates and Panthea*, London, 1821

P. Ayres, *Classical Culture and the Idea of Rome in Eighteenth-Century England*, Cambridge, 1997

S. Bann, 'Envisioning Rome: Granet and Gibbon in Dialogue', in C. Edwards, ed., 1999, pp.35–52

J. Barrier, 'Chambers in France and Italy', in J. Harris and M. Snodin, eds, *Sir William Chambers: Architect to George III*, New Haven and London, 1996, pp.19–33

A. Barry, *The Life and Work of Sir Charles Barry*, London, 1867

W. Basevi, 'The Grand Tour of an Architect', in *The Architect*, 1922, pp.5–6, 43–4, 70–71, 117–18, 156–7

J. Bassin, *Architectural Competitions in Nineteenth-Century England*, Ann Arbor, 1984

S. Bayley, 'A British Schinkel', in *Architectural Association Quarterly*, 7, April–June 1975, pp.28–32

D. Beales, *Joseph II [Vol. I]: In the Shadow of Maria Theresa*, Cambridge, 1987

B. Bergdoll, *Léon Vaudoyer: Historicism in the Service of Industry*, Cambridge, Mass., 1994

J. Bettley, 'A Design by Stephen Riou for an Academy of Painting, Sculpture and Architecture', in *The Burlington Magazine*, 128, August 1986, pp.581–2

N. Bingham, 'Architecture at the Royal Academy Schools, 1768–1836', in N. Bingham, ed., *The Education of the Architect: Proceedings of the 22nd Annual Symposium of the Society of Architectural Historians of Great Britain 1993*, 1993, pp.5–14

M. Binney, 'The Making of an Architect: The Travels of Sir Charles Barry', in *Country Life*, 146, 28 August, 4 September and 11 September 1969, pp.494–8, 550–52 and 622–4

M. Binney, *Sir Robert Taylor: From Rococo to Neoclassicism*, London, 1984

J. Black, *The British Abroad: The Grand Tour in the Eighteenth Century*, Stroud, 1992

The Countess of Blessington, *An Idler in Italy*, 3 vols, 2nd edn, London, 1839–40

G.-A. Blouet, *Restauration des Thermes d'Anthonin Caracalla à Rome, Présentée en 1826 et Dédiée en 1827 à l'Académie des Beaux-Arts de l'Institut de France*, Paris, 1828

S. Blutman, 'The Father of the Profession', in *RIBA Journal*, 74, December 1967, pp.542–4

A. Bolton, *Architectural Education a Century Ago*, Soane Museum Publication 12 (no date)

——, *The Portrait of Sir John Soane, R.A.*, London, 1927

A. Boëthius, *Etruscan and Early Roman Architecture*, Harmondsworth, 1978

C. Bonucci, *Pompei Descritta*, Naples, 1824

A. Braham, 'Piranesi as Archaeologist and French Architecture in the late Eighteenth Century', in G. Brunel, ed., *Piranèse et les Français*, Rome, 1978, pp.67–8

——, *The Architecture of the French Enlightenment*, London, 1980

C. Brand, *Italy and the English Romantics: The Italianate Fashion in Early Nineteenth-Century England*, Cambridge, 1957

A. Briggs, *Victorian Cities*, 2nd edn, Harmondsworth, 1968 [1963]

I. Bristow, *Architectural Colour in British Interiors 1615–1840*, New Haven and London, 1996

D. Brooks, *Thomas Allom (1804–1872)*, RIBA: London, 1998

P. Broucke, *The Archaeology of Architecture: Charles Robert Cockerell in Southern Europe and the Levant, 1810–1817*, Yale Center for British Art: New Haven, CT, 1993

I. Gordon Brown, 'The Fittest Place in Europe for our Profession: George Richardson in Rome', in *Architectural Heritage II: Scottish Architects Abroad*, 1991, pp.29–40

——, *Monumental Reputation: Robert Adam & the Emperor's Palace*, Edinburgh, 1992

R. Brown, *Domestic Architecture: Containing a History of the Science, and the Principles of Designing Public Edifices, Private Dwelling-Houses, Country Mansions, and Suburban Villas*, London, 1842

E. Bulwer-Lytton, *England and the English*, 2 vols, London, 1833

——, *The Last Days of Pompeii*, 3 vols, London, 1834

R. Burgess, *The Topography and Antiquities of Rome, Including the Recent Discoveries Made About the Forum and the Via Sacra*, 2 vols, London, 1831

E. Burton, *A Description of the Antiquities and Other Curiosities of Rome: From Personal Observation During a Visit to Italy in the Years 1818–19*, 2 vols, 2nd edn, London, 1828 [1821]

C. Cameron, *The Baths of the Romans Explained and Illustrated*, London, 1772

Charles Cameron c.1740–1812: Architectural Drawings and Photographs from the Hermitage Collection, Leningrad, and Architectural Museum, Moscow, The Arts Council: 1967–8

M. Campbell, *John Martin: Visionary Printmaker*, Campbell Fine Art in association with York City Art Gallery: 1992

L. Canina, *Descrizione storico del Foro Romano*, Rome, 1834

——, *L'Architettura romana*, 2nd edn, Rome, 1844 [1830]

A. Caristie, *Plan et coupe d'une partie du Forum Romain et des monumens sur la voie sacrée*, Paris, 1821

G. Carletti and L. Mirri, *Le antiche camere delle Terme di Tito e le loro pitture*, Rome, 1776

W. Chambers, *A Treatise on the Decorative Part of Civil Architecture*, 3rd edn, London, 1791 [1759]

R. Chandler, et al., *Ionian Antiquities*, 4 vols, London, 1769–1881

E. Chaney, 'Inigo Jones in Naples', in *The Evolution of the Grand Tour: Anglo-Italian Cultural Relations since the Renaissance*, London and Portland, Oregon, 1998, pp.168–202

J. Clark, 'The Mysterious Mr Buck', in *Apollo*, 129, May, 1989, pp.317–22

M. Clarke, *Classical Education in Britain 1500–1900*, Cambridge, 1959

[W. Clarke], *Pompeii: Its Past and Present State; Its Public and Private Buildings, etc., Compiled in Part from the Great Work of M. Mazois; the Museo Borbonico; the Publications of Sir W. Gell, and T. L. Donaldson*, 2 vols, 2nd edn, London, 1846 [1831]

E. Clay and M. Frederiksen, eds, *Sir William Gell in Italy: Letters to the Society of Dilettanti 1831–1835*, London, 1976

F. Coarelli, *Il Foro Romano*, Rome, 1985

C.-N. Cochin, *Observations sur les antiquités de la ville d'Herculanum*, Paris, 1753; 2nd edn 1755; 3rd edn 1757, translated as *Observations upon the Antiquities of Herculaneum*, 2nd edn, London, 1756 [1753]

L. Colley, *Britons: Forging the Nation 1707–1837*, New Haven and London, 1992

H. Colvin, 'What we mean by Amateur', in G. Worsley, ed., 1994, pp.4–6

——, *A Biographical Dictionary of British Architects, 1600–1840*, 3rd edn, New Haven and London, 1995 [1954]

G. Consoli, *Il Museo Pio-Clementino: La Scena dell' Antico in Vaticano*, Modena, 1996

J. Cornforth, 'The Fitzwilliam Museum, Cambridge', in *Country Life*, 132, 22 and 29 November 1962, pp.1278–81, 1340–43

E. Corti, *The Destruction and Resurrection of Pompeii and Herculaneum*, London, 1951

E. Cox, *A Reference Guide to the Literature of Travel*, 3 vols, Seattle, 1935–49

M. Crinson and J. Lubbock, *Architecture: Art or Profession? Three Hundred Years of Architectural Education in Britain*, Manchester, 1994

J. Mordaunt Crook, *The Dilemma of Style: Architectural Ideas from the Picturesque to the Post-Modern*, 2nd edn, London, 1989 [1987]

——, *The Greek Revival: Neo-Classical Attitudes in British Architecture 1760–1870*, 2nd edn, London, 1995 [1972]

G. Cuisset, 'Jean-Pierre and François Fouquet, Artistes Modeleurs', in *Gazette des Beaux-Arts*, May–June 1990, pp.227–40

J. Stevens Curl, *The Life and Work of Henry Roberts*, Chichester, 1983

P. Curtis, ed., *Patronage and Practice: Sculpture on Merseyside*, National Museums and Galleries on Merseyside: 1989

L. Cust and S. Colvin, *History of the Society of Dilettanti*, London, 1898

G. Darley, *John Soane: An Accidental Romantic*, New Haven and London, 1999

P. Davies and D. Hemsoll, 'Renaissance Balusters and the Antique', in *Architectural History*, 26, 1983, pp.1–23

E. de Albentiis, 'La casa del'Accademia di Musica (VI 3,7–25–26) e le Tabernae', in *Le Insulae 3 e 4 della Regio VI di Pompei – Un'analisi storico-urbanistica*, Archaeologia Perusina 5, Rome, 1990, pp.57–110

H. d'Espouy, *Monuments Antiques Relevés et Restaurés par les Architectes Pensionnaires de l'Académie de France à Rome*, 3 vols and Supplement, Paris, 1912–23

N. Thomson de Grummond, ed., *An Encyclopedia of the History of Classical Archaeology*, 2 vols, London, 1996

A. de Jorio, *Notizie su gli scavi di Ercolano*, Naples, 1827

——, *Plan de Pompéi et remarques sur ses édifices*, Naples, 1828

P. de la Ruffinière du Prey, 'Soane and Hardwick in Rome: A Neo-Classical Partnership', in *Architectural History*, 15, 1972, pp.51–67

——, *John Soane: The Making of an Architect*, Chicago and London, 1982

——, *The Villas of Pliny: From Antiquity to Posterity*, Chicago and London, 1994

A. de Montaiglon and J. Guiffrey, eds, *Correspondance des Directeurs de l'Académie de France à Rome*, 17 vols, Paris, 1887–1908

A. de' Romanis, *Le antiche camere esquiline dette comunemente delle Terme di Tito*, Rome, 1822

R. Abbé de Saint-Non, *Voyage pittoresque de Naples et de Sicile*, 5 vols, Paris, 1781–6

J. Delaine, 'The *Romanitas* of the Railway Station', in M. Biddiss and M. Wyke, eds, *The Uses and Abuses of Antiquity*, Bern, 1999, pp.145–52

C. Denison, et al., *Exploring Rome: Piranesi and His Contemporaries*, Cambridge, Mass., and London, 1993

A. Desgodetz, *Les Edifices antiques de Rome dessinés et mesurés très exactement*, Paris, 1682, 2nd edn, Paris, 1779

C. Dezobry, *Rome au siècle d'Auguste*, 2nd edn, Paris, 1846

R. Dixon and S. Muthesius, *Victorian Architecture*, 2nd edn, London, 1985 [1978]

T. L. Donaldson, *Pompeii, Illustrated with Picturesque Views*, 2 vols, London, 1827

——, *A Collection of the Most Approved Examples of Doorways from Ancient and Modern Buildings in Greece and Italy*, London, 1833

——, *Architectura Numismatica, or Architectural Medals of Classic Antiquity*, London, 1859

——, *Temple à la Victoire: Monument Commémoratif des Jeux Sacrés des Anciens Grecs et Romains*, Paris, 1876

I. Doolittle, *The Mercers' Company, 1579–1959*, London, 1994

A. Drexler, ed., *The Architecture of the Ecole des Beaux-Arts*, Museum of Modern Art: New York, 1977

J. Dunbar, 'An English Architect at Naples', in *The Burlington Magazine*, 110, May 1968, pp.265–6

T. Algernon Earle, 'Earle of Allerton Tower', in *Transactions of the Historic Society of Lancashire and Cheshire*, 42, 1890, pp.57–60

C. Edwards, ed., *Roman Presences: Receptions of Rome in European Culture, 1789–1945*, Cambridge, 1999

——, 'Translating Empire? Macaulay's Rome', in C. Edwards, ed., *Roman Presences* (see above ref.), pp.70–87

J. Elmes, *Lectures on Architecture*, London, 1821

——, *Metropolitan Improvements; or London in the Nineteenth Century*, London, 1829

J. Epstein, *Radical Expression: Political Language, Ritual and Symbol in England 1790–1850*, New York, 1994

H. Erskine-Hill, *The Augustan Idea in English Literature*, London, 1983

H. Eschebach, *Die städtebauliche Entwicklung des antiken Pompeji*, Heidelberg, 1970

K. Esdaile, 'Battles Royal: No. 1 – Some Great Architectural Controversies of the Past', in *The Architect and Building News*, 9 January 1931, pp.47–9

J. Chetwode Eustace, *A Classical Tour through Italy*, London, 1813

J. Evans, *A History of the Society of Antiquaries*, Oxford, 1956

Fabbriche antiche disegnata da Andrea Palladio Vicentino e date in luce da Riccardo Conte di Burlington, London, c.1736–40

La Fascination de l'antique 1700–1770: Rome découverte, Rome inventée, Musée de la Civilisation Gallo Romaine: Lyon, 1998

C. Fea, *Nuova descrizione di Roma antica e moderna*, Rome, 1820

A. Felstead, et al., *Directory of British Architects 1834–1900*, London, 1993

N. Figgis, 'The Roman Property of Frederick Augustus Hervey, 4th Earl of Bristol and Bishop of Derry (1730–1803)', in *The Walpole Society*, 55, 1993, pp.77–103

G. Fiorelli, *Pompeianarum Antiquitatum Historia*, 3 vols, Naples, 1860–64

J. Fleming, *Robert Adam and his Circle in Edinburgh and Rome*, London, 1962

C. Flick, *The Birmingham Political Union and the Movements for Reform in Britain 1830–1839*, Hamden, CT, 1978

B. Ford, 'The Grand Tour', in *Apollo*, 114, December 1981, pp.390–400

B. Fothergill, *Sir William Hamilton: Envoy Extraordinary*, London, 1969

C. Fox, ed., *London – World City 1800–1840*, New Haven and London, 1992

D. Fraser, H. Hibbard and M. Lewine, eds, *Essays in the History of Architecture Presented to Rudolf Wittkower*, London, 1967

T. Friedman, *James Gibbs*, London, 1984

L. Garcia y Garcia, *Nova Bibliotheca Pompeiana: 250 anni di bibliografia archeologica (Soprintendenza Archeologica di Pompei Monografie 14)*, 2 vols, Rome, 1998

K. Garlick, *Sir Thomas Lawrence: A Complete Catalogue of the Oil Paintings*, Oxford, 1989

K. Garlick, et al., eds, *The Diary of Joseph Farington*, 17 vols, New Haven and London, 1978–98

W. Gell, *Pompeiana: The Topography, Edifices, and Ornaments of Pompeii – The Result of Excavations since 1819*, 2 vols, London, 1830–32

——, *Topography of Rome and its Vicinity*, 2 vols, London, 1834

W. Gell and J. P. Gandy, *Pompeiana: The Topography, Edifices and Ornaments of Pompeii*, London, 1817–19

K. Gibson, '"The Kingdom's Marble Chronicle": The Embellishment of the First and Second Buildings, 1600–1690', in A. Saunders, ed., 1997, pp.138–73

C. Gill, *History of Birmingham, I, Manor and Borough to 1865*, London, 1952

J. Goldicutt, *Antiquities of Sicily*, London, 1818

——, *Specimens of Ancient Decorations from Pompeii*, London, 1825

O. Goldsmith, *The Roman History, from the Foundation of the City of Rome to the Destruction of the Western Empire*, 2 vols, London, 1769

L. Goldstein, *Ruins and Empire: The Evolution of a Theme in Augustan and Romantic Literature*, Pittsburgh, 1977

G. Goodfellow, 'George Hadfield', in *The Architectural Review*, 138, July 1965, pp.85–6

L. Goro, *Wanderungen durch Pompeji*, Vienna, 1825

C. Gotch, 'The Missing Years of Robert Mylne', in *The Architectural Review*, 110, September 1951, pp.179–82

I. Gow, 'David Rhind: The Master of Mercantile Ornament', in R. Brown, ed., *The Architectural Outsiders*, London, 1985, pp.153–71

A. Graves, *The Royal Academy of Arts: A Complete Dictionary of Contributors and their Works from its Foundation in 1769 to 1904*, 8 vols in 4, East Ardsley, 1970

K. Grenville, *The Private Diary of Richard, Duke of Buckingham and Chandos*, 3 vols, London, 1862

J. Gwilt, *Notitia Architectonica Italiana*, London, 1818

J. Gwynn, *London and Westminster Improved*, London, 1766

J. Hale, ed., *The Italian Journal of Samuel Rogers*, London, 1956

J. Hall, 'The Site of the Royal Exchange in the Roman Period', in A. Saunders, ed., 1997, pp.3–10

W. Hamilton, 'Account of the Discoveries at Pompeii', in *Archaeologia*, 4, 1777, pp.160–75

J. Hansom, *A Statement of Facts Relative to the Birmingham Town Hall with an Appeal to the Rate-Payers and Inhabitants of Birmimgham*, Birmingham, 1834

T. Hardwick, 'Observations on the Remains of the Amphitheatre of Flavius Vespasian at Rome, as it was in the Year 1777', in *Archaeologia*, 7, 1785, pp.369–73

E. Harris, assisted by N. Savage, *British Architectural Books and Writers, 1556–1785*, Cambridge, 1990

J. Harris, 'Robert Mylne at the Academy of St. Luke', in *The Architectural Review*, 130, November 1961, pp.341–2

——, 'Le Geay, Piranesi and International Neo-classicism in Rome 1740–1750', in D. Fraser, et al., eds, 1967, pp.189–96

——, *Sir William Chambers: Knight of the Polar Star*, London, 1970

——, *A Catalogue of British Drawings for Architecture ... in American Collections*, Upper Saddle River, NJ, 1971

——, 'The Transformation of Lord Burlington: From the Palladio and Jones of his Time to the New Vitruvius', in D. Arnold, ed., 1998, pp.41–7

L. Harris, *Robert Adam and Kedleston: The Making of a Neo-Classical Masterpiece*, The National Trust, 1987

F. Haskell and N. Penny, *Taste and the Antique: The Lure of Classical Sculpture 1500–1900*, New Haven and London, 1981

L. Hautecoeur, *Histoire de l'Architecture Classique en France*, 7 vols, Paris, 1943–57

F. Hawcroft, *Travels in Italy 1776–1783, Based on the Memoirs of Thomas Jones*, Whitworth Art Gallery: Manchester, 1988

[D. Hemsoll and E. Caplin], *Palestrina: The Temple of Fortune as an Inspiration to Architects*, RIBA: London, 1989

W. Herrmann, 'Antoine Desgodets and the Académie royale d'Architecture', in *The Art Bulletin*, 40, 1958, pp.23–53

R. Hewlings, 'A Palmyra Ceiling in Lincoln', in *Architectural History*, 31, 1988, pp.166–9

——, 'Chiswick House and Gardens: Appearance and Meaning', in T. Barnard and J. Clark, eds, *Lord Burlington: Architecture, Art and Life*, London and Rio Grande, Ohio, 1995, pp.1–149

C. Hibbert, *The Grand Tour*, London, 1969

H.-R. Hitchcock, *Early Victorian Architecture in Britain*, 2 vols, New Haven, CT, 1954

——, *Architecture Nineteenth and Twentieth Centuries*, 4th edn, Harmondsworth, 1977 [1958]

J. Hodgson and F. Eaton, *The Royal Academy and its Members 1768–1830*, London, 1905

H. Honour, 'The Rome of Vincenzo Pacetti: Leaves from a Sculptor's Diary' in *Apollo*, 78, 1963, pp.368–76

——, *Neo-classicism*, Harmondsworth, 1968

——, *Romanticism*, Harmondsworth, 1981 [1979]

N. Hooke, *The Roman History from the Building of Rome to the Ruin of the Commonwealth*, 4 vols, London, 1738–71

W. Hope, ed., *The Diary of Benjamin Robert Haydon*, 5 vols, Cambridge, Mass., 1960–63

V. Huet, 'Napoleon I: A New Augustus?', in C. Edwards, ed., 1999, pp.53–69

J.-N. Huyot, *Forum Romanum*, Paris, 1841

R. Hyde, *Panoramania! The Art and Entertainment of the 'All-Embracing' View*, London, 1988

J. Ingamells, *A Dictionary of British and Irish Travellers in Italy 1701–1800, Compiled from the Brinsley Ford Archive*, New Haven and London, 1997

D. Irwin, *Neoclassicism*, London, 1997

A. Jacques, *Les Desseins d'Architecture du XIXe Siècle*, Paris, 1995

A. James, 'Rickman and the Fitzwilliam Competition', in *The Architectural Review*, 121, 1957, pp.270–71

I. Jenkins, *Archaeologists & Aesthetes in the Sculpture Galleries of the British Museum 1800–1939*, London, 1992

I. Jenkins and K. Sloan, eds, *Vases and Volcanoes: Sir William Hamilton and his Collection*, The British Museum: London, 1996

J. Jenkins and W. Hosking, *A Selection of Architectural and other Ornament: Greek, Roman and Italian, Drawn from the Originals in Various Museums and Buildings in Italy*, London, 1827

R. Jenkyns, *The Victorians and Ancient Greece*, Oxford, 1980

——, *Dignity and Decadence: Victorian Art and the Classical Inheritance*, London, 1991

——, ed., *The Legacy of Rome: A New Appraisal*, Oxford, 1992

O. Jones, *Designs for Mosaic and Tessellated Pavements*, London, 1842

R. Lambert Jones, *Reminiscences of the Public Life of Richard Lambert Jones*, London, 1863

H. Joyce, 'The Ancient Frescoes from the Villa Negroni and their Influence in the Eighteenth and Nineteenth Centuries', in *The Art Bulletin*, 65, 1983, pp.423–40

E. Kaufman, 'Architecture and Travel in the Age of British Eclecticism', in E. Blau and E. Kaufman, eds, *Architecture and its Image: Four Centuries of Architectural Representation*, Montreal, 1989, pp.59–80

E. Kaufmann, *Architecture in the Age of Reason: Baroque and Post-Baroque in England, Italy, France*, 2nd edn, New York, 1968 [1955]

J. Kenworthy-Browne, 'Matthew Brettingham's Rome Account Book 1747–1754', in *The Walpole Society*, 49, 1983, pp.37–132

J. Kilpin, 'The Late Mr Elmes and St George's Hall', in *Transactions of the Historic Society of Lancashire and Cheshire*, new series, 9, 1868–9, pp.233–52

D. King, *The Complete Works of Robert and James Adam*, Oxford, 1991

P. Kirby, *The Grand Tour in Italy, 1700–1800*, New York, 1952

L. Knowles, *St George's Hall, Liverpool*, Liverpool, 1988

V. Kockel, 'Rom über die Alpen tragen', in W. Helmberger and V. Kockel, eds, *Rom über die Alpen tragen: Fürsten sammeln antike Architektur – die Aschaffenburger Korkmodelle*, Bayerische Verwaltung der Staatlichen Schlösser, Gärten und Seen: 1993, pp.1–24

H.-W. Kruft, *A History of Architectural Theory from Vitruvius to the Present*, London, 1994

D. Kynaston, *The City of London: I – A World of its Own 1815–1890*, London, 1994

P. Lamers, *Il Viaggio nel sud dell' Abbé de Saint-Non*, Naples, 1992

A. W. Lawrence, *Greek Architecture*, Harmondsworth, 1957

P. Leach, *James Paine*, London, 1988

E. Leedham-Green, *A Concise History of the University of Cambridge*, Cambridge, 1996

W. Leeds, *Studies and Examples of the Modern School of English Architecture: The Travellers' Club House*, 1839

I. Leith, 'The Sculpture of the Third Exchange', in A. Saunders, ed., 1997, pp.336–48

W. Leppmann, *Pompeii in Fact and Fiction*, London, 1968

J. Lewis, *Original Designs in Architecture*, London, 1780; 2nd vol. 1797

W. Light, *Views of Pompeii*, London, 1828

R. Liscombe, *William Wilkins, 1778–1839*, Cambridge, 1980

M. Liversidge and C. Edwards, eds, *Imagining Rome: British Artists and Rome in the Nineteenth Century*, London, 1996

N. Llewellyn, 'Those Loose and Immodest Pieces: Italian Art and the British Point of View', in S. West, ed., *Italian Culture in Northern Europe in the Eighteenth Century*, Cambridge, 1999, pp.67–100

J. G. Lockhart, *Valerius: A Roman Story*, Edinburgh, 1821

Louis-François Cassas 1756–1827, Musée des Beaux-Arts de Tours and Waldruf-Richartz-Museum: Cologne, 1994

T. B. Macaulay, *Lays of Ancient Rome with Illustrations Original and from the Antique by George Scharf Jun.*, 2nd edn, London, 1847 [1842]

——, *Critical and Historical Essays*, 2 vols, London and New York, 1907

W. MacDonald, *The Architecture of the Roman Empire, I, An Introductory Study*, New Haven and London, 1965

W. MacDonald and J. Pinto, *Hadrian's Villa and its Legacy*, New Haven and London, 1995

J. Marciari, *The Grand Tour: An Exhibition held at the Beinecke Rare Book and Manuscript Library*, The Beinecke Library: New Haven, CT, 1998

——, ed., *Grand Tour Diaries and other Travel Manuscripts in the James Marshall and Marie-Louise Osborn Collection*, The Beinecke Library: New Haven, CT, 1999

P. Marconi, A. Cipriani and E. Valeriani, eds, *I disegni di architettura dell' Archivio storico dell' Accademia di San Luca*, 2 vols, Rome, 1974

P. Marsden, 'The Excavation for the Third Exchange', in A. Saunders, ed., 1997, pp.272–5

G. Marshall, *The Ancient Buildings of Rome by Antony Desgodetz*, 2 vols, London, 1771–95

[F. Mazois], *Le Palais de Scaurus, ou description d'une maison romaine*, Paris, 1819, 2nd edn, 1822

F. Mazois, 'Considérations sur la forme et la distribution des théâtres antiques', in J.-B. Levée, ed., *Théâtre complet des Latins*, 15 vols, Paris, 1820, I, pp.xlix–lxvi

F. Mazois [and F. C. Gau], *Les Ruines de Pompéi*, 4 vols, Paris, 1824–38

M. McCarthy, 'The Education in Architecture of the Man of Taste', in *Studies in Eighteenth-Century Culture*, 5, 1976, pp.337–53.

——, 'Art Education and the Grand Tour', in M. Barasch and L. Sandler, eds, *Art the Ape of Nature: Studies in Honor of H. W. Janson*, New York, 1981, pp.477–94

T. McCormick, *Charles-Louis Clérisseau and the Genesis of Neo-Classicism*, Cambridge, Mass., 1990

E. McParland, 'Sir Thomas Hewett and the New Junta for Architecture', in G. Worsley, ed., 1994, pp.21–6

W. Mead, *The Grand Tour in the Eighteenth Century*, Boston, 1914

C. Meeks, *Italian Architecture 1750–1914*, New Haven and London, 1966

P. Metcalf, *The Halls of the Fishmongers' Company: An Architectural History of a Riverside Site*, London and Chichester, 1977

R. Middleton, 'Hittorff's Polychrome Campaign', in R. Middleton, ed., *The Beaux-Arts and Nineteenth-Century French Architecture*, London, 1982, pp.175–88

R. Middleton and D. Watkin, *Neoclassical and 19th Century Architecture*, 2 vols, London, 1987 [1977]

R. Millington, *The House in the Park*, Liverpool, 1937

D. Moss, *Thomas Attwood: The Biography of a Radical*, Montreal and Kingston, 1990

T. Mowl, 'The Williamane: Architecture for the Sailor King', in R. White and C. Lightburn, eds, 1988, pp.92–106

——, 'A Roman Palace for a Welsh Prince: Byres' Designs for Sir Watkin Williams-Wynn', in *Apollo*, 142, 1995, pp.33–41

P. Murray, 'Archer Abroad', in *The Architectural Review*, 122, August 1957, p.88

A. Musiari, *Neoclassicismo senza modelli: L'Accademia di Belle Arti di Parma tra il periodo napoleonico e la Restaurazione (1796–1820)*, Parma, 1986

F. Nardini, *Roma Antica*, Rome, 1666; 2nd edn, 1704; 3rd edn, 1771; 4th edn, A. Nibby, ed., 1818–20

Neapolis: Temi progettuali (Soprintendenza Archeologica di Pompei Monografie 7), Rome, 1994

W. Newton, *The Architecture of M. Vitruvius Pollio*, 2 vols, London, 1771 and 1791

A. Nibby, *Del Foro Romano*, Rome, 1819

B. G. Niebuhr, *The History of Rome*, trans. by J. Hare, C. Thirlwall and W. Smith, 3 vols, Cambridge, 1828–32

E. Nigris, 'Robert Mylne all'Accademia di San Luca', in *Ricerche di Storia dell'Arte*, 22, 1984, pp.23–36

W. Oechslin, 'Pyramide et Sphère: Notes sur l'Architecture Révolutionnaire du XVIIIe Siècle et ses Sources Italiennes', in *Gazette des Beaux-Arts*, 77, 1971, pp.201–38

K. Ohr, *Die Basilika in Pompeji*, Berlin, 1991

J. Olley, 'St George's Hall, Liverpool', in *The Architects' Journal*, 183, 18 and 25 June 1986, I, pp.36–57 and II, pp.36–61

——, 'University Library', in *The Architects' Journal*, 186, 8 February 1989, pp.34–63

A. Oppé, 'Memoirs of Thomas Jones', in *The Walpole Society*, 32, 1951, pp.i–162

J. Paine, *Plans, Elevations and Sections of Noblemen and Gentlemen's Houses*, London, 1767

A. Palladio, *I quattro libri dell'architettura*, Venice, 1570

Paris – Rome – Athènes: Le Voyage en Grèce des Architectes Français au XIXe et XXe Siècles, Paris, 1982

C. Parker, *Villa Rustica, Selected from Buildings and Scenes in the Vicinity of Rome and Florence*, 3 vols, London, 1832–41

C. Parslow, *Rediscovering Antiquity: Karl Weber and the Excavation of Herculaneum, Pompeii, and Stabiae*, Cambridge, 1995

M. Pellegri, ed., *Concorsi dell' Accademia Reale di Belle Arti di Parma dal 1757 al 1796*, Parma, 1988

E. Pernice, *Die Hellenistische Kunst in Pompeji, VI: Pavimente und Figürliche Mosaiken*, Berlin, 1938

J.-M. Pérouse de Montclos, *Les Prix de Rome: Concours de l'Académie royale d'architecture au XVIIIe siècle*, Paris, 1984

P. Petrini, *Memorie Prenestine*, Rome, 1795

N. Pevsner, *The Buildings of England: South Lancashire*, Harmondsworth, 1969

M.-J. Peyre, *Œuvres d'Architecture*, Paris, 1765

C. Phipps, Marquis of Normanby, *The English in Italy*, 3 vols, London, 1825

S. Piale, *Del Foro Romano – sua posizione e grandezza non bene intese dal Nardini e non ostante generalmente seguite da' Moderni*, Rome, 1832

——, *Della Basilica Giulia*, Rome, 1833

J. Picton, *Memorials of Liverpool*, 2 vols, London, 1873

S. Rowland Pierce, 'Thomas Jenkins in Rome', in *The Antiquaries Journal*, 45, 1965, pp.200–229

C. Pietrangeli, *Scavi e scoperte di antichità sotto il Pontificato di Pio VI*, 2nd edn, Rome, 1958 [1956]

——, 'Archaeological Excavations in Italy, 1750–1850', in *The Age of Neo-Classicism*, 1972, pp.xlvi–lii

C. Pietrangeli and A. Diotallevi, 'La Pontificia Accademia Romana di Archeologia: Note Storiche', in *Memorie della Pontificia Accademia Romana di Archeologia*, Series III, 4, 1983, pp.5–92

R. Pine-Coffin, *Bibliography of British and American Travel to Italy to 1860*, Florence, 1974

P. Pinon and F.-X. Amprimoz, *Les Envois de Rome (1778–1968): Architecture et Archéologie*, Collection de l'Ecole française de Rome, 110, Rome, 1988

G. B. Piranesi, *Varie vedute di Roma antica e moderna*, Rome, 1741–8

——, *Prima parte di architetture, e prospettive inventate*, Rome, 1743

——, *Antichità romane*, Rome, 1748

——, *Le antichità romane*, 4 vols, Rome, 1756

——, *Della magnificenza ed architettura de 'romani*, Rome, 1761

——, *Il Campo Marzio dell' antica Roma*, Rome, 1762

L. Pirotta, 'Thomas Harrison architetto inglese, accademico di San Luca per sovrano motu proprio', in *Strenna dei Romanisti*, 21, 1960, pp.257–63

Pompei, pitture e mosaici, Instituto dell' Enciclopedia Italiana: Rome, 1990–

Pompéi: travaux et envois des architectes français au XIXe siècle, Paris and Rome, 1981

M. Port, 'The New Law Courts Competition, 1866–67', in *Architectural History*, 11, 1968, pp.75–93

——, 'The New Houses of Parliament', in J. Mordaunt Crook and M. Port, *The History of the King's Works, VI, 1782–1851*, London, 1973

——, ed., *The Houses of Parliament*, New Haven and London, 1976

——, *Imperial London: Civil Government Buildings in London 1850–1914*, New Haven and London, 1995

——, 'Destruction, Competition and Rebuilding: The Royal Exchange 1838–1884', in A. Saunders, ed., 1997, pp.279–305

C. Powell, *Turner in the South: Rome, Naples, Florence*, New Haven and London, 1987

M. Praz, *On Neoclassicism*, London, 1969 [1940]

J. Prest, *Lord John Russell*, London, 1972

A. W. N. Pugin, *Contrasts: or a Parallel between the Noble Edifices of the Fourteenth and Fifteenth Centuries and Similar Buildings of the Present Day; Shewing the Present Decay of Taste*, London, 1836

——, *An Apology for the Revival of Christian Architecture in England*, London, 1843

R. Quinault, 'Westminster and the Victorian Constitution', in *Transactions of the Royal Historical Society*, 6th series, 2, 1992, pp.79–104

I. Rae, *Charles Cameron: Architect to the Court of Russia*, London, 1971

D. Raoul-Rochette, *Pompéi: choix d'édifices inédits*, Paris 1828

[R. Rawlinson], *Correspondence Relative to St George's Hall Liverpool*, London, 1871

B. Read, 'From Basilica to Walhalla', in P. Curtis, ed., 1989, pp.32–41

'Report … from the Committee appointed at the Annual General Meeting in May 1852 for the purpose of promoting the Improvement of the Town', in *Proceedings of the Liverpool Architectural and Archaeological Society*, II, Part III, Session 1852–3, 1857, pp.367–83

A. Richardson, *Monumental Classic Architecture in Great Britain and Ireland during the Eighteenth and Nineteenth Centuries*, New York and London, 1982 [1914]

G. Richardson, *Capitals of Columns and Friezes, Measured from the Antique*, London, 1793

L. Richardson, *Pompeii: An Architectural History*, Baltimore and London, 1988

——, *A New Topographical Dictionary of Ancient Rome*, Baltimore and London, 1992

M. Richardson, 'Model Architecture', in *Country Life*, 183, 21 September 1989, pp.224–7.

——, 'Learning in the Soane Office', in N. Bingham, ed., 1993, pp.15–21

M. Richardson and M. Stevens, eds, *John Soane Architect: Master of Space and Light*, Royal Academy: London, 1999

J. Ridley, *Lord Palmerston*, London, 1970

R. Ridley, 'The Monuments of the Roman Forum: The Struggle for Identity', in *Xenia*, 17, 1989, pp.71–90

——, *The Eagle and the Spade: Archaeology in Rome during the Napoleonic Era*, Cambridge, 1992

——, 'To Protect the Monuments: The Papal Antiquarian (1534–1870), in *Xenia Antiqua*, I, 1992, pp.117–54

——, 'The Founding of the German Archaeological Institute: Unpublished Documents', in *Mitteilungen des Deutschen Archäologischen Instituts: Römische Abteilung*, 103, 1996, pp.275–94

D. Robertson, *Greek and Roman Architecture*, 2nd edn, Cambridge, 1943 [1929]

D. Robertson, *Sir Charles Eastlake and the Victorian Art World*, Princeton, 1978

J. Martin Robinson, *The Wyatts: An Architectural Dynasty*, Oxford, 1979

——, 'A Dazzling Adventurer: Charles Cameron – The Lost Early Years', in *Apollo*, new series, 135, 1992, pp.31–5

R. Rodd, *Rome of the Renaissance and To-day*, London, 1932

P. Rogers, *The Augustan Vision*, London, 1978 [1974]

Roma antiqua: envois des architectes français (1788–1924) – Forum, Colisée, Palatin, Rome and Paris, 1985

Roma antiqua: 'envois' degli architetti francesi (1786–1901) – Grande edifici pubblici, Rome, 1992

D. Romanelli, *Viaggio a Pompei a Pesto e di ritorno ad Ercolano*, 2nd edn, Naples, 1817 [1811]

W. Rorabaugh, 'Politics and the Architectural Competition for the Houses of Parliament 1834–7', in *Victorian Studies*, 18, 1973, pp.155–75

H. Rosenau, 'The Engravings of the *Grands Prix* of the French Academy of Architecture', in *Architectural History*, 3, 1960, pp.15–180.

R. Rosenblum, *Transformations in Late Eighteenth Century Art*, Princeton, 1967

L. Rossini, *Vedute di Roma – Antichità romane divise in cento tavole*, Rome, 1819–23

'Royal Exchange: Report of Sir Robert Smirke, Mr Joseph Gwilt and Mr Philip Hardwick on the Designs and Plans', 1839

J. Rykwert, *The First Moderns: The Architects of the Eighteenth Century*, Cambridge, Mass., 1980

A. Saint, 'The Marble Arch', in *The Georgian Group Journal*, 7, 1997, pp.75–93

F. Salmon, 'British Architects and the Florentine Academy, 1753–1794', in *Mitteilungen des Kunsthistorischen Institutes in Florenz*, 34, 1990, pp.199–214

——, 'Charles Cameron and Nero's Domus Aurea: una piccola esplorazione', in *Architectural History*, 36, 1993, pp.69–93

——, 'Storming the Campo Vaccino: British Architects and the Antique Buildings of Rome after Waterloo', in *Architectural History*, 38, 1995, pp.146–75

——, 'An Unaccountable Enemy: Joseph Michael Gandy and the Accademia di San Luca in Rome', in *The Georgian Group Journal*, 5, 1995, pp.25–36

——, 'British Architects, Italian Fine Arts Academies and the Foundation of the RIBA, 1816–43', in *Architectural History*, 39, 1996, pp.77–113

——, 'Heretical and Presumptuous: British Architects Visiting Palladio's Villas in the Later Georgian Period', in D. Arnold, ed., 1998, pp.61–74

——, 'Charles Heathcote Tatham and the Accademia di S. Luca, Rome', in *The Burlington Magazine*, 140, 1998, pp.85–92

F. Salmon and P. de Figueiredo, 'The South Front of St George's Hall, Liverpool', in *Architectural History*, 43, 2000, pp.195–218

S. Sande, 'History of Excavation and Research', in I. Nielsen and B. Poulsen, eds, *The Temple of Castor and Pollux, I: Lavori e Studi di Archeologia Pubblicati dalla Soprintendenza di Roma*, 17, Rome, 1992, pp.5–29

A. Saunders, ed., *The Royal Exchange*, London Topographical Society, Publication 152, 1997

G. Saunders, *A Treatise on Theatres*, London, 1790

N. Savage, et al., *Early Printed Books 1478–1840: Catalogue of the British Architectural Library Early Imprints Collection*, vol.1, 'A–D', London, 1994; vol.2, 'E–L', London, 1995; vol.3, 'M–R', London, 1999

S. Sawyer, 'Sir John Soane's Symbolic Westminster: The Apotheosis of George IV', in *Architectural History*, 39, 1996, pp.54–76

O. Bertotti Scamozzi, *Le fabbriche e i disegni di Andrea Palladio*, 4 vols, Vicenza, 1776–83

Scottish Architects at Home and Abroad, National Library of Scotland: Edinburgh, 1978

F. Sear, *Roman Architecture*, 2nd edn, London, 1989 [1982]

J. Serra, ed., *Paestum and the Doric Revival 1750–1830*, Florence, 1986

Sessional Papers of the Royal Institute of British Architects, 1864

D. Shvidkovsky, *The Empress and the Architect: British Architecture and Gardens at the Court of Catherine the Great*, New Haven and London, 1996

C. Sicca, *Committed to Classicism: The Building of Downing College Cambridge*, Downing College, 1987

B. Skinner, *Scots in Italy in the Eighteenth Century*, Edinburgh, 1966

R. Smirke, *Specimens of Continental Architecture*, London, 1806

M. Snodin, ed., *Catalogue of Architectural Drawings in the Victoria and Albert Museum: Sir William Chambers*, London, 1996

J. Soane, *Designs for Public and Private Buildings*, London, 1828

——, *Memoirs of the Professional Life of an Architect between the Years 1768 and 1835*, London, 1835

——, *Description of the House and Museum on the North Side of Lincoln's Inn Fields*, London, 1835–6 [1830]

R. Spiers, 'Cockerell's Restorations of Ancient Rome', in *The Architectural Review*, 29, 1911, pp.123–8

C. Springer, *The Marble Wilderness: Ruins and Representation in Italian Romanticism, 1775–1850*, Cambridge, 1987

L. Stainton, 'Hayward's List: British Visitors to Rome 1753–1775', *The Walpole Society*, 49, 1983, pp.3–36

J. Spencer Stanhope, *Topography Illustrative of the Battle of Platea*, London, 1817

——, *Olympia, or, Topography Illustrative of the Actual State of the Plain of Olympia and the Ruins of the City of Elis*, London, 1824

G. Stamp, 'Architectural Sculpture in Liverpool', in P. Curtis, ed., 1989, pp.8–12

M. Steinby, ed., *Lexicon Topographicum Urbis Romae*, 5 vols, Rome, 1993–

D. Stillman, *The Decorative Work of Robert Adam*, London, 1966

——, 'Robert Adam and Piranesi', in D. Fraser et al., eds, 1967, pp.197–206

——, 'British Architects and Italian Architectural Competitions, 1758–1780', in *Journal of the Society of Architectural Historians*, 32, March 1973, pp.43–66

——, 'Chimney-pieces for the English Market: A Thriving Business in Late Eighteenth-Century Rome', in *The Art Bulletin*, 59, March 1977, pp.85–94

——, *English Neo-classical Architecture*, 2 vols, London, 1988

J. Stoye, *English Travellers Abroad, 1604–1667: Their Influence in English Society and Politics*, revised edn, New Haven and London, 1989 [1952]

E. Strong, 'Istituti stranieri in Roma', *Annales Institutorum*, I, *1928*, 1929, pp.15–60

D. Stroud, *Henry Holland: His Life and Architecture*, London, 1966

——, *George Dance, Architect, 1741–1825*, London, 1971

J. Stuart, *De Obelisco Caesaris Augusti*, Rome, 1750

J. Stuart and N. Revett, *The Antiquities of Athens*, 4 vols, London, 1762 [1763]–1816, revised edn by W. Kinnard, London, 1825–30

J. Summerson, 'L'Architettura Neoclassica in Inghilterra', in *Bollettino del Centro Internazionale di Studi di Architettura Andrea Palladio*, 13, 1971, pp.249–60

——, *The Life and Work of John Nash, Architect*, London, 1980

——, *The Architecture of the Eighteenth Century*, London, 1986

——, *Architecture in Britain 1530–1830*, 9th edn, New Haven and London, 1993 [1953]

A. Tait, 'Reading the Ruins: Robert Adam and Piranesi in Rome', in *Architectural History*, 27, 1984, pp.524–33

——, *Robert Adam: Drawings and Imagination*, Cambridge, 1993

——, *Robert Adam – The Creative Mind: From the Sketch to the Finished Drawing*, The Soane Gallery: London, 1996

G. Tappen, *A Short Description of a Tour through France and Italy … by George Tappen, Architect*, London, 1804

——, *Professional Observations on the Architecture of the Principal Ancient and Modern Buildings in France and Italy*, London, 1806

C. H. Tatham, *Etchings Representing the Best Examples of Ancient Ornamental Architecture, Drawn from the Originals in Rome and other Parts of Italy during the Years 1794, 1795 and 1796*, London, 1799

——, *Etchings Representing Fragments of Antique Grecian and Roman Architectural Ornament, Chiefly Collected in Italy before the Late Revolutions in that Country*, London, 1806

R. Tavernor, *Palladio and Palladianism*, London, 1991

G. L. Taylor, *The Autobiography of an Octogenarian Architect*, 2 vols, London, 1870–72

G. L. Taylor and E. Cresy, *The Architectural Antiquities of Rome*, 2 vols, London, 1821–2, 2nd edn, 1874

——, *Architecture of the Middle Ages in Italy*, London, 1829

——, *The Stones of Etruria and Marbles of Antient Rome*, London, 1859.

G. M. Trevelyan, 'Englishmen and Italians: Some Aspects of their Relations Past and Present', *Proceedings of the British Academy*, 1919–20, pp.91–108

G. Tyack, *Sir James Pennethorne and the Making of Victorian London*, Cambridge, 1992

D. Udy, 'The Neo-Classicism of Charles Heathcote Tatham', in *The Connoisseur*, 177, August 1971, pp.269–76

G. Valadier, *Raccolta delle più insigni fabbriche di Roma antica e sue adjacenze*, 7 vols, Rome, 1810–26

N. Vance, *The Victorians and Ancient Rome*, Oxford, 1997

H. van der Poel, *Corpus Topographicum Pompeianum*, vol.4 (Bibliography), Rome, 1977, vol.5 (Cartography), Rome, 1981

D. van Zanten, *Designing Paris: The Architecture of Duban, Labrouste, Duc, and Vaudoyer*, Cambridge, Mass., 1987

——, 'The Harmony of Landscape, Architecture and Community: Schinkel's Encounter with Huyot, 1826', in J. Zukowsky, ed., *Karl Friedrich Schinkel: The Drama of Architecture*, Chicago, 1994

R. Venuti, *Accurata e succinta descrizione topografica delle antichità di Roma*, 3rd edn, Rome, 1824 (ed. S. Piale) [1763]

Visions of Ruin: Architectural Fantasies & Designs for Garden Follies, The Soane Gallery: London, 1999

V. W. von Hagen, *Frederick Catherwood Architect*, New York, 1950

L. Vulliamy, *Examples of Ornamental Sculpture drawn from the Originals in Bronze, Marble and Terracotta in Greece, Asia Minor and Italy by Lewis Vulliamy, Architect, in the Years 1818, 1819, 1820 and 1821*, London, 1823–6

C. Wakefield, *Life of Thomas Attwood*, London, 1885

[B. Walker, et al.], *The Birmingham Town Hall 1834–1934*, Birmingham, 1934

D. Walker and C. McWilliam, 'Cairness, Aberdeenshire', in *Country Life*, 149, 28 January and 4 February 1971, pp.184–7, 248–51

J. Ward-Perkins, 'Veii: The Historical Topography of the Ancient City', in *Papers of the British School at Rome*, 29, 1961, pp.1–123

——, *Roman Imperial Architecture*, Harmondsworth, 1981

——, *Roman Architecture*, London, 1988 [1979]

D. Watkin, *Thomas Hope (1769–1831) and the Neo-Classical Idea*, London, 1968

——, *The Life and Work of C. R. Cockerell*, London, 1974

——, *The Triumph of the Classical: Cambridge Architecture 1804–1834*, Cambridge, 1977

——, *Athenian Stuart: Pioneer of the Greek Revival*, London, 1982

——, *The English Vision: The Picturesque in Architecture, Landscape and Garden Design*, London, 1982

——, *Regency: A Guide and Gazetteer*, London, 1982

——, 'Newly Discovered Drawings by C. R. Cockerell for Cambridge University Library', in *Architectural History*, 26, 1983, pp.87–91

——, 'Architecture', in R. Jenkyns, ed., 1992, pp.329–65

——, *Sir John Soane: Enlightenment Thought and the Royal Academy Lectures*, Cambridge, 1996

——, 'The Travellers' Club and the Grand Tour: Correcting Raphael …', in *The British Art Journal*, I, autumn 1999, pp.56–62

D. Watkin and T. Mellinghoff, *German Architecture and the Classical Ideal 1740–1840*, London, 1987

D. Watkin and C. Proudfoot, 'A Pioneer of English Neo-Classicism: C. H. Tatham', in *Country Life*, 151, 13–20 April 1972, pp.918–21

H. Weinbrot, *Augustus Caesar in 'Augustan' England: The Decline of a Classical Norm*, Princeton, 1978

[E. Welch] writing as 'A Resident of Birmingham', 'A Descriptive Account, Accompanied by Plans, Elevations, Sections etc. of the Birmingham New Town Hall', in *The Architectural Magazine and Journal*, 2, January 1835, pp.16–27

R. Wetten, *Designs for Villas in the Italian Style of Architecture*, London, 1830

R. White and C. Lightburn, eds, *Late Georgian Classicism: Papers Given at the Georgian Group Symposium 1987*, 1988

D. Wiebenson, *Sources of Greek Revival Architecture*, London, 1969

G. Wightwick, *Select Views of the Roman Antiquities*, London, 1827

——, 'Sketches by a Travelling Architect', in *Library of the Fine Arts*, 2, 1831, pp.14–30, 111–20, 345–57; 3, 1832, pp.37–48, 136–46, 209–16, 391–7

——, *Hints to Young Architects, Comprising advice to those who, while yet at school, are destined to the profession; to such as, having passed their pupillage, are about to travel; and to those who, having completed their education, are about to practice*, London, 1846

H. Wilkins, *Suite de vues pittoresques des ruines de Pompeii*, Rome, 1819

W. Wilkins, *The Antiquities of Magna Graecia*, London, 1807

——, *The Civil Architecture of Vitruvius*, London, 1812

R. Willis and J. Willis Clark, *The Architectural History of the University of Cambridge*, 3 vols, Cambridge, 1886

C. Willsdon, 'The Mural Decoration of the Royal Exchange', in A. Saunders, ed., 1997, pp.311–35

M. Wilson Jones, 'Designing the Roman Corinthian Order', in *Journal of Roman Archaeology*, 2, 1989, pp.35–69

——, 'Designing the Roman Corinthian Capital', in *Papers of the British School at Rome*, 49, 1991, pp.89–150

A. Wilton and I. Bignamini, eds, *Grand Tour: The Lure of Italy in the Eighteenth Century*, Tate Gallery: London, 1996

J. Wilton-Ely, *The Mind and Art of Giovanni Battista Piranesi*, London, 1988

——, 'Soane and Piranesi', in R. White and C. Lightburn, eds, 1988, pp.43–57

——, *Piranesi as Architect and Designer*, New Haven and London, 1993

——, ed., *Giovanni Battista Piranesi: The Complete Etchings*, 2 vols, San Francisco, 1994

R. Wittkower, *Palladio and English Palladianism*, London, 1974

R. Wood, *The Ruins of Palmyra, otherwise Tedmor in the Desart*, London, 1753

——, *The Ruins of Balbec, otherwise Heliopolis in Coelosyria*, London, 1757

J. Woods, *Letters of an Architect from France, Italy and Greece*, 2 vols, London, 1828

S. Woolf, *A History of Italy 1700–1860*, London, 1986 [1979]

C. Wordsworth, *Inscriptiones Pompeianae*, London, 1837

G. Worsley, *Architectural Drawings of the Regency Period 1790–1837*, London, 1991

G. Worsley, ed., *The Role of the Amateur Architect: Papers Given at The Georgian Group Symposium 1993*, London, 1994

——, *Classical Architecture in Britain: The Heroic Age*, New Haven and London, 1995

M. Digby Wyatt, 'On the Architectural Career of the Late Sir Charles Barry', in *The Builder*, 18, 26 May 1860, pp.322–4

F. Yegül, *Baths and Bathing in Classical Antiquity*, Cambridge, Mass. and London, 1992

Dissertations

D. Blissett, 'Sir Charles Barry: A Reassessment of his Travels and Early Career', Ph.D, Oxford Polytechnic, 1984

J. Mordaunt Crook, 'The Career of Sir Robert Smirke, RA', D.Phil., University of Oxford, 1961

P. de la Ruffinière du Prey, 'John Soane's Architectural Education 1753–1780', Ph.D, Princeton University, 1972

D. Evinson, 'Joseph Hansom', M.A., Courtauld Institute of Art, University of London, 1966

R. John, 'T. L. Donaldson: The Last of the Old Gods?', B.A., University of Cambridge, Department of History of Art, 1987

H. Kalman, 'The Architecture of George Dance the Younger', Ph.D, Princeton University, 1971

B. Lukacher, 'Joseph Michael Gandy: The Poetical Representation and Mythography of Architecture', Ph.D, University of Delaware, 1987

M. Okrim, 'The Life and Work of Thomas Harrison of Chester', Ph.D, Courtauld Institute of Art, University of London, 1988

M. Rivlin, 'A Nineteenth Century Classical Forum: William Brown Street, Liverpool', M.A., University of Manchester, 1999

E. Tollfree, 'Napoleon and the "New Rome": Rebuilding Imperial Rome in Late Eighteenth- and Early Nineteenth-Century Paris', Ph.D, University of Bristol, 1999

A. Yarrington, 'The Commemoration of the Hero 1800–1864: Monuments to the British Victors of the Napoleonic Wars', Ph.D, University of Cambridge, 1980

Index

References in italics are to pages on which black and white illustrations appear